Benedict XVI and the Roman Missal

FOTA LITURGY SERIES

General Editor: D. Vincent Twomey SVD

Benedict XVI and the Roman Missal

Proceedings of the Fourth Fota International Liturgical Conference, 2011

Janet Elaine Rutherford & James O'Brien

EDITORS

FOUR COURTS PRESS • DUBLIN
SCEPTER PUBLISHERS • NEW YORK

Typeset in 11 pt on 14 pt AGaramond by
Carrigboy Typesetting Services for
FOUR COURTS PRESS LTD
7 Malpas Street, Dublin 8, Ireland
www.fourcourtspress.ie
and in North America for
SCEPTER PUBLISHERS, INC.
P.O. Box 211, New York, NY 10018–0004
www.scepterpub.org

A catalogue record for this title is available
from the British Library.

ISBN 978-1-84682-371-8

Printed in England
by CPI Antony Rowe, Chippenham, Wilts.

Contents

Editors' Preface

The Fourth Fota International Liturgy Conference explored the topic: 'Benedict XVI and the Roman Missal'. Its objective was to examine the approach of Benedict XVI/Joseph Ratzinger to understanding and appreciating the Roman Missal as one of the central texts of Catholic Worship. That task required an exploration of the historical evolution of the Roman Missal, beginning in eighth-century Rome, traversing the Romano-Frankish period, to arrive at the missal published by St Pope Pius V (1570) and its further development as embodied in the missals published by Pope John XXIII (1962), that of Pope Paul VI (1970) and the third edition of the revised missal published by Pope John Paul II (2000).

Given the various revisions and reforms of the Missal which have been carried out during this time span, it was necessary to sketch the theological and liturgical principles by which they were guided, as well as to look at some of their concrete applications in specific historical situations so as to appreciate the nuances often determining their application. As every consideration of liturgy begins in the context of the objective relationship between God and man, an outline of the principles underlying the juridical matrix governing that relationship and the operation of the missal was an essential aspect of the proceedings.

Within this general context, the specific interest to the Conference focused on the contribution of Benedict XVI/Joseph Ratzinger in clarifying the dogmatic foundations of the liturgy, particularly of the Eucharistic Celebration, and on his contribution to the renewal of the liturgy (specifically of the Roman Missal) since the Second Vatican Council.

In the light of Benedict XVI/Joseph Ratzinger's theological understanding of the form of the Mass, the Conference's attention moved to consider its implications towards resolving contemporary questions which have arisen with regard to the Roman Missal. These include the development of liturgical languages in the vernacular, the co-existence of two forms of the one Roman Rite, the recovery of sacred music in the Western liturgy, the relationship between the Roman Missal and eventual liturgical books proper to the Anglican Ordinariates, and the objectives and evaluation of the new English language translation of the *Missale Romanum*.

The editors wish to record with gratitude the munificent sponsorship made available to the Fourth Fota International Liturgy Conference by the Supreme Council of the Knights of Columbus, New Haven, Connecticut, US. Particular thanks are due to Dr Carl Anderson, Supreme Knight, and to Mr Stephen Feiler for their interest in and commitment to the propagation of Benedict XVI's writings through the Fota Liturgical Conferences and their published Proceedings.

Special thanks go to the *Ratzinger/Benedikt XVI Stiftung* in Munich, and to Fr Stephan Horn, for the foundation's financial assistance; to the Knights of Malta; to a number of benefactors in Germany, Ireland and in the United States; and to a number of priests of the diocese of Cloyne for generous financial contributions towards defraying the expenses of the Conference.

St Colman's Society for Catholic Liturgy, particularly its President, Norma Crosbie, once again accomplished small miracles in organizing the Conference and individuating the speakers who contributed papers. The officers of the Society, Terry Pender, Adrian O'Donovan, James O'Sullivan and Sylvia Wilmott, did sterling work to ensure that everything ran smoothly and according to plan.

The editors also wish to thank Fr Patrick McCarthy, parish priest of the church of Sts Peter and Paul, Cork, for kindly making it available for the liturgical functions attendant on the Conference, for which members of the Institute of Christ the King generously took charge of all aspects of liturgical preparations. Thanks are also due to the Lassus Scholars under the direction of Ite O'Donovan, the members of the Priestly Fraternity of St Peter who assisted at the Pontifical High Mass, as well as to the many other persons who acted as ministers and servers.

James O'Brien   Janet E. Rutherford
Buttevant, Co. Cork   *Julianstown, Co. Meath*

Verbum Domini: word and rite in Ratzinger's sacramental theology

D. VINCENT TWOMEY SVD

INTRODUCTION

The ongoing development of the initial liturgical reform carried out in the aftermath of the Second Vatican Council was the theme of the First Fota Conference (2008).[1] This 'reform of the reform' has been inspired primarily (but not exclusively) by the writings of Joseph Ratzinger, now Pope Benedict XVI. It is predicated on the realization that the initial attempts to reform the liturgy were, to put it mildly, not always entirely in harmony with what the Council had in fact intended. Joseph Ratzinger has in various writings undertaken a critical review of that initial reform and has been indefatigable in advocating a more profound reform based on richer theological principles.[2] The second and third conferences focused primarily on the significance of beauty for any such reform – more precisely, the expression of beauty in sacred art and architecture (2009)[3] and in sacred music (2010).[4]

On the first Sunday of Advent, 2011, the new English translation of the revised Latin exemplar of the Roman Missal was introduced to the English-speaking local churches worldwide, replacing the vernacular text of the Mass, to which in the course of four decades we have grown accustomed, and which many, including this writer, came to love, despite its banality of expression and rather thin theological content. Familiarity can also breed affection. With this in mind, the Fourth Fota International Liturgical Conference was devoted to the topic of the Roman Missal.

---

1 N.J. Roy and J.E. Rutherford (eds), *Benedict XVI and the sacred liturgy. Proceedings of the First Fota International Conference* (Dublin, 2010); see also A. Nichols, *The thought of Pope Benedict XVI. An introduction to the theology of Joseph Ratzinger, new edition* (London–New York, 2007), pp 147–59; J. Murphy, *Christ our joy. The theological vision of Pope Benedict XVI* (San Francisco, 2008), pp 171–83; E. de Gaál, *The theology of Pope Benedict XVI. The christocentric shift* (New York, 2010), pp 239–67.   2 To highlight the priority that the theologian, Joseph Ratzinger, gave to the theology of the liturgy, he decided that the first volume of his projected collected works should be Volume 11, *Theologie der Liturgie. Die sakramentale Begründung christlicher Existenz* [= *Gesammelte Schriften*, Vol. 11] (Freiburg–Basel–Vienna, 2008), 757 pages, including Indices.   3 D.V. Twomey SVD and J.E. Rutherford (eds), *Benedict XVI and beauty in sacred art. Proceedings of the Second Fota International Conference* (Dublin, 2011).   4 J.E. Rutherford (ed.), *Benedict XVI and beauty in sacred music. Proceedings of the Third Fota International*

After dealing extensively with the history of the Roman Missal, up to and including the third revision of the *Novus Ordo*, the Conference explored the long and complicated process that went into the new translation. The international *Vox Clara* Commission chaired by George Cardinal Pell (one of the keynote speakers at the Conference), followed new principles of translation, the aim of which was to render the revised Latin text into a language that would be faithful to the original and yet be suitable for use in the English-speaking Catholic Church spread throughout the whole world. The Missal thus became central to the reform of the reform. It should be noted, however, that the complicated process of achieving a text acceptable to all the English-speaking Episcopal Conferences long predated the election of Joseph Ratzinger to the See of Peter in 2005.

As a background to the theme of this conference, I wish to explore in rather general terms the unique role played by the 'word' (and thus language) in Christian liturgy. This role, according to the Pope, arises from the very form of the sacraments which the liturgy articulates and celebrates. And so we must examine, however briefly, the underlying sacramental theology that underpins all of Ratzinger's writings on liturgy.

RATZINGER'S SACRAMENTAL THEOLOGY

In his introduction to his twelve-volume collected writings on the liturgy, the Pope explains why he decided that the volume on the liturgy (volume 11 in the series) should be the first to be published.[5] He recalls how, more or less by accident, the Second Vatican Council began its task of enabling Christianity to engage more effectively with a changed world by taking up the topic of the Divine Liturgy. *The Constitution on the Sacred Liturgy (Sacrosanctum concilium)* was formally promulgated at the end of the Second Session, on 4 December 1963. The Council could do so, the Pope comments, since the document on the liturgy was the least controversial of all the preparatory texts. It also enabled the Council Fathers to gain the conciliar expertise needed to tackle other, more controversial, documents. But, Pope Benedict notes, what appeared to be an accident was in fact of great significance with regard to the Council's

Conference (Dublin, 2012).   5 J. Ratzinger, *Gesammelte Schriften*, pp 5–8.

true order of preference. By giving their attention first to the theme of liturgy, the Council Fathers highlighted in no uncertain terms the primacy of God.

God First

This is the true significance of the decision of the Council Fathers to devote their attention to the Divine Liturgy. When God is no longer the focus of our attention, everything else gets out of focus. The Pope quotes the Rule of St Benedict: 'Nothing is to be preferred to the worship of God', and applies this monastic dictum to the life of the Church as a whole as well as to each one personally. He also recalled the etymology of the term 'orthodoxy', the second half of which comes from the Greek word *doxa* meaning not opinion, but glory. Orthodoxy is not about the right *opinion* about God but the right way to *glorify* God, to respond to Him. For that is the fundamental question posed by anyone, who begins to come to terms with himself: how should I encounter God? Learning the right way to adore – orthodoxy – that, above all, is what we receive from the Faith.

The Council's document on the liturgy was the least controversial of all the documents it produced. As Ratzinger and others have commented, it was the mature fruit of the earlier liturgical movement that spanned over half a century before the Council was assembled. The Council Fathers did not foresee that the reforms it initiated would cause such turbulence. Nor did they expect a controversy that would, in effect, end in schism.[6] The objective of the pre-Conciliar liturgical movement, Ratzinger pointed out, was to overcome the reductionism of the neo-scholastic sacramental theology sundered from its actual realization in liturgical form.[7] That theology had reduced the sacrament of the altar to its constituents of matter and form: bread and wine being the matter, the words of institution the form; only these are necessary, everything else can be changed.[8] On this point, Ratzinger comments rather pointedly, both traditionalists and modernists could shake hands with each other. The object of the earlier liturgical reform was to overcome such reductionism and help us understand liturgy as the rich, complex product of a living organic tradition, whose inner form had been shaped, and so had matured, over time. For this reason, it cannot be hacked into pieces but must be seen and lived in its authentic wholeness:

---

6 The first volume of Proceedings in this series examined the aftermath of the initial reform.   7 See T. Rowland, *Ratzinger's faith. The theology of Pope Benedict XVI* (Oxford, 2008), Chapter 7, especially pp 125–6.   8 *Gesammelte Schriften*, p. 716; see also p. 660.

Anyone like me, who on the eve of the Second Vatican Council had
been moved by this insight at the time of the liturgical movement, can
only contemplate in profound sorrow the destruction precisely of that
which was the object of its concern.[9]

A second general comment by the Pope is related to this. Liturgy is
communal worship: the habitat of the sacraments, the oxygen they need to
breathe. Liturgy is something living, a communal expression of our human
response to Christ's offer of grace which we call sacrament:

> Sacraments are divine-worship events (*Vollzüge*) of the Church, in which
> the Church as Church is engaged, that is, one in which she acts not
> simply as a club but rather on the basis of that which she has not made
> herself. In these acts, she gives more than she herself can give: namely the
> inclusion of man in the Gift she herself receives. This means that in the
> sacrament the entire continuity of history is present: past, present and
> future. As *memoria* it must reach down into the roots of the entire
> human history, and so encounter man in the present moment and give
> him a Presence, a making-present of salvation whose essence is that it
> opens up a future beyond death.[10]

In his concluding comments at the conference held in the Benedictine
Abbey of Fontgombault on 24 July 2001, the then Cardinal Ratzinger called
on his audience to rediscover the truth that liturgy is not simply a complex of
ceremonies aimed at giving the transubstantiation of the species a certain
permanence and ceremony; it is rather the world of the sacrament as such.[11]
Accordingly, liturgy presupposes a proper understanding of what is meant by
sacrament. It presupposes a sacramental theology – and it is his unique
sacramental theology, it seems to me, that lies at the heart of all Ratzinger's
many writings on liturgy. Reflecting on these writing in his introduction to his
collected works on the liturgy, he informs us as to why he first gave his
attention to liturgy. Fundamental theology was his initial choice of theological
discipline, because, as he confesses, he wanted to get to the root of the
question: Why do we believe? Implicit in that question is another question,
namely: What is the right answer we must give to God? – which, evidently,
includes the question, What is the true nature of worship? 'I was not

9 Ibid.   **10** *Gesammelte Schriften*, p. 232.   **11** Cf. *Gesammelte Schriften*, p. 660.

concerned with specific problems of liturgy as a discipline', he admits, 'but rather with the way liturgy is anchored in the fundamental act of our faith and thus with its place in the whole of our human existence.'[12]

SACRAMENT – TYPOS – MYSTERION

Though Ratzinger lectured on the topic in Regensburg, he never got an opportunity to write a full-blown sacramental theology. This is to be found in fragments scattered throughout his volume on the liturgy in his *Gesammelte Schriften*. That volume includes two remarkable papers devoted expressly to sacramental theology, one at the Salzburg Hochshulwochen in 1965[13] and the other in 1978 at the Catholic University of Eichstätt.[14] In his collected works on the liturgy, he has placed them in a section of their own (Section B), immediately after his key publication: *The spirit of the liturgy*, under the title: 'Sacrament – Typos – Mysterion', a title that sums up their content.

In his introduction to his collected writings on liturgy, the Pope stresses that the aim of all his earlier writings on this subject was to get beyond the often petty questions about this or that form so as to situate liturgy in its wider context.[15] This he achieved by working out the implications of three fundamental principles or themes[16] for understanding Christian liturgy.

Unity of the Old and New Testaments

In the first instance, we have the inner relationship between the Old and the New Testaments.[17] If one fails to see the intrinsic connection of Christian worship with the heritage of the Old Testament, Ratzinger claims, the liturgy simply cannot be understood. This is the most basic of all three principles and is summed up in the title: *Sacrament – typos – mysterion*. To be more precise, Ratzinger shows why the Christian understanding of sacrament can only be understood when the Old Testament is understood first of all typologically, that is seeing its events, words and rites as representing types of Christ, who fulfilled them (see 1 Corinthians 10:11). Related to this is the central Greek

---

12 *Gesammelte Schriften*, p. 6. 13 *Gesammelte Schriften*, pp 197–214. 14 *Gesammelte Schriften*, pp 215–32. 15 See in particular de Gaál, *Theology of Pope Benedict XVI*. 16 Ratzinger uses the loose term *Kreise* (circles), which I have translated as 'principles', which does not do justice to the notion of a cluster of themes implied in the term 'Kreis'. 17 See Joseph Cardinal Ratzinger/Pope Benedict XVI, *God's word. Scripture–tradition–office*, P. Hünermann and T. Söding (eds), tr. H. Taylor (San Francisco, 2008), in particular pp 91–126; see also de Gaál, *Theology of Pope Benedict XVI*, pp 111–17; S.W. Hahn, *Covenant and communion. The biblical theology of Pope Benedict XVI* (Grand Rapids MI, 2009), especially pp 91–113.

term *mysterion*, namely the secret that God had prepared from the beginning (to unite man with God and so to unite all things in Christ; see Ephesians 1:9–10). In the course of the centuries this term would come to mean sacrament as we understand it today.

Liturgy and cosmos

Another principle is the cosmic character of the liturgy.[18] The liturgy, he tells us, celebrates the breadth and reaches into the depth of the cosmos, encompassing at the same time creation and history. This, for example, was the intent behind the orientation of prayer, namely prayer facing the Rising Sun in the East: it signifies 'that the Saviour, to whom we pray, is also the Creator; consequently, love of creation and responsibility for it is also intrinsic to the liturgy'.[19]

Liturgy and world religions

More *ad rem* to the subject of this Conference is perhaps the third theme, namely world religions.[20] Ratzinger's original interest, we saw, was 'with the way liturgy is anchored in the fundamental act of our faith and thus with its place in the whole of our human existence'.[21] The paper on sacramental theology he gave in Salzburg (1965) was entitled 'The sacramental foundation of Christian existence'. It was one of the few publications (more a pamphlet than a book) I brought with me to Papua New Guinea and the Solomon Islands, where I was to teach a course on the sacraments. There I encountered the aboriginal rites and myths that gave cohesion and meaning to the numerous indigenous tribes so that they (and the members of the tribes) could survive and flourish for tens of thousands of years. They – or rites of a similar kind – are at the root of the rituals of all the world religions. I wondered about what possible connection they might have with the Christian rites. So did my students, many of whom had taken part in various rites of initiation. Looking for help, I turned to the work of the anthropologists, Victor Turner and Mary Douglas, as well as the comparative religious studies of Mircea Eliade. Turner

---

18 See Hahn, *Covenant and communion*, pp 163–85; Cardinal Joseph Ratzinger, *'In the beginning ...'* *A Catholic understanding of the story of creation and the fall*, tr. B. Ramsey (Edinburgh, 1995), in particular pp 27–32; see also U.M. Lang, 'Benedict XVI and church architecture' in D.V. Twomey and J.E. Rutherford (eds), *Benedict XVI and beauty in sacred art and architecture*, pp 116–19.   **19** *Gesammelte Schriften*, pp 7–8; see U.M. Lang, *Turning towards the Lord. Second edition* with an introduction by Joseph Ratzinger (Pope Benedict XVI) (San Francisco, 2008).   **20** Ratzinger's comprehensive theology of the world religions is to be found especially in his book *Truth and tolerance, Christian belief and world religions*, tr. H. Taylor (San Francisco, 2004).   **21** *Gesammelte Schriften*, p. 6.

in particular discovered that ritual, though always particular, shares universal patterns that reflect and express the most basic human/religious experiences of mankind.

But it was Ratzinger who provided me with the key to both interpreting the aboriginal rituals and making the connection with liturgy, the celebration of the sacraments. He shows how certain moments in human life – birth and death, meals and marriage – touch us so deeply that, following an insight of Schleiermacher, they open up fissures in our souls that let in the light of eternity. Turner discovered in his field-work in Africa that aboriginal rites both express and have their source in these primal human experiences. Turner coined the term 'liminal'[22] to describe the effect on the participants of such ritual celebrations.

These liminal moments, Ratzinger stresses (though he does not use the term as such), are related to *bios*, that is, to physical life, which for man is always shot through with spirit, with meaning. He illustrates this by examining the universal experience of meals, which properly understood involve more than physical nourishment – they create community, fellowship, not only horizontally, with our fellows, but with God, the Giver of all. In another context he recalls how in the world religions sacrifice, the core of worship, invariably involves a meal, communion with the divinity and with those participating in offering the sacrifice, to show that there is no opposition between meal and sacrifice in the world of ritual. Ratzinger recalls Bonaventure's insight into what the mediaeval theologians called the sacraments of creation, namely marriage and repentance. The nature of marriage as a natural sacrament rooted in *bios* is obvious. And though repentance is a specifically spiritual experience, it expresses itself bodily, in tears, and craves absolution – the many ritual washings and purifications that are to be found in all religions and were incorporated into the Old Testament rites, including that of the scapegoat. And finally there are the primordial social sacraments, kingship and priesthood, which expressed the transcendent dimension of society that unites past, present and future and so gives society its inner coherence. It is a profoundly significant characteristic of the New Testament that the sacral nature of kingship was *not* recognized – political authority is essentially a profane activity.[23] It is worth noting in passing that

22 From the Latin, *limen* = threshold.   23 See also Joseph Ratzinger/Pope Benedict XVI, *Church, ecumenism, and politics: new endeavours in ecclesiology*, tr. M.J. Millar et al. (San Francisco, 2008), pp 155–7, 203–4. There is, of course, no denying that, in the course of the Church's history, attempts were made to

Ratzinger's theology of political life draws out the many implications for the contemporary world of this radical break with the religious traditions of humanity.[24]

In the Old Testament we find that these primordial cultic actions or rites common to all the world religions – such as first fruits – have been transformed into celebratory links to (memorials of) those historical events which shaped the Chosen People in the past and which at the same time point to their future expectations of God's design for them. Those rituals were shaped anew by the prophetic word that transformed primordial rituals into history-shaping ritual actions that opened up the future. This process eventually found expression in the Temple sacrifices, until such time as the Temple was destroyed at the time of the Babylonian captivity. In Exile, the prophets discovered a new form of sacrifice to make up for the absence of the Temple worship – namely a contrite and broken heart. And with this more spiritual kind of sacrifice grew the hope for the restoration of the Temple in Jerusalem.

Since none of the subsequent stone buildings could satisfy that hope, the way was left open for the expectation of a new Temple, an expectation that in the consciousness of the early Christians was realized in the Church, the Body of Christ, at the core of which is the Paschal Mystery, the source of all the sacraments. The post-Exilic discovery of worship in the spirit encountered a similar movement in Greek thought when the Greek thinkers literally saw through their own inherited myths and rites to discover the eternal Logos. Evidence of this growing convergence of Hebrew prophecy with Greek thought can be found to the Wisdom literature of the Old Testament. Both strands merged into one in the New Testament, as in St Paul's description of the new form of worship inaugurated by the Paschal Mystery: λογική λατρεία (θυσία) – literally a word-like worship.[25] This term is found in the letter to the Romans 12:1f.[26]

turn political authority into a sacral entity, expressed above all in the coronation ceremonies of Byzantium and the Holy Roman Empire, the last survivor of these elaborate ceremonies is probably the magnificent coronation rite of the English monarch last used for the coronation of Queen Elizabeth II on 2 June 1953. **24** See above all, Joseph Cardinal Ratzinger, *Church, ecumenism and politics*, especially pp 193–208; see also T. Rowland, *Ratzinger's faith*, pp 105–22; D.V. Twomey, 'An introduction to Ratzinger's theology of political life' in K.D. Whitehead (ed.), *The thought of Joseph Ratzinger, Pope Benedict XVI: Proceedings from the 32nd annual convention of the Fellowship of Catholic Scholars, Providence, Rhode Island, September 25–27, 2009* (Chicago, 2009), pp 23–65. **25** In Latin: *rationale obsequim*, which is echoed in the Roman Canon: *Quam oblationem tu, Deus, in omnibus, quaesimus, benedictam, adscriptam, ratam, rationalilem, acceptabilemque facere digneris ut nobis Corpus et Sanguis fiat dilectissimi Filii tui, Domini nostril Jesu Christi …* **26** The CTS New Catholic Bible translates: 'Think of God's mercy, my brothers, and worship him, I beg you in a way that is worthy of thinking beings, by offering your living bodies as a holy sacrifice, truly pleasing to God.'

… as the Christian answer to the cultic crisis of the whole antique world: the 'Word' is the sacrifice, the word of prayer, which rises out of the heart of man and takes up the entire existence of man and allows his very self to become 'Word'.[27]

In his programmatic speech at the Liturgical Institute, Trier (2003), to mark the fortieth anniversary of the promulgation of the Liturgy Constitution by the Council. Ratzinger stressed the sacrificial nature of Christian worship. 'For it is the liturgy through which, especially in the divine sacrifice of the Eucharist, "the work of our redemption is accomplished", and it is through the liturgy, especially, that the faithful are enabled to express in their lives and manifest to others the mystery of Christ and the real nature of the true Church' (*SC* 2). Ratzinger comments:

Because [liturgy] is the realization (*Vollzug*) of redemption, it conveys its dynamic to humanity – from the visible to the invisible, from activity to contemplation; from the present to the future City we seek.[28]

He quotes Origen: 'In fact, we must go beyond everything', and in this context refers to the final temptation as expressed by Goethe's Faust: 'Verweile doch, du bist so schön' ['Stay, please, you are so fair']. This, Ratzinger says, shows an ultimate awareness of the need to keep alive what he calls the dynamic thrust 'to go beyond' this world intrinsic to human existence – a central concern of the Fathers of the Church:

The liturgy, according to the Council, leads us right into this dynamic of going beyond, which Augustine in his theology of the *Sursum corda* tried to bring home to his hearers in his sermons. Liturgy snatches us out of what is visible, what is present, what is comfortable – and transfers us into the future City [the City of God].[29]

What happened to this vision?

'CREATIVITY' AND THE CONCILIAR REFORM

In an interview with the periodical, *Communio*, in 1977, Ratzinger commented on the way 'creativity' took over the liturgical reform. Bourgeois forms of politeness began to infiltrate into the liturgy like the banal greetings at the

27 *Gesammelte Schriften*, p. 57. **28** Here Ratzinger summarizes SC 2. **29** *Gesammelte Schriften*, p. 698.

beginning of Mass or the priest waiting until all had received Communion before he did, or avoiding to say, 'I bless *you*' – the avoidance of which undermines the basic liturgical relationship of priest and congregation.

> In the period in which the new missal had not yet appeared and the old one had already been rejected as 'old', the consciousness was lost that there is such a thing as a 'rite', that is, a pre-given liturgical form, and that liturgy is something that of its very nature is not at the disposal of those who celebrate it. Even the new official missals, as good as they are in many respects, allow us here and there to detect too easily the considered planning of the professors and so give weight to the opinion that a liturgical book is 'made' the way other books are made.[30]

In other words, of its very nature the liturgy is not at our disposal; it is not even at the disposal of the celebrant. It is something objective, something that has grown out of the experience of the whole Church down through the ages. This, however, does not mean that a liturgical rite is fixed in stone: '[T]he missal can be mummified as little as the Church herself.'[31]

As is well known, the Council highlighted the notion of *participatio actuosa* – active participation – in the liturgy. Behind that notion, according to Ratzinger, is the idea that the Christian liturgy in its essence and form is a coming-to-be [*Vollzug*] of community. It involves reciprocal prayers, acclamations, proclamation and common worship. Liturgical texts are characterized by terms such as 'we', 'you' (singular and plural) and the whole is described as part of an *actio* ('drama'), in which all are active in a common endeavour. This insight of the liturgical movement was, as it were, canonized by the Council. Unfortunately it was often interpreted in a one-sided fashion:

> Some pragmatic exponents of the liturgical reform appear to hold the view that what was needed to make the liturgy attractive and effective is to express everything out loud and as much as possible to involve the community by getting them to perform various tasks. They forget that the spoken words also have a *meaning*, the realization (*vollziehen*) of which belongs together with *participatio actuosa*. They had overlooked the deeper insight that *actio* does not only, and does not primarily, consist of changing one's posture, such as standing, sitting, kneeling, but

---

30 *Gesammelte Schriften*, p. 618.   **31** *Gesammelte Schriften*, p. 619.

rather in the inner processes that constitute the actual drama of it all. 'Let us pray' – that is an invitation to a process that is interior in its reach. 'Lift up your heart' – the words and the standing that accompanies them are here, as it were, but the 'tip of the iceberg'. What actually happens takes place in the depth [of the soul] where it is raised up to the heights. 'See the Lamb of God' – refers to a particular kind of seeing that does not take place simply by seeing the visible Host.[32]

And so on. This leads to the unavoidable conclusion that liturgy needs catechesis – we have to learn the deeper significance of the language and gestures that make up the rite.

Learning the deeper meaning of the words and symbolic actions is central to active participation in the liturgy. And it is for this reason that catechesis is essential. Even before it appeared, the new translation was rejected on the grounds that it was too difficult for the 'average' person (in effect children below the age of twelve) to understand. Behind this contention, it could be argued, lies a rather superficial rationalism that assumes that we can actually understand what the liturgy (or indeed the Faith) is all about. But Christian liturgy celebrates mysteries that are almost beyond comprehension. For this reason, the text should be a never-ending invitation to probe more deeply into the mysteries we share in through the Divine Liturgy. To respond, however inadequately, to this invitation, we need the grace of humility: docility of heart. The initial attempt at rendering the Latin into English, following the principles of dynamic equivalence, tended to reduce the text to what could be immediately understood by all – and so fostered banality as it sought the lowest common denominator. It is precisely this character of the first translation that is now being glorified by those who reject the new one. It is to be hoped that the somewhat awkward syntax of the new translation might help to overcome the temptation to embellish the liturgy with one's own additions of an even more banal nature, what Ratzinger referred to as 'creativity'. Liturgical language is not colloquial. The real question is: should it be colloquial? This could be phrased in another, more positive way: does the new translation foster a more sacral approach to the celebration of the liturgy? Does it promote real *participatio actuosa*, as intended by the Council?

The challenges faced by any attempt to translate the Latin text are enormous. As Daniel Gallagher in his contribution to the conference shows,

32 *Gesammelte Schriften*, p. 622.

the syntactical differences between Latin and English are so great as to render it almost impossible for any translation to do justice to both.[33] Whatever criticism one may have of the literary quality of the new translation, or indeed its suitability for singing or reading out loud (two very important aspects), there is no doubting the fact that both priest and people now have to *think* about and reflect on the meaning of the text. Now that the Latin text of the *Novus Ordo* which is at the basis of the new English translation has been enriched by the inclusion of more ancient prayers with their profound scriptural and patristic allusions, it has become a greater challenge to all, but above all to the celebrant, to search for the deeper meaning of the text. In short, the text is not self-explanatory. Like Scripture, which, incidentally, is the source of most of the texts used in the Mass, the words of the new translation have a depth and a richness that needs to be discovered over and over again. The very awkwardness of the more literal translation, though at times rather off-putting, can be an invitation to 'go beyond' the letter to the spirit of the written word. It is to be hoped that it will promote a more 'sacral' approach to the celebration of the Liturgy by directing the attention of both priest and faithful to what is beyond, to God.

In the meantime, for many older priests, long familiar with the earlier translation, who find the new translations difficult to accept – or even to read without stumbling at times – the act of obedience involved in submitting to the new translation is itself a kind of spiritual sacrifice that surely must be pleasing to God.

---

33 See also the perceptive comments from an Anglican perspective by J.E. Rutherford, '"Putting ashes on our heads": Anglican reflections on the problem of liturgical English' in *One in Christ* 45:2 (Winter, 2011), 182–99.

Ius Divinum and the sacred liturgy

RAYMOND LEO CARDINAL BURKE

INTRODUCTION

This essay addresses a fundamental concept that underlies the study of the *Missale Romanum*. The relationship of the *ius divinum*, the divine right (or right of God) and the Sacred Liturgy must be clarified if we are to understand the nature of the book containing the texts for the celebration of the Holy Eucharist in which, in the words of the Decree of the Second Vatican Ecumenical Council (drawing upon a text of Saint Thomas Aquinas):

> is contained the whole spiritual good of the Church, namely Christ himself our Pasch and the living bread that gives life to men through his flesh – that flesh that is given life and gives life through the Holy Spirit.[1]

In the celebration of the Holy Eucharist, in the words of the same Decree, 'men are invited and led to offer themselves, their works and all creation with Christ'.[2] The Holy Eucharist, therefore, is the fundamental and pre-eminent manifestation of the relationship of the *ius divinum* and the Sacred Liturgy.

This essay is a further development of two previous presentations, one given during the *incontro di studio* hosted by the Faculty of Jurisprudence at the University of Bari, on the theme '*Liturgie secolarizzate e diritto*', 'Secularized liturgies and the law', on 25 March 2011, and the other given to the Thomistic Circle of the Pontifical Faculty of the Immaculate Conception at the Dominican House of Studies in Washington DC, on the theme 'St Thomas Aquinas and theo-centric ecclesiology', on 11 May 2011. The subject that I addressed on those two occasions and am addressing here is one that merits a much more profound study that I hope to make in the future. This essay represents the fruits of my study up to the present, in the hope that it

---

1 *totum bonum spirituale Ecclesiae continetur, ipse scilicet Christus, Pascha nostrum panisque vivus per Carnem suam Spiritu Sancto vivificatam et vivificantem vitam praestans hominibus* … Concilium Oecumenicum Vaticanum II, Decretum *Presbyterorum Ordinis*, 'de Presbyterorum ministerio et vita', 7 Decembris 1965, *Acta Apostolicae Sedis* 58 (1966), p. 997, no. 5. English translation, A. Flannery OP (ed.), *Vatican Council II: The Conciliar and Post Conciliar documents* (Collegeville, MN, 1975), p. 871. **2** *qui ita invitantur et adducuntur ad seipsos, suos labores cunctasque res creatas una cum ipso offerendos.* Ibid.

will be helpful in understanding the nature of the *Missale Romanum*, especially as it is presented in the teaching of Pope Benedict XVI.

FUNDAMENTAL CONCEPTS

To speak of the *ius divinum*, the divine right, is, in the most simple terms, to speak of the right relationship between God and his creation, especially mankind, the only earthly creature created in the image of God himself. It is clear that such discourse has to do, first of all, with the Sacred Liturgy, as the highest and most perfect expression of the relationship between God and man. There is no aspect of the life of the Church in which the truth about God's relationship with man should be more visible than in the Sacred Liturgy.

But in recent years it is a discourse that has rarely been engaged in, so much so that it generates wonder among not a few to hear divine right and Sacred Liturgy spoken of in the same context. In the time since the Second Vatican Ecumenical Council, but certainly not because of the teaching of the Council, there has been an exaggerated attention on the human aspect of the Sacred Liturgy, which has overlooked the essence of the Sacred Liturgy as the encounter of God with us by means of sacramental signs – that is, as the direct action of the glorious Christ in the Church to give us the grace of the Holy Spirit.

I am addressing the subject from the perspective of a student of Canon Law. It should be clear, however, that the canonical treatment of the subject, to the degree that it is true, must necessarily be securely grounded in the theological reality of the Church. For that reason, I will first treat the subject with reference to the Sacred Scriptures and the Magisterium, and only then with reference to its place in canonical discipline. In other words, since the canonical order is at the service of the objective order of our life in Christ in the Church, it is fundamental to understand the objective relationship of the *ius divinum* and the Sacred Liturgy, in its essentials at least, in order to understand the deepest significance of the canonical norms that govern the Sacred Liturgy.

The then Cardinal Joseph Ratzinger, in his classic work, *The spirit of the liturgy*, reminds us of the relationship of man's worship of God to his moral rectitude in general, observing:

Ultimately, it is the very life of man, man himself as living righteously, that is the true worship of God, but life only becomes real life when it receives its form from looking toward God. Cult exists in order to communicate this vision and to give life in such a way that glory is given to God.[3]

The right understanding of the Sacred Liturgy is in fact key to understanding every dimension of life. That right understanding is safeguarded by the law – the discipline which safeguards, first, the relationship of man with God. Cardinal Ratzinger concludes:

When human affairs are so ordered that there is no recognition of God, there is a belittling of man. That is why, in the final analysis, worship and law cannot be completely separated from each other. God has a right to a response from man, to man himself, and where that right of God totally disappears, the order of law among men is dissolved, because there is no cornerstone to keep the whole structure together.[4]

Clearly, the knowledge and observance of the *ius divinum* has fundamentally to do with man's own self-knowledge and the self-respect that it demands.

Reflecting on the relationship of law and sacred worship, Cardinal Ratzinger further observed:

Worship, that is, the right kind of cult, of relationship with God, is essential for the right kind of human existence in the world. It is so precisely because it reaches beyond everyday life. Worship gives us a share in heaven's mode of existence, in the world of God, and allows light to fall from that divine world into ours ... It lays hold in advance of a more perfect life and, in so doing, gives our present life its proper measure.[5]

---

3 'Letzlich ist das Leben des Menschen selbst, der recht lebende Mensch die wahre Anbetung Gottes, aber das Leben wird zu wirklichem Leben nur, wenn es seine Form aus dem Blick auf Gott hin empfängt. Der Kult ist dazu da, diesen Blick zu vermitteln und so Leben zu geben, das Ehre wird für Gott.' J. Ratzinger, *Theologie der Liturgie: Die sakramentale Begründung christlicher Existenz* (Gesammelte Schriften, Band 11) (Freiburg, 2008), p. 36; tr. J. Saward, *The spirit of the liturgy* (San Francisco, 2000), p. 18. 4 'Eine Ordnung der menschlichen Dinge, die Gott nicht kennt, verkleinert den Menschen. Darum sind letzlich auch Kult und Recht nicht gänzlich voneinander zu trennen: Gott hat ein Recht auf die Antwort des Menschen, auf den Menschen selbst, und wo dieses Recht Gottes gänzlich verschwindet, löst sich auch die menschliche Rechtsordnung auf, weil ihr der Eckstein fehlt, der das Ganze zusammenhält.' *Theologie der Liturgie*, pp 36–7; *The spirit of the liturgy*, p. 19. 5 'Anbetung, die richtige Weise des Kultes, der

Cardinal Ratzinger's reflection on the *lex orandi* and the *lex vivendi* points to the fundamental importance of the study of the *ius divinum* in its relationship to the Sacred Liturgy for a right understanding of our life in Christ in the Church and in the world.

SACRED SCRIPTURE

When God offered the covenant of faithful and enduring love between himself and his people to restore the covenant that had been radically broken by the sin of Adam and Eve, he founded it on the Decalogue, the Ten Commandments. The first three of the Commandments, in fact, express the essence of the *ius divinum*, the right of God to be recognized as the Creator of the world and the Lord of history and, therefore, as the exclusive recipient of the worship of man.

One recalls that Satan tempted Adam and Eve to sin against the one and only commandment that the Lord had given to them, that is, 'of the fruit of the tree of the knowledge of good and evil you shall not eat, for in the day that you eat of it you shall die',[6] with the words:

> You will not die. For God knows that when you eat of it your eyes will be opened, and you will be like God, knowing good and evil.[7]

Our first parents were led into a lie by Satan, not recognizing God as the source of their being and of their every good but taking on the pretence of being equal to God. The first three commandments of the Decalogue re-establish the just relationship between God and man, based on divine right.

The Decalogue begins with the identification of the Lord as the only God, Creator and Saviour: 'I am the Lord your God, who brought you out of the land of Egypt, out of the house of bondage.'[8] Then there follows immediately the prohibition of every form of idolatry: 'You shall have no other gods before me';[9] the commandment always to honour the holy name of the Lord in speech: 'You shall not take the name of the Lord your God in vain';[10] and the

---

Gottesbeziehung, ist konstitutiv für die rechte menschliche Existenz in der Welt; sie ist es gerade dadurch, dass sie über das Leben im Alltag hinausreicht, indem sie uns an der Existenzweise des »Himmels«, der Welt Gottes, beteiligt und damit das Licht der göttlichen Welt in die unsrige fallen lässt … Er greift voraus auf ein endgültigeres Leben und gibt gerade so dem gegenwärtigen Leben sein Maß.' *Theologie der Liturgie*, p. 38; *The spirit of the liturgy*, p. 21.   **6** Gen 2:17; cf. Gen 3:3.   **7** Gen 3:4–5.   **8** Ex 20:2.   **9** Ex 20:3.   **10** Ex 20:7.

precept of the observance of the day of the Lord: 'Remember the Sabbath day, to keep it holy'.[11] The other seven commandments derive from these first commandments, which establish and safeguard the divine right and, thereby, the foundation of man's relationship with God. In other words, the worship of God 'in spirit and truth' is, at the same time, the sanctification of the people.[12]

In the Code of the Covenant, which follows the declaration of the Decalogue, the first attention is dedicated to divine worship and specifically to the altar. God, reminding the people of the truth that he has come from heaven to speak to them, commands: 'An altar of earth you shall make for me and sacrifice on it your burnt offerings and your peace offerings, your sheep and your oxen; in every place where I cause my name to be remembered I will come to you and bless you.'[13] After the ratification of the covenant detailed norms for divine worship are listed.[14] Following upon the account of the offering of the covenant and its ratification in the *Book of Exodus*, the *Book of Leviticus* contains the detailed norms for the priests and Levites, in order that they might fulfil their responsibility for divine worship and, therefore, for the sanctification of the people.

From this brief look at the content of the covenant between God and man, one sees as the fundamental principle the *ius divinum*, the right of God to receive man's worship in the manner that God desires and commands. It is clear that divine worship and the sanctification of the people, which is its fruit, are ordained by God himself. Divine worship is not the invention of man, but the gift of God to man, by which God makes it possible for man to offer 'the sacrifice of communion' with him.

Cardinal Ratzinger has reminded us that God has created us in order to enter into a covenant of faithful and enduring love with us, and that this relationship of faithful and enduring love on the part of man means, first and foremost, divine worship. The Sabbath rest is the concrete manifestation of the covenant finality of God's creative work:

> The Sabbath is the sign of the covenant between God and man; it sums up the inward essence of the covenant. If this is so, then we can now define the intention of the account of creation as follows: creation exists to be a place for the covenant that God wants to make with man. The goal of creation is the covenant, the love story of God and man. The freedom and equality of men, which the Sabbath is meant to bring

---

11 Ex 20:8.   **12** Jn 4:24.   **13** Ex 20:24.   **14** Cf. Gen 25:1–31:18.

about, is not a merely anthropological or sociological vision; it can only be understood *theo*-logically. Only when man is in covenant with God does he become free. Only then are the equality and dignity of all men made manifest. If, then, everything is directed to the covenant, it is important that the covenant is a relationship: God's gift of himself to man, but also man's response to God. Man's response to the God who is good to him is love, and loving God means worshipping him. If creation is meant to be a space for the covenant, the place where God and man meet one another, then it must be thought of as space for worship.[15]

Clearly, unless man recognizes and respects the *ius divinum* in what pertains to the Sacred Liturgy, he fails to recognize and respect the truth about creation. The failure to recognize and respect the *ius divinum* leads to idolatry, as the story of the golden calf eloquently illustrates. Cardinal Ratzinger has articulated the two causes of the act of idolatry:

1. Man's refusal to recognize God as other, and his subsequent attempt to reduce God to man's dimensions;
2. Man's pretence of creating his own worship, instead of worshiping in accord with the *ius divinum*.[16]

In the Sermon on the Mount, in which Our Lord Jesus communicated the law of the New Covenant, the first Beatitude is the poverty of spirit, which recognizes the Lord as the source of being itself and of every good: 'Blessed are the poor in spirit, for theirs is the kingdom of heaven.'[17] All of the other Beatitudes depend upon the first and fundamental recognition of our relationship with God and the effective expression of the same.

---

15 'Der Sabbat ist das Zeichen des Bundes zwischen Gott und Mensch; er fasst das Wesen des Bundes von innen her zusammen. Von da aus können wir jetzt die Intention des Schöpfungsberichte schon so definieren: Schöpfung ist, damit ein Ort sei für den Bund, den Gott mit den Menschen schließen will. Das Ziel der Schöpfung ist der Bund, die Liebesgeschichte zwischen Gott und Mensch. Die Freiheit und die Gleichheit der Menschen, die der Sabbat wirken soll, ist keine rein antropologische oder soziologische Vision; sie ist nur theologisch denkbar: Nur wenn der Mensch im Bund mit Gott steht, wird er frei, erscheint die Gleichheit und die Würde aller Menschen. Wenn also alles auf den »Bund« ankommt, dann ist wichtig zu sehen, dass der Bund Beziehung ist: ein Sich-Schenken Gottes an den Menschen, aber auch ein Antworten des Menschen auf ihn. Die Antwort des Menschen auf einen Gott, der ihm gut ist, heißt: Liebe, und Gott lieben heißt: ihn anbeten. Wenn Schöpfung als ein Raum des Bundes, als Ort der Begegnung von Gott und Mensch gemeint ist, dann heißt das auch, dass sie als Raum der Anbetung gedacht ist.' *Theologie der Liturgie*, p. 42; *The spirit of the liturgy*, p. 26.   **16** See *Theologie der Liturgie*, pp 39–40; *The spirit of the liturgy*, pp 22–3.   **17** Mt 5:3.

After having announced the Beatitudes as the law of the New Covenant and after having exhorted the disciples to be 'the salt of the earth' and 'the light of the world', so that others, seeing the holiness of the people, might give 'glory to [their] Father who is in heaven',[18] the Lord declared His mission in what pertains to the Law:

> Think not that I have come to abolish the law and the prophets; I have come not to abolish them but to fulfil them. For truly, I say to you, till heaven and earth pass away, not an iota, not a dot, will pass from the law until all is accomplished. Whoever then relaxes one of the least of these commandments and teaches men so, shall be called least in the kingdom of heaven; but he who does them and teaches them shall be called great in the kingdom of heaven.[19]

The words of the Lord confirm the fundamental service of the Law, which is to honour and to safeguard the *ius divinum*, the divine right, and, thereby, to honour and safeguard the order written by God in His creation.

All of the norms of the Law are directed to the just relationship between God and man, upon which depends the salvation of the world, and thus they must be respected as the commandment of God and not the invention of man. Otherwise, the Law of God is corrupted for human purposes. After having declared the holiness of the Law, the Lord exhorted the disciples with these words: 'For I tell you, unless your righteousness exceeds that of the scribes and Pharisees, you will never enter the kingdom of heaven.'[20] Only by observing and honouring the divine right that God be known, adored and served, as he desires and commands, does man find his happiness in this life and in the life to come.

When Our Lord encountered the Samaritan woman at the Well of Jacob, He revealed himself as the Messiah with these words: 'I who speak to you am he'.[21] In the conversation with the Samaritan woman that precedes the revelation, Our Lord instructs her on the true worship of God, the adoration of God 'in spirit and truth'.[22] It is clear from his teaching that faith in him as Messiah, as God the Son made man, is expressed, first of all, in the worship owed to God.

At the Last Supper, when Our Lord instituted the Eucharistic Sacrifice, he directly gave the command: 'Do this in remembrance of me … Do this, as

---

18 Mt 5:16.　**19** Mt 5:17–19.　**20** Mt 5:20.　**21** Jn 4:26.　**22** Jn 4:23–4.

often as you drink it, in remembrance of me'.[23] It is clear that the Holy Eucharist, the worship offered to God 'in spirit and truth', is not an invention of man, but a gift of God to man. In a similar manner, when Christ was about to ascend to the right hand of the Father in heaven, He gave the command to the disciples:

> All authority in heaven and on earth has been given to me. Go therefore and make disciples of all nations, baptizing them in the name of the Father and of the Son and of the Holy Spirit, teaching them to observe all that I have commanded you.[24]

It is evident that true worship, for example, the rebirth of christians through the sacrament of Baptism, is an act of respect for the right of God, carried out in accord with the indications given by him.

THE CATECHISM

Before considering some texts of the Magisterium, it will be helpful to look at the Catechism, the instrument for the understanding and application of the Sacred Scriptures and the Magisterium in daily living. Regarding the First Commandment, we read in the *Roman Catechism*, edited after the Council of Trent:

> It should also be noted here that this is indeed the First Commandment, not just because it is first in order, but because it is first in rank by its very nature and excellence. God is entitled to a love and an obedience infinitely greater than what is owed to any other king or superior. He created us, he governs us. He nurtured us even in the womb of our mother and brought us into the world and still provides for us in all that we need for life.[25]

The language of the *Catechism* underlines the truth that worship is owed to God, that is, that worship is part of the divine right.

---

23 I Cor 11:24–5.   **24** Mt 28:18–20.   **25** *[H]oc praeceptum esse omnium primum et maximum: non ordine tantum ipso, sed ratione, dignitate, praestantia. Debet enim Deus obtinere apud nos infinitis partibus majorem quam domini, quam regis charitatem et auctoritatem. Ipse nos creavit, idem gubernat; ab eo in utero matris nutriti, atque inde hanc in lucem ducti sumus: ipse nobis ad vitam victumque res suppeditat necessarias. Catechismus Romanus ad Parochos*, Coloniae Agrippinae: Apud Franciscum Balth. Neuwirth, 1765. Pars III,

In presenting the obligation to observe the Decalogue, the *Catechism of Saint Pius X* declares: 'We are obliged to observe the commandments of God, because they are imposed by him, our supreme Master, and dictated by nature and sound reason.'[26] Father C.T. Dragone, in his classical presentation of the same Catechism for catechists, comments on the First Commandment with these words:

> Religion is a duty and a fundamental need of every intelligent being. By the fact itself that we are creatures, we must recognize and fittingly honour our Creator and Lord, offer adoration, praise, thanksgiving and reparation to Him, and implore from him what we need. Religion is the virtue which makes us recognize God as our absolute sovereign, our total dependence on him, and inclines us to render to him the worship and honour which is owed to him.[27]

Divine worship therefore is the first and most perfect way to observe the divine right.

The *Catechism of the Catholic Church* puts the duty of divine worship among the rights and duties 'inherent in the nature of the human person'.[28] Divine worship constitutes the fundamental duty of man toward God; the First Commandment, like the others, is 'engraved by God in the human heart'.[29] In the words of the *Catechism*, 'God's first call and just demand is that man accept him and worship him'.[30] By God's first call or commandment, he establishes the order of his relationship with man, which is safeguarded by the other commandments.

SAINT THOMAS AQUINAS

Saint Thomas Aquinas, in the *Summa theologiae* and in the *Summa contra gentiles*, presents divine worship as an act of religion,[31] the virtue by which we

Caput II, Quaestio II, n. IV, p. 479; tr. R.I. Bradley and E. Kevane, *The Roman Catechism* (Boston, 1985), p. 359, no. 6. **26** *Siamo obbligati a osservare i comandamenti di Dio, perché sono imposti da Lui, nostro Padrone supremo, e dettati dalla natura e dalla sana ragione.* C.T. Dragone, S.S.P., *Spiegazione del Catechismo di San Pio X per catechisti*, 4ª ed. (Torino, 1964), p. 258. English translation by author. **27** *La religione è un dovere e un bisogno fondamentale per ogni essere intelligente. Dal fatto stesso che siamo creature, dobbiamo riconoscere e onorare convenientemente il nostro Creatore e Signore, offrire a Lui adorazione, lode, ringraziamento, riparazione e implorare quanto ci occorre. La religione è la virtù che ci fa riconoscere Dio come nostro sovrano assoluto, la nostra totale dipendenza da Lui e inclina a rendergli il culto e l'onore che gli è dovuto.* Ibid., p. 262; English translation by author. **28** *Catechism of the Catholic Church*, no. 2070. **29** *Catechism of the Catholic Church*, no. 2072. **30** *Catechism of the Catholic Church*, no. 2084. **31** Cf. *Summa theologica*,

render the honour owed to God.[32] He responds to the question whether religion is a theological virtue, with these words:

> *I answer that,* As stated above (A. 4) religion pays due worship to God. Hence two things are to be considered in religion: first that which it offers to God, viz. worship, and this is by way of matter and object in religion; secondly, that to which something is offered, viz. God, to whom worship is paid. And yet the acts whereby God is worshiped do not reach out to God himself, as when we believe God we reach out to Him by believing; for which reason it was stated (Q. a, AA. 1, 2, 4) that God is the object of faith, not only because we believe in a God, but because we believe God. Now due worship is paid to God, in so far as certain acts whereby God is worshipped, such as the offering of sacrifices and so forth, are done out of reverence for God. Hence it is evident that God is related to religion not as matter or object, but as end; and consequently religion is not a theological virtue whose object is the last end, but a moral virtue which is properly about things referred to the end.[33]

The text of the Angelic Doctor shows how divine worship is the expression of the moral virtue of religion, by which man offers to God acts of reverence, in accord with the objective relationship between God and man.

In the *Summa contra gentiles*, Saint Thomas explains that the objective relationship between God and man, the relationship between Creator and the creature capable of knowing and loving him, capable of offering to the Creator due reverence, not only interiorly but also with the body, with words and gestures, postulates three norms, as they are enunciated in chapter 20 of the *Book of Exodus*. Above all, the worship of other gods or idolatry is prohibited. In the second place, the divine name may not be pronounced without due

---

II-II, q. 81, art. 1. **32** Cf. *Summa theologica*, II-II, q. 81, art. 2. **33** *Respondeo dicendum quod, sicut dictum est, religio est quae Deo debitum cultum affert. Duo igitur in religione considerantur. Unum quidem quod religio Deo affert, cultus scilicet; et hoc se habet per modum materiae et obiecti ad religionem. Aliud autem est id cui affertur, scilicet Deus. Cui cultus exhibetur non quasi actus quibus Deus colitur ipsum Deum attingunt, sicut cum credimus Deo, credendo Deum attingimus (propter quod supra dictum est quod Deus est fidei objectum non solum inquantum credimus Deum, sed inquantum credimus Deo): affertur autem Deo debitus cultus inquantum actus quidam, quibus Deus colitur, in Dei reverentiam fiunt, puta sacrificiorum oblationes et alia huiusmodi. Unde manifestum est quod Deus non comparatur ad virtutem religionis sicut materia vel obiectum, sed sicut finis. Et ideo religio non est virtus theologica, cuius obiectum est ultimus finis: sed est virtus moralis, cuius est esse circa ea quae sunt ad finem. Summa theologica*, II-II, q. 81, art. 5. English version: St Thomas Aquinas, *Summa theologica*, Complete English edition, vol. 3 (Westminster MD, 1948), p. 1526.

reverence. And, finally, the rest on the Day of the Lord is prescribed, in order that man may dedicate his soul to contemplation.[34]

THE MAGISTERIUM

Time does not permit the review of all of the texts of the Magisterium which indicate the irreplaceable relationship between divine right and liturgical law. I limit myself to some examples.

The Council of Trent, in treating the question of doctrine on Holy Communion *sub utraque specie et parvulorum*, declared that the Church from the beginning has had the authority to order the administration of the Sacraments, but that she has no authority to touch the substance of the Sacraments in any manner. Here is the text from Session 19 of the Council:

> [The Holy Council] furthermore declares that in the dispensation of the sacraments, provided their substance is preserved, the Church has always had the power to determine or change, according to circumstances, times and places, what she judges more expedient for the benefit of those receiving them or for the veneration of the sacrament.[35]

The substance of the Sacraments cannot be touched because they are instituted by Christ and entrusted to the Church, as the worship of God the Father 'in spirit and truth'.[36]

The Second Vatican Ecumenical Council has repeated the constant teaching on the exclusive authority of the Church for the right discipline of the Sacred Liturgy, distinguishing two parts of the liturgy, 'unchangeable elements divinely instituted' and 'elements subject to change', which 'not only may be changed but ought to be changed with the passage of time, if they have suffered from the intrusion of anything out of harmony with the inner nature of the liturgy or have become less suitable'.[37] Regarding the elements susceptible to change, the Council enunciated clear rules, namely:

---

34 *Summa contra gentiles*, cap. 120, no. 25. 35 *Praeterea declarat, hanc potestatem perpetuo in Ecclesia fuisse, ut in sacramentorum dispensatione, salva illorum substantia, ea statueret vel mutaret, quae suscipientium utilitati seu ipsorum sacramentorum venerationi, pro rerum, temporum et locorum varietate, magis expedire iudicaret.* H. Denzinger et A. Schönmetzer, *Enchiridion Symbolorum* (Rome, 1967), pp 405–6, no. 1728; tr. J. Neuner and J. Dupuis (eds), *The Christian Faith in the doctrinal documents of the Catholic Church*, 7th ed. (Staten Island NY, 2001), p. 56, no. 1324. 36 Jn 4:24. 37 *parte immutabili, utpote divinitus instituta, ... partibus mutationi obnoxiis, ... decursu temporum variare possunt vel etiam debent, si in eas forte irrepserint quae minus*

22. § 1. Regulation of the sacred liturgy depends solely on the authority of the Church, that is, on the Apostolic See, and, as laws may determine, on the bishop.

§ 2. In virtue of power conceded by law, the regulation of the liturgy within certain defined limits belongs also to various kinds of bishops' conferences, legitimately established, with competence in given territories.

§ 3. Therefore no other person, not even a priest, may add, remove, or change anything in the liturgy on his own authority.[38]

The Sacred Liturgy is the worship owed to God, as he himself has instituted it. As the Church has always taught, it cannot be reduced to the activity of any individual, not even a priest, but must be governed, in respect for the divine right, by the law of the Church, by the supreme authority, that is, by the Roman Pontiff and by the bishops in communion with him.

Blessed Pope John Paul II underlined the divine right in what pertains to the Sacrament of Penance in his first Encyclical Letter *Redemptor hominis*. Confronting a certain tendency to substitute communal forms of penance and conversion for individual confession, he called to mind that the act of conversion has always to be personal. These are his words:

> Although the participation by the fraternal community of the faithful in the penitential celebration is a great help for the act of personal conversion, nevertheless, in the final analysis, it is necessary that in this act there should be a pronouncement by the individual himself with the whole depth of his conscience and with the whole of his sense of guilt and of trust in God, placing himself like the Psalmist before God to confess: 'Against you ... have I sinned'. In faithfully observing the centuries-old practice of the Sacrament of Penance – the practice of individual confession with a personal act of sorrow and the intention to amend and make satisfaction – the Church is therefore defending the human soul's individual right: man's right to a more personal encounter

---

bene ipsius Liturgiae intimae naturae respondeant, vel minus aptae factae sint. Constitution on the Sacred Liturgy *Sacrosanctum concilium*, 4 December 1963, *Acta Apostolicae Sedis* 56 (1964), pp 105–106, no. 21; tr. A. Flannery (ed.), *Vatican Council II: The Conciliar and Post Conciliar Documents* (Collegeville MN, 1975), p. 9. **38** Ibid., p. 106, no. 22. English version, pp 9–10. 22. § 1. *Sacrae Liturgiae moderatio ab Ecclesiae auctoritate unice pendet: quae quidem est apud Apostolicam Sedem et, ad normam iuris, apud*

with the crucified forgiving Christ, with Christ saying, through the minister of the Sacrament of Reconciliation: 'Your sins are forgiven'; 'Go, and do not sin again'.[39]

Having noted the right of the individual penitent 'to a more personal encounter' with Christ in the Sacrament of Penance, the Holy Father quickly adds that it is also a question of 'a right on Christ's part with regard to every human being redeemed by him'.[40]

He continues, explaining the right and also the duty of the Church to insist on the observance of the divine right, that is:

> [Christ's] right to meet each one of us in that key moment in the soul's life constituted by the moment of conversion and forgiveness. By guarding the sacrament of Penance, the Church expressly affirms her faith in the mystery of the Redemption as a living and life-giving reality that fits in with man's inward truth, with human guilt and also with the desire of the human conscience. 'Blessed are those who hunger and thirst for righteousness, for they shall be satisfied'. The sacrament of Penance is the means to satisfy man with the righteousness that comes from the Redeemer himself.[41]

Episcopum. § 2. *Ex potestate a iure concessa, rei liturgicae moderatio inter limites statutos pertinet quoque ad competentes varii generis territoriales Episcoporum coetus legitime constitutos. § 3. Quapropter nemo omnino alius, etiamsi sit sacerdos, quidquam proprio marte in Liturgia addat, demat, aut mutet.* **39** Ioannes Paulus PP II, Litterae Encyclicae *Redemptor hominis, pontificali eius ministerio ineunte*, 4 martii 1979, *Acta Apostolicae Sedis*, 71, p. 314. English version: Pope John Paul II, *Encyclicals* (Kerala, India, 2005), p. 1115. *Etsi fraterna communitas fidelium celebrationem paenitentialem simul peragentium insigniter provehit actum conversionis singulorum, nihilo minus oportet denique in hoc eodem actu se exprimat quisque homo ex intimis penetralibus conscientiae suae, immo cum toto sensu culpae suae fiduciaeque Dei, coram quo sistat psalmistae similis, ut confiteatur: «Tibi, tibi soli peccavi». Propterea Ecclesia, dum fideliter asservat productum plura per saecula usum Sacramenti Paenitentiae – hoc est usum confessionis singularis, copulatae cum actu doloris propositoque emendationis et satisfactionis – ius particulare animae humanae tuetur; quod scilicet ius refertur ad congressionem, uniuscuiusque hominis magis propriam, cum Christo Cruci affixo, qui ignoscit, cum Christo, qui per Sacramenti Reconciliationis ministrum declarat: «dimittuntur peccata tua»; «vade, et amplius iam noli peccare».* **40** Ibid. English version, p. 1115. ... *ius Christi est, quod is habet erga quemque hominem a se redemptum.* **41** Ibid. English version, pp 314–15. *Est nempe ius conveniendi unumquemque nostrum in illo decretorio tempore vitae animae, quod est momentum conversionis et condonationis. Ecclesia Sacramento Paenitentiae custodiendo profitetur aperte fidem suam in Redemptionis mysterium, ut in rem veram et vivificantem, quae etiam cum interiore veritate hominis congruit, cum humano culpae sensu et etiam cum humanae conscientiae desideriis. «Beati, qui esuriunt et sitiunt iustitiam, quoniam ipsi saturabuntur». Paenitentiae Sacramentum est instrumentum, quo homo illa iustitia satietur, quae ex eodem Redemptore emanat.*

The solicitude of the Church for the correct celebration of the Sacrament of Penance corresponds to the divine right, to the right of Christ, who, at the moment of his death on the Cross, expressed the reality of his redemptive Incarnation with one only word: 'Sitio', 'I thirst'.[42] The discipline of the Sacrament of Penance ought always to correspond to the objective relationship between God and man, which is constituted by the unceasing love of God for all men, without boundary, expressed so eloquently and powerfully with the word 'Sitio'.

THE CANONICAL DISCIPLINE

In the canonical tradition, the discipline of the worship owed to God has been regulated by the highest authority, that is, the Apostolic See. Canon 1247 of the Pio-Benedictine Code enunciated the perennial discipline of the Church: 'It belongs only to the Apostolic See to order sacred liturgy and to approve liturgical books.'[43] The Code also enunciated the responsibility of the bishops to exercise vigilance over the correct observance of the norms regarding divine worship[44] and against the introduction of abuses into ecclesiastical discipline, especially in what pertains to divine worship and the Sacred Liturgy.[45]

The present Code, promulgated by the Blessed Pope John Paul II on 25 January 1983, enunciates in Canon 838 the discipline formulated in the Second Vatican Ecumenical Council. In the second paragraph of the canon, we read:

> It is for the Apostolic See to order the sacred liturgy of the universal Church, publish liturgical books and review their translations in vernacular languages, and exercise vigilance that liturgical regulations are observed faithfully everywhere.[46]

---

42 Jn 19:28.   **43** *Unius Apostolicae Sedis est tum sacram ordinare liturgiam, tum liturgicos approbare libros. Codex Iuris Canonici Pii X Pontificis Maximi iussu digestus Benedicti Papae XV auctoritate promulgatus,* Can. 1257. English translation in E.N. Peters (ed.), *The 1917 or Pio-Benedictine Code of Canon Law in English translation* (San Francisco, 2001), p. 426. Hereafter, CIC–1917.   **44** See CIC–1917, Can. 1261, § 1. **45** See CIC–1917, Can. 336, § 2.   **46** *Apostolicae Sedis est sacram liturgiam Ecclesiae universae ordinare, libros liturgicos edere eorumque versiones in linguas vernaculas recognoscere, necnon advigilare ut ordinationes liturgicae ubique fideliter observentur. Codex Iuris Canonici auctoritate Ioannis Pauli PP II promulgatus,* 25 ianuarii 1983, *Acta Apostolicae Sedis* 75, Pars II (1983), p. 153, Can. 838, § 2; tr.: *Code of Canon Law: Latin-English edition* (Washington DC, 1998), p. 276.

In the second paragraph of Canon 392 of the 1983 Code, the responsibility of the bishop to 'promote the common discipline of the whole Church and therefore to urge the observance of all ecclesiastical laws'[47] is treated. It reads:

> He is to exercise vigilance so that abuses do not creep into ecclesiastical discipline, especially regarding the ministry of the word, the celebration of the sacraments and sacramentals, the worship of God and the veneration of the saints, and the administration of goods.[48]

The present Code puts together the various objects of the vigilance of the bishop over ecclesiastical discipline and has lost a bit the particular emphasis on the vigilance over the discipline of the Sacred Liturgy which is found in the Pio-Benedictine Code.

In fact, after the Second Vatican Ecumenical Council, but certainly not because of the teaching of the Council, many abuses in the celebration of the Sacred Liturgy took place. Pope Benedict XVI made explicit reference to the situation in his *Letter to the bishops of the world*, at the time of the promulgation of the Apostolic Letter, given *motu proprio, Summorum pontificum*. Writing about the desire of some of the faithful for the form of the Sacred Liturgy existing before the post-Conciliar reforms, he affirmed:

> Many people who clearly accepted the binding character of the Second Vatican Council, and were faithful to the Pope and the bishops, nonetheless also desired to recover the form of the sacred liturgy that was dear to them. This occurred above all because in many places celebrations were not faithful to the prescriptions of the new Missal, but the latter actually was understood as authorizing or even requiring creativity, which frequently led to deformations of the liturgy which were hard to bear. I am speaking from experience, since I too lived through that period with all its hopes and its confusion. And I have seen how arbitrary deformations of the liturgy caused deep pain to individuals totally rooted in the faith of the Church.[49]

---

47 Ibid., Can. 392: *disciplinam cunctae Ecclesiae communem promovere et ideo observantiam omnium legum ecclesiasticarum urgere tueatur.* 48 Ibid., Can. 392 § 2: *Advigilet ne abusus in ecclesiasticam disciplinam irrepant, praesertim circa ministerium verbi, celebrationem sacramentorum et sacramentalium, cultum Dei et Sanctorum, necnon bonorum administrationem.* 49 *Molte persone, che accettavano chiaramente il carattere vincolante del Concilio Vaticano II e che erano fedeli al Papa e ai Vescovi, desideravano tuttavia anche ritrovare la forma, a loro cara, della sacra Liturgia; questo avvenne anzitutto perché in molti luoghi non si celebrava in modo fedele alle prescrizioni del nuovo Messale, ma esso veniva addirittura inteso come un'autorizzazione o perfino*

There is no doubt that in many places, at the time of the post-Conciliar reform of the Sacred Liturgy, a lack of discipline was found and many abuses were introduced.

Blessed Pope John Paul II, as has been noted before, confronted the abuses regarding the celebration of the Sacrament of Penance in his first Encyclical Letter *Redemptor hominis*. Also, in his last Encyclical Letter *Ecclesia de Eucharistia*, published on Holy Thursday of 2003, he once again confronted liturgical abuses. Commenting on the benefits of the post-Conciliar liturgical reform, he also noted the deficiencies which have followed it, with these words:

> Unfortunately, alongside these lights, *there are also shadows*. In some places the practice of eucharistic adoration has been almost completely abandoned. In various parts of the Church abuses have occurred, leading to confusion with regard to sound faith and Catholic doctrine concerning this wonderful sacrament. At times one encounters an extremely reductive understanding of the eucharistic mystery. Stripped of its sacrificial meaning, it is celebrated as if it were simply a fraternal banquet. Furthermore, the necessity of the ministerial priesthood, grounded in apostolic succession, is at times obscured and the sacramental nature of the Eucharist is reduced to its mere effectiveness as a form of proclamation.[50]

The pressing concern of the Supreme Pontiff is most evident.

In fact, at the end of the introductory part of the Encyclical Letter *Ecclesia de Eucharistia* he declared:

---

come un obbligo alla creatività, la quale portò spesso a deformazioni della Liturgia al limite del sopportabile. Parlo per esperienza, perché ho vissuto anch'io quel periodo con tutte le sue attese e confusioni. E ho visto quanto profondamente siano state ferite, dalle deformazioni arbitrarie della Liturgia, persone che erano totalmente radicate nella fede della Chiesa. Benedictus PP XVI, Epistula 'Ad Episcopos Catholicae Ecclesiae Ritus Romani', *Acta Apostolicae Sedis* 99 (2007), p. 796.   **50** *Dolendum tamen est quod iuxta lucida haec umbrae non desunt. Etenim est ubi fere tota neglegentia cultus adorationis eucharisticae deprehendatur. Accedunt in hoc vel illo ecclesiali ambitu abusus qui ad rectam obscurandam fidem doctrinamque catholicam super hoc mirabili Sacramento aliquid conferunt. Nonnumquam reperitur intellectus valde circumscriptus Mysterii eucharistici. Sua enim significatione et vi sacrificii destitutum, mysterium retinetur tamquam si sensum ac momentum alicuius fraterni convivii non excedat. Praeterea sacerdotii ministerialis necessitas, quae successioni apostolicae innititur, nonnumquam absconditur atque eucharistiae sacramentalitas ad solam nuntiationis efficacitatem redigitur.* Ioannes Paulus PP II, Litterae Encyclicae *Ecclesia de Eucharistia, de Eucharistia eiusque necessitudine cum Ecclesia*, 17 aprilis 2003, *Acta Apostolicae Sedis* 95 (2003), p. 439, no. 10. English translation: *Encyclicals*, pp 9–10.

It is my hope that the present Encyclical Letter will effectively help to banish the dark clouds of unacceptable doctrine and practice, so that the Eucharist will continue to shine forth in all its radiant mystery.[51]

Toward the end of the Encyclical Letter, Blessed Pope John Paul II wrote again about the abuses introduced with the post-Conciliar reform, in the perspective of the responsibility of priests for the correct celebration of the Sacred Liturgy. He made an urgent appeal 'that the liturgical norms for the celebration of the Eucharist be observed with great fidelity.'[52] In this context, he requested the competent Dicasteries of the Roman Curia 'to prepare a more specific document, including prescriptions of a juridical nature',[53] on the liturgical norms and their profound meaning, which we may define, in a summary manner, as respect for the divine right. Thus, Blessed Pope John Paul II concluded the discussion of the norms of the discipline of the Sacred Liturgy with these words:

No one is permitted to undervalue the mystery entrusted to our hands: it is too great for anyone to feel free to treat it lightly and with disregard for its sacredness and its universality.[54]

As he had done in his first Encyclical Letter, so in his last, he taught the divine right, the *ius divinum* of sacred worship, in accord with the objective reality of man's relationship with God.

On 25 March 2004, the Congregation for Divine Worship and the Discipline of the Sacraments published the document requested by Blessed Pope John Paul II, the Instruction *Redemptionis sacramentum*, 'On certain matters to be observed or to be avoided regarding the Most Holy Eucharist'.[55] The eighth and last chapter of the Instruction treats remedies of the delicts and abuses in the celebration of the Sacred Liturgy. After having listed the most serious delicts and the relative sanctions,[56] the Instruction treats other abuses,

---

51 Ibid., no. 10: *Litteras has Encyclicas Nostras conducere efficaciter posse confidimus ut doctrinarum umbrae dissipentur et usus reprobati submoveantur, unde omni in sui mysterii fulgore Eucharistia resplendere pergat.*
52 Ibid., no. 52, p. 468: *ut in eucharistica Celebratione magna quidem fidelitate liturgicae observentur regulae.*
53 Ibid., no. 52: *ut proprium appararent documentum cum monitionibus etiam generis iuridici.* **54** Ibid., no. 52: *Nulli quidem parvi pendere licet Mysterium nostris manibus concreditum: maius quidem illud est quam ut quisquam sibi permittat proprio id arbitratu tractare, unde nec sacra eius natura observetur nec universalis ratio.*
55 Congregatio de Cultu Divino et Disciplina Sacramentorum, Instructio *Redemptionis sacramentum, de quibusdam observandis et vitandis circa sanctissimam Eucharistiam,* 25 martii 2004, *Acta Apostolicae Sedis,* 96 (2004), 549–601. English translation, Vatican Polyglot Press. **56** See ibid., pp 597–8, nos. 172–3.

indicating that they are not to be considered 'of little account', but 'are to be numbered among the other abuses to be carefully avoided and corrected'.[57] The Instruction then indicates that all liturgical norms are to be observed and all errors correctd:

> The things set forth in this Instruction obviously do not encompass all the violations against the Church and its discipline that are defined in the canons, in the liturgical laws and in other norms of the Church for the sake of the teaching of the Magisterium or sound tradition. Where something wrong has been committed, it is to be corrected according to the norm of law.[58]

The right attention to liturgical norms does not constitute a sort of legalism or rubricism, but an act of profound respect and love for our Lord who has given us the gift of divine worship, an act of profound love which has as its irreplaceable foundation the respect for the divine right.

CONCLUSION

I hope that this brief reflection on the *ius divinum* and the Sacred Liturgy has indicated the necessity of beginning every consideration of the Sacred Liturgy in the context of the objective relationship of God with man, a relationship which demands the worship of God on the part of man, as God himself has taught in the Sacred Scriptures and in the Tradition. In this sense, I also hope that the reflection has underlined the fundamental disposition of man in the act of worship of God, that is, care to offer worship to God in the manner that God himself asks. Father Nicola Bux has observed:

> What more is there to say? The Church has established the matters that are to be observed in the liturgy and those that are not to be done, but the crisis and the uncertainty of the authority and of ecclesiastical and liturgical discipline, connected to the conviction that to manipulate

---

57 Ibid., no. 174, p. 505: *leviter non sunt aestimandae, sed inter eos abusus sedulo vitandos et corrigendos adnumerentur.* 58 Ibid., no. 175: *Quae in hac Instructione exponuntur, ut patet, haud omnes contra Ecclesiam eiusque disciplinam referunt violationes, quae in canonibus, in legibus liturgicis atque in aliis normis Ecclesiae ob doctrinam Magisterii sanamve traditionem definiuntur. Ubi quid mali patratum est, corrigendum erit ad normam iuris.*

Sacred Liturgy is not a serious sin, renders the norms a dead letter. This follows from having trampled upon the divine right and the juridical dimension of the liturgy.[59]

It is in the liturgical act, above all, that man must put into practice the way of the Beatitudes, the poverty of spirit that recognizes the Lord as Creator of the world and Lord of history, and with humility and total fidelity offers him due worship.

---

59 *Che dire di più? La Chiesa ha stabilito le cose che si devono osservare nella liturgia e quelle che non si devono fare, ma la crisi e l'incertezza dell'autorità e della disciplina ecclesiale e liturgica, unite alla convinzione che manipolare il culto non sia peccato grave, rendono le norme lettera morta. Questo dipende proprio dall'aver conculcato il diritto divino e la dimensione giuridica della liturgia.* N. Bux, *Come andare a Messa e non perdere la Fede* (Milan, 2010), p. 43. English translation by author.

Sacerdos paratus and *populo congregato*: the historical development of the Roman Missal

PAUL GUNTER OSB

For those who have witnessed Mass being celebrated, the vested priest and the assembled congregation appear as connected components of the eucharistic celebration. This is because the person attending is part of the congregation that sees what is done by the celebrating priest, who wears sacred vestments to celebrate Mass. The terms *sacerdos paratus* and *populo congregato*, however, suggest different theological understandings and pastoral priorities within the eucharistic liturgy. They are the opening words of the rubrics of the missals of 1570 and 1970 respectively.[1] The rubric prior to the celebrant beginning Mass in the missal of 1962 states that the vested priest, having arrived at the altar and made the customary reverences, makes the sign of the cross and (unless another rubric prescribes otherwise) says in a clear voice: *In nomine patris, et filii, et spiritus sancti. Amen.*[2] While the missal envisages ministers who reply in dialogue, there is no specific role for the assembly described here; and in the absence of this concept there is also a rubric attached to the *Orate fratres* that allows the celebrant to answer it himself when there are no servers.[3] From a juridical perspective, it should be observed that *sacerdos paratus* referred as much to the vested priest in the liturgical sense, as to the requirement that the priest should be qualified to celebrate Mass. It can therefore be argued that *sacerdos paratus* includes the requirement that the celebrant be *sacerdos idoneus*.[4]

Conversely, the opening rubric of the missal of 1970 states as the first premise that the people have assembled: *populo congregato*. Only then does the priest arrive at the altar with the ministers during the Introit, bowing profoundly to the altar, and possibly censing the cross and altar before going to the chair with the ministers. When the Introit has been sung, the priest and

---

1 A. Ward and C. Johnson, *Missalis romani editio princeps mediolani* (Rome, 1996), p. 165. In the missal of 1474 beneath the heading *Ordo missae is: paratus sacerdos cum intrat ad altare dicat.* 2 *Missalis romanum: Ex decreto sacrosancti concilii tridentini restitutum summorum pontificum cura recognitum, editio prima iuxta typicam* (Barcinone, 1962), p. 307: *Sacerdos paratus cum ingreditur ad altare, facta debita reverentia, signat se signo crucis a fronte ad pectus, et clara voce dicit, nisi peculiari rubrica alter statuatur.* 3 Ibid., p. 313: *Minister, seu circumstantes, respondent; alioquim ipsemet sacerdos; Suscipiat … (vel meis).* 4 See CIC 807 in the 1917 Code of Canon Law and CIC 916 in the 1983 Code. The term *sacerdos idoneus* is used in the *motu*

the faithful make the sign of the cross standing, while the priest is turned to the people (*ad populum conversus*), who answer '*Amen*'.[5] A reservation about private Masses is reinforced in the transition from the missal of 1970 to that of 2002 – the latter of which renames the separate section found in the missal of 1970, *Ordo missae sine populo*.[6] While acknowledging the existence of legitimate circumstances for saying Mass privately, the missal of 2002 refers to its corresponding section as *Ordo missae cuius unus tantum minister participat*.[7] This development of emphasis is illustrated in the differences contained in the respective versions of the *Institutio generalis* that support the missals of 1970 and 2002. The missal of 1970 states that Mass should not be celebrated without a minister unless there is grave necessity. The missal of 2002 mentions the importance of the minister and the faithful interchangeably: *Celebratio sine ministro vel aliquo saltem fideli ne fiat nisi iusta et rationabili de causa.* Nonetheless, by the third typical edition of the missal in 2002, the disposition of the faithful was deemed to require clarification of the missal of 1970. In the section on the Eucharistic Prayer in the *Instituto generalis* there is this additional note: *Prex eucharistica exigit ut omnes reverentia et silentio auscultent*; illustrating that reverent silence forms an intrinsic part of the *participatio actuosa* of the faithful.

In the light of these observations about contrasting characteristic features, it is my intention in this essay to consider the historical development of the Missal. In order to avoid the misconception that the Ordinary Form of the Mass in its 2002 edition and the Extraordinary Form of 1962 are two distinct entities irreconcilably at odds with each other (since each, in its distinctive form, represents the Roman Rite), we need to trace the historical developments out of which the missal of 1570 arose. A similar *excursus* is necessary to appreciate the missal of Paul VI in its three editions. Points of convergence and divergence between the two Forms of the Roman Rite will indicate some of the challenges and opportunities that lie ahead in a Liturgical Movement spurred onwards in growing maturity.

---

proprio *Summorum pontificum* 2007, art. 5, para. 4.   **5** *Missale romanum: Ex decreto sacrosancti concilii oecumenici Vaticani II instauratum auctoritate Pauli PP.VI promulgatum Ioannis PP.II* (Vatican City, 2002), p. 503: *Populo congregato, sacerdos cum ministris ad altare accedit dum cantus ad introitum peragitur. Cum ad altare pervenerit, facta cum ministris profunda inclinatione, osculo altare veneratur et, pro opportunitate, crucem et pro opportunitate, crucem et altare incensat. Postea cum ministris sedem petit. Cantu ad introitum absoluto, sacerdos et fideles, stantes, signant se signo crucis, dum sacerdos, ad populum conversus, dicit: ... Populus respondet: Amen.*   **6** *Missale romanum: Ex decreto sacrosancti oecumenici concilii vaticani II instauratum auctoritate Paulii PP.VI editio typica* (Vatican City, 1970), pp 479–86.   **7** *Missale romanum*, 2002, pp 663–72: 'The order of Mass at which only one minister participates.'

The French Canadian Abbé, Emmanuel Bourque, wrote prosaically, 'On n'arrête pas l'histoire!'[8] We have all watched history unfold in the course of our lives. Could we imagine working without electric light, or without computers? The historical development of the Roman Missal, in all its complexity, has involved changes in the contexts of both its celebration and its attendant scholarship, with the inevitable result that it is difficult from a modern perspective to understand the conditions under which the members of the Tridentine Commission were working. Such as they were, however, the results of the Commission made few changes to the Curial missal that had first been printed in 1474. The priority for the missal of 1570 was to affirm the centrality of the celebration of the Eucharist as the essential and permanent link between *lex orandi* and *lex credendi*.

THE HISTORICAL DEVELOPMENT OF THE GELASIANIZED GREGORIAN SACRAMENTARIES

The first phase of the historical development of the Roman Missal was that of the 'Gelasianized' Gregorian sacramentaries (to use the expression of the medieval sources scholar Cyrille Vogel) – because the Gregorian sacramentaries were mixed. Bourque described this phenomenon as 'L'histoire de ce type syncrétiste';[9] and although the title of his second article is 'Une énigme à résoudre', he clearly states that by 1952 there was a scholarly consensus that the eighth-century Gelasian sacramentary was a fusion of an earlier Gelasian sacramentary with the Gregorian sacramentary,[10] based on the *Hadrianum*, together with a supplement. The calendar was that of the *Gregorianum*, with small sections taken from the eighth-century *Gelasianum*.

The development of the *Hadrianum* and its supplement in the Franco-Germanic countries gave rise to three types of sacramentary. The first is the 'direct type' – that is, sacramentaries in a direct line from the thirteenth-century missal of the Roman Curia. The Proper of Saints from the supplement of Benedict of Aniane was added to this, together with additional votive Masses, requiem Masses, and a reduced number of Prefaces, while it retained substantial fidelity to the *Hadrianum* and the *Supplementum*. Examples of this type of missal are the Sacramentary of St Vaas of Arras, the Canterbury Missal,

---

8 E. Bourque, *Étude sur les sacramentaires romains* (Quebec, 1952), p. 395.   **9** Bourque, *Étude*, pp 33–251. **10** Ibid., p. 255.

and the Lateran Missal.[11] The second type added to the *Hadrianum* with its supplement many votive Masses and other kinds of Masses which do not appear in the *Missale Romanum*. Examples are the *Sacramentarium Rossianum* and the Sacramentary of Noyon. The third type (which has left no direct heirs) included sacramentaries with the outward appearance of the *Hadrianum* with its supplement, but whose contents had been significantly re-worked. Examples are the Sacramentaries of Echternach, Fulda and Eligius.[12]

The adjustments made to the *Hadrianum* and *Supplementum* were motivated by a desire for a single volume, edited in such a way as to eliminate duplications. The result safeguarded the heritage of the *Gregorianum*, and addressed some of its shortcomings, even though this required a lengthy process. The direct line of the Roman Missal has remained relatively pure since the tenth and eleventh centuries. The Missal incorporated elements of the *Gelasianum* of the eighth century, but mostly through the *Supplementum* and the votive Masses, and those *ad diversa* came largely from the *Supplementum*. Since the *Gelasianum* is characterized by a Gregorian *Paduense* influence, its dependence on the Gregorian sacramentary is clear; but the *ordo missae* shows significant changes, despite the fact that the Canon of the Mass was carefully preserved.[13]

In the second half of the tenth century, the cultural centres of Europe were in France and Germany, since Rome was at a low ebb in terms of religious culture. With the fall of the Carolingian Empire in 887, the situation deteriorated even further. There were no scribes to copy liturgical books, and while the life was drained out of her liturgy the Church went into material and spiritual decline. The reduction of liturgical life to a minimum was a sign of this decay.

It is therefore hardly surprising that the books brought to Rome by the Ottos of Germany were received so positively, with the additional patronage of a series of German popes during the eleventh century, whose liturgical formation would have been based on the mixed Gregorian liturgical books. Pope Gregory V, nephew of Emperor Otto III, commissioned the monastery of Reichenau to produce all the books necessary for the papal liturgy. Reichenau continued to supply these books for a hundred years, which made it an influential force. In particular, on 22 April 998 Gregory V commanded the scriptorium of Reichenau to provide him with a copy of the *codex sacramentorum* each year. As Vogel states:

11 C. Vogel, *Mediaeval liturgy: an introduction to the sources* (Portland OR, 1986), p. 103.   **12** Ibid., p. 104.
13 Ibid., pp 104–5.

The *vetus missale lateranense* of Azevedo (eleventh to twelfth century), the missal of the Papal Curia of the thriteenth century, and the Sacramentary of St Peter's (twelfth century) all belong to the family of the Gelasiano-Gregorian sacramentaries.[14]

The missal of the Papal Curia in the thirteenth century thus comes directly from the Gelasianized Gregorian line.

The second stage of development is represented by the missals of the thirteenth century. It has been suggested that by the year 1275 there were four different liturgical traditions in use:

A. That of the papal court
B. The urban tradition (as represented by St Peter's)
C. The reform of Cardinal Orsini (the future Nicholas III)
D. That of the Lateran basilica.

The papal court at that date was, for the most part, to be found at the Lateran Palace, the private chapel of the pope, the *sancta sanctorum*, and not in the basilica itself (since the basilica was under the care of canons). The tradition of the papal court underwent four important changes during the thirteenth century. Between 1213 and 1216, in the last years of his pontificate, Pope Innocent III had reorganized the Divine Office, but not the Missal. Pope Honorius worked on the Breviary again, and the resulting breviary was adopted by the Franciscans in 1230. Later, this would be known as the 'Breviary of the Rule'. Honorius III did not change anything in the Mass, though he promulgated a new missal. The missal of Honorius III was also adopted by the Franciscans in the same year and is known as the 'Missal of the Rule'. It was updated in the papal court because, unlike the breviary, it was deemed to lack substance. Aimon of Faversham, the fourth Minister General of the Franciscans, adjusted the breviary and missal between 1243 and 1244, and a second edition was published in 1260. The result of these revisions was confusion. Each church or community that followed the tradition of the papal court had its own combination of older and newer books.

The urban tradition focused mainly on St Peter's, through its books. This tradition represents the ancient Roman rite, which the basilica of St Peter had maintained for centuries in distinction from the papal liturgy. Other churches

14 Ibid., p. 104.

of the city also followed the urban tradition until the middle of the thirteenth century, and in some cases the tradition continued to be observed even longer. Then a sudden change took place that involved the disappearance of the ancient books.

From about 1250, the liturgy of the papal court was beginning to have a strong influence over the urban liturgy. According to Van Dijk, Cardinal Orsini resisted this influence and, wanting to protect the urban tradition, arrived at a compromise.[15] This reform consisted in a new urban usage that combined the previous urban liturgy with that of the papal court and that of the Lateran Palace. But because Nicholas II died in 1280, and the papal court moved to Avignon during the following century, this reform died out.

The tradition of the Lateran basilica, as distinct from that of the papal court, had been in the care of the canons of St Fridianus of Lucca since 1105. These canons had their own liturgical traditions based on the urban tradition. The difference in the context of the Lateran, however, is that when the canons celebrated, they followed the use of the papal court.[16]

These four different Roman liturgical traditions influenced each other during the thirteenth century. While the papal tradition would be destined to dominate, the urban tradition almost disappeared. The missal that had been updated by the Franciscans and approved by Pope Clement V became the missal of the papal court at Avignon, and formed the basis of the first printed missal, the *editio princeps* of 1474, with the title *Incipit ordo missalis secundum consuetudinem romanae curiae.*

The third stage of development concerned the missal of Pius V. This provided a context for liturgical unity arguably unknown elsewhere, despite a gradual unification of the liturgy of Rome during the thirteenth century. While newer religious orders such as the Cistercians, Premonstratensians, Dominicans and Franciscans contributed to a new liturgical stability by establishing uniformity of liturgical practice in their houses throughout Europe, various dioceses clung to their local uses. There were various *ordines missae* in existence, which contained threads of varied origin, all indicative of diversity.

The lack of a united and strong force to rein in or moderate liturgical developments of the Missal during the fourteenth and fifteenth centuries

15 See S. van Dijk, 'The legend of the missal of the papal chapel and the fact of Cardinal Orsini's reform', *Sacris Erudiri*, 8 (1956), 76–142. See also S. van Dijk and J. Hazleden-Walker, *The origins of the modern Roman liturgy: the liturgy of the papal court and the Franciscan order in the thirteenth century* (London, 1960).
16 *Missale romanum: editio princeps* (1570) (Vatican City 1998), XIV, n. 17.

(when the Church was so sorely tried by the exigencies surrounding the Avignon papacy and the Western Schism) meant that personal initiatives thrived. During this testing time, albeit in good faith, rectors of churches, abbots and even bishops added formulas and rites to the traditional texts, the origins of which were less than clear, and at times even superstitious.[17] Inconsistencies and indeed abuses circulated between dioceses. Ernest, archbishop of Prague, acknowledged this state of affairs, and in 1349 he forbade the introduction of Mass formulas that had not been authorized by Rome. During the synod of 1453, Cardinal Nicolò di Kues, bishop of Bressanone, placed copies of the corrected missal in the principal churches of the diocese, and instructed that others make the same adjustments to their own.[18]

At the end of the fifteenth century, the need for corrected liturgical books, particularly the Missal, was evident given the pressure that bishops and synods exerted on the Holy See about the problem. Writing for the Church in Spain in 1588, Charles V referred to the strange and historically unsound provenance of some of the more innovative collects, sequences and prefaces, and stressed that they were having a negative affect on the reception of the faith. Furthermore, he wrote that bishops were, by virtue of their office, responsible for clarifying ambiguities, and that it was their duty to give direction and correct any texts used within the liturgy, making them pure, certain and solid.[19] Similar *cris de cœur* came from the Synod of Cologne (1536) and Augsburg (1548), as well as other places.

THE COUNCIL OF TRENT

Opening in 1543, the Council of Trent concerned itself (among other things) with liturgical books, and was particularly concerned with the Missal. In 1562, a commission was established under the Archbishop of Lanciano, Leonardo Marini, to deal with this.[20] However, the members of the commission were divided over what criteria to adopt for the reform, and whether to demand absolute uniformity throughout the whole Church at the expense of local uses. Faced with these uncertainties, and given the need to conclude the already prolonged sessions of the Council, the fathers in Session XXV took the

17 See A. Franz, *Die Messe im deutschen Mittelalter* (Freiburg i. B., 1902), pp 300–2.   18 See M. Righetti, *Manuale di storia liturgica* (Milan, 1950), vol. 1, p. 275, fn. 206.   19 See J. Harzheim, *Concilia Germaniae* VI, p. 755.   20 See Righetti, *Manuale di storia liturgica*, vol. 1, p. 279.

opportunity to delay making any decision about the projected reform and submitted the *acta* (such as they were) to Pius IV in 1564.

Pius IV died in 1565 and was succeeded by Pius V, who showed particular interest in the Tridentine Commission, whose numbers grew and whose work was brought to fruition in the bull *Quo primum*. This bull presented the authentic text of the new missal to the whole Church, and it was promulgated on 14 July 1570. It also imposed the obligation of every church and religious order to adopt the new missal, unless it could be demonstrated that their own had a record of antiquity of more than two humdred years. Some churches, such as those in Toledo, Aquileia and Ravenna, accepted the new missal and imposed it with rigour, even though they would have had grounds for retaining their own time-honoured traditions.

The text that became the basis of the reform was the missal that had been in use in the papal chapel, and its *ordinarium missae*. This type of missal, described as being *secundum consuetudinem romanae curiae* or *romanae ecclesiae*, started to appear during the thirteenth century, and multiplied in an extraordinary way during the fourteenth and fifteenth centuries. Its diffusion was greatly assisted by the Order of Friars Minor, which, having been founded in 1209 and needing to organize its own liturgical life, adopted the *ordinarium missae* with the missal used in the papal chapel. As a consequence, the missal of the Franciscans bore the title: *Incipit ordo missalis fratrum minorum secundum consuetudinem romanae curiae*. Indeed, certain modifications and additions introduced by the Friars Minor were approved by Clement V and inserted into the *ordo* of the pontifical chapel. It was, therefore, this missal (as amended by the Franciscans) that formed the basis of the *editio princeps*, which was issued in 1474.

The differences between the missals of 1474 and 1570 were few. In the edition of 1474, the Mass finishes with the blessing by the priest, followed by the *Placeat tibi sancta trinitas* and the kissing of the altar; whereas in the missal of 1570 it anticipates the blessing. Furthermore, the missal of 1570 makes the reading of the prologue to the Gospel of John at the end of the Mass compulsory, where it had previously been optional.[21] According to Frutaz, it was Cardinal Sirletto who was responsible for the reform of the Missal. In the Vatican library the corrections of Cardinal Sirleto can be seen in the margins of the 1497 *Missale secundum morem sanctae romanae ecclesiae*, which is almost identical to the *editio princeps* of 1474.[22]

21 Ibid., p. 280. 22 A.P. Frutaz, 'Sirleto e la riforma del messale romano di S. Pio V', *Regnum Dei.*

THE *MISSALE ROMANUM* OF 1570 AND ITS SUBSEQUENT EDITIONS

The most notable change affecting the missal of 1570 was its calendar, which eliminated many sanctoral celebrations in favour of restoring a sense of the *cursus de tempore*. This calendar developed the organization of the liturgical year, while providing information about the history of the liturgy, stating when and how specific celebrations came into being, particularly at the level of the local church. The older liturgical books – the sacramentary, lectionary and antiphonal – didn't have a calendar at the beginning. This custom arose in the early Middle Ages. From the eleventh century calendars appeared in France, but not in Rome until a century later.[23] Two types of calendar appeared; one was independent of liturgical books, while the other was a fascicule in the missal, and thus intrinsic to it.[24] Nonetheless, according to Frere,[25] evidence of various celebrations can be found in the records of the *tituli*, that is, the original parish churches, station churches, and seven deaneries of Rome. The sanctoral cycle and the sense of *de tempore* emerged during the sixth and seventh centuries, though without specific calendars. A direct line to the calendar of the missal of Pius V can however be traced from that of the papal court in the thirteenth century.[26]

The word *missale* in its earliest sense was synonymous with 'sacramentary'. Though a sacramentary was intended for use by the celebrant, it contained not only the texts of the Mass but also everything he needed to celebrate the sacrament.[27] Amalarius, in 827, referred to '*missale, liber ubi continetur mysterium missae*'. Even earlier, Egbert of York (who died in 766) had referred in his *Dialogue* to a collection *antiphonaria cum missalibus* that he had consulted in Rome.[28] These antiphonals and missals developed in a complementary way,

Collectanea Theatina a clericis regularibus edita, 30 (Rome, 1974), 84–111.   **23** See P. Jounel, *Le culte des saints dans les basiliques du lateran et du Vatican au douzième siècle* (Turin, 1977), ch. 1; E. Palazzo, *A history of liturgical books from the beginning to the thirteenth century* (Collegeville MN, 1993), pp 49–50; A. Nocent, 'I libri liturgici', *Anamnesis*, 2 (Genoa, 1978), 170–1; C. Folsom, 'Liturgical books' in A. Chupungco (ed.), *Handbook for liturgical studies*, vol. 1 (Collegeville MN, 1997), pp 261 and 307.   **24** As a fascicule independent of the missal, it was either a simple list of feasts celebrated by a particular church or diocese, or a martyrology that, in addition to the list of feasts, contained details about the life, death and burial place of the saints mentioned. Ancient evidence of a Roman calendar can be found in two lists of the Chronograph of Philocalus (*c.*336–54), which refers to the *depositio episcoporum*, which commenorated the days of death and burial of the popes, and the *depositio martyrum*, which marked the day and place of burial and/or veneration of martyrs in Rome.   **25** W.H. Frere, *The Kalendar* (Oxford, 1930), vol. 1, p. 17. **26** See S. van Dijk and J.H. Walker, 'The Ordinal of the papal court from Innocent III to Boniface VIII and related documents' in *Spicilegium Friburgense* (Fribourg, 1975), (page numbers unknown).   **27** See P. Jounel, 'Missel' in *Catholicisme: Hier, aujourd'hui, demain* (Paris, 1982), vol. 9, p. 294.   **28** Righetti, *Manuale di storia liturgica*, p. 275 fn. 204.

and eventually missals became interchangeable with sacramentaries. When referring to the Gelasian and Gregorian missals we are thus referring to sacramentaries. The 'missal', in the sense of the Tridentine missal, is a book designed to contain all texts pertinent to the celebration of the Mass. Not only does it include the three Orations, Prefaces and the Canon for use by the celebrant, but also the singing parts for the *schola*: the Introit, Gradual, Alleluia, Offertory, and Communion. It also has the pericopes of the Epistles and Gospels for all the Masses of the year. This missal was described as the *missale plenum*, a title given to this sort of compendium between the eleventh and thirteenth centuries. According to Ebner,[29] the Ambrosian missal is the oldest of this kind and dates from the tenth century. The reason for the development of the sacramentary into a missal was the phenomenon of the private Mass. The assumption that the celebration of Mass involved a church and many priests (as was the case in important cities) gradually gave way to the practice of celebrating Mass in rural churches, or even in private houses, by a single priest.[30]

The order of the missal of 1570 reflects its relationship to the *missale plenum* of the thirteenth century.[31] After the decree, the constitutional bulls of respective editions, and (in the case of the missal of 1962) the Apostolic Letter *Rubricarum instructum*, the Missal opens with the general rubrics – those specific to the year and its particular times: *De anno et eius partibus*. Thus the principal parts of the Missal are as follows:

A. The calendar, containing the feasts of the year and those of saints, indicating their respective liturgical ranks. Until the end of the eleventh century, the Roman calendar was essentially local. It was limited to Roman saints and to those with cults in Roman churches or oratories. During the twelfth and thirteenth centuries, as a result of the adoption of the breviary and missal of the Curia by the Friars Minor, the Roman calendar was increasingly mixed up with the martyrology. Then the number of sanctoral celebrations expanded rapidly, with vigils and octaves. The calendar became increasingly international, with a growing tendency to expand until the reform of Pius V (which seemed to reduce this trend) – only for it to resume under future popes.[32]

29 A. Ebner, *Quellen und Forschungen zur Geschichte und Kungstgeschichte des Missale Romanum im Mittelalter* (Freiburg i. B., 1896), pp 359–63.   **30** Righetti, *Manuale di storia liturgica*, p. 275 fn. 205.   **31** Ibid., p. 280 fn. 209.   **32** Ibid., pp 280–1.

B. The general rubrics of the Missal, whose primitive nucleus comes from the *ordines romani*, were the work of Giovanni Burcardo, Master of Ceremonies of Sixtus IV and Innocent VIII, and were published in 1502 with the title *Ordo servandus per sacerdotem in celebratione missae*. This *ordo* or *ritus servandus in celebratione missae* finishes with the section *De defectibus in celebratione missae occurrentibus*, which identifies potential mistakes in the celebration of Mass. The final section of the introductory part includes the *Praeparatio ad missam*, the *Gratiarum actio post missam*, and diagrammes explaining the schemes for censing the altar and *oblata*.

C. The Proper of Times containing the Mass formulas from the first Sunday of Advent until the twenty-fourth Sunday after Pentecost, which concluded the *annus ecclesiasticus*. It also contains formulas composed for the feasts of the Lord, around which the year revolves. After the Mass of Holy Saturday there is the fascicule of the *ordo missae* together with its Prefaces and Canon. This position, which is more or less at the centre of the missal, was conveneint for the celebrant both because it preserved book bindings, and also because it retained the position it had had in the sacramentaries of the eleventh and twelfth centuries. Prior to this period, the Canon was placed at the beginning of the book, while in the Gelasian sacramentaries it was located at the back among the *missae cotidianae*.

Though I will deal with the subject of the *ordo missae* separately, it is worth noting here that its location in the missal could give the impression of dividing the *proprium de tempore* in two halves. But before the missal of Paul VI, Eastertide only began with Mass, not with the entire liturgy of the Easter Vigil. After the litanies, the ministers changed from violet to white vestments for Mass. Indeed, in the missal of 1962 this division was emphasized by the heading *Tempus paschalis*, before the section *De missa solemni vigiliae paschalis*, which separated the Mass from what had gone before.

The formulas of the *Proprium de tempore* occupy the first and most important section of the missal. In the Mass of the early Church, while there were few recognized liturgical feasts, the basis of the eucharistic liturgy was the Canon of the Mass, while the Scriptures selected for that day formed the unique feature of each feast. While there was no *lectio continua*, the celebrant would read scriptural verses pertinent to the feast being celebrated, and comment on them in his homily. Particular formulas did not exist prior to the fifth century – that is, before the Ordinary of the Mass was enriched by providing each feast with its own formulas, and prescribing the texts for the celebrant and schola respectively. Probst has sought to demonstrate that Pope Damasus was the author of these innovations, which in turn instigated a huge liturgical evolution from the fifth/sixth centuries. During this evolution Advent and Lent became established in the ninth century, involving the compilation of formulas for some Sundays which had not previously been fixed.[33] It should be noted that in the East, the themes of specific feasts were only represented in the *cursus* of the readings and chants; because by the end of the fourth century the antiphons, readings and psalms in Jerusalem were those appropriate to the hour of the day in which one was celebrating. But in the West (apart from Gallican liturgies) specific feasts influenced not only the proper prayers of the sacrifice, but in some cases even the Canon itself.[34]

There are certain things that are distinctive about this missal (whether in red or black print, depending on the edition). Advent, which finishes with the Mass *in vigilia nativitatis domini*, only provides formulas for four other Sundays and for the three days of the *quattro tempora*. The *tempus nativitatis* opens with the Mass *in nocte* and closes with the formula of the Mass of the Holy Name and the commemoration of St Telosforus. The *tempus epiphaniae* opens with the Mass of that feast and continues until 13 January. The *tempus per annum ante septuagesimae* closes with the Sundays II–VI after Epiphany. The *tempus septuagesimae* includes the three Sundays that immediately precede Lent. The *tempus quadragesimae* begins with Ash Wednesday and passes through four Sundays, with formulas also provided for weekdays and for the *quattro tempora* before Passiontide. Passiontide comprises the formula of the first week and continues into the second week, which begins under the title *Domenica II passionis seu in palmis* or *hebdomada sancta*. *Hebdomada sancta* reflects the importance of this special week, from the references to *de solemni palmarum processione in honorem Christi regis* until the Easter Vigil. No specific references to the Paschal Triduum appear in the titles.

The structure of the *Proprium de tempore* continues after the *ordo missae* with the formula of Easter Sunday and subsequent post-Easter texts until the Mass of the Vigil of the Ascension. A short *tempus ascensionis* begins with the formula of the Feast of the Ascension. It includes the Sunday after the Ascension and concludes with *sabbato in vigilia pentecostes*. The *tempus per annum post pentecostem* with its formula for Trinity Sunday and those of the

---

33 F. Probst, *Liturgie des vierien Jahrhunderts und deren reform* (Münster, 1893), pp 445–70. 34 See Righetti, *Manuale di storia liturgica*, p. 109.

twenty-four Sundays after Pentecost joins the formula of Corpus Christi in the week of Trinity Sunday and that of the Feast of the Most Sacred Heart of Jesus in the following week. After the seventeenth Sunday there are formulas for the three days of the *quattro tempora* of September. Between the twenty-third and the twenty-fourth Sundays are the formulas of the third, fourth, fifth and sixth Sundays *quae superfuit post epiphanium*. The section is completed by a table of orations to be used on ferial days during the *Proprium de tempore*:

A. The *sanctorale* whose cycle began on 29 November, the Vigil of St Andrew (extended to 26 November), and the feast of St Peter of Alexandria. As a result of the addition of new feasts by various popes, thirteen new formularies were added to the sanctoral at the end of the sixteenth century, forty-nine at the end of the seventeenth, thirty-two in the eighteenth, twenty-five in the nineteenth, and twenty-six between 1900 and 1960.

B. The Common of Saints consisted of Masses for one or more bishops, martyrs, confessors, holy virgins, and 'non-virgins'.[35] These were applicable to saints whose celebrations lacked proper prayers. The Common of Dedication of a church and the Masses for feasts of Our Lady are followed by formulas for Our Lady on Saturday, distributed according to the times of the liturgical year.

It might seem more logical for the Common of Saints to have preceded the Proper. Originally each saint had his or her own particular Mass. But once the number of saints had grown to such an extent it became less feasible for each to have a specific formula. As a result a generic formula for each category developed from the texts of well-known ancient saints, and these were used for newer saints. These texts are, substantially, those found in the *Missale Gregorianum*. However, as Dom Antoine Wilmart has explained,[36] they were taken from earlier Mass formulas that had disappeared from the *Hadrianum*, but which regained prominence in the supplement compiled by Alcuin, and which were later joined by other formulas deriving from eight Masses from the ancient Gelasian sacramentary. Righetti lists the series and indicates the source and position they occupied in the *Missale Romanum*:[37]

35 See Jounel, 'Missel', p. 295.   **36** A. Wilmart, 'Un Missel grégorien ancien', *Revue Bénédictine*, 26 (1909), 294.   **37** Righetti, *Manuale di storia liturgica*, pp 111–13.

1. Unius Apostoli   Vigil of St Andrew   Vigil of an Apostle
2. Plurim. Apostolorum Ss Philip and James   (Ss Philip and James)
3. Unius Martyris   St Menna (11 Nov)   Martyr non Pontif.
4. Plurim. Martyrum   Ss Felicissimus & Agapitus Plurim. Martyrum (II)
5. Unius Confessoris   St Sylvester (31 Dec)   Confess. Pontif. (I)
6. Plurim. Confess.   Ss Processus &   Ss Processus &
       Martinianus   Martinianus
7. Virginum   St Agatha   Virginum (I)

8. Votive Masses or *missae votivae de mysteriis domini aut de angelis vel sanctis singulis hebdomadae diebus dispositae* would have comprised Masses of the Trinity, the Blesses Sacrament, Angels, Ss Peter & Paul, and the Masses of Virgins. This section expanded due to the growing popularity of particular devotions, with particular votive Masses assigned to different days of the week, applicable when free days in the calendar allowed. The section *ad diversa* was made up of twenty-nine formulas and completed by a series of thirty-four formulas of *orationes diversae*.

9. The Masses for the Dead also include the *ordo absolutionis in exsequiis* from the Roman Ritual.

10. The diocesan Proper, or *Proprium sanctorum pro aliquibus locis*, provides a collection of Masses in honour of those saints not found in the universal calendar, who nevertheless enjoy special devotion in a particular diocese.

11. Blessings from the Ritual were included in the Missal because they were frequently convenient to the celebrant – such as the Blessing of Water, the Asperges ceremony, and a small section of texts set to music. In the 1962 edition a series of blessings from the Ritual was conveniently arranged, including the Confirmation rite, and the rite for the blessing of a paten and chalice from the Roman Pontifical.

The use of the expression *ordo missae* needs some clarification. In the context of the 1590 missal, Luykx,[38] and later Baroffio and Dell'Oro[39] (who were both influenced by Luykx) held that:

> By the *ordo missae* we mean a collection of personal prayers for the use of the celebrant, to help him express his devotion during the celebration of Mass. Therefore it is not a sacramentary but a collection of private formulas.[40]

38 B. Luykx, 'Der Ursprung der gleichbiebenden Teile der heiligen Messe (*Ordinarium missae*)', in T. Bogler (ed.), *Priestertum und Mönchtum* (Maria Laach, 1961), pp 72–119. **39** B. Baroffio and F. Dell'Oro, 'L'*Ordo missae* di Warmondo d'Ivrea', *Studi Medievali*, 16 (1975), 795–823. **40** Ibid., 801–2.

Luykx himself distinguished between three types of *ordines missae*:

1. The apologetic type
2. The French type
3. The type of the area around the Rhine.

According to him, the apologetic type consisted of apologetic or personal prayers that the priest recited privately, which arose from more-or-less homogeneous nuclei that were inserted into Carolingian *libelli precum*.[41] He noted that 'early on, three groups of apologetic prayers arose, which corresponded to the three key moments of the celebration: *ad communionem, ad munus offerendum*, and *ante altare*.'[42] Also that:

> the series of prayers *ad communionem* constitute the most ancient nucleus of the specifically named *ordo missae*; that is, of all the personal prayers of the priest with which he transforms the course of the Mass from an almost impersonal 'objective act' to a moment of subjective experience.[43]

The French type (*franco*) developed from the primitive type. Baroffio and Dell'Oro state that in the French type:

> the three groups are linked between themselves organically with the insertion of new prayers introduced by the rubrics which expressed their purpose, while the *ordines missae* of the apologetic type were beginning to lose influence.[44]

Indeed, they assert that:

> The most ancient testimony is to be found in the Gregorian sacramentary of Amiens from the tenth century. Most others emerge during the eleventh century when this *ordo* achieved its maximum diffusion, a few years before being marginalized by the *ordo renano* [the *ordo* from the area around the Rhine]. However, it survived its apparent isolation, above all in central France, for example in Lyons, where it remains in use to this day. It is also known outside France, and there are scholars find

---

41 These were collections of devotional prayers.   **42** Baroffio and Dell'Oro, 'L'*Ordo missae* di Warmondo', 805.   **43** Ibid., 805.   **44** Ibid., 805.

some of its elements in Spain, Milan, and also in the *ordo* of the *Missale Romanum*.[45]

The type from the area of the Rhine was more precisely from the Abbey of St Gallen in Switzerland. It spread from Lake Constance and the wetlands up to Mainz, following the division of the eastern and western Carolingian empire – a division that is also evident in their respective traditions of chant. The diversification of the *ordo missae* between the French type and the Rhine type thus mainly reflects linguistic differences between French and German.

In the *ordo franco*, the order of the prayers and of the successive rites is as follows:

1. The preparatory prayers before Mass (Psalm 50, prayers and orations), for the washing of hands and while vesting.
2. The prayers while the priest approaches the altar.
3. The prayers for the blessing of incense, before and after the Gospel.
4. The prayers while the priest places the bread and wine on the altar.
5. The prayers of the *Orate fratres*.
6. The prayers to be recited while the *Sanctus* is being sung, and other prayers that precede the *Te igitur*.
7. The personal *memento* of the celebrant for the living and the dead.
8. The prayers during the *commixtio*.
9. The prayers before and after Communion.
10. The prayers at the end of Mass (*Placeat*) and after removing vestments.[46]

The principal characteristics of the *ordo renano* that distingush it from the *ordo franco* are as follows:

1. The purification of hands is accompanied by the oration *Largire sensibus nostris*, while the *ordo franco* prefers the *Lavabo*.
2. The recitation of psalms, which are generally three: Psalm 83 *Quam dilecta*, Psalm 84 *Benedixisti* and Psalm 85 *Inclina*, with versicles and prayers *Fac me quaeso* and *Aures tuae pietatis*.
3. While the priest approaches the altar he recites Psalm 42 *Iudica me* with the antiphon *Introibo ad altare Dei*. There follows the oration *Aufer a nobis*.

45 Ibid., 806. **46** Ibid., 795–824.

4. The prayers during the singing of the *Gloria in excelsis* and after the collect *Usque ad evangelium prout sibi videatur.*

5. The prayers before the presentation of the gifts.

6. After the *Sanctus*, during the Canon, the assistants continue their prayer, which usually consisted of five psalms: Psalm 19 *Exaudiet te dominus*, Psalm 24 *Ad te domine levavi*, Psalm 50 *Miserere*, Psalm 89 *Domine refugium* and Psalm 90 *Qui habitat*, together with versicles and orations.

7. The formulas *Habete vinculum pacis* and *Pax Christi et ecclesiae* in the rite of the Peace.

8. Some prayers at Communion such as *Panem caelestem accipiam.*

9. The dismissal from the altar, sometimes accompanied by the prayer *Meritis et intercessionibus.*

10. While the priest returns to the sacristy, he recites the canticle *Benedicite* and Psalm 150 *Laudate dominum*, followed by versicles with one or more oration.

We are told that through the Romano-Germanic Pontifical:

> The *ordo missae* spread into Italy in the second half of the tenth century and into other European regions until it characterized and in some sense unified the mediaeval eucharistic liturgy of the West.

So one can confidently assert that:

> [the] *ordo renano* in the form in which it was received in Italy is the direct model of the Roman *ordinarium missae* which would subsequently be re-worked in some particulars and disseminated through the liturgical books *secundum consuetudinem romanae curiae* of the thirteenth century [subsequently revised by Giovanni Burcardo in 1502] and sanctioned definitively in the *Missale Romanum* of Pius V.[47]

After Pius V, the Missal received other modifications, most significantly under Pope Clement VIII in 1604, and Urban VIII in 1634 – both within a relatively few decades of its original promulgation in 1570. Then there was the missal promulgated under Leo XIII in 1884.[48]

---

47 Ibid., 806.   48 *Missale Romanum, ex decreto Concilii Tridentini restitutum S. Pii V pontificis maximi iussu editum, Clementis VIII, Urbani VIII et Leonis XIII, auctoritate vulgatum* (Mechlin, 1884).

Not everyone responded favourably to the reforms of the Council of Trent, and ferments arose against the missal at various times in the course of the following centuries. In France, Gallican uses survived in many places. During the eighteenth century, some French Jansenist bishops attempted to compromise the unity of the reformed liturgy by claiming competences and prerogatives independent of the Holy See. They tried to introduce different rubrics, such as the audible recitation of the Canon and the arbitrary insertion of *Amen* at various points. They also altered some texts, introduced new compositions, and suppressed texts. Most notably, they tried to return to the simplicity of the ancient sanctuary by removing the cross and candles from the *mensa*. Concerned bishops, together with great scholars such as Mabillon and Le Brun, protested against these practices, but in vain. There was even a missal promulgated for the diocese of Paris in 1738 that included many such localized practices.[49] This French sense of autonomy also spread into dioceses in Germany like Cologne and Münster, and gathered momentum at the Synod of Pistoia in Italy in 1786. In the end Pius VI condemned both the practices and the doctrines of the Jansenists in the bull *Auctorem fidei* of 7 September 1974. However, in the middle of the nineteenth century dissidents reacted against the Tridentine missal once again.[50]

During the twentieth century, the missals of Benedict XV in 1920 and of John XXIII merit particular mention. With the exception of the 1962 missal, the differences were largely to do with rubrics, but new formulas were included in response to various canonizations, as well as four new Prefaces, two introduced by Benedict XV and two by Pius XI.[51] In 1948, the year following the promulgation of *Mediator Dei*, Pius XII began to move towards a liturgical reform that was in turn taken up by the Congregation of Rites, and involved consultation with bishops from all over the world. The five volumes of proceedings, published in an edition by Carlo Braga, illustrate that for the most part the envisaged reform concerned the Calendar and Breviary, with only a few pages dealing with the Missal. In the typical edition of 1952 the name of Pius V disappeared from the title page of the Roman Missal, though his bull *Quo primum* remained at the front.[52] Between the pontificates of Pius XI and Pius XII new high-ranking feasts appeared, such as those of the

---

49 *Missale Romanum editio princeps (1570)*, XVI, nn 25–6 list the printed editions of the *missale Pariense*. **50** See P. Gueranger, *Institutiones liturgicae* (Paris, 1878), vol. 2. **51** Benedict XV introduced the Prefaces of the Dead and of St Joseph in 1919, and Pius XI those of Christ the King and the Sacred Heart in 1925 and 1928 respectively. **52** See Jounel, 'Missel', p. 295.

Precious Blood and of Christ the King, while other formulas saw significant changes to their texts, such as those of Holy Week, the Sacred Heart, the Immaculate Conception and the Assumption. At the beginning of the pontificate of John XXIII, the rubrics of the Missal and Breviary were simplified. Having announced the forthcoming Second Vatican Council, Pope John decided not to wait to its conclusion before moving ahead. The first sentence of the Introduction of *Sacrosanctum concilium* clearly indicated the intended direction of the reform: 'The sacred Council has set out to impart an ever-increasing vigour to the Christian life of the faithful'.[53]

After the reform of the Breviary, Pius had intended to proceed to that of the Missal. He wanted the rubrics of the Missal to be harmonized with those of the Breviary, without changing *substantium ipsius missalis*, thereby expressing his deep sensitivity to the integrity of the Missal, with the Canon of the Mass at its heart. In addition, according to Righetti, the Pontifical Commission for the revision of the text of the Vulgate had not yet completed its task. This missal would not be published until 1920, some six years after the death of Pius X.

Although Pius XII issued no new typical edition of the Roman Missal, he gave authorization for missals to include the changes he made to the Holy Week liturgies, which had begun in 1951 with the new Easter Vigil and which continued as a result of the decree *Maxima redemptionis nostrae mysteria* in 1955.[54] The series of six Old Testament readings was also removed from the Vigil of Pentecost, though for some reason they continued to be printed. Subsequently, John XXIII promulgated the *motu proprio Rubricarum instructum* in 1960, which arose from the *coetus* of *periti* established by Pius XII in 1956. The formation of this committee arguably constituted a preamble to the general liturgical reform that would follow in the next decade. In any case, it set out to simplify the rubrics of both the Missal and the Breviary. The 1962 missal included the new rubrics that the commission of Pius XII had prepared, which had been obligatory since 1 January 1961. Most notably, it also included new texts for the Holy Week liturgies, and the insertion of the name of St Joseph in the Canon of the Mass. *Rubricarum instructum* displaced two of the documents found in the 1920 edition of Benedict XV, and superseded the Apostolic Constitution of Pope Pius X, *Divino afflatu*.

---

53 *SC* 1, 4 December 1963, AAS, 56 (1964), 97–144. 54 AAS, 47 (1955), 838–47.

THE *MISSALE ROMANUM* OF 1970 AND ITS SUBSEQUENT EDITIONS

The Tridentine missal functioned as the book used by priests, since in it the celebrant had in one volume everything he needed to celebrate Mass without ministers. The reform of the liturgy promulgated by the Second Vatican Council in *Sacrosanctum concilium* articulated different priorities. It stated that in the liturgy:

> Pastors of souls must therefore realize that when the liturgy is celebrated, something more is required than mere observation of the laws governing valid and licit celebration. It is their duty also to ensure that the faithful take part fully aware of what they are doing, actively engaged in the rite, and enriched by its effects.[55]

After instructing that the liturgy should be taught in its theological, historical, spiritual and pastoral aspects, *Sacrosanctum concilium* 16 states that the liturgy should be taught in its juridical aspects. Likewise, *SC* 11 could be interpreted as having a negative attitude to law in the liturgy, since it discusses the juridical dimension last in its list of priorities. One receives the impression that liturgical law has been pushed aside to accommodate the full participation of the faithful, who are to be consciously aware of what they are doing. The catechetical emphasis also often stresses that the faithful were to concentrate on 'what they were doing' – which might arguably distract them from participating in and cooperating with 'what God is doing'.[56] Interpreted disproportionately there is thus the risk that focusing on 'active participation' might overshadow the enrichment of the faithful by sacramental grace. While potentially diminishing liturgical law (without explicitly disparaging it), *SC* 11 did not explain how it was to be replaced. It explained that the law was not sufficient to fulfil the requirements of a liturgical celebration, but it did not clarify precisely what the necessary 'something more' should be. One consequence of this has been that those who place primary importance on the people taking an active part in the liturgy have introduced a proliferation of liturgical abuses that disregard the law that governs them.

Despite such challenges, *Sacrosanctum concilium* had acknowledged that parts of the Missal could be changed, whereas others were immutable. The new missal was designed for the restoration of concelebration and for the full

---

55 *SC* 11.　56 See *SC* 21.

and proper exercise of respective ministries within the celebration – such as those of deacons, lectors and cantors. The reason for proclaiming Sacred Scripture in word and song was now no longer solely for the worship of God, but also for the purpose of catechesis. The Scripture became specifically directed at the faithful. *SC* 51 states:

> The treasures of the Bible are to be opened up more lavishly, so that richer fare may be provided for the faithful at the table of God's Word. In this way a more representative portion of the Holy Scriptures will be read to the people in the course of a prescribed number of years.

The missal is thus crowned by its lectionary, rather than by its *Graduale romanun*, whose appeal remains specialized. It was not intended that the missal of 1970 would mirror the *Missale plenum*. It was promulgated by Paul VI, and after the Apostolic Constitution of 6 April 1969 there is a very important general presentation. In eight chapters it expounds the structure of the Mass and the different kinds of celebration, rather than the manner in which the priest might use the texts placed before him.

The great development was the introduction of three additional Eucharistic Prayers to complement the Roman Canon. Eucharistic Prayer II is modelled on the third-century prayer of St Hippolytus, while Eucharistic Prayer IV presents a summary of the mystery of salvation, drawing imagery from the anaphoras of the East. There are eighty-four Prefaces compared to a smaller number in the missal of 1570, and the number of Collects in the missal of 1970 has almost doubled.

The thinking behind the Collects of the missal of 1970 has also changed. It is clear that they have been adapted to illustrate the specific mission of a given saint, honoured in the all-encompassing celebration of the Paschal Mystery. The *memoria* of 11 February provides a useful example. We celebrate 'Our Lady of Lourdes' rather than the apparitions, as was the case in the missal of 1962. The prayers for the dead have likewise been reworked to reflect the teaching of *Lumen gentium* and *Gaudium et spes* from Vatican II, and view the deceased from the perspective of the Paschal character of Christian death. Matias Augè expressed an awareness that a conflict had arisen between the sanctoral cycle and the Proper of Time or the Christological cycle, and that a reform would be needed to re-establish the balance that had been lost.[57]

---

57 M. Augè, 'I santi nella celebrazione del mistero di Cristo', *Anamnesis*, 6 (1988), 254: *Explode così il*

The *ordo missae* has also changed its emphasis in a number of ways. The priest leads everyone in a communal act of penitence. The Tridentine offertory prayers have given way to an adaptation of the Jewish blessing of a table. The *Orate fratres* has become a communal mode of offering, since the *meum et vestrum* that distinguishes the priest's offering of the sacrifice from the offering of the faithful has been blurred. The dismissal of the assembly closes the celebration.[58]

1970

The missal of 1970 received definitive approval on 11 March of that year and was officially published with a decree by the Congretation of Divine Worship dated 26 March. It was ready for 17 May, the day on which Paul VI celebrated his Golden Jubilee of ordination. Like the missal of 1570, the missal of 1970 was the product of a Council – and significantly, a pastoral council. Correspondingly, the *Consilium* responded with a pastoral agenda. In the first paragraph of the first chapter ('The key to the liturgical reform') in his book *The reform of the liturgy, 1948–1975*, Bugnini stated:

> The reform that the Second Vatican Council inaugurated is differentiated from all others in the history of the liturgy by its pastoral emphasis. The participation and active involvement of the people of God in the liturgical celebration is the ultimate goal of the reform, just as it was the goal of the liturgical movement.[59]

The missal begins with the Apostolic Constitution *Missale Romanum* of 3 April 1969, and the section that deals with the Missal from the *motu proprio* on the Liturgical Year, *Mysterii paschalis* of 14 February 1969. The import of its introduction into the Roman Missal (it is consulted for the General Norms of the Liturgical Year and the Calendar) is often less appreciated than that of the *Institutio generalis* that follows. But it focuses on three points. The first, in giving a history of the Roman Missal from the Council of Trent until Vatican II, explains the changes that have been made. The second emphasizes the continuity of faith in the sacrifice of the Mass, the real presence of Christ in the Eucharist, and the hierarchical nature of the ministerial priesthood,

conflitto tra sanctorale e temporale o ciclo cristologico. Lentamente si delinea il bisogno di una riforma che cherchi di ristabilire l'equilibrio perduto. **58** See P. Jounel, 'La composition des nouvelles prières eucharistiques', *Maison Dieu*, 94 (1968), 38–76; M. Thurian, 'La théologie des nouvelles prières eucharistiques', *Maison Dieu*, 94 (1968), 77–102. **59** A. Bugnini, *The reform of the liturgy, 1948–1975* (Collegeville MN, 1990), p. 5.

together with the essential relationship between the ministerial priesthood and
that of the faithful. The third is concerned with attendant norms. There is a
change in the way the hermeneutics of tradition is described. Its importance is
no longer presented as consisting in the maintenance of a particular position
through the centuries, but rather the historical context of each stage. The
'Introduction to the Roman Missal' exhibits this interpretation clearly,
referring to it as a 'broader prospect':

> 'The tradition of the Fathers' does not require merely the preservation of
> what our immediate predecessors have passed on to us. There must also
> be profound study and understanding of the Church's entire past and of
> all the ways in which its single faith has been expressed in quite diverse
> human and social forms prevailing in Semitic, Greek, and Latin cultures.[60]

Part three of Bugnini's *Reform of the liturgy* is devoted to the Roman Missal,
and he emphasizes that a clear division was made between the contents of the
Missal and those of the Lectionary. The Missal, containing euchological and
sacramental formulas, was for the altar, while the Lectionary, containing the
Word of God, was for the lectern. The missal drew upon extensive sources
from East and West, and other prayers were created that had no precedent –
such as the prayer for non-believers on Good Friday, and some of the collects
for particular occasions. Consequently, while the missal was a harmonization
of texts, it was also the creative work of the *Consilium*. The relevant *coetus* was
18 bis, and its director was Fr Placide Bruylants of Mont-César, who died in
1966. The patrology scholar Fr Henry Ashworth of Quarr was also a member,
and he too died before the full results of his labours were realized. *Coetus* 18
bis studies the problems of the structure of the Commons, which provided the
Common of the Dedication of a Church, six formulas of the Blessed Virgin
Mary, ten formulas for martyrs and three other specialized sets for martyrs,
twelve formulas for pastors, two formulas for doctors, four for virgins and
twelve for holy men and women. Some of these twelve were appropriate to a
variety of classes, while others were intended for specific groups such as
religious, teachers, mothers of families, and those who work with the
underprivileged.[61] The Masses for Various Needs were divided into Masses for
Various Occasions, in four groups that included the needs of the Church, civil
needs, various public needs and particular needs. A large collection of votive

---

60 'Introduction', *Missale Romanum* 1970, no. 9.   61 See Bugnini, *The reform of the liturgy*, pp 397–9.

Masses was followed by the Masses for the Dead with five general formulas and fourteen formulas for particular circumstances.

After the special rites for 2 February, Ash Wednesday and Holy Week, an appendix to the missal gives specimens of the Prayer of the Faithful. It was the instruction *Inter oecumenici* of 26 September 1964 that established general norms for a modern prayer, constructed according to the practices of antiquity. In practice this has proved to be an unwieldy innovation, and it has rarely retained its envisaged structure. A second appendix of musical settings for the parts of the Mass has remained under-employed, as well as the 1972 decree of the Congregation for Divine Worship which produced the volume, *Ordo cantus missae* for the singing of the Order of the Mass in Latin but with the new liturgical books in mind.

The *Institutio generalis* of the Roman Missal has been amended in response to particular juridical and pastoral exigencies in recent decades. In synthesis: after its first promulgation by the Sacred Congregation of Rites on 6 April 1969, it was inserted into the missal of 1970 with some adjustments, including a decree from the Congregation for Divine Worship dated 26 March 1970. It was revised in 1972 because of the discontinuation of ordinations to the subdiaconate, and the re-evaluation of the ministries of lector and acolyte. It was updated again in 1975 and published in the *editio altera typica*, and again in 1983 to reflect the norms of the new Code of Canon Law. The *Institutio generalis* of 2002 saw considerable changes in the third typical edition.[62]

Implementation and results

Imitating the practice of the Church of the first six or seven centuries, when liturgy was understood as a corporate act with a plurality of ministers, each of whom required his particular book, the renewal of the liturgical books of the post-Conciliar rites nonetheless includes some compromises. The lectionary carries responsorial psalms that pertain to a cantor. The missal resisted the title of sacramentary, even though it contains only the prayers of the priest. Whether or not there was a cantor for the Introit, the priest could 'incorporate' the entrance antiphon into his introduction. It was this incorporation that justified the presence of the text in the missal, but it is hard to imagine what the communion antiphon might be incorporated into by the celebrant. The offertory chant, however, was either discontinued, or its text sung according to the *Graduale*.

62 See M. Barba, *Institutio generalis missalis romani* (Vatican City, 2006), XXIII.

The General Instruction and the *ordo missae* are well co-ordinated, though discrepancies do exist. Unlike the Tridentine missal, they mention what the people do and say. In the three typical editions, the people say 'Amen', the priest sits, and the priest continues with the people. Seeds had already been sown for this in Pius XII's reform of Holy Week in 1955. For example, the priest was directed to sit at the *sedilia* and listen, but not to read the texts separately. He was to face the people to bless palms. The renewal of baptismal vows took place facing the people. Early in the liturgical reform, then, it was suggested that the people must be able to see liturgical actions.

Integral to this concern that the people be able to see what was happening was that they should understand what was being done – even though there were also recommendations that the people should be listening while the liturgy was being proclaimed. Currently, some publishing houses produce a disposable monthly series of booklets with all the texts included. Given that they sell, they must be meeting a need. This illustrates that many lay people have not realized the importance of each minister having his own book for a liturgy that is proclaimed, and that their own personal missals diminish the roles of the ministers.

There are various sorts of literary aids that also indicate how the reception of the Missal has evolved. Individually held missals were the means by which the people participated in Mass before the Second Vatican Council, being a feature of the liturgical movement of the twentieth century. Whether we like it or not, the missal of the people gave way to the missalette after the Second Vatican Council, which is now the norm in many places. Their popularity arose from the use of the St Andrew's missal of Gaspar Lefebvre, which also contained Sunday Vespers. The idea was to bring Mass to the people. The ministers had their book; with the layman's missal, the people were to have theirs. Unfortunately the new translations provide an excuse for the revival of missalettes; but their coming into being was inevitable. If liturgy was to be a corporate undertaking by a community led by a group of ministers, each with his own duties, the missalette was bound to become the book of the assembly. Although the missal was no longer the only book necessary for the celebration of Mass (due to the variety of forms of liturgical participation), the *novus ordo* retained this name for the book used by the priest at the altar. The personal hand-missal has survived much as before, containing the texts of the Liturgies of Word and Sacrament. Though the new form of the liturgy is a corporate act involving all, people still often want to hold something in their hands.

COMPARING THE TWO MISSALS

As I stated at the beginning of this essay, the rubrics *Sacerdos paratus* and *Populo congregato* begin the two forms of a shared Roman Rite that are founded on very different mentalities. In antiquity, we know that the books were put together according to their respective ministries; thus the priest had his, the lectors theirs, and the singers theirs in the context of the *Antiphonale*. The liturgy thus assumed an interaction among a plurality of ministries.

The counterpart of the Missal is of course the Breviary. The texts here are not put together on the basis of a diversity of ministries, but of a liturgical diversity. The Missal had all the texts necessary for Mass, while the Breviary contained those necessary for the Divine Office, all of which were to be used by a single person. This is important in the context of the significant development in the Mass that began around the ninth century and continued into the twelfth. From a liturgical act involving a variety of ministries there arose an act performed by one person, who therefore needed all the texts in one book. The missal for the use of one person goes hand in hand with the private Mass. Monks played a large part in this process, often because of the requirement for Masses of suffrage offered for the prince who built an abbey (for example). In these cases monks had to celebrate their own masses. Mendicants were also responsible for the diffusion of the private Mass. Since they were itinerate preachers, they were less bound to the common life, which influenced both the Breviary and the Missal.

The underlying causes of these developments are particularly interesting. In the ninth-century Carolingian and Frankish kingdoms there was an explosion of the building of gigantic monasteries, which had processional liturgies. The exhortation of St Paul to 'pray without ceasing'[63] encouraged a form of incessant liturgical activity in Rome, Jerusalem and Constantinople (to give three examples) which involved all priests, throughout the day. Why, then, would these priests have felt it necessary to say Mass privately as well? Certainly, the requirement to honour Masses of suffrage was considerable. But in addition, a new understanding of priesthood was developing. Before Trent, ordinations took place because of pastoral commitments that needed to be fulfilled. After Trent, the thinking shifted to the idea of absolute ordination, whereby the fact of having been ordained required the offering of Mass each day.

---

63 I Thess. 5:17.

This idea of 'absolute ordination' and the need for the priest to celebrate daily Mass evokes a variety of responses. Some see the fulfilment of this duty as a feature of Carolingian monasticism.[64] Others have suggested that perhaps there were canons in the ninth and tenth centuries that encouraged priests to say secretly what others were reading or singing aloud. Another theory is that the missal arose from the private Mass; or that priests felt obliged at least to read secretly what others were doing. This assumes an understanding of priesthood that requires each priest to do everything, precisely because Mass is what a priest does. Thus Mass and priesthood go together, and the priest himself is more important than his liturgical context. His dignity, his responsibility, is to celebrate Mass every day. The *Orate fratres*, which distinguishes the priest's sacrifice from lay participation in the sacrifice, together with the priestly apologetic prayers, give the suggestion that despite an individual priest's unworthiness he should perform that to which he was called. It is his right to do this, approaching the eucharistic celebration with joy and faith.

The effects of the provision of the 1962 missal on how new priests viewed themselves after *Summorum pontificum* in 2007 and *Universae ecclesia* of 2011 is evident. There is a marked difference between older priests who celebrate the *novus ordo* now, but who had previously been used to the Tridentine rite, and younger priests who have never known anything other than the missal of Paul VI. The passions aroused from each of these perspectives is well known. But we need to resist the temptation to believe that everything before 1965 was perfect, and that everything since has been unfortunate. The missal of 1962 carries a more cultic view of priesthood, understood through its links to the Tridentine Mass and that Mass's theology and beauty of form and artifact. Priests who prefer the Tridentine missal find confirmation of their priestly identity within this entire context. The missal of 1970, by contrast, with its emphasis on the assembly, requires that the content of the celebration and its rites should be self-explanatory. Achieving noble simplicity in rites that are intrinsically connected to the assembly (as stated in *SC* 34) continues to be an uphill struggle. There are many factors involved in making the texts and *ars celebrandi* of rites 'noble', 'short', 'clear', 'within the people's powers of comprehension', and 'normally not requiring much explanation'. In addition, as I have indicated, each liturgical book needs to be understood within its own theological context, so that we can be conscious of the breadth of what is being conveyed in its proclamation.

64 See A.A. Haussling, *Mönchskonvent und Eucharistiefeier* (Münster, 1973), pp 298–347.

The need for choice, particularly in liturgy, is symptomatic of post-modernism precisely because post-modernism denies that things can be precisely defined. It is probable that post-modernism will continue to encourage picking and choosing favourite parts of what had previously been an organic whole, and placing them into new contexts where they do not belong. This danger highlights the need for absolute integrity in the celebration of each of the two forms of the Roman rite, so that they speak of salvation rather than bow to the often subtle agendas of post-modernism.[65]

It is impossible to separate the implementation of Vatican II from its context of the 1960s. Before the Council, a tightly controlled liturgy with no variations, changes or options was the corollory of an equally unchanging dogmatic and moral understanding of canonical systems, which together comprised a whole world-view. For many, this world-view was not only adequate, it inspired faith, and for this reason seemed wonderful. It was a vivid and reassuring means to truth, and it was thus missionary, and presumed a cosmos organized around poles of the *perichoresis* that made up the Catholic world. The loss of this liturgical cosmos after Vatican II was thus only one part of the wider dismemberment of its morally and dogmatically defined unity, which was itself symptomatic of the implosion that disconnected many areas of Catholic life from others. The 'pick and mix' Catholic came to the fore, who chose one thing while rejecting another. And yet he called himself a Catholic, refusing to acknowledge that he was caught up in a cognitive deviance, rather than engaged in mature reflection.

CONCLUSION

No liturgy this side of heaven will be structurally perfect. The *aggiornamento* of the sanctoral cycle of the Extraordinary Form called for in *Summorum pontificum* indicates that one cannot arrest liturgical development, and recognizes that there are defects in the missal of 1962. But once one updates the missal of 1962, it is no longer the 1962 missal (even though other updated missals were promulgated as simply being 'new editions'). The view that what was being read in Latin by the priest should be read to the people in English was already gaining prominence. On the other hand, for some people the

---

65 On the affects of post-modernism on modern liturgical practice see, e.g., J.E. Rutherford, '"Putting ashes on our heads": Anglican reflections on the problem of liturgical English', *One in Christ*, 45:2 (2011), 182–200.

slightest addition or change to the missal was seen as simply being the thin end of the wedge. The schemes piloted in the reformed Holy Week of the 1950s had not envisaged the extent to which they would be surpassed in the missal of 1970. The expectation that the fire at Easter Vigil might be struck from flint, even in the twentieth century, suggests that few people anticipated the future extent of the process that had been unleashed. And this is to say nothing of the unique beauty and history of ecclesiastical Latin as a language in which to recite or sing the formulas that sanctify people and make things holy. It is impossible to calculate the cost to more than a generation of people that has been excluded from appreciating Latin as the language of the Church – when a draw-bridge was raised, separating them from the heritage which explains the culture of the Roman Missal.

When addressing the Pontifical Institute of Liturgy on 6 May 2011 on the occasion of the fiftieth anniversary of its foundation, Benedict XVI connected the prospects of these apparently divergent perspectives. He repeated this when he spoke to the Pontifical Institute of Sacred Music on 31 May 2011 on the occasion of its centenary, which suggests that he attaches considerable importance to it:

> The liturgy, summit to which the action of the Church tends and at the same time source from which her virtue springs [cf. *SC* 10], with its celebratory universe, thus becomes the great educator in the primacy of the faith and of grace. The liturgy, privileged witness to the living Tradition of the Church, faithful to its original duty to reveal and make present in the *hodie* of human vicissitudes the *opus redemptionis*, lives from a correct and constant relationship between healthy tradition and legitimate *progressio*.

We are at a unique time in the history of liturgy in the Roman Missal. Though there have been simultaneously maintained rites in the Latin Church, never before have there been two forms of the one Roman rite. Theodore Klauser, though writing about the history of liturgical books, expresses the opportunity that is before us: *Romana est sed etiam nostra.*[66] The liturgy that we perform today is truly Roman, but it is at the same time also our own. *Summorum pontificum*, promulgated by Benedict XVI, explains the perennial need to find fruit in this notion:

---

66 Vogel, 'Mediaeval liurgy', p. 3.

Since time immemorial it has been necessary – as it is also for the future – to maintain the principle according to which 'each particular church must concur with the universal Church, not only as regards the doctrine of the faith and the sacramental signs, but also as regards the uses universally accepted by uninterrupted apostolic tradition, which must be observed not only to avoid errors, but also to transmit the integrity of the faith; because the Church's law of prayer corresponds to her law of faith'.[67]

This statement provides an ongoing context in which to reaffirm the themes expressed in the first paragraph of *Sacrosanctum concilium* to govern our minds today and in the future towards the coherent celebration of the liturgy of the Roman rite from the two missals entrusted to us that will:

desire to impart an ever-increasing vigour to the Christian life of the faithful; to adapt more suitably to the needs of our own times those institutions that are subject to change; to foster whatever can promote union among all who believe in Christ; to strengthen whatever can help to call the whole of mankind into the household of the Church.[68]

Thus *sacerdos paratus* and *populo congregato* can genuinely share the same objectives from the respective historical development of the two missals of 1570 and 1970, because in the holiness of the Mass, which both celebrates the work of the Lord and calls us to conversion, 'our way of thinking is attuned to the Eucharist, and the Eucharist in turn confirms our way of thinking.'[69]

---

67 *Summorum pontificum* para. 2.   68 *SC* 1.   69 Irenaeus, *Adversus haereses*, 4.

The 'basic structure' (*Grundgestalt*) of the eucharistic celebration according to Joseph Ratzinger

MANFRED HAUKE

Up to now, the discussion concerning the 'basic structure' of the Holy Mass has taken place primarily in the German-speaking countries.[1] We find a certain foreshadowing of the debate already in a controversy in the years before the First World War. Franz Seraph Renz (1884–1916), in a substantial monograph on the history of the eucharistic sacrifice,[2] proposed the thesis that the eucharistic sacrifice, in its essence, is a meal (1902). As Ratzinger does not refer to the controversy that sprang from this suggestion (especially in the years 1906–10) or to its connection with a certain condemned proposition in the decree *Lamentabili* (1907) of Pope Pius X against Modernism, we mention it here only briefly.

The 'tendency towards an increasing importance of the meal aspect of the Holy Mass' begins with the Augsburg theologian Franz Seraph Renz.[3] Renz 'confused the nature of the sacrificial act with the purpose of union with God'[4] and states that 'eucharistic worship is essentially a meal with a sacrificial character'.[5] The ideas described here would be re-elaborated by a student of Renz, Franz Sales Wieland (1877–1957),[6] according to whom the eucharistic celebration was understood before Irenaeus as a meal. Only after Irenaeus did the thanksgiving sacrifice [*Danksagungsopfer*] become a presentation/offering sacrifice [*Darbringungsopfer*].[7] Wieland was challenged by the Innsbruck dogmatic and fundamental theologian Emil Dorsch SJ (1867–934).[8] The relevant

---

1 See in particular the overview in H.B. Meyer, *Eucharistie. Geschichte, Theologie, Pastoral* (Regensburg, 1989), pp 441–60; M. Hauke, 'La Santa Messa – che cosa è? La „struttura fondamentale" della celebrazione eucaristica' in G. Borgonovo and K. Charamsa (eds), *Eucaristia e libertà. Percorsi di formazione sacerdotale*, vol. 2 (Vatican City, 2006), pp 37–52. 2 F.S. Renz, *Geschichte des Messopferbegriffs* (Freising, 1902). 3 Cf. W. Imkamp, 'Die katholische Theologie in Bayern von der Jahrhundertwende bis zum Ende des Zweiten Weltkrieges' in W. Brandmüller (ed.), *Handbuch der bayerischen Kirchengeschichte* III (St Ottilien, 1991), pp 539–651 (at p. 578); on Renz see G. Rauschen, *Eucharistie und Bußsakrament in den ersten sechs Jahrhunderten der Kirche* (Freiburg i.Br., 1910), pp 60–17; Imkamp, pp 576–8. 4 Imkamp, p. 578. 5 Renz, *Geschichte des Messopferbegriffs*, p. 500. 6 See Imkamp, pp 578–80; a tendentious presentation of the conflict can be found in O. Weiss, *Der Modernismus in Deutschland. Ein Beitrag zur Theologiegeschichte* (Regensburg, 1995), pp 410–25. 7 See F.S. Wieland, *Der vornizänische Opferbegriff* (Munich, 1909), XIf. 8 Cf. Imkamp, p. 579. On the Wieland–Dorsch controversy (1906–10), see Rauschen, pp 71–95. Against Wieland, Dorsch stressed (and here Rauschen agrees) that the Eucharist is an offering of the body and blood

works of Wieland were put on the Index because they were seen to be connected to proposition 49 of the anti-Modernist decree *Lamentabili* of Pius X:

> When the Christian supper gradually assumed the nature of a liturgical action those who customarily presided over the supper acquired the sacerdotal character. (DH 3449)

The topic is probably also familiar to Ratzinger from a doctoral dissertation supervised by him, which contradicts the interpretations of Renz and Wieland.[9]

The discussion of our topic in its stricter sense begins in 1939 with some meditations of Romano Guardini, and culminates in the contributions of Joseph Ratzinger and Walter Kasper in the decade after 1980. While the debate over the 'basic structure' of the eucharistic celebration has so far not numbered among the top themes treated by contemporary theologians at a worldwide level, we are nevertheless touching here a central point to which Ratzinger has made vital contributions.[10]

The most important contribution is an article that appeared for the first time in the German edition of the journal *Communio* in 1977.[11] This article, supplemented by two addenda, then entered into the collection entitled *The feast of faith* (1981),[12] and now appears as part of the collected works of Ratzinger (in German), in the volume dedicated to the theology of the liturgy (2008).[13] The importance of this contribution is evident in the remark of Ratzinger that:

---

of Christ already in the pre-Irenaeian testimonies. According to H. Schürmann, the Wieland–Dorsch controversy was 'objectively and humanly unsatisfactory': H. Schürmann, 'Die Gestalt der urchristlichen Eucharistiefeier' in idem, *Ursprung und Gestalt. Erörterungen und Besinnungen zum Neuen Testament* (Düsseldorf, 1970), pp 77–99 (78, fn. 6). For Ratzinger's evaluation of this contribution by Schürmann, see below pp 87f. Alongside the Wieland–Dorsch controversy Schürmann also mentions studies on the Agape meals: A. Arnold, *Der Ursprung des christlichen Abendmahls* (Freiburg i.Br., 1937), pp 100ff. **9** H. Moll, *Die Lehre von der Eucharistie als Opfer. Eine dogmengeschichtliche Untersuchung vom Neuen Testament bis Irenäus von Lyon* (Köln and Bonn, 1975), p. 33. **10** This must be taken into consideration in order to understand Ratzinger's eucharistic theology. See P. Blanco, 'Liturgia e Eucaristía en la obra de Joseph Ratzinger', *Scripta Theologica*, 38 (2006), 103–30; E. Duffy, 'Benedict XVI and the Eucharist', *New Blackfriars*, 88 (2007), 195–212; A. Centurelli, *L'Eucaristia nel pensiero di Joseph Ratzinger Benedetto XVI* (Turin, 2011), pp 41–5; M. Becker, 'Eucharistie – Mitte des Lebens. Theologische Reflexionen mit Benedikt XVI', *Theologisches*, 41 (2011), 165–90 (at 174–7). **11** J. Ratzinger, 'Gestalt und Gehalt der eucharistischen Feier', *Internationale Katholische Zeitschrift Communio*, 6 (1977), 385–96. **12** J. Ratzinger, *Das Fest des Glaubens* (Einsiedeln, 1981), pp 31–54; English tr: *The feast of faith* (San Francisco, 1986). **13** J. Ratzinger, *Theologie der Liturgie* (Freiburg i.Br., 2008), pp 359–82.

[with] the concept of form or structure [*Gestalt*], a hitherto unknown category entered the theological dialogue, clearly recognizable as a power for reform. Indeed, it can be said that it was this category that gave birth to liturgical scholarship in the modern sense.[14]

As the Erfurt exegete Heinz Schürmann (cited by Ratzinger) put it in the early 1950s:

> Under the veil of ceremonies and rubrics the basic structures [*Grundgestalten*] of the holy events are being discovered once more, and this discovery inspires liturgical change.[15]

The core of the discussion revolves around the idea that, according to Guardini, the 'structure' (or 'form/figure/shape', in German *Gestalt*) and its 'content' (*Gehalt*) are entirely different things: the Holy Mass in its 'structure' is a meal, but its 'content' is a sacrifice. This divergence between liturgical structure and dogmatic content, according to Ratzinger:

> must be regarded as the central problem of the liturgical reform. Failure to deal with it has resulted in a great many of the individual problems that have since preoccupied us.[16]

This essay, then, first describes the beginning of the discussion in the liturgical movement of the German-speaking lands in the 1930s and 1940s. It looks next at the above-mentioned article of Ratzinger and its reception in contemporary theology. We will then take a glance at some related topics in the theological work of Ratzinger, before concluding with some recommendations for formulating this topic in a systematic framework.

THE PHILOSOPHICAL CONCEPT OF *GESTALT*

The German word *Gestalt*, in its philosophical sense, goes back to Greek philosophy, especially to the concept of *eidos* in Plato and *morphé* in Aristotle.[17] *Eidos* means the appearance (which can be seen) or the 'form' (figure, shape, species, quality, nature) that characterizes a single being. *Morphé* in Aristotle

---

14 Ratzinger, *Feast of faith*, p. 34.   **15** Schürmann, p. 77.   **16** Ratzinger, *Feast of faith*, p. 36.   **17** Cf. P. Janssen, *Gestalt*, in *Lexikon für Theologie und Kirche*, 4 (1995), pp 600f (at 600).

signifies the 'form' that determines the 'matter' (*hyle*) and constitutes it as a being that can be described. In the phenomenology of Edmund Husserl, *eidos* is identified with 'essence', that is, with a 'universal object that can be manifested by the "intuition of the essence" (*Wesenserschauung*)'.[18]

The concept of *Gestalt* has a notable role in the philosophy of art and literature. Johann Wolfgang von Goethe, the most renowned German poet, defines *Gestalt* as the visible manifestation of the essence.[19] Similarly, for Hegel *Gestalt* is:

> the name for the direct sensible expression of an interior and therefore necessary condition of the beautiful, as the sensible appearance of the idea: 'beauty can devolve only on the *Gestalt*'.[20]

It is especially in so-called 'Gestalt psychology' (*Gestaltpsychologie*) that *Gestalt*, the holistic structure or form, is presented as an expression of an 'interior essence'. *Gestalt* was introduced into psychology as a technical term in 1890 by Christian von Ehrenfels (1859–1932),[21] a disciple of the neo-Aristotelian philosopher Franz Brentano.[22] Contrary to empirical approaches that reduce every perception to its individual material elements, *Gestalt* psychology underlines the fact that the perception of a totality, of a whole, is more than the addition of single perceptions. The 'quality of form' (*Gestalt-Qualität*), according to von Ehrenfels, is not an aggregate of concepts, 'but a complex of elements based on a spiritual principle (with the tendency to form a totality)'.[23] Von Ehrenfels for instance gives the example of the melody whose progression remains the same even if every tone is changed (as when it is transposed into another key).[24] Its nature appears as a structured totality which is formed by an equilibrium of forces. The *Gestalt* can be destroyed if even just one part is changed. 'Not only does the whole have qualities that are not visible in its "parts", but every single element changes, gains and likewise loses

---

18 J. Szaif, *Eidos, eidetisch*, in *Lexikon für Theologie und Kirche*, 3 (1995), pp 525f (at 525).   **19** Cf. W. Strube and W. Metzger, 'Gestalt' in J. Ritter (ed.), *Historisches Wörterbuch der Philosophie*, 3 (Darmstadt, 1974), pp 540–8 (at 543).   **20** Ibid., p. 543, citing G.W.F. Hegel, *Ästhetik*, I (Berlin, 1965), p. 408.   **21** Cf. Strube and Metzger, p. 547, with reference to C. von Ehrenfels, *Gestaltqualitäten*, *Vierteljahresschrift für wissenschaftliche Philosophie*, 14 (1890), 249–92; see C. von Ehrenfels, 'On Gestalt qualities' in B. Smith (ed.), *Foundations of Gestalt theory* (Munich and Vienna, 1988), pp 82–117.   **22** See F. Austeda, *Wörterbuch der Philosophie* (Munich, 1981), p. 65; R. Fabian, *Christian von Ehrenfels: Leben und Werk* (Amsterdam, 1986); B. Smith, *Austrian philosophy. The legacy of Franz Brentano* (Chicago, 1994), chs. 8–9. On the philosophy of Brentano, cf. W. Stegmüller, *Hauptströmungen der Gegenwartsphilosophie* (Stuttgart, 1975), pp 1–48.   **23** Strube and Metzger, p. 545.   **24** See E. Zellinger, *Gestalt*, in *Lexikon für Theologie und Kirche*, 4 (1960), pp 838–43 (at 838f).

certain attributes' in relation to the whole in which it is integrated.[25] The concept of *Gestalt* is therefore defined with reference to a 'whole' or 'totality' (*Ganzheit*).

The philosophical discussion is very well summarized in the philosophical dictionary edited by the German Jesuit Walter Brugger: '*Gestalt* is the structured totality of sensible realities (in a figurative way also of spiritual realities) that can be articulated in space (such as mathematical figures or pictures) or in time in a rhythmic way (such as melodies).'[26] From this definition we can deduce that the concept of *Gestalt* can be applied to realities that we can see or hear. This observation is important in evaluating the exposition of Guardini, who orients himself to the visible part of the Eucharist (bespeaking a 'meal'), but who does not consider the things we can hear (especially the eucharistic prayer). 'Guardini was not attentive to the fact that it is not only visible things that are part of the *Gestalt*, but also audible realities'.[27]

THE APPLICATION OF THE CONCEPT OF *GESTALT* TO THE HOLY MASS
BY ROMANO GUARDINI: THE MEAL AS *GRUNDGESTALT* (BASIC
STRUCTURE)

The philosophical concerns of Gestalt psychology are also evident in phenomenology, which, following Edmund Husserl (1859–1938), attempts to apprehend the integrated structure of beings in the 'vision of essence' (*Wesensschau*).[28] Related to the phenomenological style of thinking is Romano Guardini (1885–1968), who sought to grasp mentally the living and concrete reality in its structured totality.[29] His intentions are well described in the foreword written by Ildefons Herwegen to Guardini's work *On the spirit of the liturgy* (1918). According to Herwegen, the abbot of Maria Laach, individualism is 'finished'. The human being 'longs for *community* ... The age of

25 Strube and Metzger, p. 547. 26 A. Willwoll, 'Gestalt' in W. Brugger (ed.), *Philosophisches Wörterbuch* (Freiburg i.Br., 1976), pp 143f (at 143). 27 Th. Maas-Ewerd, *Die Krise der Liturgischen Bewegung in Deutschland und Österreich. Zu den Auseinandersetzungen um die „liturgische Frage" in den Jahren 1939 bis 1944* (Regensburg, 1981), p. 344, fn. 328. 28 See for example the introductory overview in Stegmüller, pp 49–95; J. Hirschberger, *Geschichte der Philosophie* II (Freiburg i. Br., 1991), pp 593–605. Like von Ehrenfels, Husserl was also a student of Brentano: see Stegmüller, p. 49. 29 See H.R. Schlette, *Guardini*, in *Theologische Realenzyklopädie*, 14 (1985), pp 294–7 (at 295f); A. Schilson, *Perspektiven theologischer Erneuerung. Studien zum Werk Romano Guardinis* (Düsseldorf, 1986), pp 17f; H.-B. Gerl-Falkowitz, *Romano Guardini. Konturen des Lebens und Denkens* (Kevelaer, 2010).

socialism certainly knows communities, but only such communities as are formed by an accumulation of atoms, of individuals. Our desire, however, looks for the *organic reality*, for *fully-lived community'* whose supreme form is the Church.[30]

Just as Gestalt psychology overcomes the fragmentation of the individual elements of human impressions, so the Church can overcome the individualism that reduces human community to a mere collection of individuals. The Church appears as an organic whole that manifests itself as such in the liturgy. Hence comes the readiness to perceive liturgical 'forms' or 'structures' (*Gestalten*) in the prayer life of the Church. This disposition is reflected, for example, in the following remark:

> Piece by piece, the mountain range of the Mass reveals itself; and just as the peaks, crests and slopes of a mountain emerge pure and bright from the receding mist, so we think that we see it for the first time.[31]

Later on, Guardini writes:

> One of the main concerns of authentic liturgical work is to bring out once more every structure [*Gestalt*] in the liturgical actions[32] ... The *Gestalt* is what is 'comprehensible by itself', which reveals itself by its own signifying power and which can be easily apprehended by the receptive eye.[33]

Joseph Ratzinger has been very much influenced by the theological approach of Romano Guardini. In his foreword to the volume dedicated to the *Theology of the liturgy* in his collected works, he specifically mentions the importance of four theologians: Schmaus, Söhngen, Pascher and Guardini.[34] As to the concept of *Gestalt*, we should also note the influence of Guardini on Hans Urs von Balthasar;[35] the first volume of his main work, the theological

---

30 I. Herwegen, 'Zur Einführung' in R. Guardini, *Vom Geist der Liturgie* (Freiburg i.Br., 1934), VII–XIII. 31 Guardini, *Vom Geist der Liturgie*, p. 79. 32 R. Guardini, *Versuche über die Gestaltung der hl. Messe* (Basel, 1946), p. 17. 33 R. Guardini, *Besinnung vor der Feier der heiligen Messe* (Mainz, 1939), p. 74. 34 Ratzinger, *Theologie der Liturgie*, p. 6: 'The liturgy of the Church was for me since my childhood the central reality of my life, and in the theological school of teachers like Schmaus, Söhngen, Pascher, and Guardini it became the centre of my theological endeavours as well'. See also J. Ratzinger, 'Von der Liturgie zur Christologie. Romano Guardinis theologischer Grundansatz und seine Aussagekraft' in E. Biser (ed.), *Wege zur Wahrheit. Die bleibende Bedeutung von Romano Guardini* (Düsseldorf, 1985), pp 121–44. 35 See E. Guerriero, *Hans Urs von Balthasar. Eine Monographie* (Einsiedeln and Freiburg i.Br., 1993), pp 37–9.

trilogy (*Glory, Theo-drama, Theo-logic*) is entitled *Glory: A theological aesthetics*, vol. I: *Seeing the form*.[36] The 'form' [*Gestalt*] perceived by the faith finds its centre in Christ, whose glory is revealed on the Cross.[37] The aesthetic approach of von Balthasar, and thus also the concept of form centered on Christ, has had a lasting influence on the theology of Ratzinger.[38]

The most important work of Ratzinger on the theology of the liturgy, closely following the example of Guardini, is entitled *The spirit of the liturgy*. In his introduction he writes:

> One of the first books I read after starting my theological studies at the beginning of 1946 was Romano Guardini's first little book, *On the spirit of the liturgy* ... This slim volume ... has contributed decisively to the fact that the liturgy ... was discovered once more as the animating centre of the Church and as the centre of Christian life.

It had the effect that people wanted to understand the liturgy:

> from its inner form [*Gestalt*] as the prayer of the Church, a prayer moved and guided by the Holy Spirit himself, in which Christ himself unceasingly becomes contemporary with us, entering into our life.[39]

Ratzinger thus shares the approach of Guardini in disclosing the liturgical form of the Church's prayer, but at the same time he is not uncritical of Guardini's remarks concerning the basic structure of the Holy Mass. The starting point of our discussion is the appearance of a devotional book by Guardini in 1939, entitled *Meditations before Mass* (*Besinnung vor der Feier der heiligen Messe*).[40] This work goes back to a series of short meditations for young people given by Guardini between 1930 and 1932 at Burg Rothenfels in Bavaria.[41] According to Guardini, every 'authentic liturgical action ...

---

36 H.U. von Balthasar, *Herrlichkeit. Eine theologische Ästhetik I. Schau der Gestalt* (Einsiedeln and Trier, 1988).   37 See Balthasar, *Herrlichkeit* I, pp 445–505.   38 See E. de Gáal, *The theology of Pope Benedict XVI. The Christocentric shift* (New York, 2010), pp 38f.   39 J. Ratzinger, *Der Geist der Liturgie* (Freiburg i. Br., 2000), p. 7 = Ratzinger, *Theologie der Liturgie*, p. 30, English tr. *The spirit of the liturgy* (San Francisco, 2000). On the relationship between Ratzinger and Guardini see G. Brüske, *Spiel oder Anbetung? Romano Guardini und Joseph Ratzinger über den Sinn der Liturgie*, in R. Voderholzer (ed.), *Der Logos-gemäße Gottesdienst. Theologie der Liturgie bei Joseph Ratzinger* (Regensburg, 2009), pp 91–110; Gáal, *Theology of Benedict XVI*, pp 39–43.   40 R. Guardini, *Besinnung vor der Feier der heiligen Messe* (Mainz, 1939), pp 70–80. On which, see F. Debuyst, *Romano Guardini. Einführung in sein liturgisches Denken* (Regensburg, 2009), pp 54–62, or. *L'Entrée en Liturgie. Introduction à l'œuvre liturgique de Romano Guardini* (Paris, 2008).   41 See Debuyst, *Romano Guardini*, pp 54f. For background, see also W. Zahner, 'Raumkonzepte der

contains a basic structure [*Grundgestalt*] which supports it and which gives it its specific life'.[42] The sacraments, especially:

> are no mere apportionments of divine gifts, but life events, constructed according to the essence of man, whose soul expresses itself in the body, and whose body is formed by the soul. 'Form' [*Gestalt*] is the manner in which the human essence is alive ... Therefore one of the most important tasks of liturgical education is to reveal as clearly and as vigorously as possible the interior structure of the divine events. So what is the basic structure of the Mass? It is that of the meal.[43]

In support of this thesis, Guardini refers especially to the Last Supper, and then continues:

> The supporting structure of the Mass is the meal. The sacrifice does not emerge as structure, but remains behind the whole. In this way, it is not pushed back. Already in the history of religion, every cultic meal, or even ultimately every meal, depends on it ... The animal that should serve for food must be immolated, properly speaking, before the altar, because blood and life belong to God ... From the altar, from the hands of the Lord, man then receives the immolated victim and uses it as nourishment.

Applied to the Mass, this means: 'Its structure is the meal; behind it – not as structure, but as reality, as fountain, as condition – is the sacrifice.'[44]

In the fourth edition of 1947, Guardini omits his expositions on the 'structure' of the Holy Mass. He explains this omission in his preface, writing:

> the chapter 'The form of commemoration, the meal' ... had to be omitted because it gave rise to certain misunderstandings ... The reflections of the chapter dealt with ... a pure problem of form [*Formproblem*]. They were not, however, understood in this way, but they were implicated in the old controversy in which Catholic doctrine says that the Mass is 'a true and proper sacrifice' ... The reflections of the mentioned chapter did not concern this controversy even in a minimal

Liturgischen Bewegung' in A. Gerhards, T. Sternberg, W. Zahner (eds), *Communio-Räume. Auf der Suche nach der angemessenen Raumgestalt katholischer Liturgie* (Regensburg, 2003), pp 70–94 (at 79–85). **42** Guardini, *Besinnung vor der Feier der heiligen Messe*, p. 70. **43** Ibid., pp 72f. **44** Ibid., pp 76f.

way. They ... posed ... the question of what structure or form of appearance is to be attributed in the liturgy to the action which, in itself, is a sacrifice ... It appears, however, that there is little interest in form problems of this kind; this is the only way to explain how the whole could be so misunderstood.

In order to remedy this, a more detailed presentation than is possible in the present context would be necessary. So I must wait for another opportunity and omit the chapter entirely.[45]

The 'more detailed presentation' that Guardini considered writing was, however, never realized. In the editions of 1961 and 1965 of the cited work, that is, still during Guardini's lifetime, the pages omitted in 1947 were simply re-inserted.[46]

Nevertheless when, at a 1943 symposium at Vienna, he was confronted with the view of Jungmann that the Mass in the primitive Church contains 'not only the essence, but also already the expressive shape [*Gestaltausdruck*] of the sacrifice', Guardini stressed the hypothetical character of his own exposition and remarked:

> it cannot by any means be a question of us changing anything on our own initiative. I proposed only to consider whether it is not correct and possible to make more prominent, besides the aspect of sacrifice, also the other aspects present in the entirety of the Holy Mass, such as the meal and the commemoration, so as to gain a more balanced picture.[47]

Already in 1942 Guardini had published a letter in which he conceded 'that it is probably not possible to accept only one form [*Gestalt*] and that, at certain points, the form of the sacrifice enters into the form of the meal'.[48] 'In this way, Guardini admitted that the essence of the Eucharist as sacrifice finds expression also in its exterior structure.'[49]

Guardini's concern to accentuate the 'meal' as the 'structure' or 'basic form' of the Holy Mass was influenced by the liturgical movement at the beginning

45 R. Guardini, *Besinnung vor der Feier der heiligen Messe* (Mainz, 1947), pp 14f.   **46** Cf. Debuyst, *Romano Guardini*, pp 58f.   **47** R. Guardini, *Zu meinem Vortrag im Wiener Seelsorgeinstitut über Wesen und Gestalt der heiligen Messe am 19.1.43* (2 February 1943) (Nachlass Dr. Karl Rudolf): Th. Maas-Ewerd, *Die Krise der liturgischen Bewegung in Deutschland und Österreich* (Regensburg, 1981), pp 613f.   **48** R. Guardini, 'Die mystagogische Predigt' in K. Borgmann (ed.), *Volksliturgie und Seelsorge* (Kolmar im Elsass o. J., 1942), pp 159–61 (at 161), cited by Maas-Ewerd, *Die Krise der liturgischen Bewegung*, p. 346.   **49** Maas-Ewerd, *Die Krise der liturgischen Bewegung*, p. 346.

of the twentieth century. At the end of the nineteenth century, the faithful received Holy Communion only a few times a year. Pope Pius X, however, encouraged the faithful to communicate more frequently, even inviting children. In order to emphasize the active participation (*participatio actuosa*) of the faithful in the liturgy, common communion became the focus of attention.[50]

Guardini's proposal went further, however, inasmuch as it described the eucharistic banquet, Holy Communion, as the basic structure of the entire eucharistic mystery. This approach would also influence church architecture: the sacred space was structured in a way to accentuate the aspect of the meal, especially by orientating the celebration toward the people. Guardini was one of the first and most influential supporters of the Mass being celebrated *versus populum*.[51] The theological problem in all this does not consist in the first place in the rediscovery of the 'meal' as a partial aspect of the Eucharist, but rather in the divergence between the content and the form of the Holy Mass, between 'exterior' and 'interior'. As Ratzinger observes, the explication according to which the structure of meal and the content of sacrifice were juxtaposed:

> could not provide a satisfactory answer in the long term. Particularly since if the structure is not merely a ceremonial form, but at its core is an indispensable manifestation of its essential content, it makes absolutely no sense to separate the one from the other. The lack of clarity that has prevailed in this area, even during the Council, regarding the relation between the dogmatic and liturgical levels, must be regarded as the central problem of the liturgical reform. Failure to deal with it has resulted in a great many of the individual problems that have since preoccupied us.[52]

A concept similar to that of Guardini was developed in the same period (1937–46) by a teacher of Ratzinger, Gottlieb Söhngen (1892–1971).[53] His

50 Cf. Meyer, *Eucharistie. Geschichte, Theologie, Pastoral*, pp 280f; A. Ziegenaus, *Die Heilsgegenwart in der Kirche. Sakramentenlehre* (Aachen, 2003), p. 344. For the liturgical movement in general see Th. Maas-Ewerd, 'Was wollte die liturgische Bewegung?', *Erbe und Auftrag*, 69 (1993), 223–46.   **51** See A. Reid, *The organic development of the liturgy. The principles of liturgical reform and their relation to the twentieth-century liturgical movement prior to the Second Vatican Council* (San Francisco, 2005), p. 93; H.R. Kuehn, 'Introduction' in H.R. Kuehn (ed.), *The essential Guardini: an anthology of the writings of Romano Guardini* (Chicago, 1997), pp 1–12 (at 7f).   **52** Ratzinger, *Feast of faith*, pp 35–6.   **53** On the contribution of Söhngen generally see E.P.D. Martasudjita, *Die Gegenwart des Mysteriums Christi. Zum Sakramentenverständnis*

liturgical works are influenced by the 'theology of mysteries' developed by Odo Casel.[54] Whereas Casel presupposes an objective presence (as mystery) of the sacrifice of Christ in the Holy Mass, Söhngen identifies the presence of Christ's sacrifice with its effects in the faithful who participate in the celebration of the Eucharist.[55] For his account of the meal, he draws on French theologians who explained the sacrifice of the Mass (in distinction to the sacrifice of the Cross) by the meal ('*théorie du banquet*').[56] In the remarks of Söhngen, who is essentially following Guardini, the systematic tension becomes particularly obvious: the objection that 'a meal as such is not a sacrifice', according to Söhngen, is valid only for the non-sacramental realm:

> A sacramental sacrifice can have the form [*Gestalt*] of a meal, because a sacramental sacrifice is a sacrifice not in its proper form, but in a different form.[57]

Also following Guardini's line was Michael Schmaus (1897–1993), professor of dogmatic theology at Munich. As we already noted, besides that of Guardini, Söhngen and Pascher, Ratzinger emphasizes the influence of Schmaus on his own liturgical thought.[58] According to Schmaus, the basic structure of the eucharistic sacrifice is the meal.[59]

bei Gottlieb Söhngen (Frankfurt a. M., 1996), pp 42–53; W. Klausnitzer, 'Gottlieb Söhngen', *Biographisch-Bibliographisches Kirchenlexikon* 21 (2003), pp 1446–54. On Söhngen's influence on Ratzinger cf. Gáal, *Theology of Benedict XVI*, pp 33–6.   **54** See Martasudjita, *Die Gegenwart des Mysteriums Christi*, pp 62–5, 201–4 and passim; R. Berger, *Erlebte Liturgie in Ratzingers Studienzeit. Erinnerungen aus gemeinsamen Tagen*, in Voderholzer (2009), 78–90 (at 86).   **55** In this sense, Söhngen is interpreted by A. García Ibáñez, *L'Eucaristia, dono e mistero. Trattato storico-dogmatico sul mistero eucaristico* (Rome, 2006), p. 346f, fn. 85. Cf. G. Söhngen, *Das sakramentale Wesen des Messopfers* (Essen, 1946), p. 38: 'The Mass is the sacrifice of the Cross in the basic structure of a holy meal (…) whose gifts, the body and blood of the Lord under the species of bread and wine, are made present as the sacrifice of the Cross and are received as nourishment … The sacrifice of the Mass is the holy banquet which is celebrated as a memory of Christ's passion …' (ibid., p. 55). 'I see the essence of the Mass in the sacramental or symbolically real representation (*repraesentatio*) of the sacrifice of the Cross … This sacramental essence of the sacrifice of the Mass (*sakramentale Opferwesen der Messe*), the *memoria passionis Christi*, appears in the structure of a holy meal, the *sacrum convivium*' (ibid., p. 58). However, Söhngen also stresses the importance of the double consecration, 'the most essential sacrificial act', by which body and blood are made present separately (ibid., p. 19) and therefore contain a 'mystical immolation' (cf. ibid., p. 47).   **56** Cf. Söhngen, *Das sakramentale Wesen*, p. 57; idem, '„Tut das zu meinem Gedächtnis". Wesen und Form der Eucharistiefeier als Stiftung Jesu', in K. Rudolf (ed.), *Pascha Domini. Fragen zu Liturgie und Seelsorge* (Vienna, 1959), pp 64–90 (85–8). Anyway, Söhngen stresses going his own way here (*Das sakramentale Wesen*, p. 57). On the conception of Söhngen about the meal as basic structure of the Eucharist see also Schürmann, 'Die Gestalt der urchristlichen Eucharistiefeier', p. 77, fn. 4; Martasudjita, *Die Gegenwart des Mysteriums Christi*, pp 305–10. On the origin of the 'banquet theory' to explain the sacrifice of the Mass see A. Piolanti, *Il Mistero Eucaristico* (Città del Vaticano, 1983), pp 424–6 (the German theologian F.S. Renz, 1902, appears here at the beginning).   **57** Söhngen, *Das sakramentale Wesen*, p. 59; G. Söhngen, '„Tut das zu meinem Gedächtnis"', p. 86.   **58** Cf. Ratzinger, *Theologie der Liturgie*, p. 6; Berger, *Erlebte Liturgie in Ratzingers Studienzeit*, p. 86.   **59** M. Schmaus, *Die Lehre von den*

THE CONTRIBUTION OF JOSEPH PASCHER: A MEAL STRUCTURE
WITH SACRIFICIAL SYMBOLISM

For Ratzinger, the separation between meal structure and sacrificial content is problematic, and renders the basic thesis that the Eucharist is fundamentally a meal 'highly questionable'. He therefore attempts 'to trace the stages of the dispute and bring some light to bear on the problem'.[60] As 'a first attempt at reconciliation', he recalls the work of the Munich liturgist, Joseph Pascher,[61] who also finds a place in his memoirs:

> Pascher ... had first studied mathematics and additionally learned oriental languages, he then occupied himself with pedagogy and religious studies, investigated the mysticism of Philo of Alexandria, and then finally, by way of pastoral theology, he found his way to liturgical science ... As director of the Georgianum, he was responsible for our human and priestly formation; he performed this task entirely from the spirit of the liturgy and influenced all of us profoundly on our spiritual way.[62]

In 1960 Joseph Maria Pascher (1893–1979) was named a member of the preparatory commission for Vatican II. In 1962 and 1963 he was a *peritus* of Cardinal Döpfner, and from 1964 to 1969 he was active as consultor to the Roman Liturgy Council (*Consilium ad exsequendam constitutionem de sacra liturgia*).[63]

Pascher was one of the first liturgists to treat the topic of the 'basic structure' of the Eucharist in a separate publication, an article in 1950.[64] Here, instead of distinguishing the 'sacrificial Mass' from the foregoing 'preparative Mass', he speaks of the 'holy meal' that begins with the preparation of the

Sakramenten (Munich, 1957), p. 386: 'The meal, in a broad sense, is the basic shape of the eucharistic sacrifice' (Guardini); see ibid., p. 252. The same opinion remains unchanged in the last edition of his Dogmatik: idem, *Der Glaube der Kirche* V/3 (St Ottilien, 1982), p. 241.   **60** Ratzinger, *Feast of faith*, p. 36. **61** Ibid., p. 36.   **62** J. Ratzinger, *Aus meinem Leben. Erinnerungen (1927–1977)* (Stuttgart, 1998), p. 55 (my translation). See also J. Ratzinger, *Milestones: Memoirs, 1927–1977* (San Francisco, 1998).   **63** See R. Kaczynski, 'Pascher', *Lexikon für Theologie und Kirche*, 7 (Freiburg i.Br., 1998), pp 1412f; R. Berger, *Erlebte Liturgie in Ratzingers Studienzeit*, 78–90 (at 80–5); R. Berger, *Joseph Pascher*, in B. Kranemann and K. Raschzok (eds), *Gottesdienst als Feld theologischer Wissenschaft im 20. Jahrhundert. Deutschsprachige Liturgiewissenschaft in 94 Einzelportraits* (Münster, 2011).   **64** J. Pascher, 'Um die Grundgestalt der Eucharistie', *Münchener Theologische Zeitschrift* 1 (1950), 64–75. The topic is also treated in J. Pascher, *Eucharistia. Gestalt und Vollzug* (Münster and Krailling, 1947), especially pp 14–30 (Münster and Freiburg i.Br., 1953, pp 14–40); idem, *Form und Formenwandel sakramentaler Feier. Ein Beitrag zur Gestaltenlehre der heiligen Zeichen* (Münster, 1949), pp 41–62.

eucharistic table, continues with the 'eucharistic table grace' [*eucharistischen Tischgebet*] or thanksgiving, and reaches its completion with the 'feeding'. 'The structure of the Holy Mass is that of a meal.'[65] Nevertheless there is an exterior sign of the sacrifice in the consecration of the two species and the words of the Lord. Pascher, in Ratzinger's words:

> speaks of sacrificial symbolism being introduced into the meal structure. The separation of the gifts of bread and wine, symbolically indicating the fatal spilling of Jesus' blood, introduces the mark of sacrifice into the basic structure of the meal.[66]

The reference here is to Pascher's 1947 book on the 'structure and execution' of the Eucharist.[67]

In 1958, on the occasion of his becoming the rector of the university of Munich, Pascher held a solemn academic address on the eucharistic celebration as 'dramatic representation of the historical Last Supper'.[68] The liturgist stressed (just as Guardini had in 1947) that he was not treating 'the dogmatic doctrine of the Lord's Supper', and especially 'not the sacrificial aspect of the sacred action', which is methodologically bracketed.[69] In any case, the 'sacrificial character' of the Holy Mass does 'not change its central structure'.[70]

THE CRITICAL POSITION OF JOSEF ANDREAS JUNGMANN: THE PREDOMINANCE OF *EUCHARISTIA* RELATIVE TO THE MEAL

Ratzinger mentions the renowned Innsbruck professor of education, catechesis and liturgy, the Jesuit Josef Andreas Jungmann (1889–1975) as developing a position of 'far-reaching significance' in response to Guardini and Pascher.[71]

---

65 Pascher, *Eucharistia* (1953), p. 31.   **66** Ratzinger, *Feast of faith*, p. 36.   **67** Ratzinger does not cite any of the works just mentioned, but refers to Pascher, *Eucharistia*: cf. Ratzinger, *Feast of faith*, pp 34–5, 37. **68** J. Pascher, *Die christliche Eucharistiefeier als dramatische Darstellung des geschichtlichen Abendmahles* (Munich, 1958); cf. J. Rothkranz, *Mahl- oder Opfercharakter der heiligen Messe? Ein Klärungsversuch auf der Grundlage der Theologie des hl. Thomas von Aquin und J.A. Berrenbergs* (Frankfurt a. M., 1987), pp 25–7. Ratzinger was 'habilitated' in February 1957 in Munich and had already taken up the chair of Fundamental Theology at the University of Bonn in the summer of 1958, so he was probably not present at Pascher's keynote address in November 1958. For biographical data, see Ratzinger, *Aus meinem Leben*, pp 8–9. **69** Pascher, *Die christliche Eucharistiefeier*, pp 3f.   **70** Ibid., p. 7.   **71** See H.B. Meyer, 'Jungmann, Josef Andreas', *Theologische Realenzyklopädie*, 17 (Berlin, 1988), pp 465–7; R. Pacik, 'Liturgische Forschung als Mittel religiöser Reform', *Liturgisches Jahrbuch* 43 (1993), pp 62–84; G. Bitter, 'Jungmann, Josef Andreas', *Lexikon für Theologie und Kirche*, 5 (Freiburg i. Br, 1996), p. 1099f.

His *magnum opus*, the widely known *Missarum sollemnia* (1948; fifth edition 1962), offers a 'genetic explanation of the Roman Mass'.[72] In 1960 Jungmann became, like Pascher, a member of the preparatory commission for the Second Vatican Council. In 1962 he was made a member of the commission for liturgy at the Council itself, and in 1964 consultor of the Roman Liturgy Council. His 'main concern was … the concentration of pastoral care and ecclesiastical life on salvation history and Christology'; the liturgy made up part of this aim. Together with some Innsbruck colleagues (Dander, Lakner and Hugo Rahner), Jungmann was a leading figure in the development of the so-called 'theology of proclamation', which stressed the catechetic aim of theology. As a liturgist, as early as the 1930s he showed himself 'never interested in scholarship as such, but always in the fundamental ideas and structures on which Christian liturgy is based and from which the Church lives and can renew herself'.[73] Typical of this concern is his small monograph of 1939 on *The liturgical celebration: principles and history of the laws of liturgical form*.[74]

In January of 1943, Jungmann participated together with Guardini in a 'discussion among specialists' in Vienna about the 'structure' (*Gestalt*) of the Holy Mass.[75] As already mentioned, Guardini qualified his opinions, while Jungmann emphasized that 'the expression of the form of sacrifice' can be found already in the primitive Church.[76] In his subsequent comment on the liturgical memorandum of the Archbishop of Freiburg, Gröber, the Austrian Jesuit noted in February 1944 that the symposium at Vienna led to a 'fruitful understanding'. Besides the (obviously primary) sacrificial character of the Mass, 'other aspects of the mystery also, such as the meal and the commemoration, should be taken more strongly into account'.[77]

In 1949 Jungmann published an article dedicated entirely to the 'basic structure' (*Grundgestalt*) of the Eucharist.[78] Other writings on this theme followed, especially in 1967, 1970 and 1971.[79] Already in a contribution of

---

72 J.A. Jungmann, *Missarum sollemnia. Eine genetische Erklärung der römischen Messe*, 2 vols, (Vienna, 1948; 1962).　**73** Meyer, 'Jungmann', p. 466.　**74** J.A. Jungmann, *Die liturgische Feier. Grundsätzliches und Geschichtliches über Formgesetze der Liturgie* (Regensburg, 1939).　**75** Söhngen, *Der Weg der abendländischen Theologie*, p. 85. For a detailed account of the relevant sources, see Maas-Ewerd, *Die Krise der Liturgischen Bewegung*, pp 343–8.　**76** Guardini, *Zu meinem Vortrag im Wiener Seelsorgeinstitut*: Maas-Ewerd, *Die Krise der liturgischen Bewegung*, p. 613, fn. 11.　**77** J.A. Jungmann, 'Zu liturgischen Fragen im Freiburger Memorandum (1944)' in Maas-Ewerd, *Die Krise der liturgischen Bewegung*, pp 609–16 (at 612f).　**78** J.A. Jungmann, 'Um die Grundgestalt der Messfeier', *Stimmen der Zeit*, 143 (1949), 310–12; see the updated version in: idem, *Liturgisches Erbe und pastorale Gegenwart* (Innsbruck, 1960), pp 373–8.　**79** J.A. Jungmann, 'Von der „Eucharistia" zur Messe', *Zeitschrift für Katholische Theologie*, 89 (1967), 29–40; *Messe*

1943 he had shown that in the ancient Jewish banquet, on the occasion of the great feasts, a gesture of offering could be found when the father of the family elevated the chalice. The liturgy of Saint Basil, in the institution narrative, ascribes this gesture to the Last Supper itself, a reference which 'very probably' corresponds to the historical reality.[80] 'The Lord takes the bread in his holy hands and holds it, showing it as he offers it towards the heavenly Father.'[81] The sacrificial symbolism manifests itself therefore not only in the separation of the holy species, but also in the elevation of the gifts which can be observed already in the offertorium: there the offered gifts 'receive that movement towards God ... that is ultimately due to the transubstantiated gifts, the body and blood of the Lord'.[82] The 'thanksgiving' is at the same time an 'offering-up' that appears in the early Middle Ages in the elevation of the chalice before the consecration. Since the twelfth century, the elevation is first of all an invitation to adore and to salute the Lord,[83] but it must be taken into account that it originally contained a sacrificial symbolism:

> It is also not enough to say that the sacrifice becomes present under the structure of the meal; for even in this case, the Mass would not be the visible sacrifice of which the Council of Trent ... and the whole Tradition speaks.[84]

In his article on the 'basic structure of the Mass', Jungmann stresses that:

> in all liturgies, without exception, the basic structure of the celebration is formed as a thanksgiving *to God*, and indeed as a thanksgiving from which the offering springs: we give thanks to you and so we offer to you.[85] ... Everything that expresses the giving, the movement of the gifts

---

im Gottesvolk. Ein nachkonziliarer Durchblick durch Missarum solemnia (Freiburg i. Br., 1970), pp 23–6; '„Abendmahl" als Name der Eucharistie', *Zeitschrift für Katholische Theologie*, 93 (1971), 91–4. The findings of Jungmann are supported especially by J.H. Emminghaus, 'Hausmessen II. Bemerkungen zur „Mahlgestalt der Eucharistie"', *Theologisch-praktische Quartalschrift*, 117 (1969), 321–6; idem, *Die Messe. Wesen – Gestalt – Vollzug* (Klosterneuburg, 1992). **80** J.A. Jungmann, 'Accepit panem. Liturgiewissenschaftliches zur Eucharistie als Opfer im Abendmahlssaale' in J.A. Jungmann, *Liturgisches Erbe und pastorale Gegenwart* (Innsbruck, 1960), pp 366–72 (at 370–2); cf. *Zeitschrift für Katholische Theologie*, 67 (1943), 162–5. **81** Jungmann, *Liturgisches Erbe und pastorale Gegenwart*, p. 366. Cf. F.E. Brightman, *Liturgies eastern and western* (Oxford, 1896), p. 327: *labôn árton epi tôn hagíon autoû kai achrántôn cheirôn kai anadeíxas soi tô Theô kai Patrì*. **82** Jungmann, *Liturgisches Erbe und pastorale Gegenwart*, p. 367. **83** Cf. Jungmann, *Liturgisches Erbe und pastorale Gegenwart*, pp 368–70. **84** Jungmann, *Messe im Gottesvolk*, pp 23f. Cf. DH 1740 (*visibile sacrificium*; Sessio XII, cap. 1). **85** Jungmann, *Liturgisches Erbe und pastorale Gegenwart*, p. 376.

towards God belongs to the exterior gestures that manifest this idea. ...
In this sense, the whole rite between the Liturgy of the Word and the
Communion is clearly referred, also as structure (*Gestalt*), not merely to
the togetherness of a common table, but to the movement towards God
that begins in the preparatory part of the Mass and comes to rest in the
Communion rite ... [This] ritual expression is not the fruit of a late and
secondary development, but was impressed already in the primitive
Church in the institution of Jesus.[86]

The great historical study of Jungmann on the Roman Mass, *Missarum
solemnia*, is also important for our topic. Here he presents the earliest names
of the Holy Mass.[87] As Ratzinger comments:

On the basis of the liturgical texts themselves, Jungmann shows that,
even in the most ancient forms, the *eucharistia* – the prayer of *anamnesis*
in the shape of a thanksgiving – is more prominent than the meal aspect.
According to Jungmann, the basic structure, at least from the end of the
first century, is not the meal but the *eucharistia*; even in Ignatius of
Antioch this is the term given to the whole action.[88]

Ratzinger's interpretation seems to accentuate the concept of 'eucharist'
more strongly than does the presentation of Jungmann, according to whom
the thanksgiving finds its consummation in the offering. After the reference to
the biblical concepts of 'breaking bread' and the 'Lord's banquet', Jungmann
mentions first of all the importance of the title 'eucharist' as already present in
the early post-biblical sources. Immediately after it, however, he reports a
whole series of concepts that revolve around the notion of 'sacrifice'. We
should also mention here the early testimonies of the *Didache* and of the First
Letter of Clement (even if Jungmann himself does not cite these sources in his
overview). The *Didache*, a writing from ancient Syria, indicates the Eucharist
as 'sacrifice' ('*tusia*') and sees in it the fulfilment of the prophecy of Malachi
about the pure offering that must be practised at any place and at any time
(Malachi 1:11).[89] Also extremely important is the reference of the First Letter

86 Ibid., p. 377.   **87** Cf. Jungmann, *Missarum solemnia I* (1948), 217ff; the pages (I 327ff) cited by
Ratzinger (1981) 34 = (2008) are most probably a typographical error.   **88** Ratzinger, *Feast of faith*, pp
36–7.   **89** *Didache* 14,1–3 (Fontes christiani 1, 132–4). For the interpretation of the passage, see H. Moll,
*Die Lehre von der Eucharistie als Opfer. Eine dogmengeschichtliche Untersuchung vom Neuen Testament bis
Irenäus von Lyon* (Köln and Bonn, 1975), pp 109–15; G. Schöllgen, *Einleitung zur Didache*, in *Fontes*

of Clement, which Pope Clement I addressed to the Corinthians in the year 96. He is dealing with the reinstatement of the presbyters-bishops who had been driven away from their ministry without any valid motive. Their ministry has an apostolic origin. The central task of the presbyters-bishops is the 'offering of the gifts' (*prosenegkóntas tà dôra*).[90] After the concept of sacrifice, Jungmann mentions still other names of the Mass, such as 'the Holy', 'service (liturgy)', 'assembly', and 'Mass'.[91]

In a short article of 1971, cited by Ratzinger, Jungmann also shows that:

> linguistically speaking, Luther's use of the word 'supper' [*Abendmahl*] was a complete innovation. After 1 Corinthians 11:20 the designation of the Eucharist as 'meal' does not occur again until the sixteenth century, apart from direct quotations of 1 Corinthians 11:20 and references to the satisfaction of hunger (in deliberate contrast to the Eucharist).[92]

The meaning of 'eucharist' also fits with the meaning of rational verbal sacrifice (*oblatio rationabilis*), which spiritualizes the category of sacrifice and is well suited 'to interpret what is special in Jesus' sacrifice. For what we have here is death transformed into a word of acceptance and self-surrender'. Ratzinger concludes:

> This much should be clear at this stage: if the basic structure of the Mass is not the 'meal', but *eucharistia*, there remains a necessary and fruitful difference between the liturgical (structural) and the dogmatic level; but they are not estranged: each seeks and determines the other ... But the meal symbolism is subordinated to a larger whole and integrated into it.[93]

EXEGETICAL SUPPORT IN THE INVESTIGATIONS OF HEINZ
SCHÜRMANN

The evidence revealed by liturgical history that the 'basic structure' of the Mass does not consist in the 'meal' was strengthened by a contribution of Heinz

christiani, 1 (Freiburg i. Br., 1991), pp 25–94 (at 69f). **90** 'For it will be no small sin for us if we depose from the office of bishop those who blamelessly and piously have made the offerings.' (1 Clem. 44,4) (ed. J.A. Fischer, *Die Apostolischen Väter* (Darmstadt 1976), p. 81). Cf. Ignatius of Antioch, Ad Smyrn. 7,1. **91** Jungmann, *Missarum solemnia I* (1948), 219–24. For a recent detailed study see Meyer, *Eucharistie. Geschichte, Theologie, Pastoral*, pp 34–43. **92** Ratzinger, *Feast of faith*, p. 37, citing Jungmann, '„Abendmahl" als Name der Eucharistie', 93; cf. Jungmann, *Messe im Gottesvolk*, p. 23, Anm. 73. **93** Ratzinger, *Feast of faith*, p. 38.

Schürmann (1913–99),[94] a biblical scholar who for many years taught at Erfurt. It was first published in 1955 and is cited by Ratzinger from an anthology that appeared in 1970.[95] It is the inaugural lecture of Schürmann, delivered on the occasion of his habilitation at Münster in February 1952, in which, after delineating the state of the systematic discussion on the 'basic structure' of the Mass, he offers his own exegetical contribution.[96] Schürmann identifies three stages in the structural development of the Eucharistic celebration:

1. 'the Eucharist at the Last Supper of Jesus', which was an integral part of a meal-structure;
2. 'the Eucharist in connection with the apostolic community meal' (as in Saint Paul's presentation of the 'Lord's Supper' in 1 Corinthians 11);
3. 'the celebration of the Eucharist in post-apostolic times, separated from the community meal'.[97]

The Lord's institution of the Eucharist at the Last Supper:

> is something new. It is woven into an old context – that of the Jewish ritual meal – but it is clearly recognizable as an independent entity. He commanded it to be repeated, which implies that it was separable from the immediate context in which it took place.[98]

Nevertheless, Ratzinger does not adopt Schürmann's interpretation completely. With regard to the second stage, for example, he rejects Schürmann's notion that the community banquet in the primitive Church was, structurally considered, more of a 'continuation of Jesus' everyday table fellowship with his disciples' than it was a re-enactment of the ritual novelties of the Last Supper.[99] One argument Ratzinger brings against this interpretation is the festal and solemn character of the Eucharist, which from the earliest times was seen to transcend an everyday event and was placed, for this reason, on Sunday, the Lord's Day.[1] Another objection is the exclusive character of the Eucharist, again 'right from the apostolic period':

94 See C.-P. März, 'Schürmann, Heinz', *Neue Deutsche Biographie*, 23 (Munich, 2007), pp 647f.   **95** H. Schürmann, 'Die Gestalt der urchristlichen Eucharistiefeier', *Münchener Theologische Zeitschrift*, 6 (1955), 107–31; also in P. Bormann and H.-J. Degenhardt (eds), *Liturgie in der Gemeinde* (Lippstadt and Salzkotten, 1964), pp 69–93; H. Schürmann, *Ursprung und Gestalt. Erörterungen und Besinnungen zum Neuen Testament* (Düsseldorf, 1970), pp 77–99.   **96** Ibid., pp 77–9.   **97** Ratzinger, *Feast of faith*, p. 40, with reference to Schürmann, 'Die Gestalt der urchristlichen Eucharistiefeier', pp 77–99.   **98** Ratzinger, *Feast of faith*, p. 40.   **99** Schürmann, 'Die Gestalt der urchristlichen Eucharistiefeier', p. 85.   **1** Ratzinger

Just as the Passover meal was celebrated in a clearly defined household, the Eucharist too, from the beginning, had definite conditions for admission. From the start, the Eucharist was celebrated in what one might call the household of Jesus Christ, and thus it built the 'Church'.[2]

'EUCHARIST' AS THE 'DEFINITIVE FORM' OF THE MASS

From the foregoing discussion, Ratzinger concludes that the meal (or banquet) cannot be the 'basic structure' of the Eucharist. At the Last Supper itself, there is not yet an 'independent Christian reality, but only an open-ended form within Judaism'. For this reason:

> there cannot yet be an independent and specifically Christian form of liturgy ... the Last Supper of Jesus is indeed the basis of all Christian liturgy, but it is not yet itself a Christian liturgy ... the Last Supper is the foundation of the dogmatic content [*Gehalt*] of the Christian Eucharist, but not of its liturgical form [*Gestalt*]. The latter does not yet exist. As her separation from Israel became unavoidable, the Church had to discover an appropriate form [*Gestalt*] of her own in which to express the reality bequeathed to her.[3]

The concept of the 'meal' structure is 'an historically untenable oversimplification'. '[The] Lord's testament is correctly seen in terms of *eucharistia* ...' There is no opposition between sacrifice and meal:

> *eucharistia* is the gift of *communio* in which the Lord becomes our food; it also signifies the self-offering of Jesus Christ, perfecting his trinitarian Yes to the Father by his consent on the Cross, and reconciling us all to the Father in this 'sacrifice'. There is no opposition between 'meal' and 'sacrifice'; they belong inseparably together in the new sacrifice of the Lord.[4]

---

however emphasized that the development of the daily eucharistic celebration, traceable in the West to the third century, 'could easily have taken place once the Christian liturgy had discovered its own special form [*Gestalt*]; for this the connection with Sunday was an essential prerequisite'. Ratzinger, *Fest des Glaubens*, p. 41, n. 15. That the Sunday celebration of the Eucharist was the rule in the primitive Church appears from the sources cited by Ratzinger (Rev 1:10; Acts 20:7; 1 Cor 16:2). On the 'breaking of bread' in the primitive Church at Jerusalem (Acts 2:42), see J. Zmijewski, *Apostelgeschichte* (Regensburg, 1994), p. 158f.
2 Ratzinger, *Feast of faith*, pp 44–5.   **3** Ibid., p. 41.   **4** Ibid., pp 49–50.

The transition from the proclamation of the 'Kingdom of God' to Christology is a similar process:[5]

> In this situation, unity with Jesus has to be sought in that discontinuity which is manifested where the proclamation of the Kingdom to Israel is left behind and the Church of the Gentiles is embraced.[6]

We can add the observation that this change has its foundation in Christ, who is the Kingdom of God in his own person. As Origen formulated it, he is the '*autobasileia*', in whom the reign of God approaches us.[7]

THE CONTRIBUTION OF LOTHAR LIES: *EULOGIA* AS 'FORMAL STRUCTURE OF SIGNIFICANCE'

Ratzinger's argument was published for the first time in a 1977 article of the journal *Communio*. When he integrated it into the volume *The feast of faith* in 1981, he added two postscripts. The first postscript refers to an article of Lothar Lies (1940–2008), professor of Dogmatic Theology at Innsbruck: 'Reflections on the formal structure of significance (*formale Sinngestalt*) of the Eucharist' (1978).[8] In this contribution, Lies responds to Ratzinger's points from the preceding year (1977).[9]

What Ratzinger, 'in common with liturgical scholars of the interwar and postwar period', called form or structure [*Gestalt, Grundgestalt*], 'Lies refers to as "material structure" [*Materialgestalt*], going on to inquire as to the formal structure [*Formalgestalt*]',[10] which he defines in this way:

> By the 'formal structure' of the Eucharist we mean that structure which is able to embrace the ideas of *anamnesis*, sacramental Real Presence, sacrifice and meal, imparting to all aspects of the Eucharist their formal meaning. We also call this formal structure the 'theological structure of significance' [*theologische Sinngestalt*].[11]

---

5 Cf. Ratzinger, *Fest des Glaubens*. **6** Ratzinger, *Feast of faith*, p. 42, with reference to J. Ratzinger, *Eschatologie – Tod und ewiges Leben* (Regensburg, 1990), pp 30–42. **7** See A. Ziegenaus, *Jesus Christus, die Fülle des Heils. Christologie und Erlösungslehre* (Aachen, 2000), p. 303, with reference to Origen, In Mt 18:23 (PG 13, 1197). **8** L. Lies, 'Eulogia – Überlegungen zur formalen Sinngestalt der Eucharistie', *Zeitschrift für Katholische Theologie*, 100, 69–97. **9** See ibid., 69–71. **10** Ratzinger, *Fest des Glaubens*, p. 46. **11** Lies, 'Eulogia', 69.

Lies finds this formal structure in the concept of *eulogia*. Jesus as the self-praise (*auto-eulogia*) of God presents himself as Passover-*eulogia*:

> The concept of *eulogia* can offer a uniform model of the significance of the Christian Eucharist ... [it] embraces both the theological and the liturgical structure of significance [*Sinngestalt*].[12] ... I am in full agreement with Lies' remarks ... I find they confirm and enrich my own conclusions.[13]

There is, nevertheless, a difference of approach: Lies presupposes the developed structure of the Eucharist, whereas Ratzinger's own concern was:

> to establish the legitimacy of the transition from the Last Supper to the Mass, from Jesus to the Church's Eucharist. For this is the salient point of the whole discussion in contemporary theology. It determines the view of Jesus and the Church ... the concept of tradition and Church development.

Speaking simply of the Eucharist's 'meal structure' is based on:

> a misunderstanding of the Eucharist's origins and leads to a false view of the sacrament. There is even less excuse for the Eucharist being referred to simply as a 'meal' (or even as a 'sacrificial meal'). In this regard there is an urgent need to revise the German translation of the Missal of Paul VI, where, in the post-communion prayers, contrary to the Latin original, the word 'meal' [*Mahl*] is almost used as a regular term for the Eucharist.[14]

We should hope that this desire would be respected in the German translation of the Roman Missal of 2002.

Lothar Lies subsequently developed the points of his 1978 article in a panoramic and 'ecumenically responsible' monograph on the Eucharist published in 1996.[15] This study was based to a significant degree on the investigations of Max Thurian (1921–96),[16] a French theologian who was

---

12 Ibid., 96. He receives the impetus from the Greek patristic writers; ibid., 97, with reference to: L. Lies, *Wort und Eucharistie bei Origenes. Zur Spiritualisierung der Eucharistie* (Innsbruck, 1978).   13 Ratzinger, *Feast of faith*, p. 51.   14 Ibid., p. 51.   15 L. Lies, *Eucharistie in ökumenischer Verantwortung* (Graz, 1996).   16 See Lies, 'Eulogia', 79–82; G. Falanga, *Chiesa, liturgia ed eucaristia nel pensiero di Max Thurian* (Naples, 2006).

brought up in Calvinism, lived as a monk at Taizé, and in 1987 was ordained a priest in the Catholic Church. The World Council of Churches' 1982 *Lima Document* (on Baptism, Eucharist and Ministry) is influenced by the thought of Thurian,[17] and proposes five fundamental aspects of the Eucharist:

1. 'as thanksgiving to the Father',
2. 'as *anamnesis* or memorial of Christ',
3. 'as invocation of the Spirit' (*epiclesis*)',
4. 'as community (*communio*) of the faithful',
5. 'as meal of the reign of God'.[18]

The exposition of Lies accepts these elements, albeit with some refinements, but also stresses the sacrificial aspect. In the foreword to the book, he writes:

> Moved by ecumenical responsibility, I try to see the Eucharist simultaneously as sacrifice and sacrament ... [I treat the Eucharist] first as celebration of the memory of the concentration of salvific history of the triune God with us human beings in Jesus Christ (*anamnesis*), secondly as entreaty of the Holy Spirit, who is necessary for the sacramental presence (*epiclesis*), thirdly, as celebration of the stupendous presence of the Christ in his transfigured body, who offers himself to unite us in and to his Church as his body (*koinonia*). Fourthly, I try to present the Eucharist to the reader as a sacramental sacrifice of thanksgiving in which the expiation of Christ's offering on the Cross is abundantly dispensed (*prosphora*).[19]

Lies had distinguished in 1978 between 'material structure' (*Materialgestalt*) and 'formal structure' (*Formalgestalt*), and in 1996 he develops this terminology further. He refers to the weighty 1989 treatise on the Eucharist by his Innsbruck colleague Hans Bernhard Meyer (1924–2004), the successor of Jungmann in the chair of liturgical studies.[20] In the foreground of Meyer's attention, we find the 'structure of significance' (*Sinngestalt*), an expression also

---

17 See Lies, *Eucharistie in ökumenischer Verantwortung*, p. 46f.   18 'Kommission für Glauben und Kirchenverfassung des Ökumenischen Rates der Kirche, *Taufe, Eucharistie und Amt. Konvergenzerklärungen* (*„Lima-Dokument")* 1982' in H. Meyer, H.J. Urban, L. Vischer (eds), *Dokumente wachsender Übereinstimmung. Sämtliche Berichte und Konsenstexte interkonfessioneller Gespräche auf Weltebene, 1931–1982* (Paderborn and Frankfurt a. M., 1983), pp 545–85 (at 557–67).   19 Lies, *Eucharistie in ökumenischer Verantwortung*, p. 7.   20 See http://de.wikipedia.org/wiki/Hans_Bernhard_Meyer (accessed 10.06.2011).

used by Lies in 1978 synonymously with 'formal structure'. The concept of 'structure of significance':

> denotes the formal dynamics (form of performance) that gives a significance to the celebration and by which the single aspects receive their theological importance as they are related to each other and integrated into the whole.[21]

On the other hand, the 'structure of celebration' (*Feiergestalt*) signifies for Meyer (and then also for Lies) the 'material basic structure' (*materiale Grundstruktur*):

> It is the 'supporting basic structure', investigated by Guardini and others, that can be perceived by the senses and that precedes the single elements and the single performances of the liturgical events. It reveals the formal structure of significance in the symbolic action of the Mass. Therefore it can also be called its expressive structure ... [It must be distinguished from the] structure of significance ... but cannot be separated from it.[22]

As to the 'structure of celebration', Meyer does not want to commit himself to a single concept, but gives a 'descriptive definition of content' which limits itself to enumerating the diverse 'constitutive elements'[23] – being convened and assembling, proclaiming and commemorating, entreating, offering and receiving the gifts of the meal:

> The celebrative structure of the Eucharist consists in the proclamation of the Paschal mystery in the community assembled in the name of Christ, in the commemoration of him and his salvific work by the praising and supplicating prayer over the meal gifts, in the intercession for communion with the body of Christ, in its head and its members, and in taking his body and blood.[24]

Meyer gives a more precise definition of the 'structure of significance', explained as 'commemoration with *eulogia*'. *Eulogia* contains the praise offering to God, but also the benediction communicated by God; for this reason, the commemoration with eulogia brings forth both the aspects of

---

21 Meyer, *Eucharistie. Geschichte, Theologie, Pastoral*, p. 445. **22** Ibid., p. 457. **23** Ibid., p. 457f.
24 Ibid., p. 458.

sacrifice and of meal. Or formulated in another way: it is a connection between the catabatic and soteriological structure (sanctification) on the one hand, and the anabatic and cultic structure (glorification) on the other.[25]

In the *eulogia* as the 'structure of significance' in the Eucharist, Lies sees a connection between the contents of sacrament and sacrifice.[26] The 'structure of significance' reveals itself:

> in the inner relation between *anamnesis, epiclesis*, presence [*koinonia*] and *prosphora*. This structure of benediction with its elements can be expressed very well in Latin: *Deus benedixit* (*anamnesis*); *Deus benedicat* (*epiclesis*); *Deus benedicit* (presence and *koinonia*); *Deus benedicatur* (*prosphora*). Or in the vernacular: God has blessed; may God bless; God blesses; God be blessed.[27]

THE CONTRIBUTION OF THE PROTESTANT EXEGETE HARMUT GESE: THE EUCHARIST AS THE '*TODA*' SACRIFICE OF THE RESURRECTED CHRIST

The second postscript in Ratzinger's *Feast of faith* (1981) concerns a contribution of the Protestant exegete Harmut Gese on 'The Origin of the Lord's Supper' (1977).[28] Gese taught Old Testament at the Evangelical Theological Faculty of the University of Tübingen until 1994. In his article on the Old Testament background of the Eucharist, he brings to the foreground the 'thanksgiving sacrifice', the *toda*, and concludes: 'The Lord's Supper is the *toda* of the resurrected Christ'.[29] Christ as the sacrificial offering is also the substance of the meal.

The connection between the Eucharist and the *toda* sacrifice is not universally accepted among exegetes.[30] One biblical scholar who has accepted Gese's proposal is Peter Stuhlmacher,[31] professor of New Testament at Tübingen and a good acquaintance of Pope Benedict XVI.[32] 'It seems that the

---

25 See Meyer, *Eucharistie. Geschichte, Theologie, Pastoral*, pp 453–7.   **26** See Lies, *Eucharistie in ökumenischer Verantwortung*, p. 34f.   **27** Ibid., p. 37.   **28** H. Gese, 'Die Herkunft des Herrenmahles' in H. Gese, *Zur biblischen Theologie* (Munich, 1977), pp 107–27. Cf. Ratzinger, *Fest des Glaubens*, pp 47–54. **29** Gese (1977), p. 122; cf. Ratzinger, *Fest des Glaubens*, p. 52 = *Theologie der Liturgie*, p. 380.   **30** Cautious for example is A. Schenker, *Das Abendmahl Jesu als Brennpunkt des Alten Testaments* (Fribourg, 1977), p. 63, fn. 123.   **31** See P. Stuhlmacher, *Biblische Theologie des Neuen Testamentes* I (Göttingen, 1992), pp 208f. **32** See P. Kuhn (ed.), *Gespräch über Jesus. Benedikt XVI. mit Martin Hengel, Peter Stuhlmacher und seinen Schülern in Castelgandolfo* (Tübingen, 2010).

question of whether there is a genetico-historical connection between the Last Supper of Jesus and the *toda* meal, remains open'. Nevertheless the *toda*, according the evaluation of H.B. Meyer, 'seems to have some importance for comprehending the ritual structure of the celebration'.[33]

In any case, Ratzinger sees in the considerations of Gese about the Eucharist as a thanksgiving sacrifice of the resurrected Christ an opening for ecumenical dialogue between Catholics and Protestants; for we are given here 'a genuinely New Testament concept of sacrifice' in 'a new profundity'.[34]

In distinction to Gese, however, Ratzinger emphasizes that the Eucharist cannot be developed solely from the Last Supper. According to Gese himself, the *toda* sacrifice 'is the thanksgiving of the man who has already been delivered; in a real sense, surely, it cannot take place until after the Resurrection'. The Last Supper:

> looks to the Cross, where Jesus' words of self-offering will be fulfilled, and to the hope of Resurrection. Apart from them it would be incomplete and, indeed, unreal. Again, this means that the form of the Last Supper is not complete in itself.[35]

This speaks against both the Protestant nomenclature of 'Lord's Supper' for the Eucharist and the idea of the meal as 'basic structure' of the Holy Mass.

THE CONNECTION OF THE TOPIC WITH THE ESSENCE OF THE LITURGY

The main work of Ratzinger on liturgical theology, *The spirit of the liturgy*, does not treat the 'basic structure' of the Holy Mass further. Nevertheless, we find some allusions which place the topic in the overall context of the liturgy. As 'the most appropriate way of expressing the essential form [*Wesensgestalt*] of Christian liturgy', Ratzinger elaborates the Pauline concept of *logike latreia*, divine worship in accordance with *logos* (Romans 12:1):[36]

> This concept is the confluence of several different streams: the spiritual movement of the Old Testament, the processes of inner purification

33 Meyer, *Eucharistie. Geschichte, Theologie, Pastoral*, p. 451.   34 Ratzinger, *Feast of faith*, p. 58.   35 Ibid., p. 60 fn. 1.   36 See also M. Schneider, *Zur Beurteilung der Liturgiereform und der Tridentinischen Messe im theologischen Werk Joseph Ratzingers* (Köln, 2007), pp 16–24.

within the history of religions, the human quest and the divine response. The *logos* of creation, the *logos* in man and the true and eternal *Logos* made flesh – the Son – come together. All other definitions [*Gestaltbestimmungen*] fall short. For example, one could describe the Eucharist, in terms of the liturgical phenomenon, as an 'assembly', or, in terms of Jesus' act of institution at the Last Supper, as a 'meal'. But this seizes on individual elements while failing to grasp the great historical and theological connections. By contrast, the word 'eucharist' points to the universal form of worship that took place in the Incarnation, Cross, and Resurrection of Christ, and so it can happily serve as a summary of the idea of *logike latreia* and may legitimately serve as an appropriate designation for Christian worship.[37]

This result was already made clear by the Church Fathers, 'when they saw the Eucharist as essentially *oratio*, sacrifice in the Word ...'[38]

THE RECEPTION OF RATZINGER'S OBSERVATIONS

In more recent liturgical and dogmatic theology, the demanding systematic question about the 'basic structure' or the foundational 'structure of significance' is not treated very frequently. When the topic is addressed, Ratzinger's contribution normally finds a good reception or at least a respectful treatment. This is true in the German-speaking lands not least for the two Innsbruck theologians already mentioned, who have engaged with our theme in particular detail: the liturgist Hans-Bernhard Meyer[39] and the dogmatic theologian Lother Lies.[40] The liturgist Josip Gregur, however, sees a 'convergence between Eucharist and meal'.[41] Albert Gerhards speaks of 'three basic structures' of eucharistic celebration: 'the dialogical structure of the celebration of the Word, the directed structure of prayer, and the concentric structure of the eucharistic meal'.[42] Reinhard Messner thinks that the question of the 'basic structure' is closely related to the open question of the manifold function of the altar.[43] He comes close to the concern of Ratzinger with the critical remark:

37 Ratzinger, *Spirit of the liturgy*, p. 50.   **38** Ibid., p. 46.   **39** See Meyer, *Eucharistie. Geschichte, Theologie, Pastoral*, pp 444, 454f.   **40** See Lies, 'Eulogia', 69–71; *Eucharistie in ökumenischer Verantwortung*, 35, fn. 21, 39.   **41** See Gregur, 'Fleischwerdung des Wortes', pp 65–72.   **42** A. Gerhards, 'Wort und Sakrament – Zur Bipolarität von Liturgie und Kirchenraum' in A. Gerhards, T. Sternberg, W. Zahner (eds), *Communio-Räume. Auf der Suche nach der angemessenen Raumgestalt katholischer Liturgie* (Regensburg, 2003), pp 10–25 (at 25).   **43** R. Messner, 'Gebetsrichtung, Altar und exzentrische Mitte der Gemeinde', *Communio-Räume*, pp 27–36 (at 34–6).

The alleged function of the altar as meal table is a construction – not free of ideology – of the twentieth century.[44]

The Austrian liturgist approvingly cites Johannes M. Emminghaus:

The 'meal table ideology' should be utterly forgotten in any reflection on the shaping of altars.[45]

A significant similarity to the proposal of Ratzinger can be found in a 1985 essay of Walter Kasper.[46] Taking his starting point from the Jesus' institution of the Last Supper, the Tübingen dogmatic theologian emphasizes the '*anamnesis* of Christ' as the '*inner unity* of the different *aspects of Eucharist*'.[47] After *anamnesis*, Kasper studies the aspects of thanksgiving and of sacrifice, of *epiclesis*, of *communio*, and of the eschatological sign.[48]

With reference to the work of Jungmann,[49] Ratzinger, and Lies, as well as Louis Bouyer's work on the Eucharistic Prayer,[50] Kasper defines as the 'basic structure of the eucharistic celebration' the laudatory commemoration. He explicitly takes over the proposal of Gese (and Ratzinger) to interpret the Holy Mass in the light of the Old Testament sacrifice of thanksgiving (*toda*).[51] Presenting the Eucharist as the sacramental representation of the one sacrifice of Christ could help to overcome the controversies of the Reformation period.[52] We should note the remark of Kasper that:

the primary meaning of the eucharistic celebration is … *cultus divinus*, the glorification … of God by recalling his great deeds. This cultic-latratic aspect is becoming increasingly difficult in a society oriented to human desires and their gratification. This would seem to be the real cause of the crisis of the liturgy and of the widespread liturgical incompetence … [The] second scope of significance of the Eucharist [is] the salvation of man

and is intimately connected with the primary meaning.[53]

44 Messner, 'Gebetsrichtung, Altar und exzentrische Mitte der Gemeinde', p. 34.   **45** J.H. Emminghaus, *Die Messe. Wesen – Gestalt – Vollzug* (Klosterneuburg, 1992), 61, cited by Messner, 'Gebetsrichtung, Altar und exzentrische Mitte der Gemeinde', p. 34.   **46** W. Kasper, 'Einheit und Vielfalt der Aspekte der Eucharistie. Zur neuerlichen Diskussion um Grundgestalt und Grundsinn der Eucharistie', *Internationale Katholische Zeitschrift Communio*, 14 (1985), 196–215.   **47** Kasper, 'Einheit und Vielfalt', p. 307.   **48** See Kasper, 'Einheit und Vielfalt', pp 310–18.   **49** Jungmann, *Missarum solemnia* I (1962), p. 27f.   **50** L. Bouyer, *Eucharistie. Théologie et spiritualité de la prière eucharistique* (Paris 1966).   **51** Kasper, 'Einheit und Vielfalt', p. 308.   **52** Ibid., p 309.   **53** Ibid., p. 310.

With reasoning similar to that of Ratzinger, Kasper rejects the thesis of the meal as the 'basic structure' of the Eucharist. Talk of the 'meal character', he notes critically:

> has already resulted in liturgical practice marked sometimes by quite willful experiments, in which ... in the extreme case, the celebration of the Eucharist is hardly indistinguishable from a banquet or a party. ... Instead of the meal character, one should ... better speak of the community character and of the ecclesial dimension of Eucharist.[54]

The Eucharist:

> is at the same time the gift of God (in a catabatic way) and an offering with thanksgiving (in an anabatic way), because it represents Jesus Christ, his person and his work, he who is the self-giving of God and the self-giving response in one and the same person.[55]

The three aspects of eucharistic Real Presence, eucharistic sacrifice, and eucharistic sacrament 'form ... an *inseparable inner unity*' as the 'sacramental representation of the one salvific mystery of Jesus Christ' and a '*sacramental summary of the whole mystery of salvation*'.[56]

Finally, we should also note the consideration of Ratzinger's ideas in the Fribourg doctoral dissertation of Erwin Keller on the connection between Eucharist and Parousia.[57] Here he addresses the topic of prayer oriented to the east as a visible expression of the living hope that the Lord will return at the end of times.[58]

RELATED TOPICS IN THE WORK OF RATZINGER

The eastward-facing position of the celebrant in the Holy Mass

Related to the 'basic structure' of Eucharist is the topic of the eastward-facing position of the celebrant at the Holy Mass, about which we can give only some indications here. Beginning with a short article for the journal *Communio* in

---

54 Ibid., p. 313f.   55 Ibid., p. 318, with reference to Lies, 'Eulogia', 94–7: 'in continuation of the approaches of J. A. Jungmann and J. Ratzinger' (fn. 75).   56 Kasper, 'Einheit und Vielfalt', p. 319.   57 E. Keller, *Eucharistie und Parusie. Liturgie- und theologiegeschichtliche Untersuchungen zur eschatologischen Dimension der Eucharistie anhand ausgewählter Zeugnisse aus frühchristlicher und patristischer Zeit* (Fribourg, 1989). The work was supervised by Christoph von Schönborn.   58 See ibid., pp 137–47, 204.

1979,[59] Ratzinger later expressed his thoughts on this subject in a marked way in his 1981 work, *The feast of faith*.[60] There he corrects an article according to which the Eucharist, before the liturgical reform, had been celebrated towards the Tabernacle,[61] stressing that this was not the real significance of the practice. As with the topic of the 'basic structure', so too in this case his most important authority from the realm of liturgical theology is Josef Andreas Jungmann:[62] the original significance of the eastward-oriented prayer was 'the priest and people together facing the same way in a common act of trinitarian worship, such as, for example, Augustine introduced by the post-homiletic prayer *Conversi ad Dominum*. Priest and people were united in facing eastward' as towards Christ, who is risen from the dead and who will return gloriously at the end of times:

> Where priest and people together face the same way, what we have is a cosmic orientation and also an interpretation of the Eucharist in terms of resurrection and Trinitarian theology. Hence it is also an interpretation in terms of parousia, a theology of hope, in which every Mass is an approach to the return of Christ.[63]

The Cross at the altar contains the whole theology of eastward-facing prayer.[64] In contemporary perception, however, following the liturgical reform, the idea of community assumes the first place, when:

> priest and people face each other in a dialogue relationship. This does express *one* aspect of the Eucharist. But the danger is that it can make the congregation into a closed circle ... A truly liturgical education will have to use all its resources to counter this idea ... The community does not carry on a dialogue with itself; it is engaged on a common journey toward the returning Lord.[65]

A rediscovery of the eastward-facing celebration is desirable for a liturgy that takes the cosmos created by God seriously. During the eucharistic prayer, priest and faithful should not face each other, but orient themselves together toward

59 J. Ratzinger, 'Kleine Korrektur', *Internationale Katholische Zeitschrift Communio*, 8 (1979), 381f.
60 Ratzinger, *Das Fest des Glaubens*, pp 121–6.   **61** See E.A. Diederich, 'Das Gegenwärtigwerden Christi bei der Feier der Eucharistie', *Internationale Katholische Zeitschrift Communio*, 7 (1978), 498–508 (at 501).
62 Citing J.A. Jungmann's review of O. Nußbaum, *Der Standort des Liturgen am christlichen Altar vor dem Jahre 1000*, 2 vols (Bonn, 1965), in *Zeitschrift für Katholische Theologie*, 88 (1966), 445–50.   **63** Ratzinger, *Feast of faith*, pp 140–1.   **64** See Ratzinger, *Feast of faith*, p. 141.   **65** Ratzinger, *Feast of faith*, pp 142–3.

the Cross.[66] In a final footnote, Ratzinger mentions favorably the studies of Klaus Gamber on this topic.[67]

The topics of the 'basic structure' of Eucharist and the eastward-facing celebration come together even more closely in a short chapter of Ratzinger's main liturgical work, *The spirit of the liturgy*, 'The altar and the direction of liturgical prayer'.[68] The liturgical movement demanded celebration toward the people, whereby 'priest and people looked at each other and together formed the circle of celebrants'. This was supposedly derived from the Last Supper. The construction of new altars and the widespread celebration *versus populum* appeared, therefore, as 'the characteristic fruit of Vatican II's liturgical renewal', which also brought with it 'a new idea of the essence of the liturgy – the liturgy as a communal meal'.[69] However, the Eucharist 'really cannot adequately be described by the term 'meal',[70] and what is important is the common orientation toward the Lord: 'Looking at the priest has no importance. What matters is looking together at the Lord.'[71]

The topic of the Christian orientation of prayer has now been treated in a thorough way by Uwe Michael Lang, for whose work Cardinal Ratzinger wrote a foreword (2003).[72] He recalled the important clarification of the Congregation for Divine Worship and the Discipline of the Sacraments in 2000, according to which the erection of altars facing the people in new churches is by no means obligatory, but only a proposal; the spiritual orientation, in any case, must be *versus Deum per Iesum Christum*.[73] Ratzinger then pointed to the observation of Jungmann that the classical orientation of prayer is not turning one's back to the people, but rather assuming the same direction as the people's prayer:

> The Liturgy of the Word, as proclamation, is a dialogical event … The Eucharistic Prayer, however, is a prayer in which the priest is the first who prays, but together with the people and oriented toward the Lord.[74]

66 See Ratzinger, *Feast of faith*, pp 143f. **67** See Ratzinger, *Feast of faith*, p. 145, fn. 4. On Gamber see M. Hauke, 'Klaus Gamber, father of the 'new liturgical movement' in N.J. Roy and J.E. Rutherford (eds), *Benedict XVI and the sacred liturgy* (Dublin, 2010), pp 24–69 (at 51–6). **68** *The spirit of the liturgy*, pp 74–84. **69** Ibid., p. 77. **70** Ibid., p. 78. **71** Ibid., p. 81. **72** J. Ratzinger, 'Geleitwort' in U.M. Lang, *Conversi ad Dominum. Zu Geschichte und Theologie der christlichen Gebetsrichtung* (Einsiedeln and Freiburg i. Br., 2003), pp 7–11; English translation, *Turning towards the Lord. Orientation in Liturgical Prayer* (San Francisco, 2005). **73** See Congregatio de Cultu Divino et Disciplina Sacramentorum, 'Responsa ad quaestiones de nova Institutione Generali Missalis Romani', *Communicationes*, 32 (2000) 171f; German text in Lang, *Conversi ad Dominum*, pp 25f. **74** Ratzinger, 'Geleitwort' pp 9f.

He also mentions the unduly neglected contributions of Bouyer and Gamber. The issue is the 'opening of the liturgy forward and upward'.[75] In the preface for the inaugural volume of his collected works, dedicated to the *Theology of Liturgy* (2008), the Holy Father notes the very keen interest in the topic of eastward-facing celebration (and so also, indirectly, in the 'basic structure' of the Holy Mass).[76]

The thanksgiving prayer as the 'liturgical structure' of the Holy Mass

We should not forget the most recent work of Joseph Ratzinger on the figure of Jesus Christ (2011),[77] which contains remarks on the Last Supper. Especially important is the conclusion of the chapter entitled 'From the Last Supper of Jesus to the Eucharist on Sunday Morning'.[78] The command of Jesus, 'Do this in remembrance of me' does not refer to the Passover ('if the last meal of Jesus was such'). For the Passover is celebrated once a year:

> The command of the remembrance regards … only what Jesus had done on this evening in a new way: the breaking of bread, the prayer of blessing and thanksgiving and together with it the words of trans-formation over bread and wine.[79]

> [With the] words and gestures of Jesus' at the Last Supper, 'the essence' of the new 'cult' was given, but not yet the complete cultic structure [*Gestalt*] which had to develop first in the life of the Church. It was convenient that, following the example of the Last Supper, there first be a meal in community, and then the Eucharistic attached to it.

Such experiences as described in the First Letter to the Corinthians, however, led 'very early to a separation between the Lord's Supper and the community banquet'. The words of the Lord appeared there 'as part of his *berakha*, his prayer of thanksgiving and blessing':[80]

> Starting from the thanksgiving of Jesus, which gave a new centre to the Jewish *berakha*, the prayer of thanksgiving, the *eucharistia*, manifested itself more and more as the really decisive form, as the liturgical structure in which the words of institution have their sense, and in which the new cult appears that replaces the sacrifices of the temple.[81]

75 Ibid., p. 10. **76** See Ratzinger, *Theologie der Liturgie*, pp 6f. **77** J. Ratzinger, *Jesus von Nazareth. Zweiter Teil: Vom Einzug in Jerusalem bis zur Auferstehung* (Freiburg i. Br., 2011), pp 122–64. **78** *Jesus von Nazareth*, pp 159–64. **79** Ibid., p. 159. **80** Ibid., p. 160. **81** Ibid., p. 161.

Ratzinger goes on explicitly to cite Josef Andreas Jungmann:

> The basic structure [of the Holy Mass] is the thanksgiving prayer over bread and wine. The Mass has taken its origin from the thanksgiving prayer after the meal of the last evening, not from the meal itself. The meal was considered of so little importance, and so removable, that it was omitted even in the primitive Church. The liturgy has, however, developed .. the thanksgiving prayer ... The Church is not celebrating the Last Supper, but what the Lord instituted at the Last Supper and handed on to the Church: the memory of his sacrificial death.[82]

Likewise Ratzinger takes from Jungmann the insight that the Church, after having detached the Eucharist from a meal for satiation, did not call the Holy Mass a 'meal'; this appears, rather, as an invention of the Reformers.[83]

Already during Apostolic times (see Acts 20:6–11) the 'breaking of the bread' is 'transposed to the morning of the day of Resurrection' and so appears 'as an encounter with the Risen One'. The Sunday as the 'first day of the week' (1 Corinthians 16:2) is the 'day of the Lord' (Revelation 1:10). Therefore it was logically consistent to unite the eucharistic celebration with the Liturgy of the Word, still celebrated in the Synagogue at the beginning. 'This developmental process constitutes part of the liturgical establishment itself', a process that presupposes the Resurrection of Christ and the living community of the Church 'which, guided by the Holy Spirit, gives to the gift of the Lord its form in the life of the faithful'. 'An archaism that would go back before the Resurrection and its dynamics in order to imitate only the Last Supper, would not correspond to the essence of the gift that the Lord has bequeathed to his disciples'. Through the thanksgiving, the risen Lord makes us able to give thanks together with him and to receive his benediction.[84]

The second part of the book on Jesus brings the fruits of the discussion about the 'basic structure' of the Holy Mass to a wide audience. The Last Supper is the foundation of the Eucharist, but its 'characterizing form' and sense-giving 'liturgical structure' is the thanksgiving, which draws the Church into Christ's sacrifice and bestows on her the blessed gifts of the risen Christ.

---

82 Jungmann, *Messe im Gottesvolk*, p. 24.   83 See Ratzinger, *Jesus von Nazareth*, p. 162, citing Jungmann, *Messe im Gottesvolk*, p. 23, fn. 73.   84 Ratzinger, *Jesus von Nazareth*, pp 163f.

FURTHER REMARKS

The observations of Joseph Ratzinger have made questionable the liturgical movement's strongly time-conditioned conviction about the 'meal' as the 'basic structure' of the Holy Mass. In our view, however, the task remains of formulating the relevant issues in a more precise way. Therefore in conclusion some suggestions are outlined here.

The congruency between the 'basic structure' and the 'content of significance'

The category of the 'basic structure' (*Grundgestalt*) is quite useful, but it has been so strongly influenced by its origin in the work of Romano Guardini that it does not seem to have been generally received into the common theological language. The theological problem in Guardini's proposal consists in the opposition between exterior form (the meal structure) and interior significance (the sacrifice of Christ). Ratzinger correctly stresses that content and form must correspond to each other. Therefore it must be sufficient for theological discussion to describe systematically the significance of the Eucharist in order to have a general orientation for the liturgical structure.

The eucharistic banquet as integral part of the sacrifice of the Mass

For a successful outcome of the discussion, the decisive element is to determine the relation between the idea of sacrifice and the meal character of Eucharist. In more recent discussion the appropriateness of applying the concept of 'meal' to the Holy Mass has been challenged.[85] If we define 'meal' in a phenomenological way, as a longer process of satiation in community, the application of this concept to the Mass seems questionable. The description of the Eucharist as the 'Lord's Supper' [*Herrenmahl*] is problematic, because in Saint Paul this concept presupposes the connection with a meal for satiation, which is not essential for the Holy Mass and which lasted only a short time in the primitive Church. The Protestant description of the Eucharist as a 'Supper' [*Abendmahl*] is still more problematic: Jesus did not command us to repeat the Last Supper, but to perform the eucharistic memorial that finds its center in the sacramentally efficacious words of the Lord.

The concept of 'meal' seems acceptable, however, in the sense of nourishment by the Eucharist, when Christ unites the faithful with himself and

---

85 For a description of 'meal' from the perspective of the philosophy of religion, see Meyer, *Eucharistie. Geschichte, Theologie, Pastoral*, pp 44–7; J. Ratzinger, 'Die sakramentale Begründung christlicher Existenz', *Theologie der Liturgie*, pp 197–214 (at 200–3).

among themselves. We can note here the traditional Latin concept of *convivium*, used for instance by St Thomas Aquinas to describe the eucharistic mystery: *O sacrum convivium in quo Christus sumitur; recolitur memoria passionis eius, mens impletur gratia et futurae nobis gloriae pignus datur.*[86] For this reason, it does not seem erroneous to describe the Eucharist also with the concept of meal. Explaining the main aspects of the Eucharist, the *Catechism of the Catholic Church* cites the constitution of Vatican II on the Sacred Liturgy, which calls the Holy Mass the 'eucharistic sacrifice' by which 'the sacrifice of the Cross' is perpetuated throughout the centuries; but it also uses the expressions of 'memorial' of the death and Resurrection of Jesus, of 'sacrament', 'bond of charity' and 'Paschal meal' (*convivium Paschale*).[87] The concept of meal is realized in the clearest way in the eucharistic banquet, the communion, but reveals itself also in other elements of the celebration, for instance in the designation of the altar as *mensa*. For this reason the *Catechism* describes the Holy Mass simultaneously as 'sacrifice' and as 'sacred banquet':

> The Mass is at the same time, and inseparably, the sacrificial memorial in which the sacrifice of the Cross is perpetuated, and the sacred banquet of communion with the Lord's body and blood.[88]

It is important, however, that the liturgical constitution *Sacrosanctum concilium* and the *Catechism* mention the concept of sacrifice in the first place. From a systematic perspective, the precedence of sacrifice is motivated by the primary significance of the Eucharist, which consists in the glorification of God. The communication of salvation in the eucharistic sacrament is only a consequence of orientation towards God. From the humanity of Christ, oriented to God, flows as its effect the gift of grace, which finds a first realization in Holy Communion. For this reason, the anabatic sense of Eucharist must systematically precede the catabatic sense.[89] This is valid already for liturgy in general, as *Sacrosanctum concilium* observes: the liturgy is 'first of all glorification of the divine majesty' (*sacra Liturgia est praecipue cultus divinae maiestatis*).[90]

---

[86] Magnificat antiphon for Second Vespers of Corpus Christi: *Liturgia horarum iuxta ritum romanum*, vol. III, (Città del Vaticano, 1977), 502; cf. *Breviarium Romanum ex decreto SS. Concilii Tridentini ...*, vol. II (Bonn, 2008), p. 27. **87** CCC 1323 and *Sacrosanctum concilium* 47. **88** CCC 1382. **89** The characterization of the eucharistic liturgy as primarily worship (the glorifying of God) has been strongly criticized by some liturgical scholars in the wake of the work of Emil Josef Lengeling. According to him, the cult, seen from the history of religion, tries, through a human activity, to constrain God to impart his grace. The Christian liturgy is however first of all a healing action of God – who then opens the possibility for a praising human response in a dialogue between God and man. **90** *Sacrosanctum concilium* 33.

This becomes very clear in the observations of Ratzinger, who presents the concept of *logike latreia* (in the sense of thanksgiving and adoration) as 'the most convenient formula for the essence of Christian liturgy':[91]

> Liturgy is first of all *opus Dei*, and this in a simply way. It is our going to God, it is glorification of the living God.

At the same time, the liturgy 'presupposes the descent of God; only this descent can become for us a ladder by which we can climb up to him, together with the descending God'.[92] The primary significance of Jesus' offering is the glorification of God, the secondary significance (which depends on the first) is the communication of saving grace. What applies to the sacrifice of Christ, applies also to the meaning of the Holy Mass.

This relation can be found in a very clear way in John Paul II's 2003 encyclical *Ecclesia de eucharistia*:

> By virtue of its close relationship to the sacrifice of Golgotha, the Eucharist is *a sacrifice in the strict sense* ... The gift of his love and obedience to the point of giving his life ... is in the first place a gift to his Father. Certainly it is a gift given for our sake, and indeed that of all humanity (see Matthew 26:28; Mark 14:24; Luke 22:20; John 10:15), yet it is *first and foremost a gift to the Father*.[93]

The 2004 instruction of the Congregation for Divine Worship and the Discipline of the Sacraments *Redemptionis sacramentum* speaks in the same sense: the Eucharist is 'not only [a] meal [but] first and pre-eminently [a] Sacrifice'.[94]

Sacrifice and meal are not categories of the same level. The eucharistic sacrifice contains the banquet of Holy Communion. Therefore the pre-eminent category remains sacrifice, whose efficacy reaches its perfection in the communication of grace and in the sacramental participation in the Eucharist.

---

91 Ratzinger, *Geist der Liturgie*, p. 42.   92 J. Ratzinger, 'Grußwort' in F. Breid (ed.), *Die heilige Liturgie. Beiträge der „Internationalen Theologischen Sommerakademie 1997" des Linzer Priesterkreises in Aigen/M.* (Steyr, Austria, 1997), pp 9–12 (at 9f).   93 *Ecclesia de eucharistia* 13. See the Apostolic Letter *Dominicae coenae* (1980), 9: 'The Eucharist is above all else a sacrifice. It is the sacrifice of the Redemption and also the sacrifice of the New Covenant ...'. Similarly the Apostolic Letter *Mane nobiscum Domine* (2004), 15: 'There is no doubt that the most evident dimension of the Eucharist is that it is a meal ... Yet it must not be forgotten that the eucharistic meal also has a profoundly and primarily [*penitus et in primis*] sacrificial meaning.'   94 *Redemptionis sacramentum* 38.

The sacrifice is also the center of the sacramental memorial, the *anamnesis*. The *epiclesis*, however, belongs to the communication of salvation caused by the sacrifice. So too the Resurrection of Christ is founded on his offering at the Cross. As Cardinal Koch observes:

> the sacramental representation of the propitiating action of Christ on the Cross establishes the community character of the Eucharist, and not vice versa.[95]

Thanksgiving as part of the sacrifice

As the 'basic structure' of the Eucharist, Ratzinger designates 'thanksgiving', *eucharistia*, the blessing and benediction (*eulogia*). This description stems from the ancient concept of 'eucharist', and certainly points to a central content. The more comprehensive content, however, seems to be the 'sacrifice' that manifests itself already in the first Church Fathers in terms like *tusia* and *prosphora*. Without doubt, the sacrifice contains praise and thanksgiving, but also intercession and expiation.[96] For this reason, the concept of the 'Sacrifice of the Mass' still seems more comprehensive and accurate for the Holy Mass than simply speaking of the 'eucharistic celebration'. Thanksgiving and offering can be distinguished from one another (insofar as the words of thanksgiving are directed towards the sacrifice of Christ). Thanksgiving, however, can also be seen as a part of sacrifice. It is therefore the sacrifice which appears as the 'basic structure' or the pre-eminent significance of the Holy Mass; the sacramental communication of salvation and the eucharistic banquet make up an integral part of it.[97]

---

95 K. Koch, *Das Geheimnis des Senfkorns. Grundzüge des theologischen Denkens von Papst Benedikt XVI* (Regensburg, 2010), p. 137.   96 See Council of Trent, Decree on the Sacrifice of the Mass, Canon 3: 'If anyone says that the sacrifice of the Mass is one only of praise and thanksgiving; or that it is a mere commemoration of the sacrifice consummated on the Cross but not a propitiatory one; or that it profits him only who receives, and ought not to be offered for the living and the dead, for sins, punishments, satisfactions, and other necessities, let him be anathema.' On the four-fold intention of the Mass (*sacrificium latreuticum, eucharisticum, propitiatorium, impetratorium*) see, e.g., Diekamp – Jüssen, *Katholische Dogmatik nach den Grundsätzen des heiligen Thomas*, III (Münster, 1962), pp 216–19; A. García Ibánez, *L'Eucaristia, dono e mistero. Trattato storico-dogmatico sul mistero eucaristico* (Rome, 2006), p. 543f.   97 See García Ibánez, *L'Eucaristia*, p. 484, fn. 67: *In questa prospettiva la dimensione conviviale dell'Eucaristia è rispettata, ma va considerata non come un pasto comunitario ordinario, bensì in rapporto alla comunione con il corpo dato e col sangue sparso di Gesù Cristo e, pertanto, come partecipazione al suo sacrificio.* Similarly N. Bux, *La riforma di Benedetto XVI. La liturgia tra innovazione e tradizione* (Casale Monferrato, 2009), p. 101: *Essa [la croce] sta a ricordare che la forma dell'eucaristia è il sacrificio di Cristo.*

The prayer of priest and people versus **Deum**

The pre-eminent significance of sacrifice must manifest itself also in the concrete liturgical celebration. It is therefore particularly recommended that the celebrant at prayer (especially during the Eucharistic Prayer) be faced, together with the people, in the same direction, towards the Cross.[98] Facing the people seems appropriate for the proclamation of the Word of God and for the communication of divine gifts, for instance in the distribution of Communion. Facing the people in these ways, however, is a preparation for, and a fruit from, the orientation towards God. This God-centred liturgical structure should also be made more visible in the architectural design of Churches.

---

98 See also M. Kunzler, 'Die kosmische Dimension der Eucharistiefeier. Zu Fragen ihrer liturgischen Gestalt bei Joseph Ratzinger' in R. Voderholzer (ed.), *Der Logos-gemäße Gottesdienst. Theologie der Liturgie bei Joseph Ratzinger* (Regensburg, 2009), pp 172–204 (at 188–203); M. Gagliardi, *Liturgia fonte di vita. Prospettive teologiche* (Verona, 2009), pp 147–61; C. Barthe, *La messe à l'endroit. Un nouveau mouvement liturgique* (Paris, 2010), pp 85–7. Kunzler stresses (p. 202) that focusing on an altar cross standing between priest and congregation could only be an interim solution. For Barthe (p. 85) the common direction of prayer by priest and people is the most visible sign of an intention to 'reform the reform' ('le signe le plus visible d'une volonté de réforme de la réforme').

The Church's Eucharist, the Lord's Supper, Israel's sacrifice: reflections on Pope Benedict's axiom 'Without its coherence with its Old Testament heritage, Christian liturgy simply cannot be understood'

DIETER BÖHLER SJ

In the foreword to the first volume of his collected writings to appear – volume 11, on the liturgy – Pope Benedict writes: 'Without its coherence with its Old Testament heritage, Christian liturgy simply cannot be understood.'[1] The Pope does not develop this idea at this point but he is of course right and not primarily here as Supreme Pontiff but as a scholar and theologian.

My purpose here is simply to suggest a few concrete applications of this papal axiom. There are various elements to which we might refer. For example, the liturgical calendar. Israel's religious calendar with its basic structure of the seven-day week and the Sabbath as its high point, and indeed its annual feasts, Passover and the Festival of Weeks (Pentecost), has remained decisive for the Church. We could refer also to the priesthood. The three levels of High Priest, priest and Levite are mirrored to this day in the prefaces for the ordinations of bishops, priests and deacons. Also with regard to priesthood we might mention that Israel did have female prophets[2] and rulers,[3] in other words, women in teaching and leadership roles, but priestesses as they were to be found in practically all the other peoples around were unknown in Israel. Israel was the great exception. That this was no accident but programmatic was demonstrated when the Hasmonean high priest and King Alexander Jannai died in 103 BC. The royal authority could be passed on to his widow Salome, but not the office of high priest. This was taken over by Jannai's son John Hyrkan. The Church too from her beginnings has known the exercise of authority by women as well as women's teaching activity and indeed women doctors of the Church. But as regards the liturgical symbolism of the exclusively male priesthood that explicitly distinguished Israel from the neighbouring peoples the Church in both East and West has for 2000 years clearly considered herself bound by the precedents of the Bible and of Israel.

1 Ratzinger, Schriften, Bd.11: *Zum Eröffnungsband meiner Schriften* 8. 2 Ex 15:20; Judy 4:4; 2 Kings 22:14; Lk 2:36. 3 Judy 4:4; 2 Kings 11; Josephus, Ant XIII 407.

The polytheistic peoples symbolized their male-female pantheon through a male and female priesthood and a corresponding form of worship. Israel could not do that. In this the Church follows Israel.

A further point would be liturgical apparel. The Catholic and Orthodox vestments, just like Aaron's vestments, developed initially from everyday Mediterranean attire but then, in the course of history (in the West from the beginning of the Frankish period), they were deliberately refashioned in accordance with Exodus 28.

And finally, the ritual ablutions of the Jews in general, in particular the ablutions of the priests at the copper basin in front of the Temple at the beginning of the sacrificial rites (Exodus 30:17–21) can be seen to survive in the holy water font and the priest's lavabo at the offertory.

All this shows how the liturgy of Israel as depicted in the Old Testament lives on in many and various ways in the Church. However I do not intend to deal here with all the points I have just mentioned. I limit myself to just one question. How do the Church's Eucharist, Jesus' Last Supper and Israel's practice of sacrifice, as they are represented in Holy Scripture, relate to one another?

'DO THIS IN MEMORY OF ME' – THE GOSPELS AND THE CHURCH'S BREAKING OF BREAD

The Synoptics represent Jesus' Last Supper as a Passover sacrifice-meal. It is the generally held view that in doing so they are already using liturgical formulae that had become customary in the Christian communities. A distinction is commonly made between a Matthean–Markan and a Lukan–Pauline form of the *verba testamenti*. The already existing practice of the Church is here the basis for the biblical text in its differing forms while, conversely, the biblical text is normative for the practice of the Church from then on. The repetition command 'Do this in memory of me' emphasizes that the account of the Last Supper aims at establishing an ongoing Church practice.

What Luke in the Acts of the Apostles calls the 'breaking of bread' on the Lord's Day[4] has, according to Luke and the Synoptics, grown out of the Passover sacrifice-meal. Ignatius of Antioch will call this 'Eucharist' and designate the place of its celebration as – entirely as a matter of course – an altar.

4 Acts 2:42,46; 20:7,11.

> Take heed, then, to have but *one* Eucharist. For there is *one* flesh of our Lord Jesus Christ, and *one* cup to show forth the unity of his blood; *one* altar; as there is *one* bishop ...[5]

The evangelist John makes a connection between Jesus' death and the Jewish Passover sacrifice (John 13:1–2) but he does not represent the Last Supper as a Passover sacrifice. He does not even recount it in any detail. So already at a first glance there are different ways in the New Testament of linking Jesus' Last Supper, and with this the institution of the Church's Eucharist, with Israel's temple sacrifice. No New Testament author represents Jesus' Last Supper without such a link and this cannot be without significance for the Church's practice of liturgical celebration and, all the more so, for the Church's theory of liturgical celebration. Here I would like to consider the Pauline view of the relationship between Church practice and Jesus' farewell meal and between Jesus' farewell meal and Israel's sacrificial worship.

THE LORD'S SUPPER IN FIRST CORINTHIANS AND ISRAEL'S *MINHAH*

Paul speaks of the 'Lord's Supper', κυριακὸν δεῖπνον (1 Corinthians 11:20). He has manifestly introduced the Lord's Supper when founding his communities. Nowhere indeed does he relate what basic teaching and practice he introduces when founding a community. We see though again and again in individual cases how he falls back when appropriate on self-evident presuppositions – as when for example he has recourse to Jesus' teaching on marriage and divorce which he takes for granted but does not elucidate.[6]

Paul's founding of communities presupposes, alongside the already existing biblical knowledge of the many God-fearing individuals who have long been sympathetic to the Jewish faith, a basic oral catechesis on Jesus. At the same time Paul in founding these communities sets up sacramental institutions and ministerial structures. Nowhere in Paul's Letters are these systematically explained; at most they are touched upon in passing. In the Letters, occasionally written at a later period, Paul mentions these self-evident matters explicitly only when they have in some way become problematic. Had the Lord's Supper never become a problem in any of Paul's communities we would

---

5 *The Epistle of Ignatius to the Philadelphians*, A. Roberts and J. Donaldson (tr.), in *Ante-Nicene Fathers* vol. 1.   6 1 Cor. 7:10.

have had no idea from his Letters that the Lord's Supper was in fact practiced in his communities. And doubtless many New Testament exegetes would then have declared that the Lord's Supper, the 'breaking of bread' was unknown in the Pauline churches. But, thank God, the Lord's Supper became quite a problem in Corinth and the apostle had to deal with it comprehensively in 1 Corinthians 10 and 11. In so doing he thankfully also affords us an insight into his dogmatic understanding of the celebration, specifically an insight into his view of the relationship between the Church's Lord's Supper and the Old Testament sacrificial worship.

Perhaps it is important to mention explicitly right at the outset that Paul will not live to experience the destruction of the Jerusalem Temple. The question of possible continuity and discontinuity between Jewish and Christian worship does not therefore arise for him at least from this point of view. The Acts of the Apostles shows Paul and all the other Apostles taking part as a matter of course in the worship of the Jerusalem Temple when they are in the Holy City.[7] In the Pauline communities we must also take into account the many Synagogue sympathizers (φοβούμενοι) who although they had not had themselves circumcised nevertheless already had the Old Testament in their heads when they became Christians through Paul.

Paul does not associate Jesus' Last Supper, nor consequently the Church's Lord's Supper, with a Passover sacrifice-meal. But he does certainly relate it to the Old Testament sacrifices. He represents it namely as the *minhah*, that cereal and incense offering which according to Malachi 1:11 will one day be offered everywhere in the world by the Gentiles to the Lord, the God of Israel. This *minhah* of bread and the wine libation that goes with it is however in Israel a sacrifice in the Jerusalem Temple (Numbers 15:4–5).

Already in the salutation at the beginning of his letter Paul numbers the Corinthians among those who 'call upon the name of our Lord Jesus Christ in every place' (τοῖς ἐπικαλουμένοις τὸ ὄνομα τοῦ κυρίου ἡμῶν Ἰησοῦ Χριστοῦ ἐν παντὶ τόπῳ). The expression 'to call upon the name of the Lord' refers, in the biblical language that Paul is obviously adopting here, to the cultic worship of the God of Israel, which normally involves a sacrifice.[8] As we read for example in Genesis 12:8: 'There he [Abraham] built an altar to the Lord and invoked the name of the Lord'. The formula 'to call upon the name of the Lord' is here as also in other passages in the Old Testament (for example

7 Lk 24, 53; Acts 3; Acts 21–22.   8 J.A. Fitzmyer, *First Corinthians, The Anchor Yale Bible* (New Haven–London, 2008), p. 127.

Genesis 13:4 and 26:25) used to express the offering of a sacrifice after the building of an altar.[9]

With the fuller formula '(to call upon) the name (of the Lord) in every place' Paul is alluding in particular on the one hand to the altar law in the Torah (Exodus 20:24):

> You are to make me an altar of earth and sacrifice on this ... *In every place* in which I have my name remembered[10] I shall come to you and bless you.

The Corinth community for Paul is manifestly such a place where the Altar of the Lord stands and on it the remembrance of his name is celebrated[11] – through calling upon the name of Jesus Christ. On the other hand Paul alludes to a second passage that speaks of glorifying the name (of the Lord) 'in every place'. It is to be found in the Prophet Malachi:

> From the rising of the sun to its setting my name is great among the peoples and in *every place* an incense sacrifice will be offered and a pure sacrifice (*minhah*); yes, my name is great among the peoples, says the Lord of Hosts.

In his commentary on First Corinthians at 1 Corinthians 1:2 Dieter Zeller writes: 'That sacrifice would be made to the name of God "in every place" was foretold by Malachi 1:11.'[12] Paul thus addresses the Corinthians with the allusion to the altar law not only as a kind of Israelite worship-community in general but quite specifically as the sort of community Malachi had foretold, a community from the non-Israelite Gentile peoples offering a pure Cereal offering to the name of the Lord 'in every place'. The salutation confines itself to these hints and allusions.

In 1 Corinthians 10 Paul goes back again to Malachi 1 in relation to the problem about meat sacrificed to idols and lets us see what it is that he recognizes in Malachi's cereal offering: the Lord's Supper as it is celebrated by the Church. The prophet had complained in the name of the Lord that Israel had dishonoured the altar, the Lord's table, with defective offerings:

---

9 Cf. Gen. 4:26; 1 Kings 18:24,32; Ps 116:13,17; Zeph 3:9.　**10** LXX: ἐν παντὶ τόπῳ οὗ ἐὰν ἐπονομάσω τὸ ὄνομά μου ἐκεῖ.　**11** The linking of 'in every place' with the 'name' (of the Lord) occurs only in Ex 20, 24 and 1 Mall, 11 – on both occasions in relation to the altar.　**12** D. Zeller, *Der erste Brief an die Korinther*, KEK 5, (Göttingen 2010), 74 note 23.

You offer disgusting *foods* (literally 'loaves', ἄρτους) on my altar. You say: How have we aroused your disgust? By your saying: The table of the Lord (τράπεζα κυρίου) is not so important ...[10] If only there were someone among you to close the doors [of the Temple] so that you no longer kindle useless fire on my altar. I have no pleasure in you, says the Lord of Hosts, and I want no sacrifice from your hand.[11] For from the rising of the sun to its setting my name is great among the peoples and in every place (ἐν παντὶ τόπῳ) an *incense sacrifice* will be offered to my *name* and a pure *sacrifice* (θυσία, minhah); yes, my *name* is great among the peoples, says the Lord of Hosts.[12] But you profane it, you say: one can offer despicable *food* (ἄρτους) on the *Lord's table* (τράπεζα κυρίου), it is not so important. (Malachi 1:7,10–2).

The expression 'the Lord's table' used by Malachi Paul now employs in 1 Corinthians 10 for the table of the Lord's Supper:

Is the blessing-cup that we bless not a communion with the blood of Christ? Is the *bread* that we break not a communion with the body of Christ? The fact that there is only one *loaf* means that, though there are many of us, we form a single body because we all have a share in this one *loaf*. Look at the other Israel, the race, where those who eat the *sacrifices* are in communion with the *altar*. Does this mean that the food offered to idols has a real value, or that the idol itself is real? Not at all. It simply means that the sacrifices that they *sacrifice* they *sacrifice* to demons who are not God. I have no desire to see you in communion with demons. You cannot drink the cup of the Lord and the cup of demons. You cannot take your share at the *table of the Lord* (τράπεζα κυρίου) and at the table of demons. Do we want to make the Lord angry; are we stronger than he is? (1 Corinthians 10:16–22)

τράπεζα in the Old Testament is most often the table for the bread of the Presence in the sanctuary of the Temple (Exodus 25:23–30). Malachi calls the Jerusalem sacrifice altar the 'Lord's table' and complains that Israel is careless at the sacrifice and dishonours the Lord's table with defective foods (loaves). He announces that God will one day find his name more honoured among the other peoples by a pure cereal offering (*minhah*) that the non-Jews will one day offer in *every place*. In 1 Corinthians 10 Paul takes up this expression 'the table of the Lord', just as indeed already in the opening greeting he sees in the Corinthians those non-Jews who are fulfilling Malachi's promise 'in every place'.

Joseph Fitzmyer writes in his Commentary on First Corinthians at 1 Corinthians 10:18:

> Paul is arguing primarily from the function of the altar in the cult of Israel and the relation of worshippers who offered sacrifices at it. What he says is predicated by implication of the table of the Lord in the Christian cult.[13]

And shortly afterwards commenting on 1 Corinthians 10:21 he writes:

> The phrase *trapeza kyriou*, 'table of the Lord', is found in LXX Malachi 1:7, 12, where the post-exilic prophet inveighs against priests in Judah who offered polluted food on the altar and thus despised the name of the Lord (Yahwe). Paul adopts it and applies it to the Christian celebration of the 'Lord's Supper'.[14]

Similarly Conzelmann too observes on 1 Corinthians 10:21: '*trapeza kyriou* is presupposed as an established connotation'.[15] He refers, though only in a footnote, to Malachi 1:7,12.

In 1 Corinthians 10 Paul argues against the participation of Christians in pagan sacrifice-meals. First of all he says: In the Lord's Supper we have communion with Christ and that excludes any other communion.[16] 'You cannot take your share at the table of the Lord and at the table of demons.' An altar to idols is in truth a demons' table, in contrast to the Lord's table, which is the table of the Lord's Supper. Paul compares the table of the Lord's Supper,

---

13 J.A. Fitzmyer, *First Corinthians*, p. 392.   **14** Ibid., p. 394.   **15** H. Conzelmann, 'Der erste Brief an die Korinther', *KEK*, 5, Göttingen 1981, 214.   **16** In verses 18–22 he says concretely what alternative community he means. He refers in v. 18 to 'Israel according to the flesh', which he has already talked about in vv. 1–13. That Israel had permanently betrayed herself in the wandering in the desert, particularly in the matter of the golden calf (10:7 quotes explicitly Ex 32:6). According to Ex 32:5 Aaron had built an altar in front of the golden calf. This is what Paul is talking about in 10:18. There are people in Corinth who say: since there are no idols, there is no problem at all about taking part in the idols' sacrifice-meals. In v. 20 Paul then quotes Deut 32:17 and in v. 22 he quotes Deut 32:21, the famous Moses song in which Moses complains of Israel's idolatry. V. 17: 'They sacrificed to demons who are not God, to gods they did not know, newcomers of yesterday whom their fathers had never feared …' V. 21: 'They have roused me to jealousy with what is no god.' According to the Torah, so Paul says, whoever sacrifices to non-existent gods sacrifices in truth to demons. And since every altar creates a worship community around it, those who sacrifice to non-existent gods end up in communion with demons.

which of course was still being celebrated in private houses, with an altar in the pagan religions. Conzelmann comments on this: 'Paul is thus aware of the analogy between the Christian Supper and the pagan celebrations.'[17] These pagan celebrations were sacrifice-celebrations.

Going beyond mere analogy with the sacrifices of the pagan religions Paul however names the table of the Lord's Supper with the name of the Jerusalem sacrifice-altar (and of the table for the bread of the Presence). He does not go so far as to call the Lord's Supper a sacrifice but he sees it as a sacrificial meal in rivalry with pagan sacrifice-meals. Calling the table of the Lord's Supper 'the Lord's table', he explicitly puts on a par with the Jerusalem altar, and sees it too in rivalry with pagan altars. The Apostle of the Gentiles thus sees in the Christian Corinthians, some of whom at least he has converted to the God of Israel, that community from the pagan peoples announced by Malachi which would glorify the 'name' of the God of Israel by offering him 'in every place' a pure 'cereal offering' on the 'table of the Lord'.

VEGETABLE SACRIFICE IN THE OLD TESTAMENT WORSHIP SYSTEM

In order to explain the mostly unknown, and when known, completely under-estimated, significance of vegetable sacrifice in the Old Testament liturgy I would like briefly to outline the biblical worship system.

According to the Lord's precepts on Mount Sinai in Exodus 25–31 Moses is to erect a tent as the place of the Shekhina, God's dwelling-place among his people. When the high priest comes into the Sanctuary he comes before God. On his breast-plate he bears the names of the twelve tribes, he bears the people before God. For the tent Moses is to make an ark. Two cherubim, winged heavenly beings, mark out a throne on which God is enthroned – as the Psalmist says: 'He is enthroned on the cherubim'.[18] Where in pagan temples the statue to the god stands, Israel, forbidden the manufacture of any image, sets up an empty throne, the Ark of the Covenant. The cherubim symbolize the throne of the presence of God. The Ark is his footstool. The Ark has its place in the tent's Holy of Holies as properly the throne room. In front of it is the sanctuary as audience hall. In the sanctuary Moses is to set up three things: the altar of incense in the middle in front of the curtain, the seven-branched lamp-stand to the left on the south side and the table for the bread of the

---

17 Conzelmann, 'Der erste Brief an die Korinther', 214. 18 Ps 99:1; Ps 80:2: 'Shine forth from your

Presence on the north side opposite the Menorah. Outside in front of the tent stands the altar for holocausts. Inside in the tent and outside in front of the tent daily liturgical actions take place. Morning and evening the priests are to make the holocaust sacrifice on the altar outside in front of the tent. It consists of a lamb. And on top of that, as a supplementary vegetable offering (cereal offering, *minhah*), come wheat-flour or wheaten bread with some olive oil and incense, and then wine as a libation. According to the occasion the wheat is to be offered loose or as paste or as baked bread. The vegetable sacrifice materials – bread and wine, incense and olive oil – must be manufactured. Not grains of wheat, grapes and olives are to be offered then but bread, wine and oil – 'fruit of the earth *and work of human hands*'. In Israel there is no animal sacrifice without cereal offering and wine libation. By the same token, however, in specific cases, the vegetable part of the sacrifice can on its own take the place of the whole sacrifice, as for example, in the case of a sacrifice for sin as in Leviticus 5:11.

The significance of the vegetable sacrifice in Israel is revealed above all in the fact that the animal sacrifice takes place outside in front of the tent (together with the cereal offering pertaining to it) whereas the vegetable sacrifice alone may take place in the inner sanctuary.[19] Just as twice daily the lamb with its cereal offering is to be offered in front of the tent, so also every morning and every evening the priest is to go into the tent and renew the seven oil lamps on the lamp stand. They are an eternal light in the tent, a permanent sacrifice of olive oil.[20] The burning lamp stand symbolizes the divine presence in the burning thorn bush. Likewise, twice daily, morning and evening, Aaron is to offer an incense sacrifice on the incense altar (Exodus 30:7; Luke 1:9). This too is a vegetable sacrifice from the resin of the olibanum tree. The incense sacrifice symbolizes communication between earth and heaven (Psalm 141:2; Revelation 5:8; 8:4). Finally, the loaves of the bread of the Presence that are to be renewed every Sabbath are a bread sacrifice. Their offering is brought about through the burning of the incense that has been placed upon them, whereas the loaves themselves are consumed by the priests 'as a most holy and permanent entitlement to the Lord's burnt offerings' (Leviticus 24:9). The twelve loaves signify the table fellowship, the *communion*,

---

cherubim throne.' **19** For the significance of vegetable sacrifice in the OT see A. Marx, *Les offrandes végétales dans l'Ancient Testament: du tribut d'hommage au repas eschatologique* (Leiden 1994); C. Grappe and A. Marx, *Le sacrifice: vocation et subversion du sacrifice dans les deux testaments* (Geneva, 1998); A. Marx, *Les systèmes sacrificiels de l'Ancient Testament: formes et fonctions du culte sacrificiel à YHWH* (Leiden, 2005). **20** B. Jacob, *Das Buch Exodus* (Stuttgart, 1997), p. 898.

between God and his people, the twelve-tribes-people. According to Exodus 25:29 the cups for the libation belong to the table of the bread of the Presence. Thus, beside the loaves that were to be eaten outside, stood also the wine that was to be poured out outside as a libation. Incense, oil, bread and wine are vegetable sacrifices that represent fellowship with God. The cereal and wine offering outside in front of the tent is of course only a supplement to the animal sacrifice. Inside in the tent it is however a self-sufficient and enduring sacrifice.

The daily preparation of meat, bread, wine, oil lamps and incense is the symbolic staging of a festive banquet in the royal palace. It serves, like a state banquet, the maintenance of relations, or the restoration of relations after a breach, in this case between the King and his people. The Jerusalem Temple liturgy is the ritual staging of a reception the King grants to his people in his palace. In this way he gives them, from the tributes they have paid to him, a banquet in celebration of their mutual relationship.

That Israel's vegetable sacrifice materials – wheaten bread,[21] grape wine, olive oil and incense – are to this day the sacrifice materials of the Eucharistic liturgies of East and West is no accident but rather the continuance of the Old Testament/Israelite liturgical heritage. The Church has always felt bound by these biblical precedents even where these Mediterranean food stuffs were unknown and in fact other food and drink had a central place, like rice in Asia or maize in Mexico. For the Church's sacrifice only Israel's Mediterranean food stuffs are suitable, even in situations where the central food stuffs of a particular people would have had a highly symbolic value. Here the Church's bond with the Bible and with Israel has always taken precedence over enculturation in the cultures of the peoples. The fact that in general the materials for the Church's sacraments are wheaten bread, grape wine and olive oil (together with water) is clearly due to Church's enduring bond with Israel's liturgical practice.

In the Mosaic Tent and later in the Jerusalem Temple the cereal offering is on the one hand a necessary supplement to the lamb sacrifice and on the other hand, within the Temple interior, a self-sufficient sacrifice. Thus, in front of the Temple, a banquet is prepared appropriate to the reality of this earth. Here

---

21 J. Milgrom, Lev 1–16, AB, p. 179, comments on Lev 2:1: 'First, the term solet must refer to wheat (*Sipra*, Nedaba 10:1). So it is expressly identified *solet hittim* "semolina of wheat" the very first time it occurs in the Pentateuch (Ex 29:2) ... Moreover, *solet* is contrasted with barley in ... 2 Kings 7:16.' Milgrom refers to the rabbinic tradition which identifies the solet as wheat. According to Lev 24:5 the showbread loaves too are made from *solet*.

meat too is eaten and blood flows. In the Temple interior the vegetarian ideal of paradise is realized, according to which Adam in the beginning (before the Fall, Genesis 1:29ff; but see also Genesis 9:3) had only plant nourishment. Likewise, in accordance with the future paradise ideal, the lion eats straw like the ox (Is 11, 7). In this way the plant component of the Temple sacrifice is also an expression of a non violent Utopian paradise that is celebrated in the Temple interior.

THE CENTRALIZATION OF THE ANIMAL SACRIFICE IN JERUSALEM, AND UNIVERSALIZATION OF THE BREAD AND WINE OFFERING

Israelite worship was centralized under King Josiah in the seventh century BC. From then on animal sacrifice could only be offered in the Jerusalem Temple (Deuteronomy 12; Leviticus 17; 2 Kings 23; John 4:20). At the other altars and sanctuaries in the land henceforth only bloodless sacrifices could take place. From this time on all the Jews had to go on pilgrimage to Jerusalem at Passover because that was the only place where they were still allowed to slaughter their lambs. Heretofore they had done this at home. But from now on everyone has to go to Jerusalem and that is why later Jesus too will have to go up to Jerusalem for Passover.

When the Temple no longer existed (or in a sanctuary faraway from Jerusalem) already for the Jews the purely vegetable sacrifice could manifestly substitute for all other sacrifices.[22] To this day the Jews no longer slaughter Passover lambs because the Temple is no longer there. At Passover they celebrate still to this day with only the plant part of the sacrifice-meal: flat loaves (called matze), bitter herbs and several cups of wine. The fact that, for the Jews, the vegetable sacrifice worship can substitute for the full sacrifice worship and can spread beyond Jerusalem all over the world and indeed can also extend into the time beyond the destruction of the Temple, will once again be of great significance for Christians.

---

22 In the 5th century BC the Jews of Elephantine in Egypt asked the high priest and the Governor in Jerusalem to allow them to restore their own little temple in Egypt and so resume their worship. Jerusalem allowed the restoration and sacrifice too, but only vegetable sacrifice. The animal-sacrifices remained bound to Jerusalem. When the Babylonians had destroyed the Temple in 587 BC sacrificial worship had to stop. But Jer 41:5 reports: 'Eighty men arrived from Shechem, Shiloh and Samaria, with their beards shaved off, their garments torn and their bodies gashed; they had oblations (grain offering) and incense with them to take to the Temple of the Lord.'

EATING AS A SACRIFICIAL ACT

In the Israelite animal sacrifice the slaughtering, the butchering of the animal is not yet the act of sacrifice as such.[23] The killing of the animal is rather a preparatory act that falls to the lay person who wants to have a lamb or goat offered (Leviticus 1:5; 3:2; 4:29). In given circumstances the Levites will help him with this (2 Chronicles 30:17–9). The priests first become involved with the blood-rite with which the properly priestly sacrificial action begins. The priests catch the blood as it flows out and sprinkle it on the altar (Leviticus 1:5; 3:2; 4:30). They thereby give the animal's life back to the Lord of all life (Leviticus 17:11,14). The eating of the meat is in fact the real act of sacrifice. In the holocaust everything is consumed by fire and so symbolically by the divine side (Leviticus 1:12–3). In the sacrifice of well-being a part is consumed by fire (Leviticus 3:3–5), a part by the priests (Leviticus 7:32–6) and the remainder by the faithful (Leviticus 7:15–21). But even in the holocaust, in addition to the consumption by fire, a human meal also takes place since in any case a part of the obligatory supplementary vegetable sacrifice is eaten by the priests (Leviticus 2:3). The consumption of the consecrated gifts by fire and the priests on the one hand and the meal of the Israelites on the other hand restore communion between God and God's people. The consumption by the priests (and fire) is itself the act of sacrifice in which the faithful participate by their meal.

For the inside sacrifice the stipulations of Leviticus 24:5–9 hold good:

> You are to take wheaten flour and with it bake twelve cobs, each of two-tenths of an ephah. Then you must set them in two rows of six on the pure table that stands before the Lord. On each row you shall place pure incense. This will be the food offered as a memorial, a burnt offering for the Lord. Continually every Sabbath they shall be set before the Lord. The sons of Israel are to provide them by unending covenant. They will belong to Aaron and his sons, *who shall eat them in a holy place, for they are a most holy portion for him of the Lord's burnt offerings. This is a perpetual law.*

---

23 Thomas Aquinas is absolutely right to suggest that the killing of Christ is not the essence of his 'sacrifice': S. Th. III q 22 a2 ad 2: *Christi hominis occisio potest ad duplicem voluntatem comparari. Uno modo ad voluntatem occidentium. Et sic non habuit rationem hostiae: non enim dicuntur occisores Christi hostiam Deo obtulisse, sed graviter deliquisse ... Alio modo potest considerari occisio Christi per comparationem ad voluntatem patientis, qui voluntarie se obtulit passioni. Et ex hac parte habet rationem hostiae.* And S. Th. III q 48 a3, ad

The bread of the Presence that the priests sacrifice on the Sabbath in that they ritually eat them are called in Hebrew *qodæš qadašîm*, Holy of Holies. Since the eating of consecrated gifts by the priests in the Church is, just as in Israel, the actual act of sacrifice, the celebrants in the Christian Eucharist must in every case consume the consecrated gifts, they must, *sub utraque specie* and in every case, eat and drink of the gifts that have just been consecrated (IGMR 85; Thomas Aquinas S. Th. III q 82 a43). It is in this way that they effect the sacrifice. For the faithful on the other hand all this is optional. They can likewise participate in the sacrifice by eating and drinking but they do not have to, should they wish merely to attend the sacrifice. They may also receive sub una specie and in case of necessity even from the hosts reserved in the tabernacle. But in no case can they participate in the sacrifice by receiving communion before the celebrants have effected the sacrifice by eating and drinking. The celebrants' eating on the one hand and the faithful's eating on the other, in the Christian sacrifice just as in Israel, have each a completely different meaning. This is also given expression in that the celebrants 'take' the gifts,[24] whereas the faithful participating in the sacrifice 'receive' them.[25] The significance of the Church's liturgical prescriptions can very easily be deciphered here by reference to the Biblical symbolism.

THE CHURCH'S EUCHARIST, THE CEREAL OFFERING AND THE PASSOVER MEAL

The New Testament reconnects the Church's breaking of bread, on the one hand, with Israel's Passover meal. The rite of the breaking of bread, the drinking of wine, the western practice of the use of unleavened breads – all this derives from the Passover sacrifice-meal. On the other hand, however, Paul relates the Lord's Supper, in a general way, to the vegetable sacrifices in the Jerusalem Temple.

When the Church's Eucharist is understood according to the biblical model of the cereal offering (*minhah*) together with the libation of the blood of the grape (ἐξ αἵματος σταφυλῆς) as it is termed[26] in Sirach 50:15, then the Church's sacrifice is on the one hand the implementation of the vegetable

---

3: *passio Christi ex parte occidentium ipsum fuit maleficium; sed ex parte ipsius ex caritate patientis fuit sacrificium. Unde hoc sacrificium ipse Christus obtulisse dicitur, non autem illi, qui eum occiderunt.*
24 *Institutio generalis Missalis Romani* (IGMR) 242, 246: *acipere, sumere.* **25** IGMR 160–1: *recipere.*
26 Sir 50:15: He reaches out his hand to the cup and pours a libation of the blood of the grape.

sacrifice proper to the lamb who has been slaughtered once and for all and at the same time again and again a fresh sacrifice of bread and wine, *de tuis donis ac datis*. The many Masses relate to one sacrifice of Christ, in biblical sacrifice symbolism, as the ever repeated offering of the cereal sacrifice to the one and only lamb of which the Apostle says (1 Corinthians 5:7): 'You are already unleavened bread; for Christ has been sacrificed as our paschal lamb.' In this way the Church's cereal offering repeated again and again spreads the unique and unrepeatable sacrifice of the Lamb out from Jerusalem over the whole globe and through all days to the end of time. Since the first century the Church has seen in her celebration of the Mass the cereal offering that Malachi foretold would be offered over the whole earth.[27]

The Regensburg liturgist Klaus Gamber is absolutely right when he describes as decisive for the understanding of the Eucharist as the sacrifice of the new covenant Malachi's prophecy of the 'pure sacrifice' to come – as the Septuagint translates the Hebrew word *minhah*. He adds that there is hardly a single theological writing of the early Church in which Malachi's prophecy is not either directly or indirectly referred to in relation to the Eucharistic sacrifice. It is even to be found in some of the Anaphora texts as a quotation.[28]

In the western Church Malachi 1:11 has, most recently, been incorporated into the third Eucharistic Prayer: '*ut a solis ortu usque ad occasum oblatio munda offeratur nomini tuo*' – '... so that from the rising of the sun to its setting a pure sacrifice may be offered to your name.'

The Didache, written around AD100 perhaps in Syria, in chapter 14 describes the Sunday Eucharistic breaking of bread as a 'pure sacrifice' and quotes Mal 1, 11, the 'pure *minhah*':

> Every Lord's Day (κατὰ κυριακὴν δὲ κυρίου) gather yourselves together, and break bread, and give thanksgiving (κλάσατε ἄρτον καὶ εὐχαριστήσατε) after having confessed your transgressions, that your sacrifice may be pure (ὅπως καθαρὰ ἡ θυσία ὑμων ᾖ) ... For this is that which was spoken by the Lord: 'In every place and time offer to me a pure sacrifice (προσφέρειν μοι θυσίαν καθαράν); for I am a great King, says the Lord, and my name is wonderful among the nations.'

---

27 K.S. Frank, Maleachi 1,10ff. 'In der frühen Väterdeutung. Ein Beitrag zur Opferterminologie und zum. Opferverständnis in der alten Kirche', *ThPh*, 53 (1978), 70–8. **28** Gamber, *Das Opfer der Kirche* (Regensburg, 1982), p. 60: „Ausschlaggebend für die Auffassung von der Eucharistie als Opfer des Neuen Bundes war [...] die Weissagung des Malachias vom kommenden `reinen Opfer´, wie die Septuaginta das hebräische Wort `Mincha´ übersetzt. ... Es gibt kaum eine theologische Schrift aus der Frühkirche, in der

Similarly Justin Martyr († *c.*165) in his Dialogue with Trypho the Jew 28, 5: 'God now accepts gifts (δῶρα) and offerings (προσφοραί) also from the uncircumcised as Malachi 1:11 confirms.' In the same work (41:3) Justin calls the wheaten flour sacrifice of the healed leper (Leviticus 14:10) a prototype of the Eucharist. He then quotes the *minhah* text Malachi 1:11 and addressing the Jews continues:

> He then speaks of those Gentiles, namely us, who in every place offer sacrifices to him, i.e., the bread of the Eucharist, and also the cup of the Eucharist, affirming both that we glorify his name, and that you profane it.[29]

And similarly at 117:1:

> Accordingly, God, anticipating all the sacrifices which we offer through this name, and which Jesus the Christ enjoined us to offer, that is, in the Eucharist of the bread and the cup, and which are presented by Christians in all places throughout the world, bears witness that they are well-pleasing to him.

There follows the quotation from Malachi 1:11. At the latest from the year 100, the Church explicitly identified her Eucharistic practice with the *minhah* of Malachi 1:11 for she sees her own universality foretold in this text. In this the earliest Fathers are merely continuing what Paul had already begun.

Finally, towards the end of the second century, Irenaeus of Lyons writes in his *Against heresies* IV 17, 5:

> Again, giving directions to his disciples to offer to God the first-fruits of his own, created things – not as if he stood in need of them, but that they might be themselves neither unfruitful nor ungrateful – he took that created thing, bread, and gave thanks, and said, 'This is my body'. And the cup likewise, which is part of that creation to which we belong,

---

im Zusammenhang mit dem eucharistischen Opfer nicht direkt oder indirekt auf die Weissagung des Malachias verwiesen wird. Auch in einige Anaphora-Texte ist sie als Zitat eingegangen." **29** Περὶ δὲ τῶν ἐν παντὶ τόπῳ ὑφ' ἡμῶν τῶν ἐθνῶν προσφερομένων αὐτῷ θυσιῶν τουτέστι τοῦ ἄρτου τῆς εὐχαριστίας καὶ τοῦ ποτηρίου ὁμοίως τῆς εὐχαριστίας προλέγει τότε, εἰπὼν τὸ ὄνομα αὐτοῦ δοξάζειν ἡμᾶς ὑμᾶς δὲ βεβηλοῦν (Greek text acc. to P. Bobichon (ed.), *Justin Martyr: Dialogue avec Tryphon, vol. 1 Paradosis 47,1* (Fribourg, 2003), p. 286. English: Justin Martyr, *Dialogue with Trypho*, M. Dods and G. Reith (tr.) in *Ante-Nicene Fathers*, vol. 1).

he confessed to be his blood, and taught the new oblation of the new covenant; which the Church receiving from the apostles, offers to God throughout all the world, to him who gives us as the means of subsistence the first-fruits of his own gifts in the New Testament, concerning which Malachi, among the twelve prophets, thus spoke beforehand: *'I have no pleasure in you, says the Lord Omnipotent, and I will not accept sacrifice at your hands. For from the rising of the sun, unto the going down [of the same], my name is glorified among the Gentiles, and in every place incense is offered to my name, and a pure sacrifice; for great is My name among the Gentiles, says the Lord Omnipotent;'* (Malachi 1:10–1) – indicating in the plainest manner, by these words, that the former people [the Jews] shall indeed cease to make offerings to God, but that in every place sacrifice shall be offered to him, and that a pure one; and his name is glorified among the Gentiles.[30]

The interpretation of the vegetable sacrifice of Malachi 1 in terms of the Church's Eucharist, which has been standard in Christian theology since the second century, acquired for Christians after the destruction of the Jerusalem Temple the further implication that the sacrifice worship of the Jews had been rejected by God. Before the destruction of the Temple however it was possible for Paul, without dissociating himself from the Jerusalem worship, to relate the Church's Lord's Supper to the Old Testament worship in a positive way and so suggest a continuity between the Jewish temple sacrifice and the Christian Lord's Supper that retains its validity to this day. For Paul, the global extension of the Israelite cereal offering to all peoples spoken of by Malachi has simply been realized in the Lord's Supper.

The Church's Eucharist is the continuance of the offering of bread and wine, incense and olive oil in the forecourt of the Jerusalem Temple. The Eucharist as a biblical cereal and wine offering extends the sacrifice of the

---

30 *Sed et suis discipulis dans consilium, primitias Deo offerre ex suis creaturis, non quasi indigenti, sed ut ipsi nec infructuosi nec ingrati sint, eum qui ex creatura est panem accepit, et gratias egit dicens:* Hoc est meum corpus. *Et calicem similiter, qui est ex ea creatura, quae est secundum nos, suum sanguinem confessus est, et novi testamenti novam docuit oblationem, quam Ecclesia ab apostolis accipiens, in universo mundo offert Deo, ei qui alimenta nobis praestat, primitias suorum munerum in novo testamento, de quo in duodecim prophetis Malachias sic praesignificavit:* Non est mihi voluntas in vobis, dicit Dominus omnipotens, et sacrificium non accipiam de manibus vestris. Quoniam ab ortu solis usque ad occasum nomen meum clarificatur inter gentes, et in omni loco incensum offertur nomini meo et sacrificium purum; quoniam magnum est nomen meum in gentibus, dicit Dominus omnipotens (Mal. 1:10–1) *manifestissime significans per haec, quoniam prior quidem populus cessabit offerre Deo, omni autem loco sacrificium offeretur ei et hoc purum. Nomen autem eius glorificatur in gentibus.* Irenaeus, *Against Heresies.* A. Roberts and W. Rambaut (tr.), in *Ante-Nicene Fathers*, vol. 1.

Lamb slaughtered once and for all through all times and over the whole globe: from the rising of the sun to its setting.

Above all, however, the Church's Eucharist is the continuance of the vegetable sacrifice gifts on the 'Lord's table' in the sacrifice inside the Jerusalem Temple. These gifts represent an eschatological ideal of non-violence which has found its unsurpassable expression in Jesus' surrender on the cross, an ideal of paradise-like communion between God, his people and his creation, an ideal of untroubled homage and thanksgiving from the people of God to their King in the kingdom of God in which, in Jesus words, this meal finds its fulfilment (Luke 22:16). In one sentence: Pope Benedict is completely right when he states that without its coherence with its Old Testament heritage, Christian liturgy simply cannot be understood.

The Roman Missal in *Summorum pontificum*

CASSIAN FOLSOM OSB

The question I would like to ask in this essay is how the history of the Roman Missal can help us to understand better the *motu proprio Summorum pontificum* of Pope Benedict XVI. The *motu proprio* begins with these words: 'Up to our own times, it has been the constant concern of the supreme pontiffs to ensure that the Church of Christ offers worthy worship to the Divine Majesty …' Which Supreme Pontiffs? The text mentions Pope St Gregory the Great as one of the outstanding fathers of the Roman liturgy, then jumps to St Pius V and the post-Tridentine liturgical reforms. When specifically speaking about the Roman Missal, the *motu proprio* mentions Clement VIII, Urban VIII, St Pius X, Benedict XV, Pius XII and Blessed John XXIII. Let's examine what each of these pontiffs contributed to the development of the Roman Missal and then on the basis of this data, try to understand the larger context of *Summorum pontificium*.

THE DEVELOPMENT OF THE ROMAN MISSAL FROM 1570 TO 1962

The liturgical book we call a Missal is the result of the synthesis of three great rivers of the tradition: the orations of the Sacramentary, the chants of the Antiphonal and the readings of the Lectionary. This new synthesis came about in the thirteenth century. To this foundation must be added three other elements: the *Ordo Missae*, the calendar and various kinds of rubrical indications. During the post-Tridentine period, most of these elements of the Roman Missal remained remarkably constant. Two elements, however, were subject to frequent change: the calendar and the rubrics. The calendar develops with the history of sanctity in the Church: new saints are inserted into the Martyrology, and hence also into the Breviary and the Missal. The ranking of feasts is subject to variation. While the growth of the sanctoral cycle is a sign of the holiness and vitality of the Church, there is the consistent experience that the feasts of saints tend to crowd out the *de tempore* cycle, obscuring both Sundays and ferial days. The second element just mentioned, the rubrics, reflects the importance of an objective celebration of the Mass, excluding subjective whims, and the desire to celebrate worthily according to established norms. Some of the rubrics change in tandem with the sanctoral cycle. Other rubrical changes might reflect a desire for greater clarity on the one hand, or greater simplicity on the other.

Missale Romanum 1570 (Pope St Pius V)

The reform of the Roman Missal by Pius V was not a radical one. The behind-the-scenes work was done by Cardinal Guglielmo Sirleto.[1] In the Vatican Library, there is an *incunabulum* dated 1497 with the title *Missale secundum morem Sanctae Romane Ecclesiae* containing Cardinal Sirelto's corrections in the margins. His working text is practically identical to the *editio princeps* of 1474. The most notable change in the 1570 Missal was the calendar, with the elimination of many feasts of saints so as to return to the *de tempore* cycle. A significant difference between the MR 1474 and the MR 1570 is the presence in the post-Tridentine text of an ample introduction containing:

1. The Constitution *Quo primum tempore* of Pius V
2. The *Rubricae generales*
3. The *ritus servandus* (a more detailed explanation of the rubrics)
4. *De defectibus Missae*
5. Prayers of preparation before Mass and prayers of thanksgiving after Mass
6. The calendar and its explanation

But the structure and content of the MR 1570 is essentially the same as that of the MR 1474. The concerns are the pruning of the sanctoral cycle and the improvement of the *ars celebrandi* (to use a modern term) by the insertion of a highly developed system of rubrics and other instructions.

Missale Romanum 1604 (Pope Clement VIII)

With the Constitution *Cum sanctissimum* (7 July 1604), Pope Clement VIII wished to correct certain errors that had already crept into the Missal in the space of twenty-five years. Printers had taken liberties in changing the texts, and Missals were circulating which did not correspond to the 1570 Mass book. The question was whether or not to use the newly corrected Vulgate translation of biblical texts in the Roman Missal. The Giunta brothers, printers in

---

1 A.P. Frutaz, 'Sirleto e la riforma del Messale Romano di S. Pio V', *Regnum Dei: Collectanea Theatina a clericis regularibus edita*, 30 (1974), 84–111.

Venice, in a 1596 edition, had substituted the text of the chants (which used the ancient Itala version of the Latin Bible) with the Vulgate version. They made similar interventions in the lectionary, correcting both Epistles and Gospels. These unauthorized changes provoked the prohibition of the use of this Missal, which was put on the Index of forbidden books in 1601. Pope Clement established a commission to review the matter, which adjusted the 1570 Missal in terms of the rubrics and the text of the readings where there was some discrepancy with the Vulgate. The Constitution *Cum sanctissimum* established norms for the publishing of the Missal and imposed the severest penalties on anyone who would dare to print the Mass book without the necessary permissions and guarantees of authenticity.[2] The concerns behind the promulgation of the 1604 edition were publishing norms, the use of the Vulgate translation of the Latin Bible, and an updating of the rubrics.

Missale Romanum 1634 (Pope Urban VIII)

Thirty years later, Pope Urban VIII published a new edition of the Breviarium Romanum, and hence felt the need to update the Missal as well, so that the two books would correspond to one another. He established a commission that continued the work begun under Pope Clement VIII; that is, they updated the rubrics, adjusted the text of the readings so as to correspond better to the Vulgate, and corrected the Latin of various poetic texts.[3] Pope Urban also reiterated the sanctions of Clement VIII concerning unlawful printings of the Missale and added new structures for a closer control of the situation.[4] These arrangements were contained in the Constitution *Si quid est* (2 September 1634).

Pope Urban VIII was concerned to maintain continuity with the earlier editions of 1570 and 1604; in fact he describes himself as *Nos quoque eorum vestigiis inhaerentes*, following in the footsteps of his predecessors. The issues remain much the same as those of the 1604 Missal: publishing norms, the Latin Vulgate and rubrical updating.

Missale Romanum 1884 (Pope Leo XIII)

From the end of the seventeenth century and during the eighteenth, there were many new editions of both Missal and Breviary in France, due to the

2 A.P. Frutaz, 'Messale' in *Enciclopedia Cattolica* (Vatican City, 1952), vol. 8, p. 837. See also P. Sorci, 'Il Messale Romano come strumento della tradizione celebrativa' in C. Giraudo (ed.), *Il Messale Romano: Tradizione, traduzione, adattamento* (Rome, 2003), p. 54, fn. 65.   3 Sorci, 'Messale Romano come strumento', 54–5, fn. 65.   4 M. Noirot, 'Livres liturgiques de l'Église Romaine' in R. Naz (ed.),

Gallican preference for local custom and a spirit of independence from Roman authority.[5] For over a century these Missals circulated in France; it was only a vigorous campaign to restore the Roman rite (spearheaded, in large part, by the abbot of Solesmes, Prosper Guéranger) that gradually resulted in the conformity of the Mass book to Roman usage. This new situation of relative liturgical peace, allowed Pope Leo XIII finally to publish a new edition of the Roman Missal, which took into account all the developments and variations since the edition of Urban VIII.[6]

In the 250 years between the editions of Pope Urban VIII and Pope Leo XIII, the sanctoral cycle expanded considerably. According to a study of Pierre Jounel, over 100 new feasts had been introduced: thirteen since the end of the sixteenth century, forty-nine during the seventeenth century, thirty-two during the eighteenth century and six during the first half of the nineteenth century. In addition, other feasts could be found in the section *Proprium pro aliquibus locis* as well as additional celebrations *ad libitum*.[7] For example, during the pontificate of Pius IX, the following feasts were introduced or elevated to a higher rank: Immaculate Conception, Patronage of St Joseph, Precious Blood, Visitation of the Blessed Virgin Mary, St Titus, Sacred Heart of Jesus, St Angela Merici, St Paul of the Cross and St Boniface. Pope Leo XIII continued the expansion of the sanctoral cycle.[8] His 1884 edition is still called *typical*, even though it was not printed in Rome, but in Regensburg, by the pontifical publisher Pustet.[9] Pope Leo's concern was simply to update the Missal, especially in terms of the sanctoral cycle; an update that the political and ecclesiastical situation had not permitted until that time.

Missale Romanum 1920 (Pope Benedict XV)

By the time we come to the twentieth century, the sanctoral cycle had grown to such an extent that it was suffocating the cycle *de tempore*. Pope St Pius X did some rather severe pruning of this luxurious vine, reducing the number of octaves and suppressing or transferring feasts that fell on Sunday, so as to restore the importance of the Lord's Day.[10] This was prescribed in both the Apostolic Constitution *Divino afflatu* (1 November 1911) and the *motu*

Dictionnaire de droit canonique, vol. 6 (Paris, 1957), p. 596.   **5** In Italy the Synod of Pistoia (Sixth session, 27 September 1786) took up the question of the reform of the Missal, with the same anti-Roman spirit. **6** Frutaz, 'Messale', p. 837.   **7** P. Jounel, 'L'Évolution du Missel Romain de Pie X à Jean XXIII (1846–962)', *Notitiae*, 14 (1978), 246.   **8** Jounel, 'L'Évolution du Missel Romain', 247–50.   **9** See M. Sodi, 'Il *Missale Romanum* tra l'edizione del 1474 e quella del 1962', *Rivista Liturgica*, 95:1 (2008), 67, fn. 36.   **10** See Jounel, 'L'Évolution du Missel Romain', 250–2.

proprio Abhinc duos annos (23 October 1913). In both cases, the main focus is on the Breviary, with the instruction that the new edition of the Missal should limit itself to updating the rubrics, without making any substantial changes.[11] But the new edition of the Roman Missal desired by Pius X had to be postponed, because the Pontifical Commission for the revision of the Vulgate had not yet finished its work. Hence the new edition fell to his successor, Pope Benedict XV. The new edition was promulgated with a decree of the Congregation of Rites, *Evulgata editione* of 25 July 1920.[12] This edition contained the changes made by Pius X with some further minor adjustments. For example, proper Masses for special occasions were placed in an Appendix and the calendar was made to conform to that of the Breviary. The concerns reflected in the 1920 Missal are the pruning of the sanctoral cycle and the use of the Vulgate in biblical texts.

Missale Romanum 1962 (Pope John XXIII)

Pope Pius XII did not publish a new edition of the Missal, but worked to simplify the rubrics of the Mass in the document *De rubricis ad simpliciorem formam redigendis* of 1955. These changes included the suppression of most octaves, the reduction in rank of certain feasts, the elimination of First Vespers for most feasts, and a renewed attention to the ferial office.[13]

Pope John XXIII continued this work of simplification with the document *Rubricarum instructum* (1960), which was included in the now-expanded introductory part of the 1962 Missal. The principle contribution of John XXIII was the gathering together of rubrics from diverse places into the one text of the *Codex rubricarum* as well as the modification of the *Ritus servandus* and *De defectibus*. The 1962 Missal includes the reformed rites of Holy Week and all the variations that were introduced between 1920 and 1960. These variations have to do especially with the sanctoral cycle. Jounel presents some statistics: since the beginning of the pontificate of Pius IX, forty-five new feasts had been added: seven by Pius IX, twelve by Leo XIII, two by Pius X, five by Benedict XV, eleven by Pius XI, five by Pius XII and three by John XXIII.[14] Jounel comments on this situation:

---

11 See Frutaz, 'Messale', pp 837–38, and Sorci, 'Messale Romano come strumento', p. 55, fn. 69.   12 See Sodi, 'Il *Missale Romanum*', 67, fn. 37.   13 See Noirot, 'Livres liturgiques de l'Église Romaine', p. 603. 14 See Jounel, 'L'Évolution du Missel Romain', 256–7.

The inventory of the principle additions and variations introduced into the Missal from Pius IX to John XXIII leaves at first an impression of dizziness. The reader feels carried away by a kind of perpetual motion, and is astonished that the Roman liturgy was not able to achieve a certain stability in that period of a century.[15]

The concerns manifested in the 1962 edition are, once again, the simplification of rubrics, with some adjustments to the sanctoral cycle.

Summary

In the editions of the Roman Missal made by various supreme pontiffs between 1570 and 1962, certain repeated concerns emerge:

1. The correction of errors
2. The accuracy of Latin texts
3. Norms for publishing and printing
4. The growth and pruning of the sanctoral cycle
5. Updating rubrics to correspond to the historical moment

These kinds of changes do not require substantial or radical revisions. They represent the normal developments of the Church's liturgy and can be interpreted as growth in continuity with the tradition.

UNDERSTANDING *SUMMORUM PONTIFICUM* IN THE LIGHT OF THE
HISTORY OF THE ROMAN MISSAL

Summorum pontificum affirms that two forms or usages of the Roman rite constitute different expressions of the one *lex credendi* of the Catholic Church of the Latin rite (art.1). This is an amazing position. In fact, it would be fair to say that the Ordinary Form and the Extraordinary Form represent different theologies, different spiritualities, different ways of understanding God, the Church and the world. How can they be expressions of the same *lex credendi*? I would suggest that this affirmation represents not so much the starting point as the goal: it is our hope that, even with different ways of praying, there be a single way believing. It is clear that Pope Benedict wants to bridge the gap, and

---

15 Ibid., 257.

hence is applying his brilliantly articulated hermeneutic of continuity in order to repair a liturgical situation where the discontinuity is very obvious. If one law of belief is the goal, how can the Church get there? The argument can be developed in stages, first defining the starting point, then describing the immediate goal, thirdly the steps necessary to move from the immediate goal to the long-term goal, and finally the long-term goal itself.

The starting point

It has been shown that the history of the Roman Missal from 1570 until 1962 is one of organic growth and development. The fundamental content and structure remains the same, while minor corrections, additions and subtractions are made in order to respond to the needs of the Church at that particular historical moment. The 1970 Missal, however, is in a totally different category. The three basic elements of the Roman Missal are radically changed: that is, the orations, the readings and the chants. The corpus of orations is modified in two ways: greater recourse is made to the euchological tradition of the ancient sacramentaries, and texts are edited to reflect contemporary theological positions. The lectionary is radically altered to respond to the expressed wish of SC 51 that the treasures of the Bible be opened up more lavishly to the faithful. Whether such radical changes were necessary in order to respond to SC 51 is a question open for debate. The chant texts were not altered to the same extent as the readings and the orations, but in practice, the chant repertoire has been almost universally abandoned.

The other important elements of the Roman Missal are the *Ordo Missae*, the calendar and the rubrics. The *Ordo Missae* of the 1970 Missal was radically changed: in fact, we call it the *Novus Ordo*. Concerning the calendar, and especially the superabundant growth of the sanctoral cycle, there has always been need of periodic pruning. But in the 1970 Missal, the pruning was so radical that the original plant is sometimes unrecognizable. The protective fence of the rubrics, carefully developed over centuries in order to guard the Holy of Holies, was taken down, leading to unauthorized 'creativity' and liturgical abuse.

An unbiased observer would have to conclude that there has been a breach or rupture in the development of the Roman Missal. Cardinal Ratzinger addressed these questions already in 1981 in *The feast of faith*. Concerning the development of the Missal from 1570 to 1962 he says:

In 1614[16] [sic], under Urban VIII, there was already a new edition of the Missal, again including various improvements. In this way each century before and after Pius V left its mark on the Missal. On the one hand, it was subject to a continuous process of purification, and on the other, it continued to grow and develop, but it remained the same book throughout.[17]

In contrast, Ratzinger observed concerning the Missal of 1970, that:

> with all its advantages, the new Missal was published as if it were a book put together by professors, not a phase in a continual growth process. Such a thing has never happened before. It is absolutely contrary to the laws of liturgical growth, and it has resulted in the nonsensical notion that Trent and Pius V had 'produced' a Missal four hundred years ago. The Catholic liturgy was thus reduced to the level of a mere product of modern times. This loss of perspective is really disturbing.[18]

Cardinal Ratzinger was even more blunt in his memoirs:

> The prohibition of the Missal that was now decreed, a Missal that had known continuous growth over the centuries, starting with the sacramentaries of the ancient Church, introduced a breach into the history of the liturgy whose consequences could only be tragic ... the old building was demolished, and another was built, to be sure largely using materials from the previous one and even using the old building plans. There is no doubt that this new Missal in many respects brought with it a real improvement and enrichment; but setting it as a new construction over against what had grown historically, forbidding the results of this historical growth, thereby makes the liturgy appear to be no longer a living development but the product of erudite work and juridical authority; this has caused us enormous harm.[19]

The challenge launched by Pope Benedict is the hermeneutic of continuity. How can the breach between the 1962 edition and the 1970 edition of the Roman Missal be repaired? *Summorum pontificum* is Pope Benedict's response to this question.

16 This is a typographical error; it should be 1634.   17 J. Ratzinger, *Feast of faith* (San Francisco, 1986), p. 86.   18 Ibid., p. 86.   19 J. Ratzinger, *Milestones: memoirs, 1927–1977* (San Francisco, 1997), pp 147–8.

The immediate goal

The first step in this process of re-interpreting the reform of the Roman Missal is allowing unrestricted use of what has come to be called the 'extraordinary form'. *Summorum pontificum* establishes juridical and pastoral provisions for the *Usus antiquior*. In July 2001 at the liturgical conference of Fontgombault, Cardinal Ratzinger expressed his desire to see both Missals equally recognized:

> It seems to me essential, the basic step, to recognize that both Missals are Missals of the Church, and belong to the Church that remains the same as ever. The preface of Paul VI's Missal says explicitly that it is a Missal of the same Church, and acknowledges its continuity. And in order to emphasize that there is no essential break, that there is continuity in the Church, which retains its identity, it seems to me indispensible to continue to offer the opportunity to celebrate according to the old Missal, as a sign of the enduring identity of the Church.[20]

In the letter to bishops accompanying *Summorum pontificum*, Pope Benedict describes this desire for continuity in terms of an 'interior reconciliation in the heart of the Church'. Here he is referring not only to the reconciliation of individual people or of groups, but to the more profound healing of the Church's own sense of self-identity.

This important step has been taken. Pope Benedict, with great courage and in the face of considerable opposition, has established two usages of the one Roman rite. Where did this idea come from? It is easy to see the influence of the German liturgist Klaus Gamber, who already in the early 1970s suggested the co-existence of these two forms. He proposed that:

> The traditional *ritus Romanus* and the *ritus modernus* should both be accepted as legitimate forms of liturgical worship. The two rites are to exist as independent rites and must be kept separate and unique in such a way that the traditional Roman rite and the traditionally used *Missale Romanum*, together with all other liturgical texts (*Rituale* and *Pontificale*) be reinstated or be authorized for use in the form in which they existed prior to the Council.[21]

---

20 J. Ratzinger, 'Assessment and future prospects' in A. Reid (ed.), *Looking again at the question of the liturgy with Cardinal Ratzinger* (Farnborough, 2003), p. 149.   **21** K. Gamber, *The reform of the Roman liturgy: its problems and background* (San Juan Capistrano, 1993), p. 91.

Despite the practical difficulties involved in this arrangement, Gamber thought that in the long run, it would foster the unity of the Church's liturgical prayer:

> If we allow the traditional rite to continue unchanged and nurture it, alongside the new rite but allowing the traditional rite to exist as a living liturgy, not as a museum piece, it will manifest itself within the universe of the Church and among the different peoples as an important element: the unity of cult.[22]

While it seems very likely that Pope Benedict was influenced by Gamber's liturgical theology, there are important differences, which Manfred Hauke has pointed out in an important article:

> The proposal of Gamber, at least in its practical aspects, has been fulfilled, in essence by the *motu proprio Summorum pontificum* (7 July 2007), especially regarding the Missal. Unlike Gamber, however, the *motu proprio* does not distinguish between two rites, but recognizes, rather, an 'ordinary' and an 'extraordinary' form of the one Roman rite. Hence Pope Benedict XVI, as liturgical legislator, underscores the essential continuity that remains between the two expressions of the Roman liturgy. Another difference between Gamber's proposals and the *motu proprio* lies in the latter's preference for the new liturgy as the 'ordinary' form. Gamber, however, had wanted to treat the Missal of Paul VI not as a part of the Roman rite 'in the strict sense', but rather as a distinct rite *ad experimentum*.[23]

Of course, forty years have passed since Gamber's proposal, and it is clear that the *Novus Ordo* is here to stay. Hence Pope Benedict's pastoral provisions take into account the reality of the Church in 2007.

Moving from the immediate goal to the long-term goal

The immediate goal having been happily achieved, what is the road map for moving toward the long-term goal? Well, there isn't one, and perhaps it is presumptuous to think that there might be anything quite so specific. If the

---

22 Gamber, *Reform of the Roman Liturgy*, pp 92–3.   **23** M. Hauke, 'Klaus Gamber: father of the "new liturgical movement"' in N.J. Roy and J.E. Rutherford (eds), *Benedict XVI and the sacred liturgy* (Dublin, 2010), p. 67.

principle is that of organic development, we must allow the Church the necessary time. It is extremely disruptive to change the Church's liturgy (even for the better) every twenty-five or thirty years. Pope Benedict has enunciated the principles: organic development and the hermeneutic of continuity.[24] It remains for us to put these principles into practice. A number of key intuitions have emerged over the last few decades, such as the need for a new liturgical movement, a renewed theology of the liturgy, the reform of the reform, and the mutual enrichment of the ordinary and extraordinary forms.

Cardinal Ratzinger has frequently mentioned how much he was influenced by the liturgical movement in his youth. So it's not surprising that in 1999, in the preface to his book *The spirit of the liturgy*, he explicitly called for a new liturgical movement.

> If this book were to encourage, in a new way, something like a 'liturgical movement', a movement toward the liturgy and toward the right way of celebrating the liturgy, inwardly and outwardly, then the intention that inspired its writing would be richly fulfilled.[25]

Many individuals and groups have responded to this call. Although there is no organized structure, there are many local initiatives of both a pastoral and a scholarly nature, which are contributing effectively to a genuine liturgical renewal.

It is Pope Benedict's conviction that a proper renewal of the liturgy will only come from a proper theology of the liturgy. The recent publication of the first volume of his *Opera omnia* shows how much his theological writings are guided by this purpose. In the preface he writes:

> The liturgy of the Church has always been for me, ever since my child-hood, the central reality of my life. In the theological school of masters such as Schmaus, Söhngen, Pascher and Guardini, it also became the center of my theological work. The subject that I chose was fundamental theology, because above all, I wanted to go to the heart of the question: why do we believe? But in this question, from the beginning, the other question was intrinsically included, that of the proper response to give

24 J. Ratzinger, *Sacramentum caritatis* (Vatican City, 2007), p.6, fn. 6: 'I am referring here to the need for a hermeneutic of continuity also with regard to the correct interpretation of the liturgical development which followed the Second Vatican Council.'   25 J. Ratzinger, *The spirit of the liturgy* (San Francisco, 2000), pp 8–9.

to God and hence the question about divine worship. My studies on the liturgy should be understood from this starting point. My object was not specific problems of liturgical science, but always the anchoring of the liturgy in the fundamental act of our faith, and hence also its place in the whole of our human existence.[26]

Pope Benedict has opened up for theologians and liturgists a vast horizon of further studies that would contribute to the theological health of the Church and the Church's liturgy.

The 'reform of the reform' has been a catch-phrase now for decades, expressing the desire that the post-Conciliar liturgical reforms be subject to a careful critique and correction. There are many proposals for such reforms,[27] and such proposals are only increasing[28] since Pope Benedict's letter accompanying *Summorum pontificum* in which he affirms that the two Forms of the usage of the Roman Rite can be mutually enriching. The Holy Father himself gives some indications of how such mutual enrichment might come about:

> new Saints and some of the new Prefaces can and should be inserted in the old Missal … The celebration of the Mass according to the Missal of Paul VI will be able to demonstrate, more powerfully than has been the case hitherto, the sacrality that attracts many people to the former usage. The most sure guarantee that the Missal of Paul VI can unite parish communities and be loved by them consists in its being celebrated with great reverence in harmony with the liturgical directives. This will bring out the spiritual richness and the theological depth of this Missal.[29]

This kind of mutual influence can be seen in Pope Benedict's style of celebrating the Eucharist, and in his instructions on the *Ars celebrandi*, to which he dedicated five paragraphs in his Post-Synodal Apostolic Exhortation *Sacramentum caritatis* (38–42).[30] In regard to this mutual influence of the ordinary and extraordinary forms, it is important to point out those monasteries and religious communities that are committed to the celebration of the Eucharist *in utroque usu*. The Benedictine monastery in Norcia, Italy, is a case in point.

26 J. Ratzinger, *Teologia della Liturgia* (Vatican City, 2010), p. 6.   **27** See P. Stravinskas, 'Brick by brick: modest proposals for liturgical authenticity', *Antiphon*, 14:3 (2010), 301–1.   **28** See T. Finigan, 'Mutual enrichment in theory and practice', *Usus Antiquior*, 2:1 (January 2011), 61–8.   **29** J. Ratzinger, 'With great trust', *L'Osservatore Romano*, English edition (11 July, 2007), 9.   **30** Ratzinger, *Sacramentum caritatis*, pp 65–71.

The long-term goal

The long-term goal is hinted at in *Summorum pontificum* but not developed. In the Roman rite there are various usages: the *motu proprio* limits itself to the ordinary and extraordinary forms, but the 2011 Instruction on the Application of *Summorum pontificum* includes the rites of various religious orders (see no. 34) as well (as long as their liturgical books were in effect in 1962). These uses express their own theology and spirituality. In other words, each use has its own *lex orandi*. In order for this liturgical variety to point to a single *lex credendi*, the *lex credendi* has to be broad enough so that liturgical diversity does not harm the Church's unity of belief, but rather enriches it. Cardinal Ratzinger at the 2001 Fontgombault conference, stated that he was not trying to promote uniformity, but rather unity. His notion of unity includes a certain liturgical pluralism, which, of course, does not mean liturgical chaos or fragmentation.[31] Whether the long-term goal will ever include a new edition of the Roman Missal is an open question. Cardinal Ratzinger did refer to this possibility in *Feast of faith*:

> In my view, a new edition will need to make it quite clear that the so-called Missal of Paul VI is nothing other than a renewed form of the same Missal to which Pius X, Urban VIII, Pius V and their predecessors have contributed, right from the Church's earliest history. It is of the very essence of the Church that she should be aware of her unbroken continuity throughout the history of faith, expressed in an ever-present unity of prayer.[32]

CONCLUSION

The *summi pontifices* referred to in the opening words of Pope Benedict's 2007 *motu proprio* all laboured to promote the Church's liturgy, many of them by issuing new editions of the Roman Missal. The concern of these pontiffs was to correct, improve and regulate the Church's celebration of the Eucharist. Two major concerns that emerge are:

1. the proper relationship between the temporal and the sanctoral cycles, and
2. the rubrical indications necessary for a worthy celebration of the sacred mysteries.

---

31 See D. Bonagura, 'The future of the Roman Rite: reading Benedict in the light of Ratzinger', *Antiphon*, 13:3 (2009), 237.   32 Ratzinger, *Feast of faith*, p. 87.

In all these adjustments to the *Missale Romanum* from 1570 to 1962, the essential content remained the same. From this historical data we can conclude that the principles of organic growth and continuity are operative in this period. The Roman Missal of 1970, however, made such radical changes as to constitute a break with tradition. Pope Benedict has laboured for years to bridge this gap, and with his *motu proprio Summorum pontificum*, has laid the groundwork for a reconciliation in the heart of the Church. Time will tell whether a new liturgical movement will be able to re-interpret the *Missale Romanum* of 1970 in terms of continuity with the preceding tradition. In any case, Pope Benedict is certainly one of the great fathers of this new liturgical movement, and his liturgical teaching is already having a salutary effect in the life of the Church.

Liturgy as 'a transcending movement' (J. Ratzinger): reflections on the form and theology of the opening rites in the Roman Missal

SVEN LEO CONRAD FSSP

INTRODUCTION[1]

In 1995 the German-speaking Study Commission for the liturgy of the Mass and the Missal proposed an extensive reform of the 1975 *Missale Romanum* and the corresponding vernacular missals. On the opening rites the following observation, among others, was made: 'The opening part seems to be over-charged. Limitation of this part to a few elements should be possible'.[2] The *editio tertia* did not accept these proposals. A certain discontent regarding the opening rites of the new form has remained – and this independently of the Commission's proposals.[3]

This essay will enter the discussion of the opening rites of the *Missale Romanum*. To achieve this some important stages of the development of those rites will be outlined. Following this the rites of both the *forma extraordinaria* and the *forma ordinaria* will be presented. Finally a concluding assessment will be attempted bearing in mind the theological significance of the entrance rites.

HOW DID THE OPENING RITES EVOLVE? A LOOK AT HISTORY

From the Synagogue to the Church

In itself it is astounding that something like a formal opening to the liturgical rites of the Church, above all with an entrance (!) rite, should have been developed. The Church was instructed to celebrate the memorial of the Lord, the Eucharist.[4] The Holy Father writes simply about this in his book on Jesus:

1 Special thanks to Revd Dr Stephan Koster for his advice, Fr Lic. Benedikt Dissel OCist and Fr Jérôme Bücker FSSP. 2 E. Nagel (ed.), *Studien und Entwürfe zur Meßfeier: Texte der Studienkommission für die Meßliturgie und das Meßbuch* (Freiburg, Basel, Wien, 1995), p. 264. 3 See for example the misinterpretation of the *Kyrie* as a plea for pardon. R. Berger, *Die Feier der Heiligen Messe: Eine Einführung* (Freiburg, Basel, Wien, 2009), p. 192. 4 See J. Ratzinger, 'Gestalt und Gehalt der eucharistischen Feier' in J. Ratzinger, *Theologie der Liturgie* (Freiburg, 2008), pp 359–75, here especially p. 374.

Thus, with the words of Jesus, the essential of the 'new' cult was given, but the liturgical form was not yet prescribed. This had first to be formed in the life of the Church. In all likelihood the example of the Last Supper was followed with a common meal to which the Eucharist was added.[5]

Klaus Gamber observes that the celebration 'until the end of the second century'[6] took place according to this form. The early Eucharist was linked, 'just like the last meal of Jesus, to Jewish and Hellenistic meal usages'.[7]

What kind of an opening does such a 'domestic' celebration require?[8] Surely it needs no differentiated entrance rites. Ritual meals in Judaism were, and still are today, opened with the Kiddush-cup and the breaking of bread.[9] As Klaus Gamber states:

> Both of the introductory rites to the meal have, according to the Jewish understanding, the function of establishing a communal drinking and eating. This is the reason for the prescription of the Talmud that no one more may join the table circle.[10]

Are there other details of these early Christian eucharistic celebrations which can be identified and which would be of interest for our context? Otto Nußbaum has dealt with the question of the table used by Jesus at the Last Supper and the early form of the altar.

> With great probability the Last Supper of the Lord took place, according to the usage of the time, at a round or half round table placed before a sigma-bench.[11]

It is very likely that both the table of the Last Supper as well as that of the Eucharist 'in the first centuries of the Church ... were as a rule round or sigma-shaped'.[12] These observations are of interest to us insofar as these table arrangements required a raised place, namely 'at the left side of the sigma-couch'.[13]

5 J. Ratzinger/Benedikt XVI, *Jesus von Nazareth II: Vom Einzug in Jerusalem bis zur Auferstehung* (Freiburg, Basel, Wien, 2011), p. 160.   6 K. Gamber, *Beracha: Eucharistiegebet und Eucharistiefeier in der Urkirche* (Regensburg, 1986), p. 43.   7 H.B. Meyer, *Eucharistie. Geschichte, Theologie, Pastoral* (Regensburg, 1989), p. 75.   8 Ibid., p. 57.   9 See Gamber, *Beracha*, p. 20.   10 Ibid., p. 21.   11 O. Nußbaum, 'Zum Problem der runden und sigmaförmigen Altarplatten' in O. Nußbaum, *Geschichte und Reform des Gottesdienstes: Liturgiewissenschaftliche Untersuchungen*, (Paderborn, 1996), p. 301.   12 Ibid., p. 314.   13 O. Nußbaum, *Der Standort des Zelebranten am christlichen Altar vor dem Jahr 1000* (Bonn, 1965), p. 377.

Klaus Gamber specifies that this was the place *in cornu dextro*. 'According to ancient custom, this was the place of honour. Further places of honour were the one facing it and the one immediately next to it.'[14]

At the same time, it is interesting to remark that such a rite numerically could only take place in a small group. In the event that the number of participants was too large for one table then more sigma-shaped tables would have been brought into place.[15]

Gamber also remarks that for the early Jerusalem community, which had grown to several thousand, another form, in addition to that of the original meal-celebration, must at least be surmised. Here the Eucharist was joined to the reading of the Scriptures.[16]

This is of interest for us as it means that the opening rites in a primitive stage *must* have changed. Nevertheless, with Uwe Michael Lang we must acknowledge the fact of how hypothetical the data on early Christian worship is.[17] Still, the service of Scripture readings was for the Judaeo-Christians of the time no new creation.[18] In content it presupposes – if we wish – ceremonial stipulations, as also spatial adaptations of the domestic dining room. Elbogen remarks in his description of Jewish worship:

> The reading of the Torah and the Prophets belongs to the oldest liturgical institutions. It is even very probable that the reading of Scripture provided the cause for the first liturgical assemblies.[19]

14 K. Gamber, *Domus Ecclesiae: Die ältesten Kirchenbauten Aquilejas sowie im Alpen -und Donaugebiet bis zum Beginn des 5. Jh. liturgiegeschichtlich untersucht*, (Regensburg, 1968), p. 88. **15** Ibid., p. 92. **16** See the statement of Vincenzo Raffa on the liturgy of the early Church. He presents as a well-founded hypothesis as follows: 'A certain celebration of the Word would not have been omitted. At Troas St Paul maintained a conversation with the Christians which lasted until midnight, and at the end he accomplished the breaking of the bread (Acts 20:2–12). Presumably the assembly was instructed on the reality of Christ and of the Gospel. Besides, Acts 7:42 speaks of the breaking of the bread after having mentioned the teaching of the Apostles as a custom of the first Christians.' ('Non sarebbe mancata una certa celebrazione della parola. A Troade S. Paolo intrattenne i cristiani in una conversazione durata fino a mezzanotte e alla fine compie la frazione del pane (At 20:2–12). Presumibilmente l'adunanza fu imperniata sulle realtà del Cristo e del vangelo. Del resto At 7:42 parla della frazione del pane dopo aver menzionato l'insegnamento degli apostoli, come una consuetudine dei primi cristiani.') V. Raffa, *Liturgia eucaristica. Mistagogia della Messa; dalla storia e dalla teologia alla pastorale pratica* (Rome, 1998), p. 54. **17** U.M. Lang, *Conversi ad Dominum: Zu Geschichte und Theologie der christlichen Gebetsrichtung* (Einsiedeln, 2003), p. 63. **18** See also the observation of Felmys in his presentation on the development of the Byzantine Liturgy: 'The Divine Liturgy is a two-part unity of service of the Word (Liturgy of the Catechumens) and celebration of the Eucharist. Both are rooted in Jewish worship – also the service of the Word. The worship of the Synagogue, to which the worship of the Church largely goes back, was essentially a service of the Word.' ('Die Göttliche Liturgie ist eine Zweiheit aus Wortgottesdienst (Katechumenen – Liturgie) und Eucharistiefeier. Beides wurzelt im jüdischen Gottesdienst, – auch der Wortgottesdienst. Der Synagogen-Gottesdienst, auf den der Gottesdienst der Kirche weitgehend zurückgeht, war ja eigentlich Wortgottesdienst.') K.C. Felmay, *Vom urchristlichen Herrenmahl zur Göttlichen Liturgie* (Erlangen, 2000), p. 1. **19** I. Elbogen, *Der jüdische Gottesdienst in seiner geschichtlichen Entwicklung*

The Synagogue, as Louis Bouyer notes, had two points of reference: the Ark of the Covenant and the Seat of Moses. Yet the Torah-shrine was the real reference-point of the assembly,[20] which itself, though, pointed to Jerusalem.[21] The place for the Ark was a niche in the wall.[22] The Seat of Moses, 'in the middle of the Synagogue' was meant for 'the authentic trustee of the living tradition of the Word of God first entrusted to Moses'.[23] Only by the trustee, the Rabbi, is the assembly constituted as *Quahal*.[24]

Here we find an important indication that the assembly must be constituted through the authority of Moses, represented by the Rabbi. Thus, the assembly does not come about by itself.

Bouyer's observation is also of importance:

> Very early the Jews used for their Synagogues the typical Greek form of building for public assemblies, the basilica.[25]

In the Synagogues a fixed order of seating came about, which was orientated according to the arrangement of the basilica:

> The ancient basilica ended in a raised place on which the judges sat. We also find this again in the ancient Synagogues. A platform is joined to the Ark, which uses the name ... [bema].[26]

Erik Peterson has shown that the public as well as the private prayer of the Jews had a spatial direction.[27]

In Synagogue worship one was summoned to the reading of the Torah,[28] which was introduced and concluded by blessings.[29]

(Frankfurt am Main, 1932), p. 2. **20** 'Even the Rabbis looked, like everyone else in the Synogoge, to the Ark of the Covenant.' What is meant here is the Tora-shrine. L. Bouyer, *Liturgie und Architektur* (Einsiedeln, Freiburg im Breisgau, 1993), p. 18. **21** Ibid., p. 21. **22** Cf. Elbogen, *Der jüdische Gottesdienst*, p. 470. **23** Bouyer, *Liturgie und Architektur*, p. 18. **24** Ibid., p. 18. **25** Ibid., p. 23. **26** Elbogen, *Der jüdische Gottesdienst*, p. 473. Cf. on this the following: 'In the Tosefta the seating-order in the Synagogue is described as follows: the elders ... sit with their face turned to the congregation and their backs to the Ark. The lectern for the prayer-leader is also so placed, likewise for the priests when they give the blessing. The whole congregation, on the contrary, and the Synagogue-servants, turn their face to the Ark.' ('In der Tosefta wird die Sitzordnung in der Synagoge wie folgt beschrieben: die Presbyter ... sitzen mit dem Gesichte zur Gemeinde und dem Rücken zur Lade, das Vorbeterpult steht ebenso, desgleichen die Priester, wenn sie den Segen sprechen; die ganze Gemeinde hingegen und der Synagogendiener wenden das Gesicht der Lade zu.') Ibid., p. 475. **27** E. Peterson, 'Die geschichtliche Bedeutung der jüdischen Gebetsrichtung' in E. Peterson, *Frühkirche, Judentum und Gnosis: Studien und Untersuchungen* (Rome, 1959), pp 1–14. **28** 'He who was summoned by the leader came to the Torah and read.' Elbogen, *Der jüdische Gottesdienst*, p. 170. **29** 'First of all separate sections of the Pentateuch were put into relief, such as the songs, the Decalogue, the penal admonitions, by which the blessing was asked for at the beginning and the end. In Babylon, however, one went further and let each reader summoned pronounce the blessing before and after his Torah-section.'

Summary of the Synagogal elements

First, we have to refer to a remark of Albert Gerhards, who points out that Jewish and Christian elements of worship influenced each another. Here we are only pointing out the most basic and relevant topics that would prove a certain continuity alongside all necessary distinctions.[30] If in this sense we summarize the fundamental elements of Synagogue worship that relate to our context we find on principle a spatially orientated worship, an authority that constitutes the assembly, a fixed order of seating, and ritual formulas both to introduce and conclude the lessons.

The architectural expression consequent upon the transition from the Synagogue to the Church is to be found in the spatial architecture of the East Syrians.[31] Here we find a genuine tangible Christian understanding of liturgy and, joined to this, a new concept of sacred space.

Spatially orientated prayer is maintained but changed. Peterson has characterized the difference between this understanding and that of Judaism as follows:

> In Judaism the heavenly temple is modelled on the earthly, heavenly worship on the earthly, in Christianity it is the opposite.[32]

('Zunächst wurden einzelne Stücke des Pentateuchs, wie die verschiedenen Lieder, der Dekalog, die Strafandrohungen herausgehoben, bei ihnen am Anfang und Ende die Benediktion gefordert, in Babylonien aber ging man noch weiter und ließ *jeden Aufgerufenen* vor und nach seinem Toraabschnitte die Benediktion sprechen.') Ibid., p. 172. In this context it is interesting to note that the ambo is descended from its synagogal predecessor. 'Probably derived from the almemor of the Synagogue, in the ecclesial edifice the "ambo" designates a raised place where the lectors and deacons read the biblical texts and the prayer of the faithful, the deacon proclaims the *Exultet*; the psalmist alternates with the people a responsorial psalm; and finally from here on the feast of the Epiphany notification is given of the movable feasts and important events are communicated (on the ambo of Sancta Sophia in Constantinople the Emperors were crowned).' ('Probabilmente derivato dall'*almemor* delle sinagoghe, nell'edificio ecclesiale "ambone" designa un luogo elevato dove i lettori e i diaconi leggono i testi biblici e la preghiera dei fedeli, il diacono proclama l'*Exultet*; il salmista alterna con il popolo il salmo responsoriale; da esso, infine, vengono notificate le feste mobili nella solennità dell'Epifania, e comunicati importanti avvenimenti (sull'ambone di Santa Sofia in Constantinopoli venivano incoronati gli imperatori).') Crispino Valenziano, *L'Ambone: Aspetti Storici in L'Ambone* (Magnano, 2006), p. 89. **30** See his article, A. Gerhards, 'Vom jüdischen zum christlichen Gotteshaus?' in Rudolf Voderholzer, *Der Logos-gemäße Gottesdienst: Theologie der Liturgie bei Joseph Ratzinger* (Regensburg, 2009), pp 112–38. Gerhards refers to Martin Wallraff's study (M. Wallraf, 'Die Ursprünge der christlichen Gebetsostung', *ZKG*, 111 (2000) where Walraff states, that also in Judaism prayer facing East was known. 'Dort findet sich neben der allgemein bekannten und später allein beherrschenden Tradition des Gebets nach Jerusalem auch die Tradition, sich zum Gebet nach Osten zu wenden. Es gibt keinen Grund daran zu zweifeln, dass das sich bildende Christentum an beiden Traditionen partizipierte. Der anschließende Prozess der Ausdifferenzierung war nicht ein Prozess einseitiger Ablösung des Christentums vom Judentum, sondern ein Prozess gegenseitiger Bereicherung …' quoted in Gerhards, *Vom jüdischen zum christlichen Gotteshaus*, p. 123. **31** Bouyer recognizes the 'oldest type of a Christian church' in the 'old Syrian churches'. Bouyer, *Liturgie und Architektur*, p. 30. **32** Petersen, *Frühkirche*, p. 4.

This means that when Christians face east it is to Jerusalem descending with Christ from heaven. Petersen states that there the *apsis* occurs in pagan as well as Jewish and Christian places of worship. Where the pagans, however, prayed in the direction of the image of a god, for which the Jews substitute the Torah-shrine, the Christians interpreted the *apsis* vault as the vault of heaven.[33] According to Petersen the Christian orientation of prayer transformed 'the Jewish *apsis* or prayer-niche into the heaven of the Christian *apsis*, and turned the horizontal prayer-direction of the Jews into one directed 'to above'.[34]

As Bouyer remarks, looking to the early East Syrian churches, this eschatological and spatial orientation is related to the abandonment of sacred buildings like the Temple:

> The new Jerusalem, which the Christians await, is not some kind of reconstruction of the old one. It is a heavenly Jerusalem, whose foundations are 'above' and do not stand on a precise place in this world. For the Christians, just as for the Jews, it will be revealed at the coming of the Messiah. However, at his second and definitive *parousia* he will not return the *shekina* to where they formerly were. The heavenly City will be formed out of the gathering of the elect in his resurrected Body, which will achieve completion in the Church of the Last Days. And in this City no temple is needed; for the Lord himself in his union with the elect will be the eternal temple.[35]

The early Christians, however, saw this as the place for the Eucharist, the altar.[36]

The Service of the Word of the early East Syrians is directed from the bema in the nave towards the altar, the Ark of the New Covenant. The old Ark, fulfilled in the Gospels, was still located 'between bema and *apsis*' and, as in the Synagogue, it was decorated 'with curtain and candlesticks'.[37] Clergy and people are recognizable as two distinct groups, but fitted into the old understanding of the *Quahal*.[38] It is here that the intimate connection between the primitive Lord's Supper and the synagogal Liturgy of the Word is to be found and, at the same time, theologically highlighted. This all seems to have, on the surface, little to do with our theme of the opening rites of the Mass.

---

33 Cf. Petersen, *Frühkirche*, p. 11. 34 Cf. Petersen, *Frühkirche*, p. 12. Cf. also on this Lang, *Conversi ad Dominum*, p. 40. 35 Bouyer, *Liturgie und Architektur*, p. 33. 36 Ibid., p. 35. 37 Ibid., p. 31. 38 Cf. Bouyer, *Liturgie und Architektur*, p. 39, also p. 36.

But with these, if few, points of reference we can identify important developments at a very early stage. It is repeatedly emphasized that Christianity
exploded the traditional concept of sacred space. There existed simple
domestic gathering places, which were sanctified by 'living stones'. Despite the
fundamental correctness of this affirmation there is, nevertheless, especially
today, the danger of portraying such domestic prayer as formless, similar to
what takes place in modern 'grassroots communities'.

By joining the Supper of the Lord to the Service of the Word, and namely
at a time when the Church had not yet separated itself from all the Jewish
forms of worship, it must have developed the earliest ritualizations which went
beyond the rite of the original *eucharistia*. In the separation of the Eucharist
from the early Christian meal-community of the disciples of Jesus,[39] the ritual
meal form was surpassed and the way was opened for the development of
richer ceremonies. This first took place in private houses. On the opening rites
the following can be said; the disciples were constituted according to Jewish
usage as a meal-community. Here we can discern an original essential element
of the opening rites in the singling out and differentiation of the participants.

The community at the one table is organized. The president had the place
of honour, although descending places of honour in principle existed. Already
the *domus ecclesiae* in Dura Europos[40] had an estrade for the bishop[41] in the
actual space for worship. With regard to worship before Constantine, the
historian Kritzinger has called special attention to the central and normative
place of the bishop:

> Even if the origins of individual spatial elements in the churches and
> symbolic gestures are of pagan or Jewish provenance, it seems to me though
> that the office of bishop is bound up with the representative will of the
> Christian community, and to have enabled a conscious staging of
> ceremonial-shaped rites before the background of a deliberately arranged
> space. It is first the appearance of the bishop, who as representative of the
> congregations mediated between God and the faithful in areas expressly
> conceived for worship, that let the buildings again have representative
> character.[42]

---

39 Gamber, *Domus Ecclesiae*, p. 97.   **40** Around 240/250 for Christian customs adapted house. See R.
Krautheimer, *Early Christian and Byzantine architecture*, Revised by R. Krautheimer and S. Cureic (New
Haven, 1986), p. 27.   **41** Ibid., p. 27.   **42** Kritzinger, *Bischöfliche Repräsentation*, p. 168.

This plainly proves the ceremonial shape of the celebration.[43] The celebrating assembly accomplishes a spatially-orientated prayer,[44] directed to the east and thereby to Christ.[45]

As the Jewish so also the Christian liturgical assembly found basilical architecture especially suitable for cultic purposes. The historian Kritzinger remarks:

> Independently of the archaeological evidence there are indications which permit one to conceive the Christian churches in the third century as basilicas in the best ancient pagan sense of the word.[46]

In conclusion I would like to turn to the concept of 'ecclesia', with which the early Church designated itself and which led to the term *domus ecclesiae*. Joseph Ratzinger refers to the narrow connection of this concept with the Old Testament assembly of the People of God:

> The Greek word, which lives on in the Latin derivative, is based on the Old Testament root qahal, which is usually translated as 'assembly of the people'.[47]

According to Ratzinger this word signifies 'the spiritual and eschatological centre of the concept of people'.[48] Nevertheless, many concrete meanings can be attributed to the term:

> It means the assembly for worship as well as the local community, the Church in a larger geographical region as well as finally the sole Church of Jesus Christ itself.[49]

Beginning with the third century the concept of 'ecclesia' is found in use for Christian gathering spaces.[50] The theological conclusion of this means that the

---

43 See Kritzinger, *Bischöfliche Repräsentation*, pp 193ff.   **44** Cf. on this whole topic Lang, *Conversi ad Dominum*, especially pp 33ff.   **45** If Gamber's hypothesis proves correct, then the original seating-order of the Last Supper has been conserved in the benches for the clergy. Cf. also: 'The staging of worship went so far that already from the middle of the 3rd century the deacons indicated to the faithful their place and in the various spatial-parts of the churches provided for quiet.' ('Die Inszenierung des Gottesdienstes ging seit etwa der Mitte des 3. Jahrhunderts bereits soweit, dass Diakone den Gläubigen ihren Platz anwiesen und in den verschiedenen Raumteilen der Kirchen für Ruhe sorgten.') Kritzinger, *Bischöfliche Repräsentation*, p. 178. **46** Ibid., p. 16. Cf. also: 'Christianity adapted the most suitable form of edifice for the celebration of assemblies.' ('Das Christentum adaptierte die für die Zelebration der Versammlungen am geeignetsten scheinende Bauform.') Ibid., p. 166.   **47** J. Ratzinger, 'Ursprung und Wesen der Kirche' in J. Ratzinger, *Kirche – Zeichen unter den Völkern* (Freiburg, 2010), p. 231.   **48** Ibid., p. 232.   **49** Ibid., p. 232.   **50** See

gathering of the local community represents the gathering of the entire Church. It transcends the local community. This gathering has its own dynamism, and it is an eschatological one.[51]

To summarize: about this very early period, one can assert that at the opening of the Liturgy the assembly appears as organised, and its spatially orientated prayer is directed to Christ. At the same time the place of the bishop is especially brought to prominence. As the concept of *ecclesia* is now used for the gathering place it is clear that in the liturgical assembly the Church, of which the bishop is the visible expression, realises itself and is led to her deepest unity. The local gathering now refers to the gathering of the Church as a whole.

Evolution from Constantine the Great (272–337)

A further evolution can be discerned with the Emperor Constantine. Christianity asserted a strong public presence.[52] Already the concept of house-church itself, according to ancient understanding, necessarily emphasized the place of him who as *pater familias* led the house, namely the bishop. Now this understanding of the term evolves from meaning the family to meaning society. Karl-Heinrich Bieritz refers to the symbolism of the old Christian basilica as image of the cosmos:

> It has been shown that the basilica 'is to be regarded as *abbreviatur* of the ancient city', while the basilica itself is intended to be the image of the cosmos.[53]

The changeover from house-church to basilica would then be, at the same time, the transition from *oikos* (as social unit) to *polis*, and so, in a certain way, must be understood as the 'rendering public' of Christian worship (in the sense of *cultus publicus*).[54]

The forms of representation must also express this.[55] Bouyer makes an interesting observation about the liturgical architecture of Constantinian times:

Kritzinger, *Bischöfliche Repräsentation*, p. 161.   **51** Note: 'In der versammelten Gemeinde ereignet sich das "Heute" der kontinuierlichen Heilssorge Gottes in erinnernder Vergangenheit und antizipierter Vollendung.' ('In the gathered community occurs the *Hodie* of the continuing carrying of God in the past, which is commemorated and in the future, which is anticipated.') Gerhards, *Vom jüdischen zum christlichen Gotteshaus*, p. 117.   **52** The thesis of Constantine raising the clergy to the nobility seems to be refuted. See Kritzinger, *Bischöfliche Repräsentation*, p. 8.   **53** H.B. Meyer, *Was Kirchenbau bedeutet: Ein Führer zu Sinn, Geschichte und Gegenwart* (Freiburg, 1984), p. 34.   **54** K.H. Bieritz, *Liturgik* (Berlin, 2004), p. 97.   **55** Such a penetration of the public sphere does not result in an act of state.

Despite this fundamental transformation the original Constantinian basilica conserved as much as possible from the primitive arrangement of Christian churches, as we have found in the early Syrian Church.[56]

The bema was transformed into the *schola*, which was delimited by two ambos. The large candlestick near to the bigger ambo remains, as in the old disposition, close to the Ark.[57] Since Gregory the Great the altar is now clearly included in a genuine clerical area.[58] Nevertheless, according to the latest archaeological evidence it is probable that house-churches were maintained into the fourth century,[59] and this still even at a time in which the bishop became increasingly important and an extended clerical assistance had taken shape.[60]

Kim Bowes has researched the implementation of early Christianity in ancient Roman culture. In the course of this it is interesting to observe that Christianity brought with itself a 'crisis of sacred space'.[61] On the one hand, there was the new understanding of the holy:

> The fundamental ... of repeated assurances that God might be worshiped anywhere: the ubiquity of God's presence implied that no place, not even communal worship sites, had any particular holiness.

On the other, however, Bowes states a certain materialization of the holy, namely at the tombs of the martyrs and in the Eucharist itself:

> The eucharistic bread, wherever it was carried, likewise created spaces of particular sacredness whose purity, according to Novatian or Cyprian, had to be particularly guarded.

56 Bouyer, *Liturgie und Architektur*, p. 47. 57 Ibid., p. 48. 58 Ibid., p. 50. 59 But in addition to this it must be noted that the period of the monumental basilicas in the city of Rome first begins in the early 5th century: 'As far as the city's public Christian topography was concerned, the Constantinian "revolution" was largely an extramural affair. The great majority of the Constantinian basilicas were martyr shrines and cemetery basilicas, and even the great Lateran cathedral layed hard against the city walls ... However, it was only in the early years of the fifth century that these monumental, three-aisled basilicas appear with any frequency.' K. Bowes, *Private worship, public values and religious change in late antiquity* (Cambridge, 2008), p. 72. 'Given the slow pace of church building, it seems most likely that Christians of the fourth century continued to worship in the same places as did their ancestors of the third, namely in homes or other private spaces.' Ibid., p. 73. 60 'Even as the bishop of Rome grew in stature and the clerical and liturgical apparatus became ever more firmly established, the physical locus of worship for thousands of Christians continued to be the homes of their own elite. While these churches were not "private" in the same sense as their domestic church cousins, their domestic topography and particular domestic arrangements kept them closely bound to their individual communities, and to the influence of their founding patrons.' Ibid., pp 74ff. 61 Ibid., p. 220.

The clergy, thus, had a protective duty here towards the holy.

This also means that the insight into this holiness made no inconsiderable contribution to the development of the rites, not only in the case of the clergy but also in what concerns sacred space. Neither of these seems to me to be adequately appreciated in current debate. Both of them, however, are important in the case of the opening rites.

In this epoch the faith is joined more strongly to the conditioning factors of society. Baldovin gives us some important indications of how this should be fundamentally rated at its true value when he observes that:

> liturgy is not simply and immediately God-given, revelation in itself, but rather part of the human grace-prompted response to revelation. Any theology which exclusively emphasizes the activity of God in worship through the proclamation of the Word neglects the manifestation of God through liturgical activity itself, as well as the important human cultural factor involved in all worshipping experience. When the human response factor is minimized, the forms that worship takes will be *adiaphora*, relatively unimportant. However, if the human response to the divinely communicated grace is important, then the cultural forms in which worship is enacted must be taken seriously.[62]

The stational liturgy

At this point we must glance at the stational liturgies,[63] which developed in consequence of the religious peace in the great centres of the Roman Empire. These are to be seen 'as the natural outcome of the very nature of the Church in an urban milieu'.[64] Yet differences are due to the peculiarities of each city and to its cultural context.[65] In our context it is worth noting that the stational liturgy had a greater influence on no other part of the Mass than on the

62 J. Baldovin, *The urban character of Christian worship. The origins, development and meaning of stational liturgy* (Rome, 1987), p. 254.   63 With Baldovin we define stational liturgy thus: 'Stational liturgy is the service of worship of a designated church, shrine or public place in or near a city or town, on a designated feast, fast, or commemoration, which is presided over by the bishop or his representative, and intended as the local church's main liturgical celebration of the day.' Ibid., p. 37.   64 Ibid., p. 248. See also: 'In addition, Jerusalem, Rome and Constantinople were not the only late antique cities that developed stational systems of worship. Every large urban centre of late antiquity possessed a liturgical system that was both mobile and centred around the bishop of the city.' Ibid., p. 248.   65 'Jerusalem, Rome, and Constantinople all show some basic similarities with regard to the phenomenon of stational worship. At the same time it is important to recognize that the difference in their patterns of worship were inspired by the fact that Christians in all three places had to adapt their worship to a particular situation. Local circumstances, such as the nature of the pre-Constantinian Christian tradition, topography, and especially the historical fortunes of each city were responsible for the peculiar shape that each stational liturgy took. Worship does not develop in a vacuum, but rather between the dialectic of Christian faith

opening rites.[66] It is, moreover, of significance 'that in terms of some of their particulars the major stational systems did influence each other'.[67]

The Roman stational liturgy: the structure of Ordo romanus I *at the opening rites*

According to current research the most convenient earliest source which offers a complete ceremonial picture of the Roman Rite and its stational liturgy is the *Ordo romanus I*, which dates from the turn of the seventh to the eighth century. What does the *Ordo romanus I* say about the entrance rites?[68]

In solemn procession the pope rides to the Lateran. The greater part of the clergy awaits him in the basilica, whereby all the ranks of the clergy followed a strictly established order of seating. The pope is ritually greeted before the basilica. He goes to the sacristy. There, the Gospel Book is prepared which afterwards is brought into the church by an acolyte and laid upon the altar by a subdeacon. The pope changes his vestments, this also being ritually done.[69] The pope is informed of the ministers who will assist him. Following this he gives the arch-paraphonist the signal to begin. Incense is used.

The *schola* takes its place before the altar and begins the antiphon to the *Introitus*. During the procession the pope makes use of the former imperial *sustentatio ritualis*. The pope is preceded by the *Subdiaconus sequens* and seven acolytes. Before the altar the pope, or a deacon, greets the Sancta. Then the pope bows to the altar and a prayer is recited. He blesses himself and gives the *Pax*. Following this the pope gives a signal to the leader of the schola. An *oratorium* is brought to the pope.[70] While the Introit is being concluded the Pope prays on this *oratorium*. The deacons reverence the altar. The pope kisses the altar and the Gospel Book. He goes to his throne and faces *ad orientem*. The *Kyrie* immediately follows the *Introitus*.[71] The pope intones the Gloria *versus populum* and then turns again to the east. The liturgy changes a little if celebrated by a delegate of the pope; he receives less honour.[72] According to de Blaauw there was also a presbyteral variant for the entrance procession.[73]

---

and a particular social and cultural milieu.' Ibid., p. 234. **66** Cf. Baldovin, *The urban character*, p. 241.
67 Ibid., p. 248. **68** We follow the synopsis of Johannes Nebel, *Die Entwicklung des Römischen Meßritus im ersten Jahrtausend, anhand der Ordines Romani – eine synopstische Darstellung* (Rome, 2000), pp 86–101.
69 The exactly given order of sequence speaks for this, as also the assignment to the ministers and the petition for a blessing of the Subdiaconus sequence *Jube, domne, benedicere* and the response of the pope *Salvet nos Dominus*. **70** Nebel thinks that this could be a prayer-carpet (ibid., p. 96). Another interpretation is that it could be a *faldistorium*, which the pope subsequently always uses when kneeling down. **71** The number of alternations has not yet been fixed and is decided *ad hoc* by the pope. **72** de Blaauw, *Cultus et Decor*, p. 67. Cf. the directions of the OR II (just as old as the OR I). **73** Ibid., p. 80.

We can summarize the essential ritual elements of *Ordo romanus I* as follows:

1. Clear separation of clergy and laity at the beginning of the celebration
2. Ritual reception of the bishop before the celebration
3. Ritual vesting
4. Double opening structure:
   a. Celebrant and assisting ministers enter, prayer before the altar, *Pax*
   b. *Schola* and people are, on the contrary, occupied with the chant of the Introit
   c. *Kyrie* and *Gloria* sung with a certain alternation
   d. At the *Pax vobis* and the *Collecta* the opening acts of the pope and of the people have a common closing

It is important at this point to devote more detailed attention to the entrance procession. Paul de Clerck has refuted the thesis that the *Kyrie* at the beginning of the Roman Mass is a remainder of the so-called *Deprecatio Gelasii*.[74] He states that it owes its origins much more to the processions. In this sense Baldovin observes:

> The introduction of the *Kyrie* into the Roman Mass was due to the popularity of stational processions.[75]

At the same time the author notes the influence of the stational liturgy of Constantinople on Rome. A form of the litany accompanying the procession in Constantinople was 'the *ektene*, which ended with a three-fold *Kyrie eleison*'.[76] Baldovin arrives at the conclusion:

---

74 P. de Clerck, *La prière universelle dans les liturgies latines anciennes; temoinages patristiques et textes liturgiques* (Münster, 1977). His theses are quoted in the analysis of Baldovin, *The urban character*, pp 244ff. As evidence for this vestige of the prayer of the faithful was held to be a text of Gregory the Great, *Letter to Bishop John of Syracuse*, PL 77/956 BC. In addition Vicenzo Raffa: 'The motives adopted demonstrate the unfoundedness of the opinion advanced to interpret the text of St Gregory as a document of the presence, up until his time, of a prayer of the faithful in non-daily masses, of which the *Kyrie–Christe* would represent a trace.' ('I motivi addotti mostra l'infondatezza dell'opinione invasava di interpretare il testo di S. Gregorio come documento della presenza fino al suo tempore di una preghiera dei fedeli nelle messe non quotidiane, della quale il *Kyrie–Christe* rappresenterebbe un resto.') V. Raffa, *Liturgia eucaristica, Mistagogia della Messa: dalla storia e dalla teologia alla pratica pastorale* (Rome, 1998), p. 241.   75 Baldovin, *The urban character*, p. 245.   76 Ibid., p. 246.

Therefore, what the Roman liturgy adopted when it added the Kyrie to the entrance rite was not a form of the prayer of the faithful that had originally stood in the place of the old *orationes sollemnes*, but rather a rogational litany that had been employed in the stational processions of Constantinople, perhaps via Milan. Therefore, it is clear that the Roman *Kyrie* is the direct descendant of Constantinopolitan stational practice.[77]

The place of the *Kyrie* after the Introit justifies the author with an 'imitation of the stational practice of having the litany follow the antiphonal psalmody'.[78] In conclusion he remarks that from the middle of the sixth century the litany had fallen out of use on normal days, and that only the *Kyrie* remained.[79]

In this context, mention should be made of the actual *forma extraordinaria* of the Roman Mass at the Easter Vigil – even after the changes made by Pius XII – and what its origins are. The entrance takes place during the *Kyrie*. This *Kyrie* is simultaneously the conclusion of the litany at the blessing of the baptismal water as is also the *Kyrie* of the Mass. There is no Introit. According to Anton Baumstark's maxim of 'the maintenance of the ancient in high value liturgical time',[80] this is the oldest tangible element of the Roman liturgical heritage.

The character of the Ordo romanus primus *in relation to the opening rites*

Johannes Nebel has emphasized, as one of the characteristics of the identity of the rite which the *Ordines romani* describe, the multiplicity of clerical liturgical ministries.[81] From the beginning, the liturgical assembly is in fact hierarchically structured. Sible de Blaauw notes: 'In the Roman liturgy a strict separation of clergy and faithful was in force.'[82] Nevertheless, the people are absolutely not passive. They participate in the celebration in a different manner to the clergy, above all by singing and by participating in the processions.[83] The *schola*

---

77 Ibid., p. 247.   **78** Ibid., p. 247.   **79** Ibid., p. 247.   **80** A. Baumstark, 'Das Gesetz der Erhaltung des Alten in liturgisch hochwertiger Zeit', *JLw* (Münster, 1927).   **81** 'It concerns a celebration characterised by the complementarity of diverse ministries: the celebrant, the deacons the other clergy, the cantors the lectors, and the other inferior ministers, all have their precise task.' ('Si tratta di una celebrazione caratterizzata dalla complementarietà dei diversi ministri: Il celebrante, i diaconi, gli altri clerici, i cantori, i lettori ed i ministri inferiori, tutto hanno il loro compito preciso.') Nebel, *Il rito della Messa romana*, p. 723. **82** 'Nella liturgia romana vigeva una stretta separazione gerarchica tra clero e fedeli.' de Blaauw, *Cultus et Decor*, p. 79. The concept of *presbyterium* included the total area where the clergy stayed: 'But since in the *ordines* with this term is not only indicated that part in front of the altar assigned to the lower clergy, but also that space behind the altar reserved to the pope and the cardinals (OR I 24, OR XV, 18).' ('Poiché però negli ordines con questo termine non si indica soltanto quella parte dinanzi all'altare assegnata al basso clero, ma anche lo spazio dietro all'altare riservato al papa e ai cardinali (OR I 24, OR XV 18).') de Blaauw, *Cultus et Decor*, p. 79.   **83** Nebel, *Il rito della Messa romana*, p. 723.

consisted (at least for the greater part) of clerics.[84] The seating order of the people was also structured, namely according to public office and sex. It is interesting to observe that the people participating in the celebration are also attributed a representative position. The people represented the totality of the Christians of the City, and later at the developed pontifical liturgy, of global Christianity.[85] This means that the idea of the assembly of the People of the Covenant is still quite present, even if in a modified and more evolved form.

The entrance procession itself had a theological meaning. Baldovin clearly distinguishes between the entrance in the Roman Rite and the Byzantine usage. The Introit was never a chant accompanying the gathering of the people. Even when preceded by a procession,[86] the assembling of the people was distinct from the entry of the bishop. While in Byzantium bishop and people entered together, in Rome, however:

> Even on days when there were popular supplicatory processions the people entered the church before the bishop, and the entrance psalm was sung while he entered, but only after he changed his vestments. The more usual procedure, reflected in the *Ordo romanus I*, was to have the people gather at the stational church beforehand and await the personage-centred procession of the bishop.[87]

Therefore, the entrance procession of the Mass is person-centred. These types of processions did not have the gathering of the people for their goal but 'the focus was … rather on the progress of the bishop to the stational church at Rome and the procession of the Byzantine emperor to the Great Church for the liturgy on certain days'.[88] For it, Baldovin cites ancient pagan Roman examples.[89] But it is in the nature of things that a large number of assisting ministers has in itself a certain symbolic character, which illustrates the importance of a person. In this respect the Roman liturgy is also the heir of an

---

84 'A certain number of members of the schola were probably ordained subdeacons.' ('Un certo numero dei membri della schola era probabilmente ordinato suddiacono.') de Blaauw, *Cultus et Decor*, p. 66. **85** 'The people who assisted at the celebration symbolically represented the Christians of the City, and with the passage of the centuries, ever more those of the Globe.' ('Il popolo che assisteva alla celebrazione rappresentava simbolicamente la communità cristiana dell'Urbe e, col passare dei secoli, sempre di più quella dell'Orbe.'); de Blaauw, *Cultus et Decor*, p. 67. **86** 'Care must be taken not to confuse popular liturgical processions with the papal processions and entrance rite of the eucharist. The origins of the latter are akin to imperial practice, and their use in Rome was directly influenced Constantinople.' Baldovin, *The urban character*, pp 159ff. **87** Ibid., p. 247. He adds the observation: 'Therefore the use of the psalm in the rite of the Roman eucharist was related to the practice of stational liturgy but not directly to the stational processions.' **88** Ibid., p. 234. **89** *pompa triumphalis and pompa circenses*, ibid., p. 234.

earlier time. The entry of the bishop is already documented from the fourth century, and further developed. This statement aids us to a balanced consideration of the Roman stational liturgy as such. At the same time, it should be remembered that for some liturgists, this even today is regarded as a decadent form of liturgy. Already some of the liturgists who were pledged to the liturgical movement were precisely those who were tempted in their assessment of the Roman stational liturgy to interpret it as pure imperial ceremonial, and in fact, subsequently, as the evolution of the primitive Christian community to a state Church. In rather terse terms Johannes Wagner, who after Vatican II led the *Coetus X* for the reform of the liturgy of the Mass, states that: 'the pontifical stational liturgy ... as that form of the celebration of Mass that had already become a kind of act of state'.[90] Here the question is not even once asked whether these external forms were intended to express a genuine spiritual/theological content or not.

Sible de Blaauw treats of the spiritual significance of the ceremonies of the stational liturgy many times. Referring to the origins of the stational liturgy itself, she holds that it was able to guarantee the unity of the Church in a particular city and the special place of the bishop within the community at a time of continuous growth in the numbers of those baptised and the emergence of multiple places of worship administered by simple priests. De Blaauw concedes that many details come from the imperial ceremonial.[91] Nevertheless, it remains open if these were directly adopted in Rome or by detour from the court of Byzantium.[92] Of importance, however, is the remark:

> The pope used such forms liturgically to express the concept of primacy over the entire Church, with eventual implications of regal power, as the famous *Constitutum Constantini* of the years 754–67 claimed.[93]

The primitive idea of the gathering of the local community as a sign of gathering the entire Church in this sense is developed by stressing the importance of the one, who represents the unity of the entire church, namely, the Roman Pontiff.

---

90 J. Wagner, 'Reflexionen über Funktion und Stellenwert von Introitus, Kyrie und Gloria in der Meßfeier', *LJ* (Münster, 1967), p. 40.   **91** Ibid., p. 36.   **92** 'But is not always clear if these were taken directly from the late antique Roman tradition, or if they were reimported to Rome via the ceremonial of the Byzantine court.' ('Non è sempre chiaro però se esso sia stato preso direttamente dalla tradizione tardoantica romana, oppure se sia stato reimportato a Roma attraverso il cerimoniale della corte bizantina.') Ibid., p. 36. **93** Ibid.

Aspects of further historical evolution

A detailed consideration of the further evolution of the Roman pontifical liturgy would largely go beyond the limits we have given to our theme. At this point it will only be noted that it is the position of the bishop which expresses itself in the Roman liturgy. We find, however, an emphasis on the episcopal celebrant already in traces of earlier forms of worship. Subsequently it will logically be more and more the primacy of the pope that expresses itself in the papal liturgy. Such a form of expression, though, is not state-representation, but rather a profound spiritual representation in ancient forms.

For the period of the Gregorian reform (eleventh to twelfth centuries) De Blaauw states:

> The pontiff was no longer in the first place the bishop of Rome but the supreme pastor of the universal Church. The centre of his power no longer resided in the urban community but in the administrative apparatus of the universal Church established in the papal palace. *Curia romana* becomes synonymous with *ecclesia romana*, and the palatine chapel constituted the liturgical centre.[94]

Thus is born the concept of the *cappella papalis*, which later will designate the papal liturgy as such.[95] Historically we can note that the prayer at the altar at the conclusion of the entrance received a textual formulation in the *Confiteor*. Psalm 42 was added later, and first prayed on the way to the altar, eventually, however, being joined to the prayer at the altar steps.[96]

CHARACTERISTICS OF THE ROMAN LITURGY

The entrance rites have always distinguished the celebrant in a special way from the rest of the assembly and set him off. Yet the idea of papal representation grows in the liturgy and, at the same time, through it the insight into the teaching on the papacy itself. Let us summarize again the theological meaning of this representation with the excellent words of Ulrich Nersinger:

---

94 Ibid., p. 38. In the further development Germanic elements were added to the older forms of Byzantine representation. Cf. De Blaauw, *Cultus et Decor*, p. 39.   **95** Ibid., p. 38.   **96** Cf. Rupert Berger, *Pastoralliturgisches Handlexikon* (Freiburg, 2008), p. 491.

Not to add something to their own authority in an excessive striving after power, but conscious of a commission conditioned through history and the Good News, the popes placed themselves in the succession of the Caesars and therefore accomplished consistently and unperturbed the *imitatio imperii*. The *adventus papae* was the expression of the 'way of being of the *ecclesia triumphans*'.[97]

The Vicar of Christ on earth celebrated this triumph on behalf of the Church in which Christ lives on, as the surmounting of temporal imperfection, as the victory of life over death. The ceremonial 'appearance' of the pope was thus truly a triumphal representation.[98]

The structure of the opening rites in the present-day forma extraordinaria of the Roman Rite

When we pose the question about the entrance rites of the *forma extraordinaria* we must preface this with an important clarification of methodology, which genuinely results from the historical considerations so far: the *forma normativa* of the traditional Roman Mass is the *Missa pontificalis*, indeed properly speaking the papal Mass. We find the earliest evidence of this principle already in the use of the *fermentum* in the stational liturgy.[99] Looking at the early sources, De Blaauw notes: 'In generic terms the presbyteral liturgy can be characterized as a derivative of the official one of the bishop.'[1]

Nevertheless, in the Roman liturgy it is a question, as we have already seen, of a special case, in that it reflects the theological evolution of the teaching on the Primacy, and thereby has the character of a model for the entire Western Church. While the papal liturgy would always bring this more to the fore, the presbyteral liturgy, which derives from the papal liturgy, evolved in another direction.[2] Yet the pontifical liturgy maintained a fundamental continuity in its evolution.[3] Consequently, there are from the Roman origins, departing

---

97 J. Träger, *Der reitende Papst: Ein Beitrag zur Ikonographie des Papsttums* (München, 1973), p. 93. The word triumphans means the church as it is participating at the triumph of Christ and his Paschal Mystery. **98** U. Nersinger, *Liturgien und Zeremonien am Päpstlichen Hof* (Bonn, 2010), p. 393. **99** See above and de Blaauw, *Cultus et Decor*, p. 30. **1** de Blaauw, *Cultus et Decor*, p. 31. **2** 'For obvious reasons this conception of worship was a stranger to the presbyteral liturgy and in the long run, by way of the evolution of the pontifical liturgy, the latter and the diverse variants of the presbyteral liturgy would come to be always more understood as two independent traditions.' ('Per ovvie ragioni questa conception del culto era estranea alla liturgia presbiterale e a lungo andare, per via dell'evoluzione della liturgia pontificale, quest'ultima e le diverse varianti della litrugia presbiteriale vennero intense sempre più come due tradizioni indipendenti.'). Ibid., p. 36. **3** 'Still, the liturgical continuity of the pontifical Mass from 700 on is the characteristic the most evident of all the mutations and renovations.' ('Tuttavia, la continuità liturgica della messa pontificale a partire dal 700 è il carattere più evidente di tutti i mutamenti e i rinnovamenti.'). Ibid., p. 39.

from the fundamental pontifical form, many gradations today in the *forma extrordinaria* of the Roman liturgy. As a result the *Missa sollemnis* is that form derived from the pontifical liturgy of a priestly celebrant. In order to understand the inner structure of the rites and ceremonies the *Missa lecta* should not in any case be the point of departure. In the same way the Missal should not simply be opened at the *Ordo Missae*, which only has the beginning for the priest: *In nomine Patris ... Introibo ...* but doesn't tell, how the faithful begin Mass.

The sung Mass

The liturgy begins (as in *Ordo romanus I*) in the sacristy, where the vesting is more or less ritualized, and takes place at the very least with prayer. We observe that (also as in *Ordo romanus I*) the Mass has a double beginning. On the one hand the celebrant and his assisting ministers carry out certain actions. They enter, reverence the altar, and say the prayers at the foot of the altar. At least, of these prayers, the *Confiteor* of these prayers genuinely evolved from the prayerful silence of the pope in *Ordo romanus I*. After the prayers at the foot of the altar the celebrant kisses the altar. Then follows the rite of incensation, which is exclusively concerned with the altar and the celebrant. The celebrant silently prays the Introit and the *Kyrie*. The last two points are late developments and do not touch the identity of the rite. On the other hand we find in this double opening the joint activity of the *schola* and all other participants. They sing or hear the Introit and *Kyrie*. For the celebrant then the beginning of the Mass is as it stands in the *Ordo Missae*: 'In nomine Patris ... Introibo ad altare Dei.' For everyone else Mass begins with the singing or hearing of the Introit. This is the reason why they make the sign of the Cross accompanying the first words of the Introit. This double beginning is proper to all forms of the *Missa in cantu*.

  In the pontifical Mass there are the following peculiarities. The bishop recites the *Praeparatio Missae*. After a lavabo he is ceremonially vested, be it at a proper altar or another place. The bishop enters with a larger number of assisting ministers than a simple priest. Besides the deacon and subdeacon he has at least an assistant priest at his side. During the entrance procession the subdeacon solemnly bears the Gospel Book. In *Ordo romanus I* he would have placed it upon the altar shortly before the procession. The bishop first takes the maniple at the *Indulgentiam* of the prayers at the foot of the altar. After kissing the altar he kisses the Gospel of the day in the opened Gospel Book.

Yet the papal liturgy knows in the (momentarily not practiced) older form the same *Adventus papae*, that is, the pope enters accompanied by his court and the procurators of the religious orders. All of this constitutes a representation of the *Ecclesia universalis*, whose ideal image should be the Roman Curia.[4] At the beginning the pope visits the Blessed Sacrament Chapel for a short silent adoration of the *Sanctissimum*. We can think here of the greeting of the *Sancta* in *Ordo romanus I*. Thus the condensed heritage of *Ordo romanus I* is to be found especially in the pontifical ceremonies.

The low Mass as a down-graded simplified Solemn Mass

Structurally we find here all the elements, but in a reduced form. Above all the different tones of voice in which the texts are to be spoken show who the action-carrier is. Traditionally the prayers at the foot of the altar – even when the rubrics prescribe that they are to be spoken *clara voce* – are said a bit more softly since only the celebrant and the assisting clerics (or servers) are involved in this action. The Introit, *Kyrie*, and all the rest are, on the contrary, spoken aloud, because the whole community of the faithful is acting here. Those texts then which are chanted at a sung Mass are to be spoken at a missa lecta *clara voce*, the others either said softly or whispered. The *terminus technicus* 'High Mass rule'[5] describes this usage.

Even the said Mass stresses the hierarchical position of the celebrant. Accordingly, there is also a proper form of the *Missa lecta* for a bishop and prelates of the same rank, the *Missa praelaticia*. An essential element of emphasizing such a celebrant is here also the entrance – this time in choir habit – and a certain number of assisting ministers.

In addition it should be noted that the liturgical assembly is always structured. Clergy and religious have their place in choir, the people in the nave, the bishop on the throne, and the assisting clergy in the *presbyterium*. The allotment of the places of action of the celebrant corresponds to the *Ordines Romani I and II*.

Structure of the forma ordinaria

At the vesting we only find at the *Missa stationalis* of the bishop (that Mass that the diocesan bishop celebrates *ut sacerdos magnus sui gregis*)[6] concrete

---

4 See for the details Johannes Brinktrine, *Die feierliche Papstmesse: Die Zeremonien bei Selig- und Heiligsprechungen* (Rome, 1950), pp 3ff. **5** Berger, *Pastoralliturgisches Handlexikon*, pp 202ff. **6** *Caeremoniale episcoporum: Editio typica* (Rome, 1995), No. 119.

directions that allow the vesting to be seen as a liturgical act. Otherwise the vestments are put on without ceremony in the sacristy. The solemn entry is foreseen as usual.[7] A special adoration of the Blessed Sacrament is no longer foreseen at the entry of a solemn papal Mass.

The original double opening rite has now been replaced by a common beginning, whose core is represented by the *actus paenitentialis* (Penitential Rite). After the entry of the celebrant and those laity charged with liturgical functions there follows a common Sign of the Cross as opening and the liturgical greeting of the assembly by the celebrant.

Next *brevissimis verbis* can follow,[8] an introduction by the celebrant or someone else.[9] In principle the *actus paenitentialis* has three different forms. On Sundays it can be replaced by the Asperges, the Memorial of Baptism. The third form of the common Penitential Rite consists of a conflated *Kyrie*.[10]

How did these changes come about?

To understand these changes we must direct our attention to the praxis of the Liturgical Movement and its underlying theology. Therefore, first a look at the praxis.

At the beginning of the twentieth century representatives of the Liturgical Movement sought to enable the people actively to participate at Holy Mass. It is authenticated that the point of main effort often was not laid upon the sung liturgy, and it was forgotten that Pius X used the words *actuosa communicatio* in the context of a *motu proprio* on *Musica sacra*.[11]

Roman Stafin writes in his dissertation on Pius Parsch:

> The principle of the active participation of the people at Mass was for Pius Parsch, who directed the popular liturgical movement, decisive in the search for ... the community Mass. With the fundamental principle 'everything which does not belong to the Mass and which interferes with active participation, must be rejected', and taking into consideration the active participation of the faithful in the Mass in the early Church, Pius Parsch strove for thirty-five years to reform the existing forms of the Mass. The point of departure in this process was the *Missa recitata* (*lecta*), which was 'improved' and 'popularly moulded'.[12]

7 See R. Berger, *Die Feier der Heiligen Messe* (Freiburg, 2009), pp 196ff.   8 *Missale Romanum: Editio typica tertia* (Rome, 2002), p. 508.   9 *Sacerdos, vel diaconus vel alius minister, potest brevissimis verbis introducere fideles in Missa diei*. Ibid., p. 504.   10 *Postea sacerdos, vel diaconus, vel alius minister, sequentes, vel alias, invocationes cum Kyrie, eleison profert*. Ibid., p. 508.   11 See Pope Pius X, *Motu proprio Tra le sollecitudini*, 22 November 1903.   12 R. Stafin, *Eucharistie als Quelle der Gnade bei Pius Parsch: Ein neues Verhältnis zwischen Gott und*

A variant of this Mass was the one in which the people responded instead of the servers.[13] Let us hear again an account from that time, the year is 1928:

> In the year 1928 Pius Parsch indicated in regards to the Pray-Sing Mass that those parts of the Mass which 'were not well suited to be sung' and 'represented a very important act of prayer' were to be spoken.[14]

Among others the *Confiteor*, the *Credo*, and the first Offertory prayer, *Suscipe Sancte Pater*,[15] were to be recited in common. Parsch was fully conscientious of the problem posed by the said Mass as the basic form. But he was ready to put up with it. His goal was the 'German High Mass'.[16] So much for the historical findings on the basis of the example of Pius Parsch. This development rested upon problematical ideas, as defined by a differentiated liturgical theology:

1. The basic form of the Mass is no longer the *cappella papalis/Missa pontificalis*, but rather the parochial Mass (problematic, since the origin and standard of the Roman liturgy was the papal Mass).
2. The most important postulate is the *actuosa participatio* – important *in se*, has to be seen together with the other elements of liturgical theology.
3. This *actuosa participatio* is fixated with the texts and the speaking of the texts. Liturgical chant is not seen as *pars integralis* of the liturgy.[17]
4. The different ranks in the structured assembly are levelled. Even parts of the Offertory prayers are to be spoken by all, and phrases of the Canon are said aloud. But the Church is *societas hierarchice ordinata*.[18] The liturgy as *Epiphania Ecclesiae*[19] has to make this visible.

In general one can say that even the liturgists either did not understand the double structure of the entrance rites or wanted to simplify it, and in so doing levelled the different ranks of the various actors. The liturgical commentaries of the twentieth century no longer differentiate the actors. They also tend to neglect the way they represent the unity of the Church (compare what we have seen about the development of the rite following the developed doctrine of Papal Primacy).[20]

dem Menschen (Würzburg, 2004), pp 130ff.   **13** Ibid., especially p. 132.   **14** Ibid., pp 132ff.   **15** Ibid., especially p. 133.   **16** Ibid., pp 136ff.   **17** See *Vaticanum II: Musica traditio Ecclesiae universae thesaurum constituit pretii inaestimabilis, inter ceteras artis expressiones excellentem, eo praesertim quod ut cantus sacer qui verbis inhaeret necessariam vel integralem liturgiae sollemnis partem efficit. SC,* No. 112.   **18** *LG,* No. 20.   **19** John Paul II, *Vicesimus annus,* No. 12.   **20** Schnitzler ascribes in his commentary unequivocally everything to everyone. See T. Schnitzler, *Die Messe in der Betrachtung II* (Freiburg, 1957), pp 34ff.

As an illustration of the point we can take Theodor Schnitzler. He gives the reason for the prayers at the foot of the altar by solely (!) referring to the Frankish style-law that an action of the celebrant was to be accompanied by a prayer. The testimony of the *Ordo romanus I*, where the pope remains in silent prayer before the altar during the chant of the Introit, is not adequately acknowledged. For Schnitzler the Mass begins with the sign of the Cross, the confession of the Trinity, which he exposes from the content as embracing all the participants. He does not see that here, in principle, only the celebrant and his assisting ministers are the carriers of this very action of the making the sign of the Cross, while the faithful either listen to the Introit or sing it (or a hymn). They should in no way be orientated to the *In nomine Patris* but towards the singing, which should properly dispose them for the celebration of Mass.

In place of unreservedly leading one to a living understanding, to a co-accomplished comprehension of the Introit, Schnitzler has problems integrating this ancient entrance rite of the Roman liturgy (even when he presents interesting ideas about it):

> Still, the Introit remains even now a chant of the choir during which the people are condemned to silence. It would be 'worth the sweat of the noble' to think of forms that allow the people to be included. Could not a very simple verse be set to a tone that the people could then insert into the Introit as a refrain, such as 'to you I lift up my soul', or an *Introibo ad altare Dei*, as was so successfully done for the German Community Mass at the 1956 *Katholikentag*?[21]

Hence it follows that out of the Liturgical Movement came the demand for adaptation and change of the traditional form of the entrance rites. Schnitzler writes:

> All the little texts between the *Confiteor* and the Introit are fully overlaid at High Mass by the chant of the choir. They are devalued there to an often hardly understood murmur. In the private Mass their accomplishment is impaired by slap, dash and hurry, which not only endangers their spiritual content, but even the meaningful external form of the

---

21 Ibid., p. 6. This solution at the Katholikentag was not thought of as a liturgical principle, but was necessary because of the acoustical circumstances of the stadium.

words. On the contrary in the so-called extended community Mass these loud and solemnly common recited or declaimed texts are accorded such great importance that they even surpass the Introit in solemnity. Any future reform of the Mass will certainly be allowed to revise these texts.[22]

After the Council, Schnitzler took part in the reform of the *Ordo Missae*.

Already the Instruction on *Musica sacra* of 1958 adopted essential demands of the Liturgical Movement. The common recitation of all the texts of the opening rites up to the *Gloria* inclusively was defined as the highest step of active participation.[23]

Even before the Council demands for a reform of the liturgy were already being heard throughout the world. It is not astounding (after making the acquaintance of liturgists like Schnitzler) that changes were demanded in the entrance rites. In these wishes for reform it can be stated, as Barba notes, that the celebrations should be freed from private elements.[24] Among them he numbers the desire that in the *Missa lecta* everything should be spoken *clara voce*.[25] The prayers at the foot of the altar are purely understood as a private apology. They are to be suppressed or transferred to the sacristy. They are understood as prayers *before* the Introit, not having the sung form in view where they are prayers during the Introit. The point of departure here was not the total liturgical shape but the *Ordo Missae* as it presented itself.[26] On the other hand a penitential rite was called for with sacramental absolution for all.[27]

An understanding fixed on the *Ordo Missae* and deviating from the overall liturgical conception of a double opening made its way into the sung Mass. In

---

22 Ibid., p. 44. **23** On the participation at a said Mass it says here: 'Finally, a third and namely more perfect way consists in that the faithful give to the celebrating priest the liturgical responses, conversing with him so to speak, and speaking the parts which belong to them in a loud voice. In this more perfect form of assisting four steps can be distinguished: The first step is when the faithful give to the celebrating priest the more easy liturgical responses. The second step when the faithful speak those parts which according to the rubrics the server has to say ...' Text as found in C. Vagaggini, *Die Theologie der Liturgie* (Einsiedeln, 1959), p. 437. **24** 'The guiding thread which joins the responses contained in the paragraph regarding the modifications to be made in some rubrics, is in a certain sense the renewed conscience on the part of all, that the celebrations should be freed of the private character which covered them in the course of history, or from all the ritual layers encrusted through time that have come to make the celebration difficult to understand.' ('Il filo conduttore che lega le risposte contenute nel paragrafo riguardante le modifiche da attuare per alcune rubriche, è in un certo senso la rinnovata coscienza, da parte di tutti, che le celebrazioni dovevano essere liberate sia dal carattere privato di cui si erano rivestite nel corso della storia, sia da tutti gli strati rituali sedimentati nel tempo che arrivarono a rendere difficilmente comprensibile la celebrazione.') Maurizio Barba, *La riforma conciliare dell'Ordo Missae: Il percorso storica – redazionale dei riti d'ingresso, di offertorio, e di comunione* (Rome, 2008), p. 10. **25** *In Missa lecta omnia clara voce dicantur*. Cited after Barba, *La riforma conciliare*, p. 11. **26** *Preces ante Introitum aboleantur*. Cited after Barba, *La riforma conciliare*, p. 13. **27** *Processio introducatur dum chorus 'Introitum' cantat; in fine detur absolutio generalis*

this respect the Mass that Paul VI celebrated at the end of the Second Vatican Council is interesting. Here the rubric for the prayers at the foot of the altar says that all the clergy and faithful should respond to the pope and so begin the Mass together. The Introit antiphon follows and is responsorially arranged.[28] On this occasion then practices from the Liturgical Movement concerning the *Missa lecta* are mixed with the *Missa in cantu* (and also in its highest form, that of the papal liturgy).

The opening rites were also especially contested in the *Coetus X* of the *Consilium ad exsequendam*. The prayers at the foot of the altar were already seen in the Schema II *de Missali* as a thoroughly private prayer of the priest. But *precisely because of this* (!) they had to be suppressed since they did not concern the people. The question whether or not something historical or theological might be expressed in this differentiated beginning was not asked. Through this suppression the Introit was supposed to stand out more clearly. Many priests, moreover, desired that long texts should not have to be recited during the singing.[29] On the other hand there was also the desire to change these prayers into prayers for all.[30] In passing let it be observed that it is questionable how the various elements of the opening of the liturgy of the Mass were treated. To illustrate this let us take what Msgr Johannes Wagner, the leader of the *Coetus X*, which was charged with the reform of the *Ordo Missae*, recounts in his biography. In the course of the *Consilium*'s work, there was a debate about the *Gloria*:

> There were debates about its content as well as its place in the Mass as a whole. My personal high esteem of it was essentially based on the experiences of Catholic youth and the Catholic German people who had experienced the *Gloria* during the Nazi era as a symbol of spiritual resistance against dictatorial oppression, experiences that naturally were not shared by all.

valorem sacramentalem habens. Cited after Barba, *La riforma conciliare*, p. 14. **28** 7. *Summus Pontifex de sella gestatoria descendit ac deposita mitra, Missam incipit universo clero ac fidelibus adstantibus respondentibus … 8. Summus Pontifex, facta altare reverentia, alternatim cum omni populo preces ad gradus altaris faciendas dicit … 9. Antiphona ad Introitum cum suo psalmo dicitur a choro, aliis omnibus respondentibus … Ordo et Methodus servanda in concludendo Concilio Oecumenico Vaticano II:* Die 8 Decembris 1965 (Rome, 1965), p. 8. **29** Preces ad gradus, quamquam nunc saepius in missis lectis dialogatis a celebrante cum tota congregatione recitantur, tamen a liturgia usque adhuc non ut partes populi, sed potius preces quasi privatis celebrantis eiusque assistentiae habentur, sicut ex rubricis missae in cantu clare elucet. Proinde logicum esset in instauratione missae eas opprimere, ut clarior graviorque fieret cantus ad introitum. Merito quoque multi sacerdotes desiderant ne diutius obligentur eo tempore preces longiores ex corde proferre, quo cantus scholae vel congregationis peragitur. *Schema Nr. 16 De Missali Nr. 2,* 17 June 1964, No. 18. cited after Barba, *La riforma conciliare*, p. 342. **30** Alii vero

He then describes the content of the debate: 'If it was to be retained, then a better place in the Mass had to be sought for it, for instance at the Offertory, or as a thanksgiving after Communion'.[31] It seems truly that everything was possible ...

A critical appreciation of these changes

Even after the *a priori* double structure of the opening was transformed into a common beginning, the liturgical-theological interpretation of these rites continued to evolve into the now definitive direction. This means: no prominence is given to the priestly office, but rather to a common opening of the assembly.

It is therefore not to be wondered when already the profane theory of the assembly was brought into play in commentaries on the opening of Mass by those theologians who participated in the changes. An early example of this can again be found in the ideas of Theodor Schnitzler. He writes:

> Assemblies were held for many occasions. They always had one and the same form. The presider opens the gathering. He greets those present. The protocol of the last meeting is read: here is seen which decisions were not accomplished. The presider admonishes those present in a kind of loyalty declaration towards the aims of the community. Then he announces the programme of the actual meeting. The consultations begin. Someone reads out what a commission has considered and proposed. It is discussed and what is important is emphasized. A second proposal is read forth. Here again there are consultations and discussions. The third proposal is perhaps thought out by the president himself and he has it announced. Now the presider rises to explain all the proposals and recommend them to the assembly. Finally in a big act of resolution the proposals are accepted and confirmed. They are expressly intended for the whole association.

quaestionem movent, utrumne harum precum indoles poenitentialis sit tanti momenti pro tota communitate, ut deinceps, potius quam omittentur, pro omnis missa quae occurente populu celebratur, in partes communes totius congregationis eleventur, quod certo certius quoad missa in cantu esset innovatio. Propterea, si haec innovatio non admittenda esse videtur, censent tamen curandum esse, ut ille poenitentiae affectus, alio modo infra missam et a sacerdote et a tota congregatione de more exprimatur (e.g. in oratione fidelium). *Schema No. 16 De Missali Nr. 2*, 17 June 1964, No. 19. cited after Barba, *La riforma conciliare*, p. 342.   **31** J. Wagner, *Mein Weg zur Liturgiereform 1936–1986*: Erinnerungen (Freiburg, 1993), p. 116.

Schnitzler applies this to the Mass:

1. Introit
2. Opening: In the name of…
3. Greeting: The Lord be…
4. Reflection on the past: Penitential Rite
5. Declaration of principles: Kyrie, Gloria = Christ, Lord
6. Programme: Collect (Lord, today You have ascended into Heaven, let our minds and hearts dwell in Heaven.)
7. First Reading
8. Responsorial chant
9. Second Reading
10. Responsorial chant
11. Third Reading: Gospel
12. Explanation: Homily
13. Resolution: Creed
14. General validation: Intercessions[32]

In view of the fact that the entire liturgical tradition of the Roman Rite has been marked by the double structure of the entrance rites, the undifferentiated beginning with the common sign of the Cross and the Penitential Rite does not allow for a clear emphasis on the special relation of the celebrating priest has with the altar, which he approaches as an empowered representative. If for many the common Penitential Rite is a positive acquisition, it must nevertheless be noted that it descends from those strands of the Liturgical Movement which so stressed the *actuosa participatio* of the people that they also had them recite in parallel the most priestly part of the Mass.

By this the meaning of the *Confiteor* itself was changed. In the old form it was a prayer for worthiness of the offering priest and the ministers. The new Penitential Rite changes it into a rite of making all faithful worthy to attend Mass. This was never known by the Roman liturgy before, which emphasized from the very beginning the distinguished approach to the altar and to the offering of Mass.

In this context, it is too little when the *Institutio generalis* states that the sole reason for the opening rites is the bringing about of community.[33] It is also a

---

32 T. Schnitzler, *Was die Messe bedeutet* (Freiburg, 1990), pp 21–3. He expands this to the sacrificial part of the Mass. What has been said above suffices as example for our assessment.   **33** *Ritus qui liturgiam verbi*

question of greeting Christ in the empowered representative of the Church, without whom the sacrifice of the faithful would be impossible. The differentiation of the celebrant proper to the Roman tradition is nowhere to be found. In practice a papal entry distinguishes itself very little from that of a bishop and the latter minimally from that of the solemn entrance of a priest.

It is also really problematical that further theological development consequently brought these changes to their logical conclusions. The priest, who is empowered to offer the Body and Blood of Christ, has his position levelled. In practice the entrance is sometimes omitted and the action of the priest is reduced to pronouncing the words of Consecration.

Further theological evolution on the basis of the new form

Keeping pace with a much too strong emphasis on the holy assembly is an extremely questionable sacramental-theological interpretation of the Mass. For example, Paul Weß so presents his liturgical-theological concept, which in several respects no longer seems consonant with Catholic Dogma, precisely on the basis of No. 62 of the *Institutio generalis*.[34] This demonstrates how, on the basis of an assembly theory alone, by putting priest and people on an equal footing, important dogmatic distinctions are no longer seen. Weß says:

> Must one not really theologically more correctly say that each celebration of Mass is a concelebration, naturally not only of the priests, but of the congregation to which the one or many priests belong?[35]

Here the teaching of the whole Church as the body responsible for the liturgy[36] is reduced to the congregation assembled *hic et nunc*.[37] In the history

praecedunt, scilicet introitus, salutatio, actus paenitentialis, Kyrie, Gloria, et collecta chararacterem habent exordii, introductionis et praeparationis. Finis eorum est, ut et fideles convenientes in unum communionem constituantet recte ad verbum die audiendum digneque Eucharistiam celebrandam sesse disponant. Missale Romanum (Rome, 2002), No. 46.   **34** In the actual version of the *Missale Romanum* 2002 they are the numbers 95–7: *95. In celebratione Missae fideles efficiunt plebem sanctam, populus acquisitionis et sacerdotium regale, ut gratias Deo agant et hostiam immaculatam, non tantum per sacerdotis manus, sed etiam una cum ipso offerant et seipsos offere discant. Curent autem id manifestare per profundum sensum religiosum, et per caritatem erga fratres, qui eandem celebrationem participant. Vitent proinde omnes species vel singulariae vitae vel divisionis, prae oculis habentes se unicum Patrem hebere in caelis, omnesque propterea se inter se fratres. 96. Unum autem corpus efficiant, sive verbum die audiendo, sive in orationibus et cantu partem habendo, sive praesertim in commune oblatione sacrificii et in commune participatione mensae Domini. Haec unitas pulchre apparet ex gestibus et corporis habitibus a fidelibus communiter servatis. 97. Ne renuant autem fideles Populo Dei cum gaudio servire, quoties rogantur, ut aliquod peculiare ministerium vel munus in celebratione praestent.*   **35** Paul Weß, 'Die Stellung der Gemeinde in der Meßfeier' in *Bewahren und Erneuern: Studien zur Meßliturgie* (Innsbruck, 1995), p. 338.   **36** 'Liturgy is an "action" of the "whole Christ" (*Christus Totus*).' Catechism of the Catholic Church, No. 1136.   **37** See the observation of Weß on the 'celebration of Mass without a congregation': 'When the congregation

of the liturgy Weß does not see a more distinct elucidation of the place of the priest who offers the sacrifice but rather an obscuring of the role of the congregation. Thus he writes:

> It is probable that the actual evolution of the liturgy of the Mass exercised a great influence on the view of the role of the priest and also of the congregation and that the consequences have still to be digested. In this evolution of the liturgy there was, yet again, a decisive and causative loss of the community experience of the popular Church, as the anonymous mass of Christians were no longer held together by the personal relationship of faithful love, but through the authority of the hierarchy. Thus the Eucharist became the action of the priest.[38]

Weß has a general problems when the *Institutio* still continues to speaks of the priest apart from the congregation. This way of seeing things has consequences for the rite. Weß writes:

> Also the strong emphasis on the priest and eventually other ministers, respectively a person taking over a service through liturgical vesture, is from the view of a consequent theology of the congregation extremely questionable. Precisely when their action is to be understood as a service their special position, expressed by the vestment, is unjustified.[39]

We draw attention to these quotes to illustrate how they are at variance with all that we have seen in the development of the Roman Rite. Turning to the entrance rites, let us note the strong emphasis and accentuation of the place of the bishop (and to a lesser extent that of the priest who represents him), and a differentiation and structuring of the celebrating assembly, which partially was even an expression of its social organization. To so reform a differentiating opening of the Mass that almost only the common and simultaneous action of all is expressed risks a levelling of the theology of the priestly office. This is true too in the case of secondary elements such as the opening rites of worship. This seems to me to be the biggest problem. Here the actual praxis, and above all the interpretations resulting from it, touches the core concerns of the Protestant Reformers.

is really the body responsible for worship can something like this even be?' P. Weß, *Die Stellung der Gemeinde*, p. 338. See also the reference on D. Funke p. 344. **38** Ibid., p. 341. **39** Ibid., p. 349.

At the same time there has also been, from the outset, expert criticism of some other points of the reform. Actually, since then, the Mass has opened with the entrance of the celebrant and the incensation of the altar. The subsequent loud–sung common sign of the Cross and greeting mark a beginning, although the liturgy has already begun. Problematical also is the interpretation of the *Kyrie* as a confession of sin and a plea for mercy. Ritually, it can also be remarked that the liturgical greeting traditionally does not open but conclude. Together with the *Dominus vobiscum*, the *Collecta* concludes the opening rites.

CONCLUDING THEOLOGICAL ASSESSMENT OF THE ENTRANCE RITES OF THE ROMAN RITE

Of today's liturgical uncertainty Joseph Ratzinger writes:

> Is the opening to the world for us not just a bit too successful? Are we still conscious that we stand before the throne of the Most High? That heaven opens itself over us? That God's Angels and Saints surround us? Origen said to his faithful in one of his homilies on the Gospel of Luke: 'I have no doubts that also in our assembly angels are present, not only for the entire Church but for each individual believer.' And he imagines what it would be like when someone like the prophet Elias would pray for us: 'O Lord, open the eyes of this child …' Where bustle reigns the eyes of the heart cannot open. And yet that would be the only right participation in the liturgy, when we would begin to sense heaven laid open. All of the speaking singing, acting should, in the end, serve to lead us to this transcending movement, where silence can give its message.[40]

Looking at the tradition of the Roman Rite the opening must, on the one hand, constitute the liturgical assembly of the People of God. Here the Church is heir to the *Quahal* of Israel. And this is the first movement that the liturgy demands. Ratzinger notes that the different meanings of *ecclesia* – as we have seen – do not contradict each other but rather are interrelated, 'indeed seamlessly interlaced'.[41] They are only able to do this 'because everything is

---

40 J. Ratzinger, '40 Jahre Konstitution über die heilige Liturgie: Rückblick und Vorblick' in J. Ratzinger, *40 Jahre danach: Das Zweite Vatikanische Konzil und seine Folgen* (Trier, 2005), pp 11–26.   **41** Joseph Ratzinger, *Ursprung und Wesen der Kirche* (Freiburg, 2010), p. 232.

suspended on the Christological centre, which takes shape in the assembly of the faithful for the Supper of the Lord. It is always the Lord in his sacrifice who assembles his one and only people. In all places it is the gathering of the one.'[42] Thus the first 'transcending movement' demanded by the liturgy means the renewed and conscious going into the *ecclesia universalis* by those gathered *hic et nunc*. The people of Rome represented the globe in the papal liturgy. The entrance rites must not be inwardly closed; rather they must enable this first movement towards the whole Church.

This constitution of the celebrating assembly as representatives of the People of the Covenant and in representation of the universal Church takes place through the entrance of the empowered minister of worship, the priest, without whom the sacrifice of the faithful cannot be accomplished. In this sense the opening of the liturgy must not only impart a glance of the entire Church but also bring to expression the passage from the private prayer to the *cultus publicus* of the Mystical Body.

Finally, we accomplish in the liturgy a last movement. We enter into spatially orientated prayer, at least turned towards the Cross. In this sense the entrance explicitates the pilgrimage of the Church towards Christ, to the liturgy of Heaven. It is a transcending movement from the world of men to the world of God, and in this sense from the profane to the holy.

In this context we should mention that Ratzinger sees liturgy in it's characteristics of a movement of Exodus.[43] This exodus leads through the Paschal Mystery to communion with God.[44]

The traditional Roman Rite expresses this movement in the entry of the celebrant, in a differentiated moving towards Christ. The readying for this took place beforehand.[45] Only those who are properly ministering at the altar still need a special preparation, in order to ascend to the altar as Moses did the mountain. By this the priest represents the bishop and the bishop the pope. In a way, by this the liturgical expression transcends the local community.

Common to all is the procession towards Christ, through the *Kyrie*, *Gloria*, to the concluding *Collecta*.

---

42 Ibid., p. 232.   43 'Aber Moses besteht – dem Befehl Gottes gemäß – darauf, dass zum Kult Auszug nötig sei.' ('But Moses is insisting, following God's command, that in order to fullfill cult, exodus is necessary.') J. Ratzinger, 'Der Geist der Liturgie' in J. Ratzinger, *Theologie der Liturgie* (Freiburg, 2008), p. 34. 44 J. Ratzinger, *Ein neues Lied für den Herrn: Christusglaube und Liturgie in der Gegenwart* (Freiburg, 1995), p. 33.   45 Mediaeval architecture already did this preparation through the access to the church, which was understood as Jerusalem. The Galilee chapel often served as a point of transition. See Neil J. Roy, 'The Galilee chapel' in D.V. Twomey and J.E. Rutherford (eds), *Benedict XVI and Beauty in sacred art and architecture* (Dublin, 2011), pp 143–61.

The new form of the Roman Rite places in the Penitential Rite a transcending movement as an accent of interior renewal. Nevertheless, this form needs a supplement which brings to expression that which differentiates the action of the priest and the hierarchy such as transcending the local community.

In any case, the entrance rites of both forms must make clear the different stages of 'transcending movement' and not seal off the participants in a closed circle. The task of liturgical catechesis is to prepare for this movement of the liturgy, the essential step into the holy place of God.

The post-Vatican II revision of the Sunday collects of Paschaltide: an overview

LAUREN PRISTAS

This essay addresses the question: from where did the Vatican II corpus of Paschal Sunday collects come? It opens with an exposition that shows both what happened to the 1962 orations assigned to these days and the origins, in a general way, of the corresponding Vatican II collects. A discussion of the editorial work of the revisers follows in three sections. First, we list the policies which the *Consilium* members[1] decided would govern the revision of the proper Mass prayers. Second, we identify the source(s) of each prayer, the liturgical uses to which the sources were put prior to inclusion in the new Missal, and describe, in a general way, the editorial work that was done to bring each Vatican II prayer to its present form. From these the number and variety of the sources and the scope of editorial discretion are seen. Third, we present close textual examinations of the redactions that produced two of the collects: one, a 1962 collect that was restored in conformity with an ancient precedent and then revised; the other, a new composition produced by means of centonization.[2] A conclusion follows.

OVERVIEW

Disposition of the 1962 Orationes *in the post-Vatican II revision of the Roman Missal*

Table 1 shows, in schematic form, what happened to the Paschal Sunday *orationes* of the 1962 Missal (see Table 1 at the end of this essay). The bold typeface identifies the only *oratio* that was retained on the same day. It was edited. All the others, save one, were retained but moved to different days in the new Missal.

---

1 The fathers of Vatican II provided for a reform of the liturgy in the *Constitution on the Sacred Liturgy* (*Sacrosanctum concilium*). On 25 January 1964, Pope Paul VI issued a *motu proprio* in which he announced the establishment of a special commission whose principal task would be to implement the prescriptions of the *Constitution on the Sacred Liturgy*. The new commission was called 'the *Consilium* for carrying out the Constitution on the Sacred Liturgy'. The members of this *ad hoc* body, not the fathers of Vatican II, oversaw the editorial work that produced the new liturgical books. 2 Literary centonization is the production of a

Table 2 presents a quantitative summary. Of the eight 1962 collects under consideration, seven were transferred to ferial days and/or Sundays *per annum* and one retained in place after editing. None was retained in place without textual change (see Table 2).

Origins of the Paschal Sunday collects of Vatican II Missals

Table 3 indicates from where the post-Vatican II collects came. The small cap typeface identifies what is unique to the third typical edition (see Table 8).

Table 4 summarizes. Of the eight collects in the first two typical editions of the Vatican II Missal, only one came from the 1962 Missal. It was edited. Five came from ancient sacramentaries or collections, and three of these were edited. Two collects were new compositions. The third typical edition replaces the edited ancient prayer assigned to the fifth Sunday of the Pasch in the Missals of 1970 and 1975 with the collect assigned to Saturday after the fourth Sunday of the Pasch in the earlier Missals. This collect is a modern composition which was centonized from two ancient texts (see Table 4).

In sum, the overview finds that the post-Vatican II revisions were marked by a substantial amount of editorial activity and creativity. It is this that we wish to examine more closely.

THE EDITORIAL WORK

Revision policies

In 1966 the *Consilium* members formally approved six policies that were to govern the work of revising the Mass orations. These were:

1. Texts were to be used only once;
2. Corruptions were to be corrected;
3. References to events whose significance has been lost to the Church Universal were to be removed, and orations were to be accommodated to the customs of present day Christian life if discrepancies had arisen;
4. Proper literary genre was to be preserved in, or restored to, each prayer present in, or inserted into, the Missal;

---

new composition by assembling passages from other works. In the case of the Paschal Sunday collects, the revisers took phrases from two or more prayers and wove them together to produce a new prayer, supplying words and phrases of their own as needed.

5. In general, orations would be addressed to the Father;
6. New texts, drafted chiefly by the method of centonization, were to be added to the Missal.[3]

In the study that follows, we see three of these policies implemented: the first, the second and the sixth. The policy concerning literary genre is not in clear evidence, a matter to which we return at the end of the essay. The other two policies seem not to have pertained to the revision of this set.

Sources of the Vatican II collects for Paschal Sundays

It is best to begin our consideration of the selection and use of sources by indicating what information is, and is not, available.

To date, detailed and comprehensive records about the many specific decisions that went into the revision of the proper Mass prayers has not come to light. This is true both of the Missal as a whole and of the collects assigned to the Sundays of Paschaltide. There is nothing that explains why, for example, the revisers chose a prayer from the *Missale gothicum* that had never before served as a Mass collect to be the collect for the Second Sunday of the Pasch (later designated Divine Mercy Sunday). Nor do we know why, in specific cases, those charged with the revision of the Mass prayers composed new prayers for days that were not new feasts (for example, the third and sixth Sundays of the Pasch) or how they selected the ancient prayers that were mined to produce the new prayers by the process of centonization. Nor, except for the relatively rare cases in which revisers left published comments about the redaction of particular prayers, do we know why many of the specific ancient prayers that the revisers selected for inclusion in the new Missal were edited in ways that do not correspond to variants in the manuscript tradition.

Nor is this information preserved in the Vatican archives. In their 1986 work on the sources of proper prayers in the 1975 Missal, Cuthbert Johnson and Anthony Ward tell us:

---

3 See *Schema* n. 186, *De Missali* n. 27, 19 September 1966, pp 2–4 and *addendum* p. 1. All the Consilium schemata quoted or referred to in this essay are on file at the offices of the International Commission on English in the Liturgy, Washington, DC. I am grateful to the Revd Msgr Bruce Harbert, Executive Director of ICEL at the time, and Mr Peter Finn for permitting me access to the ICEL collection of *coetus* notes. The second and third of the above-named policies were revised in the course of the work. See Lauren Pristas, 'The orations of the Vatican II Missal: policies for revision' in *Communio: an International Catholic Review*, 30:4 (Winter, 2003), 621–53.

The material conserved in the Congregation's[4] archive documenting any particular text is uneven, depending on the work methods of a particular group (*coetus*) of revisers, the opportunities offered by distance and commitments to meet in person and so on ... Let all users of this work be therefore assured that personal access to the official archival material would reveal no further information, except of the most incidental variety. Of what is available, the fullest use has been made.[5]

What we do know or can discover is whether a prayer is from the Tridentine Missal or an earlier liturgical codex. We can also determine:

1. How widely the prayer was used in antiquity and, generally, in the course of which centuries;
2. How it was used (for example, as a collect or as a post-Communion or both);
3. Whether variant editions of the prayer exist and, if so, their individual forms;
4. Whether the prayer was redacted by the modern editors. The very helpful work of Cuthbert Johnson and Anthony Ward identifies the new compositions and, if centonized or drawn from biblical or patristic texts, their respective sources.[6]

That is, while details about the process of selecting, editing and centonizing prayers have seemingly not been preserved, we do have the final texts and their respective sources. Careful examination of each prayer with its source(s) tells us what was done even if we often do not know why. There is insufficient space here to compare the eight Sunday collects of Paschaltide either with their respective sources or with the corresponding eight prayers in the 1962 Missal. Instead we identify and describe the sources of each of the eight post-Vatican II collects and then examine closely the editorial work that went into two of them, the collects of Easter Sunday and of the sixth Sunday of the Pasch.

Sunday of the Resurrection:
To produce the collect assigned to the Sunday of the Resurrection the revisers adopted the *oratio*[7] assigned to the same day in the 1962 Missal, restored part

---

4 The Congregation for Divine Worship and the Discipline of the Sacraments.   5 'Sources of the Roman Missal (1975)', *Notitiae*, 22 (1986), 454.   6 A. Ward and C. Johnson, 'Sources of the Roman Missal (1975)', *Notitiae*, 22 (1986), 445–747; 23 (1987) 413–1009; and 32 (1996) 7–179.

of the prayer according to the form found in an eighth century codex, *Gelasianum vetus*,[8] and then revised the restored version in a way that is without warrant in the manuscript tradition. The meaning of the prayer was altered in this process. A discussion of the details is presented below.

Sunday II of the Pasch:

The collect of the second Sunday of the Pasch, or Divine Mercy Sunday, is taken from a codex known at the *Missale gothicum* which dates from the beginning of the eighth century. The prayer is a *collectio post nomina*, a variable prayer that is prayed in the midst of the Preface, assigned to Saturday in the Paschal octave. The prayer is found in no other surviving codex. The modern editors made no change to the ancient text.[9]

Sunday III of the Pasch:

The collect of the third Sunday of the Pasch is a centonized prayer confected from two ancient texts. The revisers took the opening clause of a Paschaltide prayer that appears in thirteen codices dating from the eighth century through to the eleventh.[10] In these it is used as a blessing at the end of Mass on the Paschal *Annotina*,[11] or a prayer *super sidonem*[12] on Wednesday following the third Sunday after the Pasch – that is, at the midpoint of Paschaltide. To this they joined the closing clause of a prayer for the faithful departed assigned to October in the collection of liturgical texts known as the Leonine or Veronese Sacramentary.[13] This latter prayer appears in no other codex. The new composition has twenty-three words. Fourteen words are from the Paschal prayer, six

---

7 Tridentine Missals call the first proper Mass prayer the *oratio*; the Vatican II Missals call the same prayer the *collecta*.   **8** The modern critical edition is L.C. Mohlberg, L. Eizenfoefer, P. Siffrin (eds), *Liber sacramentorum romanae ecclesiae ordinis anni circuli* (Rome, 1960), no. 463. Henceforth prayers from this volume will be designated *GeV* followed by the number assigned them in the critical edition.   **9** E. Moeller and J.M. Clément (eds), *Corpus Orationum* (hereafter *CO*, with citations given by prayer number); cited here is II D, CCSL CLX A (Turnholt, 1993), no. 1268. Between 1992 and 1999 Moeller and Clément published eleven volumes of orations that present, in alphabetical order, all the orations contained in two hundred one extant Latin liturgical codices that pre-date the Tridentine reform – 6,829 different orations in all. The editors list the codices in which each oration appears, identify the way it is used in each manuscript, and cite the textual variants. Separate lists in each volume date the codices. The eleventh volume, CLX-J, contains indices both of first lines and closing words. The modern critical edition of the *Missale gothicum* (hereafter *Gothicum*) is L.C. Mohlberg, *Missale gothicum* (Rome, 1961). *CO* 1268 = *Gothicum* 306.   **10** *CO* 4299.   **11** Catechumens were baptized at the Paschal Vigil, and the Pasch is a moveable feast. The Paschal *Annotina* is the first anniversary of baptism for those baptized at the Vigil the year before.   **12** Literally, the prayer 'over the linen' – it corresponds to the secret or prayer over the offerings in the Roman Missals.   **13** *CO* 2919 = *Ver* 1148. The modern critical edition of the Veronese or Leonine Sacramentary is L. Cunibert Mohlberg, L. Eizenhöfer, P. Siffrin (eds), *Sacramentarium Veronense*, (Rome, 1956). Prayers from this text are indicated by '*Ver*' followed by the number of the prayer. The so-called Veronese Sacramentary is not a true sacramentary for it was never used in public worship. Rather it

from the prayer for the dead and three were supplied by the modern editors. Careful examination of the new composition requires consideration of what the revisers adopted, the manner in which they adapted it in the new composition, and what they left behind. Unfortunately we cannot do this here.

Sunday IV of the Pasch:
The collect of the fourth Sunday of the Pasch appears in numerous ancient codices dating from the eighth through to the early sixteenth century. It is always assigned to Paschal or Pentecost celebrations but put to a variety of uses. In different codices it serves as a prayer at Vespers, prayer at Mass, post-Communion prayer, and prayer for all saints.[14] The revisers made three changes to the ancient text which alters its sense somewhat.[15] There exists no warrant in the extant manuscript tradition for their revisions.[16]

Sunday V of the Pasch:
The collect of the fifth Sunday of the Pasch in the first and second typical editions of the Vatican II Missals was also assigned to Saturday following the second Sunday of the Pasch and the twenty-third Sunday *per annum*. In the third typical edition it is assigned only to the latter, presumably a belated implementation of the 1966 decision not to repeat texts. The source text appears as a Paschaltide prayer in numerous ancient Missals where, with a single exception, it is assigned to Vespers.[17] The revisers made two changes to the original prayer. No warrant for either is found in the extant manuscript tradition.[18]

is a private collection of Roman formularies. The surviving manuscript dates from the first quarter of the 7th century but the prayers in it are dated variously from AD400–560. See C. Vogel, *Medieveal liturgy: an introduction to the sources* (tr. and rev. W. Storey and N. Rasmussen) (Washington DC, 1981), pp 38–45 for a description of the codex (Cod. Bibl. Capit. Veron. LXXXV [80]) and a survey of scholarly opinions concerning it. **14** *CO* 3828. **15** Compare (differences are indicated in bold type): *Omnipotens sempiterne deus, deduc nos ad societatem caelestium gaudiorum, ut, **spiritu sancto renatos, regnum tuum facias introire atque** eo perueniat humilitas gregis quo **praecessit celsitudo** pastoris // Omnipotens sempiterne Deus, deduc nos ad societatem caelestium gaudiorum, ut eo perveniat humilitas gregis, quo **processit** fortitudo pastoris:* 'Almighty, everlasting God, lead us to the communion of heavenly joys, so that **you may grant those who have been reborn in the Holy Spirit to enter your kingdom** and the lowliness of the flock may arrive there whence the **exaltedness** of the shepherd **has gone ahead** // Almighty, everlasting God, lead us to the communion of heavenly joys, so that the humility/lowliness of the flock may arrive there whence the strength of the shepherd **has come forth/gone before or ahead**.' **16** Ibid. **17** *CO* 1310a. The exception is 'another oration' at Mass on Sunday in the Paschal Octave. **18** *CO* 1310 a: *Deus, per quem nobis et redemptio venit et praestatur adoptio, **respice in opera misericoridae tuae**, ut in Christo **renatis** et aeterna tribuatur hereditas et vera libertas. 1970/1975: Deus, per quem nobis et redemptio venit et praestatur adoptio, **filios dilectionis tuae benignus intende**, ut in Christo **credentibus et vera tribuatur libertas et hereditas aeterna**.* Tr.: *CO* 1310 a: 'O God, through whom both redemption comes and adoption is granted, **look upon the works of your mercy**, that upon **those who have been reborn** in Christ, both <u>an eternal inheritance and true liberty may be bestowed</u> .' 1970/1975: 'O God, through whom

In the third typical edition, the collect originally appointed for Saturday following Sunday IV of the Pasch is assigned to this Sunday, the fifth of the Pasch. This collect is a new composition which was centonized from two ancient texts: a preface and a *super oblata* (prayer over the offerings) both from a Bergamese Sacramentary.[19] In the *Bergomense*, the preface and the prayer over the offerings are assigned to the second and first Masses, respectively, of Monday in the Paschal Octave.[20]

The new composition has thirty words: fourteen are taken from the prayer over the offerings, six from the preface and ten were supplied by the revisers. The fourteen words from the prayer over the offerings do not appear as continuous text in the new collect, but rather in three different segments. Again, a proper examination of the new composition requires consideration of what the revisers adopted, the manner in which they adapted it to the new composition, and what they left behind. Unfortunately, we are not able to present such an examination here.

Sunday VI of the Pasch:
The collect for this Sunday is a new composition centonized from three sources:

1. The preface of a Mass celebrated on the fast or ember days following Pentecost that appears in the Veronese (Leonine) Sacramentary,[21]
2. A post-Communion prayer for the feast of Saint John the Evangelist in December found in the same, and no other, collection,[22] and
3. A prayer that is used in different codices as the collect of the Mass celebrated on the Paschal *Annotina* or as a blessing prayed over the people on Wednesday following the third Sunday after the Pasch – that is, at the midpoint of Paschaltide.[23] The codices date from the eighth century through to the twelfth, and both uses span these same centuries.

The new composition has twenty-four words. Seven words were taken from the ember day preface, three from the post-Communion of Saint John, and eight from the prayer for the Paschal *Annotina*. The revisers supplied the

both redemption comes and adoption is granted to us, look kindly on the sons of your love, that upon those who believe/trust in Christ both true liberty and an eternal inheritance may be bestowed.' The changes that the revisers made in the actual wording of the prayer are indicated in bold; changes made in the word order are underlined.   **19** The Bergamese Sacramentary is a Milanese or Ambrosian text dating from the second half of the ninth century. The modern critical edition is A. Paredi and G. Fassi, *Sacramentarium Bergomense*, in *Monumenta Bergomensia*, VI (Bergamo, 1962).   **20** *Sacramentarium bergomense* 577 (preface), 571 (*super oblata*).   **21** *Ver* 229.   **22** *Ver* 1282 = *CO* 3355.   **23** *CO* 1308.

remaining six words. Examination of the new composition requires careful consideration of what the revisers adopted, the manner in which they adapted the words and thought of the source texts to the new composition, and what they left behind. (This is presented below.)

Sunday VII of the Pasch:
The Vatican II collect is an ancient prayer that is assigned to the Ascension or its vigil in numerous codices dating from the eighth through to the twelfth century, but never to the Sunday following the Ascension, which is the seventh of the Pasch.[24] The modern redactors edited the text, but since their work mainly consisted in substituting synonyms and reordering the words, the essential meaning of the prayer was not altered. There are, however, no precedents in the manuscript tradition for any of the changes they made.

Pentecost Sunday:[25]
The collect that the revisers selected for this day is found in numerous codices that date from the eighth through to the twelfth century.[26] These use the prayer in different settings: the collect for Thursday in the Pentecost octave, a prayer *post tractum* of the Pentecost vigil; and, on Pentecost Sunday itself, variously as another collect, a blessing over the people, a Vespers prayer, or 'other' prayer.

The revisers made two changes neither of which corresponds to a variant in the manuscript tradition: they omitted 'your', so that 'your Holy Spirit' becomes 'Holy Spirit', and substituted *perfunde* [pour over or fill] for *defunde* [pour down or pour out]. The meaning of the prayer is not much altered by these changes.

Examination of the texts

In this section we examine closely the editorial work that produced the Vatican II collects assigned to Easter Sunday and to the sixth Sunday of the Pasch and present an analysis of the results. We selected the Easter collect because an unusual amount of information about its restoration and revision is available. We chose the collect of the sixth Sunday because, of the centonized texts in the set we are discussing, it presents the fewest difficulties and therefore provides the best introduction to the process and its results.

---

24 *CO* 153.   **25** The collects appointed for the Vigil Masses are not considered here.   **26** *CO* 2057.

Sunday of the Resurrection:

Table 5 presents the Tridentine and Vatican II collects of Easter Sunday[27] (see Table 5).

We have the statements from both *relators* (literally, the ones who report or relate) of the *Consilium coetus* charged with the revision of the Mass prayers[28] about this prayer. In consequence we perhaps know more about its redaction than that of any other proper Mass prayer.

Placid Bruylants was the first *relator* of the *coetus* that revised the prayers and prefaces. In the course of his September 1966 discussion with the *Consilium* members about the policies which would be followed in revising the Mass orations, Bruylants identified the 1962 Paschal collect as a corrupt text and asked the members if they desired such corruptions to be corrected. I quote:

> Another change that all deplore occurred in the second part of the Paschal collect which, without doubt, very much diminishes its theological import. The old Gelasian has it thus:
>
> *Deus, qui hodierna die per Unigenitum tuum aeternitatis nobis aditum devicta morte reserasti, da nobis, quaesumus, ut, qui resurrectionis sollemnia colimus, per innovationem tui spiritus a morte animae resurgamus.*[29]

Table 6 shows the Gelasian version set next to that of the Tridentine Missals. The differences are indicated in boldface type (see Table 6).

The corruption Bruylants cites is the change from 'grant, we beseech you, that we who celebrate the solemnity of [his] Resurrection, may, through renewal of the Holy Spirit, rise from death of soul' to 'attend (or 'accompany') also our prayers (or 'solemn promises/desires'), which, by going before you inspire, with your assistance.'

Bruylants's presentation to the *Consilium* members includes the words *hodierna die* (literally, 'on today's day'; usually translated 'on this day') which appear in the *qui* clause of the Tridentine version of the prayer, but are not found in the Gelasian version – something Bruylants does not mention in his discussion with the *Consilium* members. The extant manuscript evidence

---

27 Unless otherwise noted, the translations are my own.   28 *Coetus* 18bis.   29 *Schema* n. 186, *De Missali* n. 27 (September 19, 1966), p. 2. *Alia mutatio, de qua omnes unanimiter dolent, in secunda parte collectae Paschatis, facta est, quo indubitanter momentum eius theologicum valde minuitur. In Gelasianum vetere sic sonabat:* [the Latin prayer follows as above].

suggests that these words were first introduced into the Gelasian version of the prayer in the *Sacramentaire de Gellone* which scholars date to the 'end of the eighth century'.[30] The Gelasian Sacramentary is slightly earlier; it was copied around the year 750 in the nunnery at Chelles.[31]

We shall examine the prayer in the 1962 Missal first. The references to prevenient and concommitant grace make use of Catholic theological vocabulary and concepts forged in the Pelagian and Semi-Pelagian controversies of the fifth and sixth centuries. Notwithstanding its technical character, the language of the prayer has considerable poetic force: God, acting first (*praeveniendo*), breathes into us (*aspiras*) our desires, prayers, solemn promises, vows, or longings (*vota nostra – vota* can mean any or all of these things). Having acknowledged that our longings, prayers, promises have been instilled in us by God, the collect then begs him to accompany, attend, escort (*prosequere*), one might say usher, them by his active assistance (*adjuvando*) toward their proper end: eternal life in heaven which, as we know from the prayer's opening clause, has been opened to us by Christ's definitive victory over death (*devicta morte*).

The prayer progresses from God's action in unlocking the entrance way to eternity for us through his Son's victory over death to our request for the ongoing and accompanying assistance we need from him to make our way safely from temporal to eternal life. *Vota nostra*, the prayers and longings which God breathes into us and which we ask him to accompany and assist, receive special emphasis by prominent placement at the start of the petition.[32] If we assume, and we must, that the prayers and longings are those that celebration of the Lord's Resurrection properly occasions, then the *oratio*'s petition, which at first glance seems to have been hijacked by the concerns of a doctrinal controversy, actually understands God to breathe the salvific event into the depths of our hearts and asks him to bring our hearts home to the eternity which he has opened for us.

We move now to consideration of the Gelasian collect. It begins with the same words except for this explicit reference to 'this day', and introduces the theme of Resurrection first negatively, but strikingly, with the words *devicta morte*, and then by identifying the feast being celebrated, *resurrectionis sollemnia colimus*. There follows the request that we might rise from death of soul (*a morte anime resurgamus*) through the renewal or the change (*per*

30 *CO* 1992. The information about the codex is found on p. xx of the same volume (iii).   **31** C. Vogel, *Medieveal liturgy: an introduction to the sources*, p. 65.   **32** Cf. M.G. Haessly, *Rhetoric in the Sunday Collects of the Roman Missal: with introduction, text, commentary and translation* (Saint Louis, 1938), p. 59.

innovationem) brought about by the Holy Spirit (*tui spiritus*). The movement here is from Christ's bodily Resurrection from physical death, which signals his conquest over death and all that belongs to it, to our spiritual resurrection from spiritual death (*a morte anime resurgamus*) through the renewal of the Holy Spirit (*per innovationem tui Spiritus*).

There are two extant eighth-century manuscripts and numerous later ones that present the version of the prayer found in the Tridentine Missals. Seven extant eighth-century codices with the Gelasian version, or a variant of the same, exist, but this version of the prayer is not seen after the eleventh century. Both forms are used as the Paschal collect.[33]

Antione Dumas succeeded Placide Bruylants as *relator* after the latter's death in October of 1966. Dumas mentions the revision of this collect in his 1971 article on the revision principles and the manner in which they were applied. The context is his discussion of the ways in which the revisers adapted ancient texts. He writes:

> It happened sometimes that beautiful texts, retained after a rigorous selection process or even perfectly restored, and put in the place that suits them best, still do not give complete satisfaction. In this case a slight adaptation remained necessary. The most typical case is that of the collect of Easter Sunday that, rescued from the Gregorian deformation in which it passed into the Missal of Pius V and made to conform to the best witness (Gelasian 463), ended with a regretable collapse evoking death for the second time in a few words. We believed it good to put the ending in harmony with paschal joy by replacing *a morte animae* [from death of soul] with *in lumine vitae* [in the light of life].[34]

We leave it to others to determine whether the Tridentine form of the prayer is a corruption or an authentic development. Our interest is the change made by the revisers. Table 7 presents the Gelasian collect next to its Vatican II counterpart. The differences are indicated in boldface type (see Table 7).

---

33 Cf. *CO* 1992 and the accompanying information at the front of the volume which dates each source.
34 Antoine Dumas, 'Les oraisons du nouveau Missel', *Questions Liturgiques*, 25 (1971), 263–70 at 268: 'Il est arrivé parfois que de beaux textes, retenus après une sélection sévère ou même parfaitement restaurés, et mis à la place qui leur convenait le mieux, **ne** donnent pas encore entière satisfaction. Dans ce cas, une légère adaptation demeurait nécessaire. Le cas plus typique est celui de la collecte du dimanche de Pâques qui, dégagée de sa déformation grégorienne passée dans le Missel de Pie V et rendue conforme au meilleur témoin (Gélasien 463), se terminait par une chute regrettable évoquant la mort pour la deuxième fois en quelques mots. On a cru bon de mettre la finale en harmonie ave la joie pascale en remplaçant *a morte animae* par *in lumine vitae*.'

There are three differences. *Hodierna die* is discussed above. *Dominicae* is found in all the ancient witnesses except the Gelasian Sacramentary.[35] *In lumine vitae* was introduced by the modern revisers. There is no warrant in the manuscript tradition for this last change and the substituted phrase does not come from the *Vulgate* – that is, nowhere does the *Vulgate* speak of rising in the light of life.[36]

The movement in the revised prayer is from Christ's bodily Resurrection from physical death, which signals his conquest over death and all that belongs to it, to our rising in the light of life (*in lumine vitae resurgamus*) through the renewal of the Holy Spirit.

The poetic parallelism of the Gelasian text is the literary expression of a theological truth: the bodily Resurrection of Christ from physical death, by which death itself is conquered and the gates of eternal life are opened unto us, is the source of our spiritual resurrection from the death of sin. Therefore, what Dumas describes as a 'regretable collapse evoking death for the second time in a few words' is something else entirely: an explicit acknowledgment that Christ's victory over physical death makes our escape from spiritual death possible. And since Christ was only capable of undergoing death because he assumed our mortal nature, the decision to avoid explicit mention of our vulnerability to death, either spiritual or physical, and the escape from it that God in Christ has granted, is particularly arresting.

When Bruylants told the *Consilium* members that this collect had suffered corruption, he did not suggest that there was anything unsatisfactory about the Gelasian version which, in fact, he cited as we have quoted above. Further, the first schema of Mass orations proposed for the proper seasons presents the Gelasian version of the Paschal collect without the emendation Dumas says was necessary.[37] There is no extant *Consilium* document which explains this change or whether the members explicitly approved it. We have only what Dumas states in an essay published under his own name in a scholarly journal.

Sunday VI of the Pasch

The collect assigned to the sixth Sunday of the Pasch is a centonized composition. The prayer, together with its sources, is presented in Table 8 (see Table 8).

In this essay Dumas does not refer to the revision policies agreed upon in 1966 but instead identifies them as: truth, simplicity, and pastoral awareness. He also speaks of the revision as having three aspects: the selection, the revision and the creation of texts. **35** Cf. *CO* 1992. **36** Cf. John 8:12, Jesus says that those who follow him 'will not walk in darkness but *will* have the light of life' (*non ambulabit in tenebris sed habebit lucem vitae*). I could not find a New Testament verse which brings the images of rising, light, and life together in a single thought. **37** *Schema* n. 186, *De Missali* n. 27, 19 September 1966, p. 36.

Regular type in the three left columns indicates what the revisers left behind and, in the fourth column, what they introduced. The text taken from *Ver* 229, the preface for the fast days following Pentecost, is presented in italics; that taken from *Ver* 1282, the post-Communion prayer for the feast of Saint John, is in bold typeface; and that from *GeV* 504, the collect for the Paschal *Annotina*, is in small caps. Other ancient Missals present the last prayer as a blessing over the people given at the end of Mass at the midpoint of Paschaltide.[38]

Before we examine the construction of the centonized collect and its import, we will consider each of the source texts.

Ver 229 is a preface prayed at Mass during the Ember days following the feast of Pentecost – the Wednesday, Friday and Saturday of the Pentecost octave. The prayer names three major events that the Church 'honours' during Paschaltide, the season that has just come to a close: the Lord's rising from the dead, his Ascension, and the reception of the Holy Spirit. The movement of the preface is from remembrance of the salvific events celebrated in Paschaltide, during which fasting is never done, to the necessity of fasting so that those who have been brought into the Church, that is redeemed and sanctified through the events just named, may persevere in purity of life. From this preface the revisers took the phrase 'days of joy in honour of your Son's rising'. That they deliberately omitted 'from the dead' is apparent from the word order of the original text: *laetitiae dies, quos in honorem Domini a mortuis resurgentis* [of joy the days, which in honour of the Lord from the dead rising].

Ver 1282 is a somewhat difficult text which may account for the fact that it appears in no other extant liturgical codex. The presence of the word *martyrum* (of the martyrs/witnesses) in a prayer from the Mass in honour of Saint John the Evangelist is puzzling because he is the one Apostle who, according to tradition, was not martyred. It seems best to understand *caelestium martyrum* as 'of heavenly witnesses' in the manner of Hebrews 12:1.[39] In this case, the sense of the opening portion of the prayer would be: 'Compassionate and merciful God, who never forsakes us (are always present to us) in the successive mysteries (successive celebrations of the feasts) of the heavenly witnesses, grant us we beseech you …'

The petition of this post-Communion is our chief concern. It is expressed in a balanced parallel construction that pairs the celebration and reception of the Holy Eucharist:

---

38 Cf. *CO* 1308.   **39** The Vulgate, however, has *testium* not *martyrum*.

ut	quae	sedulo		celebramus	affectu
	what	with earnest		we celebrate	love

	grato	tibi	percipiamus	obsequio
	with pleasing	to you	we may receive	reverence

The revisers took for adaptation only the first term of this bipartite parallel construction.

In different Missals *CO* 1308 [= *GeV* 504] serves as a collect on the Paschal *Annotina* and a blessing on the Wednesday following the third Sunday after the Pasch. In the first case, the celebrated [or completed] solemnity being recalled is baptism at the Paschal Vigil of a year ago; in the second, it is the Pasch itself.

The prayer, addressed to God, opens with a statement of fact about the embrace of his Providence through which he both supplies for deficiencies in our pasts and exceeds our hopes for the future. The petition is elaborated by a result clause. The simple request is that God will grant the 'abiding effect of the celebrated, accomplished, finished [*peractae*] solemnity which we recall'. The accusative participle modifying *effectum – permanentem –* comes from the verb *permanere*: to stay to the end, hold out, last, continue, endure, remain; to persist, persevere; to abide in a rule of life; to live by. The petition, depending on the liturgical use of the prayer, asks God to grant to those celebrating the first anniversary of their baptism, or to those who have reached the midpoint of the current Paschaltide, the enduring, constant, life-governing effect of the Sacrament/Pasch. The result clause follows: 'that what we traverse through in remembrance we may always uphold in action'. To put it a tad differently, the prayer asks that those celebrating not simply remember the event being liturgically recalled, but may also live it always in their every act. The revisers appropriated the result clause: that what we remember we may uphold. They did not include the petition that, in the original text, causes the result: that God may grant the abiding effect.

The revisers created a new context for the words taken from the preface, *Ver* 229, by placing what they had selected between a new introduction, *Fac nos, omnipotens Deus, hos …* ('Make, cause or grant us, almighty God, these …') and a verb *exsequimur* ('we carry out, accomplish, fulfil'). To this start they appended the words taken from the post-Communion, *Ver* 1282, after changing the verb to an infinitive: to celebrate with earnest love. In the new setting, the direct object of 'celebrate' becomes 'days of joy' – words taken from the preface. The result clause, which was attached without any changes to the text, now also refers to the days of joy. The sense is that we may not simply remember the days of joy we have been observing, but always hold fast to them in action. The result clause of the new collect is weaker than that of the source text because it is not bolstered by *tribue permanentem ... effectum* ('grant the enduring effect') of the older prayer.

We can now look at the new collect as an independent composition. The collect begins with an imperative verb – that is, with a certain intensity. There is no statement of fact about God, but he is addresses as 'almighty' and this serves the function of the statement of fact for it provides the motive for the petition. There is a statement of fact about 'us', however – we are those who are following, pursuing, performing, one might say observing 'these day of days of joy in honour of the rising of the Lord'. The petition follows: 'to celebrate [these days] with earnest love (or earnest disposition, diligent affection)'. The petition is expanded by a result clause: that what we pass through in memory we may always uphold in action.

The centonized composition implies that if God grants us to celebrate the Paschal days with earnest love or diligent devotion (however one chooses to translate the Latin), we will live what we have recalled. That is, the collect seems to assert that a particular disposition, although a gift from God, of itself obtains a good result. This is something different from what is found in the source texts. The Veronese preface presents fasting as necessary for, but not productive of, perseverance in a pure way of life. The post-Communion for Saint John understands that it is God who grants us to receive the sacraments with a reverence that pleases him. The third prayer, which was put to two different uses in antiquity, asks God to grant the abiding effect of the solemnity so that we may hold fast in practice what is liturgically recalled. The new prayer has a theology of grace that is subtly, but distinctly, different from that found in the source texts.

CONCLUSION

The eight Paschal Sunday *orationes* of the 1962 missal are an ancient set. The same prayers, with the very same wording, are assigned to the very same days in more than thirty liturgical codices dating from the eighth through the sixteenth century. The sixteenth-century compilers of the Tridentine Missal simply continued a tradition of prayer that was already very well-established – that, in fact, had been widely used for many centuries. When the post-Vatican II redactors revised the set, they departed from a tradition of usage that was at least twelve hundred years old and replaced it with, as we have seen in the foregoing, a set that is largely of their own making. For among the eight collects that we examined, there are prayers that had never before served as Paschal Sunday collects, prayers that underwent textual changes not attested in the manuscript tradition, and three new compositions.

We recall that each of the six revision policies approved in September of 1966 addresses a specific situation: prayers are not to be repeated, corruptions are to be corrected, forgotten references removed and accommodation to present day practices supplied, proper literary genre preserved or restored, address to the Father preferred, and new compositions confected chiefly by means of centonization. The first of the six gives rise to the last. Since the Tridentine Missals sometimes use the same prayers in different settings, a policy of non-repetition requires either the inclusion of prayers from other Missals, or the addition of newly composed prayers, or both.

Neither *Sacrosanctum concilium* nor the list of revision policies, however, prepares us for what we find in the revised corpus of Paschal collects. With respect to the former, the fathers of Vatican II did not call for a revision of the liturgical texts of Paschaltide as they did for Lent.[40] With respect to the latter, new or different collects were inserted where repetitions did not exist[41] and textual changes made in cases where there were no corruptions to be corrected, forgotten reference to be removed, or changes in practice to be accommodated.

Nor does the stipulation that the proper literary genre of texts be preserved or restored prepare us for what we have witnessed. On the one hand, the literary genre of prayers in antiquity seems to have been a rather fluid thing. Our identification of source prayers, for example, discovers that many ancient prayers were used on different days in different Missals and/or served different liturgical purposes in different codices. On the other, no concern for genre is

---

40 *Sacrosanctum concilium* 109.　　**41** It is true that the Tridentine Missal repeats the Paschal Sunday collect on the ferials of the following week, just as the Paul VI Missal also assigns the collects of the Sunday *per annum* to the ferial days of the week following. This is not repetition in the strict sense. And, if eliminating ferial repetition of the Sunday collect were the goal, it would have been more fitting to assign the new prayers, whether new to the missal or new compositions, to the ferial days for it is them that the repetitions occur. Further, as Table 1 shows, the revisers themselves created repetitions where they had not existed before by assigning two of the 1962 Paschal Sunday collects to both a Paschal ferial and a Sunday *per annum*.

discernible in the choices of the modern editors as they selected either whole prayers or parts of prayers for adoption, adaption or centonization. The group of source texts for just the eight Paschal collects we considered includes not only Paschal collects but also blessings, secrets or prayers over the offerings, the post-Communion of a saint honoured in December, parts of prefaces, and a prayer for the faithful departed assigned to October.

The policy that provides for insertion of new prayers composed chiefly by the method of centonization is deserving of further explanation. In 1966, when Bruylants addressed the Consilium members, he asked whether orations composed by the method called 'centonization' could be inserted into the Missal.[42]

In explanation, he told the members that one of the more difficult aspects of *Coetus* 18 *bis*'s work was selecting new prayers either to substitute for texts that are repeated in the 1962 missal or to provide orations for the *ferial days* of Advent and Paschaltide to which, formerly, proper prayers had not been assigned.

The *Coetus*' first recourse was to select suitable prayers from the ancient sacramentaries. Sometimes, however, they found it necessary to draft new orations, which they did by the method called 'centonization'. Bruylants lists three points in favour of centonization:

1. It is a very ancient (*perantiquus*) practice in Latin euchology;
2. It is conducive to preserving the unity of the corpus;
3. It allows for the preservation of beautiful elements that appear in banal contexts.

He tells the members that the revisers had centonized from sacramentaries, Sacred Scripture and the works of the Fathers.[43]

When the members voted, they granted a wider permission than Bruylants requested. Centonization was to have been the principal, not the only method of composition.[44] Schema 186, in which the policies are proposed, is a sixty-nine page document. The policy questions with the accompanying rationale are set out in the first four pages. The remaining sixty-five pages are a draft of the orations for the Masses of the Proper Seasons in which the principles Bruylants is asking the members to approve have already been applied. That

---

42 *De Missali* 27, Schema n. 186 (19 September 1966), 4: *Placetne Patribus, ut inserantur missali romano novi textus, modi 'centonis' exarati?*   **43** Ibid. All the information summarized here is to be found on page 4.   **44** See Schema n. 186, *De Missali* n. 27 (19 September 1966), Addendum I, p. 1: *Placetne Patribus, ut inserantur missali romano novi textus, modi praesertim 'centonis' exarati?* Addendum I is a six page supplement containing corrections to the original Schema.

is, when the members voted, they were able to see from the texts that they had in hand what the implementation of each policy would mean practically.

The Paschal Sunday Collects in Schema 186, however, with the exception of that assigned to Pentecost Sunday, are those found in the 1962 missal.[45] The Collect proposed for Pentecost Sunday is a centonized composition which combines the opening address of two ancient texts that begin with the same words. This new invocation replaces the *Deus, qui hodierna die* ('O God, who on this day') of the 1962 Collect for Pentecost Sunday which is otherwise left intact. Since *hotiernus* (today's, or this day's) is included in the new invocation, the proposed centonization adds to the prayer without taking anything from it. Compare the 1962 collect with the one proposed in Schema 186:

<u>*Deus, qui hodierna die*</u> *corda fidelium Sancti Spiritus illustratione docuisti: da nobis, in eodem Spiritu recta sapere; et de eius semper consolatione gaudere.*[46]

<u>*Omnipotens sempiterne Deus, qui paschale sacramentum hodierni mysteri plenitudine perfecisti et*</u> *corda fidelium Sancti Spiritus illustratione docuisti: da nobis, in eodem Spiritu recta sapere; et de eius semper consolatione gaudere.*[47]

This example of centonization is fundamentally different from the centonization which produced the new Collect of Sunday VI, in that it leaves the original sentiment of each contribution intact as it combines them to produce a new prayer.[48]

The answer to the question 'from where did the Vatican II corpus of Paschal Sunday collects come?' is that it is, essentially, new. It does not reprise a set of ancient Paschal Sunday collects that fell into disuse. To be sure, elements of the corpus are found in antiquity, but the set as a set is new. Three of the collects are new compositions, and the others never before appeared together.

Another study is needed, one which examines the content of the individual prayers of the new set – how they address God, what they seek from him, what

45 The only changes made are: 1: the Collect assigned to Easter Sunday is presented in the form in which it appears in the Gelasian Sacramentary as discussed above, and 2: a single word, *iustitiae*, is omitted from the Collect of Sunday IV in conformity with ancient variants. See *De Missale*, Schema n. 186 pp 36 and 40.
46 Traditional translation: '<u>O God, who on this day</u>, didst instruct the hearts of the faithful by the light of the Holy Spirit, grant us in the same Spirit to be truly wise and ever to rejoice in his consolation.'
47 '<u>Almighty everlasting God, who in the fulness of today's mystery didst perfect the paschal sacrament and</u> instruct the hearts of the faithful by the light of the Holy Spirit, grant us in the same Spirit to be truly wise and ever to rejoice in his consolation.' *Et* (And) was added by the revisers.   48 As Bruylants' explanation to the members leads one to expect, the other newly centonized Collects in the Paschaltide corpus of Schema 186 are assigned to ferial days.

they assume about the human condition, what posture the one who prays them assumes before God, and so forth. Further, this new study must also consider whether the post-Vatican II set of Paschal Sunday collects is substantially the same as the Tridentine set which it replaced. If the two sets are not substantially the same, it is important to know how they are different and to what effect. Because there is a reciprocal relationship between faith and prayer, these are not inconsequential questions. Particular prayers arise from particular faith convictions, and, more importantly in the present instance, our faith convictions are formed by the words that we are taught to pray.

TABLE 1. DISPOSITION OF THE 1962 PASCHAL SUNDAY *ORATIONES*

Day	Missals	Disposition	Edited?
Sunday of Resurrection	**1970–2008**	**Retained/same day or moved**	**yes**
Sunday in Albis	1970–2008	Retained/moved to ferial	no
Sunday II post Pascha	1970–1975	Retained/moved to paschal ferial and *per annum* Sunday (14th)[1]	yes
	2002–2008	Retained/moved to *per annum* Sunday (14th)	
Sunday III post Pascha	1970–2008	Retained/moved to *per annum* Sunday (15th)	yes
Sunday IV post Pascha	1970–1975	Retained/moved to paschal ferial and *per annum* Sunday (21st)	no
	2002–2008	Retained/moved to *per annum* Sunday (21st)	
Sunday V post Pascha	1970–2008	Retained/moved to *per annum* Sunday (10th)	yes[2]
Sun infra Oct/Asc	1970–2008	Retained/moved to *per annum* Sunday (29th)	no
Pentecost[3]	1970–2008	Retained/becomes the collect of votive Mass of the Holy Spirit	no

1 '*Per annum:*' means 'through the year'. The Sundays *per annum* of the Latin typical editions are called 'Sundays in ordinary time' in the current English sacramentary.   2 Changes are to word order only.   3 Collects assigned to the Vigil of Pentecost are not included in this essay.

TABLE 2. SUMMARY OF THE DISPOSITION OF 1962 PASCHAL SUNDAY AND HOLY
DAY *ORATIONES*

	Same Text	*Edited*	*Totals*
Retained on same day		1	1
Retained, but moved to Sunday per annum	2	3	5
Retained but not assigned to a Sunday	2	2	
Omitted from missal	2	2	

TABLE 3. PASCHALTIDE COLLECTS AND SOURCES IN VATICAN II MISSALS

Day	*Missals*	*Source(s)*	*Edited?*
Sunday of the Pasch[1]	1975–2008	1962	yes
Sunday II of the Pasch	1975–2008	ancient prayer	no
Sunday III of the Pasch	1975–2008	new composition; centonized from 2 texts	—
Sunday IV of the Pasch	1975–2008	ancient prayer	yes
Sunday V of the Pasch	1970–1975	ancient prayer	yes
	2002–2008	new composition; centonized from 2 texts	—
Sunday VI of the Pasch	1970–2008	new composition; centonized from 3 texts	—
Sunday VII of Pasch	1970–2008	ancient prayer	yes
Pentecost	1970–2008	ancient prayer	no

1 The pre- and post-Vatican II missals do not name the Sundays of Paschaltide in the same way. The designations of each Missal have been preserved throughout the essay.

TABLE 4. SOURCES OF PASCHAL COLLECTS IN THE VATICAN II MISSALS

	Source	*Same text*	*Edited text*	*New Comp*	*Totals*
MR 1970, 1975	1962 missal	0	1		1
	Ancient missal	2	3		5
	New Composition			2	2
	Total	2	4	2	8
MR 2002, 2008[5]	1962 missal		1		1
	Ancient missal	2	2		4
	New Composition			3	3
	Total	2	3	3	8

1 In 2008, a reimpression of *Missale Romanum* (2002) was issued.

TABLE 5.

MR 1962: Dominica Resurrectionis	MR 1970–2008: Dominica Paschae in Resurrectione Domin
Deus, qui hodierna die per Unigenitum tuum, aeternitatis nobis aditum devicta morte reserasti:	Deus, qui hodierna die, per Unigenitum tuum, aeternitatis nobis aditum, devicta morte, reserasti,
vota nostra, quae praeveniendo aspiras, etiam adiuvando prosequere.	da nobis, quaesumus, ut, qui resurrectionis **dominicae** sollemnia colimus, **per innovationem tui Spiritus in lumine vitae resurgamus**
O God, who on this day, death having been vanquished, unsealed the entrance to eternity through your only begotten Son:	O God, who this day, death having been vanquished, unseale the entrance to eternity through your only-begotten Son:
attend also our prayers (orsolemn promises), which by preceding [us] you inspire, with your assistance.	grant us, we beseech you, that we who celebrate the solemnit of the Lord's resurrection may, through the renewal of your Spirit, rise in the light of life.

TABLE 6.

MR 1962: Dominica Resurrectionis	GeV 463: Dominicum Paschae[1] = CO 1996
Deus, qui **hodierna die per** Unigenitum tuum, aeternitatis nobis aditum devicta morte reserasti:	Deus, qui per Unigenitum tuum aeternitatis nobis aditum devicta morte reserasti,
vota nostra, quae praeveniendo aspiras, etiam adiuvando prosequere.	**da nobis, quaesumus, ut, qui resurrectionis sollemnia colimus, per innovationem tui spiritus a morte animae resurgamus**
O God, who on this day, death having been vanquished, unsealed the entrance to eternity through your only begotten Son:	O God, who through your Only-begotten, unsealed for us th entrance to eternity by death having been conquered, **grant, we beseech you, that we who celebrate the solemnity of [his] resurrection, may through renewal of the Holy Spirit, rise from death of soul**
attend also our prayers [solemn promises], which by preceding us you inspire, with your assistance.	

1 Leo Cunibert Mohlberg, Leo Eizenfoefer, Peter Siffrin, eds, *Liber Sacramentorum Romane Aeclesiae ordinis anni circuli* (Rome: Herder, 1960), p. 76 #463. Henceforth prayers from this volume will be designated *GeV* followed by the number assigned them in the critical edition.

TABLE 7.

GeV 463: Dominicum Paschae Dominica	Paschae in Resurrectione Domini (Paul VI Missals, 1970–2008)
Deus, qui per Unigenitum tuum aeternitatis nobis aditum devicta morte reserasti,	Deus, qui **hodierna die**, per Unigenitum tuum, aeternitatis nobi aditum, devicta morte, reserasti,
da nobis, quaesumus, ut, qui resurrectionis sollemnia colimus, per innovationem tui spiritus **a morte animae resurgamus.**	da nobis, quaesumus, ut, qui resurrectionis **dominicae** sollemnia colimus, per innovationem tui Spiritus **in lumine vitae resurgamus**
O God, who through your Only-begotten, unsealed for us the entrance to eternity by death having been conquered,	O God, who this day, death having been vanquished, unsealed the entrance to eternity through your only-begotten Son:
grant, we beseech you, that we who celebrate the solemnity of [**his**] resurrection,	grant us, we beseech you, that we who celebrate the solemnity of the **Lord's** resurrection
may, through renewal of your Spirit, rise **from death of soul**.	may, through the renewal of your Spirit, rise **in the light of life.**

TABLE 8.

Ver 229: Mense Maio XII in Jeiunio Mensis Quarti	*Ver* 1282 = CO 3355: Mense Decembri XLI in Natale Sancti Iohannis Evang.	*GeV* 504: Orationes et Praeces de Pascha Annotina = CO 1308; super populum	Dominica VI Paschae
Uere dignum: post illos enim *laetitiae dies, quos in honorem Domini* a mortuis *resurgentis* et in caelos ascendentis exigimus, postque perceptum Sancti Spiritus donum necessariae nobis haec ieiunia sancta prouisa sunt, ut pura conuersatione uiuentibus quae diuinitus aeclesiae sunt collata permaneant.	Miserator et misericors domine, qui nos continuis caelestium martyrum non deseris sacramentis: presta, quaesumus ut quae **sedulo celebramus affectu,** grato tibi percipiamus obsequio	Deus, per cuius prouidentiam nec praeteritorum momenta deficiunt nec ulla superest expectacio futurorum, tribue permanentem peractae quae recolimus solemnitatis effectum, UT QUOD RECORDATIONE PERCURRIMUS, SEMPER IN OPERE TENEAMUS	Fac nos, omnipotens Deus, hos *laetitiae dies, quos in honorem Domini resurgentis* exsequimur, **affectu sedulo celebrare,** UT QUOD RECORDATIONE PERCURRIMUS SEMPER IN OPERE TENEAMUS.
Truly is it fitting: for after those *days of joy* which we spend *in honor of the Lord's rising* from the dead and ascending into heaven, and after the gift of the Holy Spirit has been received, necessarily these holy fasts have been provided for us who live, that they who have been brought into the church by divine providence may persevere in a pure way of life.	Compassionate and merciful God, who never forsake us in the ever present mysteries of the heavenly witnesses, grant, we beseech you, that what we **celebrate with earnest love** we may receive with a reverence that pleases you.	O God, through whose providence no moment of the past is wanting [and] no expectation for the future suffices, grant the abiding effect of the celebrated solemnity which we recall, THAT WHAT WE TRAVERSE THROUGH REMEMBRANCE WE MAY ALWAYS UPHOLD IN ACTION	Almighty God, grant us who are fulfilling [carrying out] these *days of joy in honor of the Lord's rising,* to **celebrate [them] with earnest love,** THAT WHAT WE TRAVERSE THROUGH REMEMBRANCE WE MAY ALWAYS UPHOLD IN ACTION.

Music and the sacrality of the two forms

WILLIAM MAHRT

In introducing the *motu proprio Summorum pontificum*, Pope Benedict XVI proposed a compelling reason for his view that the two forms of the liturgy should exist in mutual complementarity:

> The celebration of the Mass according to the Missal of Paul VI will be able to demonstrate, more powerfully than has been the case hitherto, the sacrality which attracts many people to the former usage. The most sure guarantee that the Missal of Paul VI can unite parish communities and be loved by them consists in its being celebrated with great reverence in harmony with the liturgical directives. This will bring out the spiritual richness and the theological depth of this Missal.[1]

Thus the frequent celebration of Mass according to the extraordinary form can hold up a mirror to the ordinary form, recalling the sacredness not always experienced in the new but a hallmark of the old.

This did not imply a criticism of the new Missal itself, but rather lamented the fact that it had been improperly celebrated. Again, quoting Pope Benedict's introductory letter:

> In many places celebrations were not faithful to the prescriptions of the new Missal, but [it] actually was understood as authorizing or even requiring creativity, which frequently led to deformations of the liturgy which were hard to bear. I am speaking from experience, since I too lived through that period with all its hopes and its confusion. And I have seen how arbitrary deformations of the liturgy caused deep pain to individuals totally rooted in the faith of the Church.[2]

The orderly celebration of the liturgy, according to the 'prescriptions of the new Missal', was the key to the hermeneutic of continuity in the liturgy, the continuity between the old and new Missals.

---

1 Benedict XVI, Letter to the Bishops of the world to present the *motu proprio* on the use of the Roman Liturgy prior to the reforms of 1970, 7 July 2007.   2 Ibid.

The secret, known to many of us, is that the ordinary form when properly celebrated as a high Mass, in Latin, with Gregorian chant, and *ad orientem* (though these are conventionally associated exclusively with the extraordinary form), bears considerable continuity with a *missa cantata* of the old usage, and is scarcely less sacral. But such celebration of the ordinary form is a rarity. The distrust of the 'new Mass' experienced by those attached to the 'traditional Mass' is principally because their consistent experience of it has been of a Mass desacralized and trivialized by improper celebration. It must be admitted, however, that some of this desacralization has taken place within the permissive rubrics of the new Missal – for example, when the celebrant of the Mass, aided by the stance facing the people, assumes the tone of a secular M.C. or a talking head of television; or when the Propers of the Mass are replaced by 'songs' in the style of pop music, etc. While refuge may be found in the extraordinary form, the preponderance of the Church attends celebrations of the ordinary form, and if Pope Benedict's hope for a recovery of the sacrality of the ordinary form is to be fulfilled, every effort should be expended to bring about a healing of the discontinuity between the forms.

Wherein lies the discontinuity? In part in the attitude toward the sacredness of the liturgy, which had been sustained largely by music, and which was lost quite quickly in the reform after the Council. And how was this lost? The rather rapid change of language, which left the liturgy bereft of its traditional music, opened the way for music to rush into the vacuum, a kind of music which was not able to carry the sacrality of the liturgy as the traditional music had in the past, or worse, which even cultivated a desacralized liturgy.

My proposal here is based upon two premises: first, that music has traditionally been the medium of the liturgy, the ordinary means of its external expression and a principal carrier of its sacrality, and second, that music and the Latin language have been a hedge against desacralization. So I propose that the frequent celebration of the extraordinary form with traditional sacred music – Gregorian chant, polyphony, and organ music – can be a model for the restoration of the sacrality in the ordinary form.

First, some definitions. 'Sacred' has the basic meaning of being set aside. Latin has two words, *sanctus*, and *sacer*. Etymologically, these terms both derive from an action of setting aside. Usage, however, establishes the distinction between something intrinsic, *sanctus*, and something purposefully set aside, *sacer*, or even *sacratus*. German terms make a more fundamental distinction: *heilig*, holy, refers to the intrinsic aspect of the other, a quality of being whole, complete, perfect, even health-giving, saving; while *geistlich* refers to the subject, the spirituality of the one perceiving the wholeness. English has a peculiar marriage of Germanic and Romance elements, in which the Germanic represents the outdoor or cosmic aspect, such as *swine* as living animals, while the Romance represents the indoor or domestic aspect, such as *pork* as a food. In this fashion, the Germanic *holy* represents a cosmic aspect and the Romance, *sacred*, its orderly access. While holy pertains to something intrinsic, sacred is an adjective denoting an action done to an object, setting it aside. We call a saint holy, but a priest sacred; the Mass holy, but the liturgy sacred. Sacred, then, includes a substantial component of reception – things not naturally taken to be sacred can become so by usage.[3] Thus, for my purposes, I define 'sacred' as things set aside for the service of the 'holy'.

Another term that needs definition is 'liturgical action'. There are two senses of this term, which roughly correspond to the holy and the sacred. 'Liturgical action' in the singular refers to that central act of Christ in the Mass, by which he makes an eternal offering to the Father, and in which we participate; this is immutable and is the holy aspect of the liturgy. 'Liturgical actions', in the plural, are the various elements of the liturgy which support that central action and by which our participation is made more palpable – lessons, processions, prayers, etc. These may change slowly and are the sacred aspect of the liturgy; I draw this distinction because music generally plays an important role in such liturgical actions.

But sacred things have two complementary aspects: an intrinsic suitability or aptness to the sacred purpose, and a process of being received as sacred. The chasuble, the principal vestment of the priest at Mass, illustrates the process of reception. As the conventional outer garment of a Roman citizen, presumably priests wore it to the celebration of Mass. But when it went out of use in secular society, its use persisted at Mass, until it had become received as a sacred garment; it had become sacred by a process of reception, much like the seventeenth-century black frock coats of Hasidic Jews became a mark of their being set apart.

But sacred things also should have an intrinsic suitability to their purpose; not everything is equally suitable to serving the holy. Thus, the chasuble is particularly suitable to its purpose, because it covers the whole man – its tent-like structure expresses the consecration of the priest being transformed from an ordinary person to an *alter Christus*.

---

3 This setting aside as sacred can be of things with secular origins, but depends upon a certain aptness of the thing to sacred use as well as a tradition of reception as sacred.

There are, however, other characteristics of the reception of sacred things. Their reception makes them ample, excellent, and distinct, with the result that their sacrality is unambiguous. Thus the chasuble may have become a more encompassing garment in its reception, symbolizing better than the secular Roman garment the encompassing character of the priestly office.[4] This was amplified by incorporating other vestments, alb and amice, dalmatic and tunicle for a bishop. Likewise, the garment came to be made of silk and sometimes with gold thread, a precious fabric, the excellence of which made it suitable for use in the worship of God, who is the source of all goodness. And it was given additional decoration, emphasizing that excellence as well. And then, the sacredness of the garment was made complete by using sacred symbols on it – crosses, *chi rho*, and even images. At this point, it was quite distinct from the original Roman garment – it became unambiguously sacred.

Reception based upon convention can be the result of a process of gradual acceptance as sacred, as in the case of the chasuble, or it can be a convention that is received as sacred from time immemorial, as in the case of incense in the Western world. Already in the Old Testament incense is an element of temple worship. Some speculate that it was for the purpose of covering the smells of animal sacrifice, and that could well have been a secondary function, but that does not explain why it was burned before the Holy of Holies, or why the psalm says, 'Let my prayer be directed as incense in thy sight'.[5] Likewise, some have said that it came from Byzantine court ceremonial and therefore had a secular origin, but the Byzantine emperor held a sacred office, and this was essentially a sacred usage. It may well have been avoided in the earliest history of the Church, but its eventual adaptation was based upon its perennial role as something sacred.

Incense is thus apt for sacred usage, because it is a symbol of prayer ascending; it is a precious item, the resin of a plant only grown in a few places in the world, and it has a distinctive fragrance, unlike any other; because it is used exclusively in sacred contexts, its distinctiveness expresses the unique character of sacred worship. If you are accustomed to attending worship where incense is regularly used, or even if you occasionally attend Benediction, where it is almost always used, you will recognize the phenomenon – catch only a whiff of incense, and the reaction is: 'Oh, I am in church!' An Irish pilgrim is reported to have said, 'I love the smell of the *Tantum ergo*'. This is an intuitive response – not the result

---

4 See the examples in E.A. Roulin, *Vestments and vesture: a manual of liturgical art*, tr. Justin McCann (Westminster, MD, 1950), pp 65–6.   5 Ps 140 (141):2.

of a reasoned conclusion, but of an immediate and instinctive recognition. The same can be said of many things which are sacred, the colours of vestments, the presence or absence of flowers, and especially, music.

Gregorian chant participates in similar characteristics of the sacred. It has always been received as sacred; the Fathers of the Church jealously guarded its sacredness, and prohibited the use of instruments, which were seen to imply a pagan context. Chant is distinct from other music; there is nothing like it in our experience, and since we experience it in church in relation to sacred actions, like incense it calls up a sacred context immediately upon being heard. It is apt for sacred use: Gregorian chants do not use regular meters as most other music. If a regular meter and a strong beat express a keen sense of the passage of time, the suspension of these regular temporal phenomena expresses the opposite – by avoiding the sense of passage of time, it can evoke an intimation of eternity. Certain Gregorian chants, as will be seen, show an ampleness that makes their purpose unambiguous – they could not be used in any other context. Moreover, they were composed when there was no musical notation and so are particularly suited to singing from memory. Singing from memory is important in sacred contexts, being called 'singing by heart'. The experience of singing by heart is quite different from singing from notation; in singing by heart, we experience music as arising from our inner depths, as belonging intimately to us as singers.

Polyphonic music derives from chant, but incorporates elements of the secular culture around it; it is therefore more like the chasuble. The Renaissance Mass is a good example; it is sometimes based upon a secular song, but the secular elements of that song have undergone a sacralization by being incorporated into a high musical style constantly received as sacred. There is something valuable in having elements of the everyday world subsumed into liturgical use, since it is analogous to our own entering into a sacred context from the secular world. Moreover, the imitative style of the Renaissance motet is apt for the expression of a sense of cosmic harmony, which expresses order and purpose analogous to the order and purpose with which the Creator endowed all of creation.

This is quite the opposite of the present-day incorporation of popular kinds of music into the liturgy. Such music is used without any transformation of style; instead of sacralizing something from the everyday, it runs the risk of desacralizing the liturgy. The message may well be, 'there is nothing set apart here, it is just like the outside world', leading to the conclusion that there is no reason to come here for it.

The organ, as well, participates in the sacredness of polyphony, its principal musical forms being derived from those of vocal polyphony. Here the question of instruments is crucial. The large organ has properly been a sacred instrument since about the ninth century. It is not regularly heard anywhere but in church.[6] Musical instruments have the property of being able to remind us of the location of their usual performance, just like incense and chant. The sound of the organ recalls the locus of the church. The piano recalls, at best, the home or the concert hall, or worse, the cocktail lounge or daytime television, depending partly upon the style of music played on it. The tone of the organ is sustained, like the singing of the voice, while the tone of the piano has a percussive beginning and an immediate decay, very unvocal. I believe it has been a serious mistake to introduce the piano into regular use in church. Needless to say, this applies to the guitar even more.

Now to my principal point. The tradition in both East and West is that whatever is to be pronounced aloud is to be sung. This tradition is so intact in the East that there is no such thing as a low Mass there. In the West, the low Mass developed in the later Middle Ages only gradually out of the private Mass, a Mass without a congregation, and was distinctly subordinate to the solemn Mass.[7] This normative status of the high Mass was expressed under Pope Pius XII in 1958, shortly before the Council:

> The more noble form of the eucharistic celebration is the solemn Mass, because in it the solemnities of ceremonies, ministers, and sacred music all combine to express the magnificence of the divine mysteries, and to impress upon the minds of the faithful the devotion with which they should contemplate them.[8]

This normative status is still the case for the extraordinary form, though it might seem not to have survived in the ordinary form. However, *Sacrosanctum concilium*, The Constitution on the Sacred Liturgy of the Second Vatican Council, restates the principle, in much the same terms as under Pius XII:

> Liturgical worship is given a more noble form when the divine offices are celebrated solemnly in song [*in cantu*], with the assistance of sacred ministers and the active participation of the people.[9]

6 House organs in the fifteenth century and theatre organs from the first part of the twentieth century had an entirely different sound, which could easily be distinguished from that of church organs. 7 See J.A. Jungmann, *The mass of the Roman rite: its origins and development (Missarum sollemnia)*, 2 vols, tr. F.A. Brunner (New York, 1950), vol. I, p. 229. 8 Sacred Congregation for Rites, *De musica sacra et sacra liturgia* (3 September 3 1958), p. 24. 9 Page 113.

It must be admitted that other elements of the ordinary form seem to have been introduced upon the paradigm of the low Mass, but these can be accommodated in the sung form.[10]

Musicam sacram (1967), the Instruction on Music in the Liturgy following *Sacrosanctum concilium*, upholds the principle more explicitly:

> The distinction between solemn, sung, and read Mass [i.e., solemn high, high, and low Mass], sanctioned by the Instruction of 1958 (¶3),[11] is retained, according to the traditional liturgical laws at present in force.[12]

The same instruction, however, proposed that there could be degrees of employment of music: 1) the priest's chants, including the orations, the dialogues with the people, the Sanctus, and the Lord's Prayer; 2) The rest of the Ordinary of the Mass along with the intercessions; and 3) the Proper of the Mass, even including the lessons.[13] This partial implementation of a singing in the Mass was explicitly permitted in order to allow the gradual accomplishment of a completely sung Mass. It resulted in exactly the opposite – what I would call a 'middle Mass', a Mass in which spoken and sung parts are thoroughly intermixed. Thus there is now a new category: added to *missa solemnis*, *missa cantata*, *and missa lecta* there is *missa mixta*. This is the musical situation in most parishes in the United States today. Often, the priests speak their parts, choir sing their parts, and congregations sing some and speak some.

The American Bishops' recent document *Sing to the Lord* goes part of the way to remedy that situation – it gives strong encouragement for the celebrant of the Mass to sing his parts.[14] If this precept alone were implemented extensively, our liturgies would be transformed. When the priest sings his part, the singing of the choir and congregation are integrated into a larger musical whole; when he does not, the singing of the choir and congregation seem extraneous to the liturgy. *Sing to the Lord*, however, also reinterprets the three degrees of incorporation of music just mentioned as degrees of solemnity[15] in which the greater feasts may be distinguished by singing more parts of the liturgy, while the normal Sunday has more of them spoken; the ideal of the

---

10 For example, the six-fold Kyrie makes sense in a spoken Mass, when the priest says the first Kyrie and the congregation responds, then Christ and so forth. This manner of performance of the Kyrie is unknown in the traditional sung Mass, where a nine-fold performance has been the norm. The rubrics, however, permit a nine-fold performance for musical or other reasons; see *General instruction on the Roman Missal* (Washington, DC, 2011), p. 52. 11 'There are two kinds of Masses: the sung Mass (*Missa in cantu*), and the read Mass (*Missa lecta*), commonly called low Mass', *De musica sacra et sacra liturgia* (1958), p. 3. 12 *De musica sacra*, p. 28. 13 *De musica sacra*, pp 29–31. 14 United States Conference of Catholic Bishops, *Sing to the Lord: music in divine worship* (Washington, 2007), p. 19. 15 *Sing to the Lord*, pp 110–44.

completely sung Mass has been forgotten, and the 'middle Mass' prevails. I contend that this was not the intention of *Musicam sacram*, which proposes these degrees as stages in the achievement of a completely sung Mass, not as means of varying the liturgy. I do not advocate turning back the clock; indeed, there have been some important gains, as imperfect as they may be, in the cultivation of congregational singing. But these gains should now be the basis of considerable further improvement, based upon the proper notion of the role of music in the liturgy and what music best fulfills that role.

Why should the completely sung Mass continue to be the ideal? There are two principal reasons. First, music elevates the liturgy out of the mode of the everyday; this is an essential component of prayer, the lifting of our hearts to God; it is an essential component of the sacred. Moreover, singing insulates the delivery of the liturgical text from the idiosyncrasies of the individual celebrant, placing the emphasis upon the text rather than the person. The liturgical text is not an everyday phenomenon to be spoken in a colloquial fashion. Fr Uwe Michael Lang CO makes an excellent case that the prayers of the liturgy show stylistic features that express their sacred character. They are distinct from ordinary language, conservative, using certain foreign words as hallmarks of the sacred, and employing rhetorical figures characteristic of oral style. The Canon of the Mass, for example, uses a high, somewhat ornate language, which Romans never spoke in everyday usage, but it was suitable to the central prayer of the Mass.[16]

Joseph Jungmann expresses this concerning the lessons:

> The performance must be stylized … The reader must never inject his own sentiments into the sacred text, but must always present it with strict objectivity, with holy reverence, as on a platter of gold.[17]

The Church of England and, for that matter, the Protestant Episcopal Church in the United States relies upon a centuries-old tradition for its manner of reading the Scriptures. In the Catholic Church, since the texts were either sung or read *sotto voce*, there was no tradition and no schooling on how to read in the vernacular. When suddenly the texts were in English, readers had to fall back upon their own devices, and the results were most often quite amateurish. The harder they tried, the worse the style of the reading became. This was because the text was approached as if it should be read in a style as

16 U.M. Lang, 'Rhetoric of salvation: The origins of Latin as the language of the Roman liturgy' in U.M. Lang (ed.), *The genius of the Roman Rite: historical, theological, and pastoral perspectives on Catholic liturgy* (Chicago, 2010), pp 22–44; at 26. **17** Jungmann, *Mass of the Roman Rite*, I, p. 409.

close to the colloquial as possible, solely for the conveying of information, thus overlooking such views as those of Lang and Jungmann that there is a poetic and expressive value to be observed in liturgical reading, and thus compromising the sacrality of the lessons. The simplest remedy to this problem is suggested by the extraordinary form: sing the lessons, according to the Latin tradition, a different tone for each type of lesson – prophesy, epistle, and gospel – whether sung in Latin or English.

I have insisted that at the Mass where my choir sings, the lessons be sung. A new pastor came, and he said, 'I don't want you to sing the lessons, this isn't opera'. When I objected, he said we should try not singing them for three months; then if we still wanted to sing the lessons, we could discuss it. The trial period was instructive: the congregation were disturbed by the loss of the sung lessons, and they attested to the fact that they could comprehend the lessons better when they were sung. I learned that the singing of the gradual and alleluia seemed disproportionate when the lessons were not sung, and that the build-up of intensity and expectation that these chants created was deflated when the Gospel was spoken, while it had seemed perfectly proportionate when the lessons were sung. The pastor was surprised when after three months, I asked to reconsider, and so he put it to a vote of the congregation; he was even more surprised when the congregation voted overwhelmingly to return to the sung lessons. Thoroughgoing singing, then, is the medium of the liturgy, the normal manner of celebrating the Mass, and a hedge against desacralization.

The second reason for the completely sung Mass is that when everything is sung, the musical style which characterizes and differentiates each piece is apparent. For example, the lessons: when spoken, all are read in about the same tone of voice; when sung, however, they are remarkably differentiated. The prophesy (see Illustration 1a at the end of this essay) is sung to a tone that creates a half-step descent at the middle of each sentence, a dissonance, slightly harsh and suitable for a prophesy; at the end the tone descends a fifth, imitating the sound of a trumpet, also suitable for a prophesy. In contrast, the epistle (see Illustration 1b) is sung to a more rhetorical tone, even a hortatory one, suitable especially to the epistles of St Paul, whose language is not anything if it is not hortatory. Its cadences are partly rising in contrast with the descending cadences of the prophesy. The Gospel tone (see Illustration 1c) is the simplest of all, in keeping with the directness and simplicity of the Gospel. It has no middle cadence, but only one at the end of the sentence, which rises a third, ending the sentence at an elevated position. Its effect is to leave the listener's attention elevated. These three tones for the lessons work subliminally; the listener does not have to recognize the technical details just mentioned; rather, when the prophesy is sung, it is intuitively recognized as a prophesy, and so for the epistle and for the gospel.

The same sort of contrast can be seen between three kinds of prayers, the orations,[18] the Preface, and the Lord's Prayer. They use a common musical vocabulary, but each is differentiated from the other in the degree of elaboration; the orations are the simplest, the Preface is more elaborate, and the Lord's Prayer is the most melodic. When the Preface is sung, the listener immediately recognizes that this will lead to the most solemn point of the Mass, while at the same time being congruent with the other prayers.

The proper Gregorian chants, processional chants (introit, offertory, and communion) and the meditational chants (gradual, tract, and alleluia) are similarly differentiated. Upon repeated hearing, these stylistic differentiations orient the listener to the unique and individual significance of each part and as well show forth its place in the organic form as a whole which is the sung Mass. Elsewhere I have pointed out that such differentiation of parts shows forth the very nature of the parts and their role in the whole; it thus fulfills a traditional definition of beauty – *splendor formae* – the showing forth of the very nature of the thing. This is surely an aspect of the view of Pope St Pius X when he defines the characteristics of sacred music, usually translated as holy, beautiful, and universal, but for the second, 'beautiful' is a translation of *bontà delle forme* (*bonitas formarum* in Latin) – the goodness of forms in the plural: the complementarity of the various chants is constitutive of the beauty of the liturgy.

When the whole Mass is sung, the difference between these chants is apparent; they suitably accompany the liturgical action and make it beautiful. When only some parts of the Mass are sung, then the most apparent aspect of the music is the contrast of the sung parts with the spoken ones, but these contrasts contribute little of beauty to the liturgy, because they are not so commensurate.[19]

How is it that Gregorian chant can be so intimately linked with the sacred liturgy? There are two principal reasons: first, it is the direct and faithful setting

---

18 Collect, secret or prayer over the offerings, and postcommunion.   **19** This view is discussed in more detail in W. Mahrt, 'Gregorian Chant as a paradigm of sacred music', *Sacred Music* 133:1 (Spring 2006), 5–14, reprinted in ibid., *The musical shape of the liturgy* (Richmond, VA, 2012), pp 115–129.

of the texts prescribed by the liturgy; second, its melodies form a suitable accompaniment of the liturgical action. To the first, the Constitution on the Sacred Liturgy speaks of 'sacred song united to the words', which 'forms a necessary or integral part of the solemn liturgy'.[20] As unison chant, it is able to project the words most directly. Its melodies arise out of the structure of the text; the *parallelismus membrorum* of its psalm texts is the foundation of Gregorian melody. The psalm tone is the simplest example (see Illustration 2a at the end of this essay). The text comprising two complete, complementary statements, rises to a peak at the end of the first and makes a pause; it then descends back to its source in the second. The melodic activity occurs on the cadences of the text, the final accented syllables of each half.

A more telling example is the psalm antiphon from the Divine Office setting the same text (see Illustration 2b). Each half of the text receives a clear melodic contour, leading to a cadence, the first a simple arch contour, the second a compound of two arch shapes, articulating the fact that it is a compound of two slightly independent grammatical elements. Moreover, the melody underlines the pattern of accent in each word: accented syllables often receive strong notes – either longer duration, higher pitch, or the final of the mode. Yet something is added to the text that goes beyond what is intrinsic to it: the contours of the melody outline notes which form harmonies. From ancient tradition, the notion of harmony does not refer so much to simultaneously sounding pitches as those presented in succession within a melody. Thus, in addition to projecting the grammar and rhythm of the text, the melody bases its contours upon triadic formations, a rising and descending major triad for the first half, and for the second half, a succession of thirds descending. This is how a simple Gregorian melody is intimately united to its text.

The second reason Gregorian melodies are intrinsic to the liturgy is their link to the liturgical action. Again, the Constitution on the Sacred Liturgy says:

> Therefore sacred music is to be considered the more holy in proportion as it is more closely connected with the liturgical action, whether it adds delight to prayer, fosters unity of minds, or confers greater solemnity upon the sacred rites.

Pope John Paul II confirms this reason in his chirograph on the hundredth anniversary of the *motu proprio* of Pope Pius X:

---

20 Even though it is speaking of sacred music in general, this description is applicable principally to Gregorian chant as the pre-eminent music of the rite.

liturgical music must meet the specific prerequisites of the Liturgy: full adherence to the text it presents, synchronization with the time and moment in the Liturgy for which it is intended, appropriately reflecting the gestures proposed by the rite. The various moments in the Liturgy require a musical expression of their own.

This means that each part of the liturgy has its own musical style, as I have already mentioned; it is particularly noticeable in the proper chants of the Mass. Consider the introit based upon the same text, *Justus ut palma* (see Illustration 2c). In comparison to the psalm antiphon, this piece is considerably more elaborated; there are more notes per syllable, and for the most part, the accented syllables receive the extra notes. The *paralellismus membrorum* is heightened by a striking contrast: the first half consists of three very discreet small arch shapes around the same notes; the second rises quickly to a remarkable peak, forming a very wide contour. Upon hearing this introit, without having to reflect upon it, the worshipper senses a greater solemnity, which suitably accompanies the entrance procession of the Mass; it projects a purposeful rhythmic motion appropriate to the procession, and at the same time suggests a sense of anticipation that something important is about to happen.[21]

Contrast the introit on *Justus ut palma* with the gradual on the same text (see Illustration 2d). This piece shows a preponderance of longer melismas (several notes on a single syllable), and the conclusion is unavoidable that the melisma is being cultivated partly for its own sake, for at the beginning of the chant, the syllables '-stus ut palma flo-' are all recited on the same pitch, while the syllable '-re-' receives a melisma of ten notes. Similarly, the word 'Líbani' receives a single note on its accented syllable, while its final unaccented syllable receives a melisma of seventeen notes. This placing of a melisma upon the final unaccented syllable of a word, what I call an end-melisma, this momentary departure from the text, is characteristic of the meditation chants of the Mass, the gradual, tract, and alleluia, and it has a very particular purpose. I sang these chants for years before I realized what this purpose was, and then I learned of it only by observing the congregation. When such a chant is sung beautifully, there occurs in the congregation an absolute stillness; the beauty of the melody elicits a sense of recollection and attentiveness, by which one can ruminate upon the text being sung or the scripture text just heard, and at the same time, be recollected and prepared to hear the next lesson.

21 Although they fulfill the text prescribed by the liturgy, simpler adaptations of chant to the vernacular do not maintain the more elaborate style necessary for the projection of this sense of solemnity.

Here the extraordinary form has something of extraordinary value to present to the ordinary form. Although the *General instruction on the Roman Missal* briefly articulates a purpose for the responsorial psalm – 'it fosters meditation on the word of God',[22] the short, insipid refrains we give our people cannot lift the listener, much less the singer, to the heights the Gregorian gradual can. Moreover, the singing of the verses of the responsorial psalm to a psalm tone is a substantial mismatch: psalm tones are designed for the chanting of the entire psalter in the course of a week by a whole community, not for a soloist to sing before a congregation.

The *General instruction on the Roman Missal* permits the singing of the gradual from the *Graduale romanum* and does not require that it be sung by the congregation.[23] The idea of the reformers to have the congregation sing the refrains to the responsorial psalm comes from very sketchy information about such singing in the early Church. One can infer from St Augustine's sermons, for example, that the congregation had just sung a refrain to a psalm, but this was in the context of a liturgy that had no Kyrie, Gloria, Creed, or Agnus Dei. If now the congregation properly sings the parts of the Ordinary, they can profitably listen to a gradual sung expertly by a choir, without being deprived of participation in the liturgy.

The extraordinary form thus provides a model for the division of singing between choir and congregation. If the congregation is to sing, it is the Ordinary chants that they sing (Kyrie, Gloria, Credo, Sanctus, Agnus Dei), leaving the Proper chants (introit, gradual, alleluia, tract, offertory, and communion) to be sung by the choir. This makes good sense, because the Ordinary chants are the liturgical action in themselves, while the Proper chants generally accompany other actions. It is true that by tradition before the Council, the Proper chants were very often all sung to psalm tones, providing very little more than a pro forma musical setting of the texts, and leaving the beautiful musical distinction between these chants based upon their liturgical functions completely unrealized. But by the strictest definition, 'Gregorian chant' includes this purposeful match of style and liturgical function, and it is not fully Gregorian chant if a Proper chant is replaced by a setting of its text to an inappropriate musical style, even if that melody may be called 'Gregorian'. The psalm tone is a rather extreme example: these melodies are suited to the chanting of the entire Psalter during the week by a whole community; they allow the elevated recitation of the text efficiently, without slowing it down.

22 *General instruction*, p. 61.   23 Ibid.

They do not accompany any other action. What melodic interest there is in this psalmody is provided by the antiphon sung before and after the psalm. To use these tones for the singing of the responsorial psalm, whose proper Gregorian genre is the gradual, a melismatic chant, is a gross mismatch of music and liturgical function. But the Proper Gregorian gradual cannot be sung by the congregation, and that is true of all the Proper chants – to sing five new chants each Sunday requires considerable rehearsal on the part of a skilled choir. It is the Ordinary, whose text remains constant from week to week that allows the congregation to be able to sing something beautiful, since they have the chance to learn it through repetition. Thus, the traditional division in the extraordinary form between the Proper sung by the choir and the Ordinary chants by the congregation is the best solution for the ordinary form as well.

There is a general difference between the extraordinary and ordinary forms in the amount that has to be sung by the celebrant. In the extraordinary form, the priest says a number of things *sotto voce*, including the prayers at the foot of the altar, the offertory prayers, most notably the Canon of the Mass, and the embolism after the Lord's Prayer. The corresponding parts are sung aloud in the ordinary form. To sing the whole Roman Canon aloud is somewhat burdensome for many priests, and this might even be burdensome for a congregation. Yet, the singing is a remedy for the histrionic delivery of the Canon heard today. In our diocese, the priests are instructed to proclaim the Gospel and the Canon. I suggest that to speak the Canon of the Mass aloud day in and day out may bring one to an understanding of why it was said silently since the eighth century, especially if it is always 'proclaimed'. An intermediate solution is to speak the Canon aloud, but in a somewhat subdued manner; this fulfills the requirement that it be said audibly, but it also maintains a sense that the text being said is a sacred one whose style of delivery is very different from that of the gospel, and it recalls the silent canon of the extraordinary form.

I therefore advocate a two-fold approach to the sung Mass in the ordinary form: paradigm and gradualism. There should always be available, at least in larger cities, a completely sung Mass in Latin with Proper and Ordinary Gregorian chants sung by a competent choir and congregation. This establishes the paradigm to which other usages can be compared. It admits of the occasional singing of a polyphonic Ordinary as well, and while this poses certain problems, I advocate singing all five movements of such an Ordinary. But not all congregations can accomplish the paradigm at once. To impose such a liturgy upon an unsuspecting congregation risks emptying out the church. Rather, as *Musicam sacram* suggests, the parts of the sung Mass can be introduced gradually, with careful catechesis while observing how well the congregation receives them. A good beginning is to have the priest sing the Preface and the congregation sing the Sanctus in Gregorian chant, perhaps beginning with the simplest chant for the Sanctus. Congregations that can sing a Sanctus by Marty Haugen can surely sing this chant; the Agnus Dei can be added as well. As for the Proper chants, the Communion is a good place to begin. There is usually plenty of time during the distribution of Communion to include a Gregorian Communion with psalm verses and still to include a hymn or organ piece as well. Each part of the Ordinary and Proper can thus be introduced in turn, always testing their reception by the congregation. I attended a parish Mass in South Carolina, in which the congregation sang all of the Ordinary, the choir sang the Proper chants, and still there were hymns. The church was packed and the singing was robust. I asked the pastor, what did you have to build on when you first came? He said nothing but the average parish music – poor music poorly performed. How long did it take you to achieve what you have now? About six months. I would have thought several years. The key is knowing what the ideal is, and knowing how quickly it can be accomplished. The completely sung Mass is the ideal, but even if the congregation sings only a Gregorian Sanctus and Agnus and the choir sings a Communion antiphon, this is sufficient Gregorian music sung in Latin to alert the congregation to the sacredness of the liturgy that these chants bring to it.

The ultimate reason that the Mass should be sung is that music, by articulating the form of the whole liturgy, integrates it and makes it persuasive. Moreover, music has the ability to touch the soul intimately. When what so touches the soul is the beauty of the liturgy, then its truth and goodness become immediately evident. The Protestant Dean of the Chapel at Stanford, upon hearing a performance with Gregorian chant, said 'this is worth a thousand of my sermons'. To paraphrase Hans Urs von Balthasar, without beauty the truth does not persuade, goodness does not compel.[24]

---

24 H.U. von Balthasar, *The glory of the Lord, vol. I: Seeing the form*, tr. E. Leiva-Merikakis (San Francisco, 1982), p. 19.

Example 1a: Prophesy

I will thrust you from your of-fice and pull you down from your sta-tion.

Example 1b: Epistle

Brethren, if we live in the spi-rit, let us also walk in the spi-rit.

Example 1c: Gospel

Blessed are the poor in spirit, for theirs is the king-dom of hea-ven.

Blessed are the meek, for they shall pos-sess the land.

Example 2a: Psalm tone

Ju-stus ut palma flo-ré-bit: sicut cedrus Libani mul-ti-pli-cá-bi-tur.

Example 2b: Psalm antiphon

Ju-stus ut pal-ma flo-ré-bit: si-cut ce-drus Li-ba-ni mul-ti-pli-cá-bi-tur.

Example 2c: Introit

Ju - stus ut pal - ma flo-ré - bit:

si-cut ce-drus Li-ba-ni mul-ti-pli-cá - bi - tur.

Example 2d: Gradual

Ju - stus ut pal-ma flo-ré - bit:

si-cut ce - drus Li-ba - ni

mul - ti-pli-cá - - - bi-tur.

The Anglican patrimony

JANET E. RUTHERFORD

INTRODUCTION

Once upon a time there was an island. It sat just a short distance to the west of a bigger neighbour, of whom it was afraid. This neighbour had very strong strategic and political interests in controlling the island, and it was also intent on imposing a different religious allegiance on its people. At one point the neighbour did occupy the island, and the outrages it inflicted on the people continue to be part of their national psyche. But the people of the island achieved independence, and through many perils, some literally by the skin of their teeth, they retained it. In the process were forged both their national and religious identity. This description will resonate with Irish people, but the island of which I speak is Britain; and more specifically, England.

Four years of watching a few Protestants a month burned under Queen Mary I left the populace with an almost paranoid fear and hatred of both the monarchy and the nobility, and an allergy to foreign occupation. It is arguable that, until the Thirty Years War, no one did more than Mary I to promote the Puritan cause in England. Even those with little religious sympathy for the Reformation felt that she had betrayed the nation by putting it in the hands of a foreign power through her marriage, and making it subject to foreign religious masters. Though the English themselves are largely unaware of it, this outrage is still present in the English psyche, not far under the surface. They might joke about it now, but under Mary I, *everyone* expected the Spanish Inquisition.

What had started out under Henry VIII as personal megalomania quickly hardened into a national obsession with remaining independent from the Continent, both politically and religiously. The result was a reformation quite different from those of the Continent. For one thing, apart from the brief reign of Edward VI, the English Reformation was led by monarchs with the assistance of theologians, not the other way round. While Swiss cities were subjected to entirely new doctrines and forms of worship by Zwingli and Calvin, successive English monarchs valued continuity, tradition, and hierarchy. This led them to assert the rights of bishops against both Roman authority and Swiss-style theocracy. As King James I snapped when offended by a Puritan Presbyterian, 'No bishop, no king'.

The 'Anglican patrimony' can thus only be understood as it developed over the course of this history – evolving from the Sarum Use of the Roman Rite and Tyndale's Bible, into the Book of Common Prayer and the King James Bible. In these two things, the Book of Common Prayer and the Bible, we encounter one of the primary characteristics of Anglicanism: beautiful liturgical English. Tyndale, Cranmer, and Shakespeare laid the basis for the English language we have inherited in both literature and speech. This is largely due to the fact that theirs was a language of public speaking, not just a literary language. When the translation committees of the King James Bible brought their final drafts to the revision committee, they didn't submit them in writing; they recited them. The rhythm, meter, phrasing and poetry of this language was intended to be heard, understood, and remembered. It was also intended to stimulate reflection and reverence through its beauty and subtlety. Both Cranmer and the King James Bible translators were masters of the subtle nuances of the multiplicity of near-synonyms that English, as a mongrel language, has inherited from its many parent languages. This is important to remember, since it is arguable that beautiful liturgical English is going to end up sounding like Cranmer and the King James Bible, whatever its dogmatic content.

Cranmer was, *par excellence*, a translator and composer of very beautiful collects and prayers, the most enduring of which are theologically inoffensive. It was only gradually that he fell under the spell of that very charming and persuasive man, Martin Bucer, and thus only after a conservative beginning that vernacular translations of rites and Bibles became the battleground between Catholic[1] and Puritan factions for the soul of the English Church.

HISTORY

1. Henry VIII

The story begins, of course, with the man once referred to as 'our national monster'. It is important to remember that Henry VIII was not a reformer; he

---

[1] For the sake of clarity I will refer to the conservative, sacramental wing within the English Church as 'Catholic', as is customary among Anglicans. I will refer to those who accept papal authority as 'Roman Catholic', though this is an anachronism before the Council of Trent. I will refer to those who followed the Swiss reformers as 'Puritan' to distinguish them from Lutherans, who were traditionally known as

simply wanted to own everything (and indeed everyone) in his kingdoms. Of all the continental reformers, he only had any respect at all for Philip Melanchthon, who inherited Luther's mantle. Like Luther, Melanchthon adamantly defended the corporeal presence of Christ in the Eucharistic elements. Also like Luther, he rejected the radical predestinationism of the Swiss reformers, and their iconoclasm (both physical and liturgical). Indeed, the radical double-predestinationism of Calvin led Melanchthon to abandon references to predestination altogether, and to speak instead of God's 'call'. But it was only late in his life that Henry gave a hearing to reformation arguments at all, and it was only gradually that arguments for vernacular worship and lay access to a vernacular Bible received a degree of cautious support from the King. He had become aware that during processions the laity had no understanding of what was being said. As a result, the first English translation of a rite for use in public worship (and the only one Henry himself authorized) was Cranmer's *Exhortation and litany*. It was such a success that it is still to be found in Books of Common Prayer in many Churches of the Anglican Communion. Drawing on Luther's *Litany* and using the Coverdale New Testament, it condensed, but did not eliminate, references to the saints. It was published in 1544, and represented the totality of Henry's liturgical reforms. His attitude to the vernacular Bible was equally cautious. Nonetheless, in 1537 the King stipulated that all doctrine should be officially stated with reference to Scripture alone, giving Cranmer the opportunity to present a vernacular Bible to him for consideration.

The only complete vernacular English Bible at the time was the so-called 'Matthew Bible'. Tyndale had translated the New Testament from Greek, and the first half of the Old Testament from Hebrew, but had been executed before he could complete the second half of the Old Testament. The Matthew Bible (named after the pseudonymous Thomas Matthew, in whose name it appeared)[2] was Tyndale's Bible completed by his colleague Myles Coverdale, who worked from Latin and German texts rather than Hebrew. The 'Matthew Bible' was however only accepted as an interim measure, while work was completed on what would be called the 'Great Bible', the first to be authorized for use in public worship and to be made available to the laity. The 'Great

'Evangelical'. The Swiss-based denominations that accept predestination and deny the corporeal presence of Christ in the Eucharist refer to themselves simply as 'Reformed', since they don't believe that either Anglicanism or Lutheranism is completely 'reformed' in their understanding of the term.   **2** This pseudepigraphal attribution was probably intended to give Henry VIII the impression that it was not Tyndale's translation.

Bible' of 1539 was also the work of Myles Coverdale, but it excised words and phrases that reflected Swiss ideas of reformation (and were thus objectionable to the King), and generally brought the translation back in a more Catholic direction.

2. Edward VI

The first, Henrician phase of the English reformation was therefore Lutheran rather than Swiss in character. Cranmer had to wait until the death of Henry before producing his first eucharistic rite in English, the 1548 *Order of Communion*. Although based largely on the Sarum Use of the Roman Rite,[3] the primary thrust of its revision was to provide for lay communication together with the clergy. This was achieved by incorporating elements of the Sarum rite for the Communion of the Sick, placed immediately after the Communion in both kinds by the priest. The other important aim of its revision was to emphasize that the eucharistic sacrifice had been made once for all by Christ, and is re-presented in the Mass by the action of God through the priest,[4] not offered to God by the priest.[5] With further refinements, it was this eucharistic rite that was included in the first Book of Common Prayer of 1549. The 1549 Prayer Book was an extraordinary achievement, in that it brought together in one volume a Calendar of readings for offices and Mass, offices of Mattins and Evensong (which were also intended for lay use), the new Order of Communion, rites for occasional services, the Litany, and a Catechism. Cranmer proudly stated in his Preface that 'by this order, the curates shall need none other books for their public service, but this book and the Bible.'

The 1549 Book of Common Prayer reveals Cranmer at his most skilled as both a translator and a composer, and his beautiful 'Prayer of Humble Access' makes its first appearance in the eucharistic rite contained here.[6] Observance of Saints' Days is provided, but prayers to them, and the lengthy devotions to the Virgin Mary of the Sarum Mass, are omitted. This reflects the continuing

3 Also consulted were the reformed Roman Breviary of Cardinal Quiñones, and a book on doctrine and liturgy by Hermann von Wied, archbishop of Cologne. 4 This understanding is in accordance with the ancient eucharistic liturgies, and remains the Anglican position. It is indeed arguable that if the eucharistic prayer and prayer of consecration of the (Alexandrian) Liturgy of St Mark were inserted into an Anglican celebration of the Eucharist, no one would notice. 5 The Roman Canon, though based on the Alexandrian anaphora, identifies the people's sacrifice of praise, and their offering of bread and wine, with the once for all sacrifice of Christ into which the Holy Spirit transforms the elements. Thus the priest offers God his own sacrifice of himself. The three eucharistic prayers added to the Roman Missal in the twentieth century were designed to restore the sense of the ancient anaphoras. 6 For clarity I will limit my comments to successive eucharistic rites in the Book of Common Prayer, since they were the focus of particular controversy between the opposing parties.

Anglican practice of joining our prayers to those of the saints (praying *with* rather than *to* them). In the same way prayers for the dead were reduced to a single reference, the departed joining the living in the 'Prayer for the Church Militant' – again, reflecting the Anglican tradition of remembering the departed before God rather than explicitly praying for them. A look at the Table of Comparative Orderings illustrates how the main purpose of the 1549 rite (lay communication) was achieved. The clergy's Confession changes to a General Confession and is moved to follow the Consecration; this in combination with the Prayer of Humble Access joins the people to the clergy for reception of the Sacrament (see the Table of Comparative Orderings at the end of this essay).

Lay communication, offering 'ourselves, our souls and bodies, to be a … living sacrifice' to God (rather than offering him his own sacrifice), giving less emphasis to the saints, and praying for the dead and living together are thus the primary distinguishing features of the 1549 Mass (for it was still referred to as that). There is no introduction of a memorialist understanding of the Sacrament, nor predestination, nor iconoclasm; nothing that is of the novelties characteristic of the Swiss Reformation. Thus the Catholic Bishop of Winchester, Stephen Gardiner, was able to observe that despite lay communication and the use of English, the 1549 Book of Common Prayer was 'patient of a Catholic understanding'; and it has remained a touchstone for Catholic Anglicans ever since. Clergy were directed to wear eucharistic vestments, and the 1549 Mass was intended to be sung. A much-loved part of the Anglican patrimony is indeed the 1549 setting composed by John Merbecke, organist at St George's Chapel, Windsor. He had also written a setting of the Sarum Mass, *Missa per arma justitiae*. Merbecke is thus an important figure in the continuity of liturgical music throughout the English Reformation; even when the Eucharist came to be said in parishes, choral music continued at court and in cathedrals. The Protestant Merbecke was saved from the stake in 1553 by none other than Stephen Gardiner, as the Catholic William Byrd would later be protected from Puritans by Elizabeth I. (Merbecke had been found in possession of a biblical concordance, and in the end they burned it instead of him.)

The 1549 eucharistic rite received a mixed reception, largely because people had come to associate receiving Communion with marriage or sickness. But it remained a reference point during subsequent revisions based on the aggressively Swiss Prayer Book of 1552. Looking at the Comparative Table again, it is easy to see how a scissor and paste method was employed in the

1552 Book, not only to glue Communion to Consecration, but indeed to make Communion (rather than Consecration) the high point of the liturgy. Yet the elements are still called the body and blood of Christ; they are 'spiritual food', but that also is 'patient of a Catholic understanding'. The new words of administration tell communicants to remember that Christ's body was given for them and his blood shed for them, which again is not explicitly anti-sacramental. This rite was the closest to the Swiss reformation that the Book of Common Prayer would ever get, but there is nonetheless still no predestination or explicit memorialism in its wording.

3. Mary I

Despite popular unease, followed by anger at her marriage, there was a reasonable amount of enthusiasm for Mary's restoration of the Sarum Mass. The papal legate, Cardinal Reginald Pole, had long desired reforms of the Church, and he was undoubtedly the man best placed to reconcile the country to a return to Roman obedience. After effecting a return of church infra-structure from the reformed model, he called a legatine synod which established diocesan seminaries in cathedral closes, to match the level of training of Protestant ministers. In other ways too the new English Catholic Church was not simply a return to pre-Reformation models. Although lectern Bibles were removed from churches, the prohibition of Bibles in English was not restored, and indeed Pole planned a new English translation of at least the New Testament. Popular devotion had also moved on. Only a few of the shrines that had been destroyed under Henry VIII and Edward VI were replaced, and there was no significant growth of gilds. Purgatory was not a popular subject of preaching, and (as Dermott MacCulloch observes) 'the Pope's name was still not a winning theme in published literature.'[7] Popular instruction followed Cranmer's model of a catechism and homilies, with Bishop Bonner of London actually pinching two of Cranmer's homilies. Clerical vocations began to rise. But all this good work was undone by Mary's implacable vengefulness, assisted, ironically, by Pope Paul IV – who declared war on her husband, and revoked Reginald Pole's legatine status, ordering him back to Rome to be tried as a Protestant heretic. Not surprisingly, Mary refused to let him go. Probably mercifully for him, he died the same day she did.

---

7 D. MacCulloch, *Reformation: Europe's house divided* (London, 2003), p. 284. The précis of the history of the English reformation that is contained in this essay is indebted to this book on many points.

4. Elizabeth I

The accession of Elizabeth brought with it the return of exiles, many of whom had been 'radicalized' by a prolonged stay in Geneva reading reports of the sufferings of Mary's victims, immortalized in what is commonly called 'Foxe's Book of Martyrs'. They arrived with a determination to have not only a Puritan Book of Common Prayer, but also a Puritan Bible, and they brought with them the Geneva Bible for this purpose. Elizabeth set herself to oppose both things, while at the same time persuading the nobility (including the bishops) to authorize the reintroduction of the Book of Common Prayer and English Bible. Her manner of reconciling these opposing factions was so subtle that it is still not widely appreciated, but it is manifest in her Settlement Prayer Book of 1559, and her choice of authorized English Bible.

Although the 1552 Book had never come into use due to the sudden death of Edward VI, the damage was done in that it had been ratified as a replacement of the 1549 Book. Elizabeth I was therefore stuck with it and its ordering, though she did her best to limit the damage. Although the 1559 Book of Common Prayer was ostensibly the 1552 Book, it appeared with small but important alterations for which Elizabeth was responsible. They all reduce the Protestantism of the 1552 Book. One of the most characteristically Anglican is her amendment of the words of administration, which remained intact throughout the subsequent history of the Prayer Book and are still present in the traditional form of the eucharistic rite. The 1552 Book had removed the 1549 words 'The body of our Lord Jesus Christ, which was given for thee, preserve thy body and soul unto everlasting life' and 'The blood of our Lord Jesus Christ which was shed for thee, preserve thy body and soul unto everlasting life', and substituted 'Eat this in remembrance that Christ died for thee, and feed on him in thy heart with faith and thanksgiving', and 'Drink this in remembrance that Christ's blood was shed for thee, and be thankful'. Elizabeth couldn't remove the new formulas, but she reintroduced the 1549 words in front of them. In fact, out of a pragmatic necessity, Elizabeth succeeded in creating a moving devotional exercise. The 1552 words now serve as a commentary on the original words, and the length of time it takes to say the entire formula lends itself to prayerful reflection during reception.

The nearest that Puritans were to get to the rites of successive Prayer Books was reflected in rubrics and additional literature tacked on the end, rather than the words. The 1552 Prayer Book had contained, at the very end of the eucharistic rite, a Swiss confection made of Zwingli lightly dusted with Knox, known as the 'Black Rubric' (of which more later). When the Settlement Prayer Book appeared, this rubric was no longer there. The only sop thrown to Puritans was the publication together with (but not as a part of) the 1559 Prayer Book of the 39 Articles of Religion, a Puritan mission statement of the most virulent sort. They are still there today in many Anglican Prayer Books, but only on the principle that it is easier to leave them there than start another row with Puritans, who are the only ones who have ever taken them seriously anyway.

But perhaps the wiliest of all Elizabeth I's alterations of the 1552 Book of Common Prayer was her attempt to legitimize the 1549 rubric on liturgical vestments. This had stipulated an alb, chasuble and all other eucharistic vestments. Tucked away at the beginning of the 1559 Prayer Book, hidden under the heading for the offices of Mattins and Evensong is this interesting rubric:

> And here it is to be noted, that the minister at the time of Communion and at all other times in his ministrations, shall use such ornaments in the church as were in use by authority of Parliament in the second year of the reign of Edward VI, according to the Act of Parliament set forth in the beginning of this book.

This is a masterpiece of double talk. The second year of Edward VI was in fact 1549; and there are two Acts of Parliament referred to in the Preface of the 1559 Settlement Book of Common Prayer – those authorizing 1552 and 1559 itself. Since the Act authorizing 1552 is referred to in the Preface as 'in the fifth and sixth years of the reign of Edward VI', the reference here must be to the Act of Settlement itself; making the phrase 'according to the Act of Parliament set forth at the beginning of this book' mean, in effect, 'this statement is authorized by its presence in this book'. Adherents of the two possible rival interpretations of this rubric were still arguing about vestments and furnishings in the twentieth century. The Caroline divines took it to authorize vestments and mediaeval plate and furnishings, and to justify the first, Laudian, Gothic revival.

Elizabeth I's efforts against the Puritans were also directed at the use of the Geneva Bible. The Geneva Bible is actually quite a good translation; the problem with it is that it comes with detailed annotations, interpreting the entire Bible on Calvinist lines. Against it Elizabeth authorized the 'Bishops'

Bible' in 1568 (revised in 1572). This was the first English translation of the entire Bible from the original Hebrew and Greek to be authorized for use in public worship. It was in some parts a new translation, but both the Great Bible and Geneva Bible owed much to Tyndale and Coverdale, as would the King James Bible. The Geneva Bible continued to be favoured for reading at home, and there was little effort made to eradicate its use. It was, ironically, the English Bible known to Shakespeare, recusant Catholic though he was. It was characteristic of Elizabeth's reign that one's private devotions were one's own business, as long as they were kept at home, and you didn't harbour agents of foreign enemies – among whom the Pope came to be numbered as a result of Pius V's Bull *Regnans in Excelsis*.

5. James I and VI, Charles I

Elizabeth I's Settlement remarkably succeeded in retaining a fragile public unity for 44 years, without ceding any further ground to Puritans. But they were simmering under the surface. When James I and VI succeeded to the English throne he was almost immediately met by a delegation of Puritans with a list of complaints against both the Prayer Book and the Bishops' Bible, bearing over 1,000 signatures. Well accustomed to quarrelling with Presbyterians in Scotland, he heard them out with his customary patience. Since it was obvious that any change in the Book of Common Prayer would make it more Puritan, there was no revision on offer from James. But he had already himself made a start at a translation of the New Testament when he was in Scotland, and the idea of a new translation of the Bible appealed to him, especially given the deficiencies of the Bishops' Bible. Thus began the seven-year process leading up to the authorization of the King James Bible. James outflanked Puritans from the outset by stacking the translation committees with what would come to be known in the reign of Charles I as 'Arminians', after the Dutch theologian Arminius.

Already during Elizabeth's reign there had been a growing weariness among the English with detailed dogmatic definitions, whether scholastic (most notably transubstantiation) or Calvinist (most notably double predestination). The Elizabethan period thus saw the first substantial development of another characteristic feature of Anglicanism: an allergy to predestination, and scepticism about attempts to explain scientifically how Christ is present in the Sacrament. In order to escape Augustine (upon whose writings Calvin developed his doctrine of predestination) and Aquinas, there grew up an increasing interest in the study of the Fathers, most particularly the eastern Fathers. Anglican Arminians were notable for their emphasis on free will, their 'high' (though dogmatically undefined) sacramental theology, and their emphasis on the divine right of both bishops and monarchs. One of the earliest was Lancelot Andrewes, who came into prominence as a translator and general editor of the King James Bible.

James I was able to combine his interest in a new translation of the Bible with continuing efforts to counter the Puritan desire to have the Geneva Bible authorized for use in public worship. The continuing influence of the Geneva Bible on private devotion remained a concern under the Stuarts, and was only stemmed when Charles I's archbishop of Canterbury, William Laud, hit on the ingenious tactic of appealing to people to stop buying Geneva Bibles because they were imported from abroad, causing English printers to be reduced to penury – buying Geneva Bibles was unpatriotic. This 'buy British' campaign was as successful then as it would prove subsequently, and led to popular acceptance of the King James Bible. After the Puritan coup and the execution of William Laud in 1645 and Charles I in 1649, the Geneva Bible was introduced for public worship; but it fell with the Puritans, and with the Restoration the King James Bible came into its own and was universally accepted for both public and private worship. It is indeed an irony that the King James Bible has since been appropriated by evangelical fundamentalists, and used as a criterion for biblical literal inerrancy. Nothing would have horrified the translators more, especially given the flaws in its underlying texts.

6. Charles II

Puritan hostility to the Book of Common Prayer led to its suppression during the years of the Commonwealth and its replacement by the Directory of Public Worship. This 'directory' was not however a book of rites, since Puritans disapproved of liturgical worship (and indeed of 'active participation' by the laity, who were only allowed to say 'Amen' at the end of prayers). But the Directory was both limited and incomplete, so that some use of the Prayer Book inevitably continued. The Puritans had been swept into power by suspicions about the monarch's loyalty to the nation, and desperation at the continued refusal of the Stuarts to intervene in the massacres of Protestant populations on the Continent during the 30 Years' War. The English were quickly disillusioned by Puritan rule, but it took some time to get free of them. By the time they were put back in their box, there were no more arguments about translations of the Bible. On the other hand, the Restoration of 1660 saw Charles II in a position to strengthen the Catholic character of the Book of Common Prayer, if circumspectly. The ordering of 1559 was retained, but with subtle alterations. The departed made their way back into the Prayer for the Church Militant, where they had last been seen in 1549. The Offertory, in its liturgical sense, made its way back, coyly attached to the collection of alms, in the offering of 'alms and oblations'. The manual acts of consecration, which again had last been seen in 1549, were reinstated, and an 'Amen' after the words of institution clearly separated consecration from communion, undoing the primary purpose of the 1552 ordering.

Puritans had come to Charles with their own wish list, but all they got was the Black Rubric tacked on the end again. He need not have bothered; they may well have taken it as a calculated insult. One may indeed wonder what the effect was on both clergy and people to be exhorted to worthy reception of Christ's body and blood, humbly pray to be joined to Christ's body through reception of his body and blood, receive the elements as his body and blood, and thank God for having been given the gift of his body and blood, then to find something like a government health warning tacked on the end of the rite that effectively says, 'Although we *call* the elements the body and blood of Christ, we don't mean they literally *are*. And though we kneel to receive them, that doesn't signify adoration.'

The 1662 Book of Common Prayer wasn't perfect. Its main defects derive from the 1552 Book, and even its admirers would have to admit that it is dry. But it has provided the Church of England with its official rites for more than 300 years, and it was the basis for the Prayer Books of Anglican churches throughout the world.

ANGLICAN LITURGY IN THE NINETEENTH AND TWENTIETH CENTURIES

The nineteenth and twentieth centuries were still characterized by arguments, now between Evangelicals and Ritualists. Desire for a Mass among Ritualists led to the creation of what is called the English Missal. Given my comments thus far, you would be forgiven for assuming that this is an English translation of the Sarum Missal. But although the Sarum Missal has been translated into English more than once (notably by Frederick Warren in 1911, using the 1526 edition), the English Missal, so beloved by extreme Anglo-Catholics and so loathed by generations of bishops, is in fact a translation into Elizabethan English of the Mass of Pius V. Episcopal efforts to stamp it out led to the Roman Canon being said secretly in English, with the Book of Common Prayer said publicly over the top. It was largely in order to curb the use of the English Missal that the English bishops devised a revision of the Prayer Book and placed it before Parliament in the 1920s, causing the last great Parliamentary row over a Book of Common Prayer. Its rubrics stipulated that the wording of the rite could neither be altered nor added to, and that everything had to be said audibly. But it also allowed ritualistic practices that had become widespread, but were objectionable to Evangelicals. The mandatory saying of the ten commandments was made optional, with the alternative given of saying what is known as the Christ's 'Summary of the Law' (Matthew 22:37–9). Permission was given to mix water with the wine. Only one of the interminable exhortations of 1662 was left in the body of the text, and even it was optional. The Prayer of Humble Access was finally pushed back before the Preface. Controversial rubrics included the stipulation that laity 'ought' to communicate with the priest rather than must, and that the 'ancient custom' of fasting before communion is permissible. For the first time since 1549 it was explicitly stipulated that traditional eucharistic vestments may be worn, and that either wafers or leavened bread are permitted. These last rubrics arose from distressing incidents of vestment-wearing, wafer-consecrating clergy being imprisoned for contempt of court, and the scandal of the much-loved bishop of Lincoln, Edward King, being tried before the archbishop of Canterbury and the Privy Council between 1888 and 1890 for the same reason.

The 1928 Prayer Book was thus intended to span the growing divide between militant Evangelicals and Ritualists. But having been approved by both convocations of the Church of England and passing through the House of Lords, it was stopped in the House of Commons by two firebrand Puritans, who called it Papistical and accused it of incorporating the doctrine of transubstantiation. When a revision of the book was blocked again, the English bishops took the unprecedented step of issuing a statement authorizing its use anyway. The legality of this was never clear however, and although there was a wide acceptance of 1928 by non-established Anglican Churches, there has not been another attempt to authorize a revision of the English Book of Common Prayer. The 1662 Book of Common Prayer remains the official Prayer Book of the Church of England, and will soon have been its authorized form of worship for 350 years. In order to revise its services, the Church of England has had to produce a legally temporary, unauthorized alternative book under a different name, *Common worship*. *Common worship* provides so very many options both of forms of rite, and of eucharistic prayers and intercessions, etc, that it is arguable that it has succeeded in overturning the purpose of the English Reformation: that is, that all English people should worship together using the same rites, whatever their disagreements. It is important therefore to remember that it is not in fact an authorized replacement for the 1662 Book of Common Prayer. When the post-modern fashion for diversity and individual choice in liturgy fades away, the possibility remains of devising a sensible revision of the English Prayer Book that remains true to the principle of worship undertaken by everyone 'in common'.

A look at the Table of Comparative Orderings will show the anomalies inherited in the 1662 Book from the 1552 Book of Common Prayer. To illustrate the thrust of liturgical revisions in more recent Books of Common Prayer I have used the 2004 Church of Ireland Book, whose alterations are conservative and generally sensible, making it one of the better examples of modern Books of Common Prayer. It has also, like previous English Prayer Books, completely replaced all earlier Irish Prayer Books. The new eucharistic order (Holy Communion 2) flows well both logically and devotionally; the Confession has returned pretty much to its place in the Sarum Missal, and it has pulled the Prayer of Humble Access back to a very good position.

At state of play then, the Church of England still has the 1662 Restoration Book as its Book of Common Prayer, but has sneaked around it by the alternative forms contained in *Common worship*. The English Missal is an Elizabethan English translation of the Tridentine Mass with elements of the Prayer Book, used by some Anglo-Catholics. The 'Anglican Use' of the Roman Rite is the Tridentine Mass incorporating bits of the Sarum Use, the English Missal, and the 1928 and 1979 American Books of Common Prayer, used by American Episcopalian converts to Rome. The Sarum Use, so profoundly part of the Anglican patrimony, is something of an orphan, but has been adopted by the Russian Orthodox Church Outside Russia and Orthodox Old Calendarists, translated into English, Spanish, French and Serbian, and is now their Western Rite. The Antiochian Western Rite Vicariate however uses an Orthodox amendment of the 1549 Book of Common Prayer. To add insult to injury, it is sung to Merbecke – though in at least one church his settings have been arranged for four-part harmony and organ accompaniment. There are other Orthodox Western Rites, based on the Roman Rite and the 1928 American Prayer Book for example. It is indeed a wise man who knows his own patrimony.

In terms of liturgical ritual, Anglicanism has a continuous legacy of doing things well and with dignity. The Sarum Use had been one of the most highly ceremonial Uses of the Roman Rite, and there was subsequently a strong continuous tradition of court and cathedral ritual and etiquette. In addition to singing or saying responses, making ritual gestures, etc., Anglican lay people participate in the liturgy by knowing what is supposed to be happening, and expecting it to be done properly. It might be supposed that this degree of scrutiny would make Anglican worship stultifyingly self-conscious, and that does happen. But in most cases it makes the liturgy enjoyable for both clergy and people. With all the devotional sincerity in the world, Anglicans find it almost impossible not to have fun going to church. An irrepressible sense of humour is undoubtedly an intrinsic part of the Anglican patrimony, and the joke is almost always at our own expense. If any Anglicans wangle invitations to the eschatological banquet, they will be easy to spot: they will be the ones at the noisy end of the table.

CONCLUSION

Although this presentation has concentrated on liturgy, I should mention the agreed tenets of belief that also constitute the Anglican patrimony. As early as Richard Hooker (1554–1600) 'Scripture, tradition, and reason' became a useful summary of the basis of Anglican authority. But in 1870 the American Episcopalian priest William Reed Huntingdon proposed four theses to serve as a basis for what he referred to as 'home reunion' with both the Orthodox churches and Rome. They are unlikely to serve that purpose, but they have proved important as unifying principles within the Anglican Communion. Passed by the American bishops in Chicago in 1886, these four principles received their final form in the Lambeth Conference of 1888. They are:

1. The Holy Scriptures of the Old and New Testaments as containing all things necessary to salvation, and as being the rule and ultimate standard of faith.

2. The Apostles' Creed as the Baptismal symbol; and the Nicene Creed, as the sufficient statement of the Christian faith.
3. The two Sacraments ordained by Christ himself – Baptism and the Supper of the Lord – ministered with unfailing use of Christ's Words of Institution, and the elements ordained by him.
4. This historic episcopate, locally adapted in the methods of its administration to the varying needs of the nations and peoples called of God into the unity of his Church.

These principles have received renewed affirmation in the recent Anglican Covenant, which is presently being considered and approved by the Churches of the Communion. In the Lambeth Quadrilateral the bishops of the Anglican Communion have agreed four Articles of Religion, without the interference of any Parliament or monarch. Although they sound minimalist, it is worth looking at them carefully:

1. By stating that the Old and New Testaments are the standard of faith, those who conscientiously object to regarding the inter-Testamental books as canonical need not do so, while those who regard them as canonical are also free to do so. How Scripture is to be interpreted is also left to individual conscience.
2. Stating that the Nicene Creed is a sufficient statement of faith might seem bare. But it places Anglicanism firmly in the tradition of the Fathers of the Councils. Moreover, it eliminates any possible claim that the 39 Articles of Religion, the Westminster Confession of Faith, or any other additional dogmatic statement, represents Anglican doctrine. The 39 Articles, as I have said, continue to haunt the back of Prayer Books, rather like a souvenir of past wars. Puritans can believe them if they want to, but to say that they are the tenets of Anglican belief is simply untrue.
3. Catholic Anglicans in their turn object to limiting the Sacraments to Baptism and the Eucharist, citing in particular the biblical claims of Marriage to that status.[8] But again, one is free to consider other rites as sacraments, without imposing that belief on everyone else. More subtly, the wording 'and the elements ordained by him' very cleverly allow Protestants to use leavened bread, as is the practice of the Church of Ireland. But since

---

8 It is arguable in any case that there is an implicit sacramental quality to everything involving a rite.

the Last Supper was a Passover meal, there can be no objection to unleavened bread in the form of wafers being used.

4. The final statement on apostolic succession isn't contentious within the Communion. The point of 'local adaptations' simply recognizes that a diocesan structure isn't the most effective in all places of the globe.

This Anglican habit of using words in a way that facilitates a variety of interpretations isn't simply a fudge; it has very good Catholic precedents, arguably the most important of which is that remarkable word *homoousios*, the cornerstone of Christian catholicity. Its success lay precisely in its ability to be interpreted in a variety of ways. It was intended to exclude only the most extreme Arians, but to be acceptable to everyone else. (Perhaps not insignificantly, this was also a monarch-driven solution.) Similarly, ambiguous Anglican language often arises from the fact that the basis of our patrimony lies in liturgical conformity, not magisterial authority. As was once said of Elizabeth I, we do not 'seek to make windows into men's souls'.[9]

It remains to be seen how much of what is distinctively Anglican will prove to be acceptable to the Roman Magisterium. Anglicanism is a reformed Christian tradition, though not in ways that the Continental reformers would have wished. It evolved through tension, conflict and dialogue (and sometimes homicidal mania), and was not the theoretical construct of a single reformer or dogmatic position. It most nearly resembles the Scandinavian and Baltic Lutheran Churches, whose histories are similar to ours, and with whom we are in full communion. But the 'Anglican Patrimony' is more elusive of definition than the Lutheran, as I hope I have illustrated. The difficulty in defining what is Catholic and what is Protestant in Anglicanism has characterized its entire history, not least because the answer varies from one Anglican to another. This has been true from the first translations of that most enigmatic character, Thomas Cranmer. In the 1552 Book of Common Prayer he had an opportunity to be as Protestant as he wanted to be. But despite the obvious Swiss influences upon it, there is a persistent emphasis on petitioning God to give us grace, on beseeching God to have mercy on us, that is inconsistent with a belief in predestination, but has rather evolved from the Sarum Missal, and has characterized Anglicanism ever since.

If I had to choose one small thing to hold up and say, 'This is the Anglican Patrimony', it might well be the Prayer of Humble Access. It is difficult to

9 Francis Bacon.

COMPARATIVE ORDERINGS

Sarum	1549	1552	1559	1662	1928	C. of I 2004 (1)	C. of I 2004 (2)
C. for Purity	C. for Purity	C. for Purity	Our Father	Our Father	Our Father	Our Father	
Our Father	Our Father		C. for Purity	C. for Purity	C. for Purity	C. for Purity	C. for Purity
Gloria	*Gloria*	Commandments	Cdments	Cdments	Summary of Law	Summary of Law	Summary of Law
CONFESSION							CONFESSION
							Gloria
Collects	Collects	Collects	Collects	Collects	Collects	Collects	Collects
Readings	Readings	Readings	Readings	Readings	Readings	Readings	Readings
							Homily
Creed	Creed	Creed	Creed	Creed	Creed	Creed	Creed
	Homily	Homily	Homily	Homily	Homily	Homily	
	Exhortation						Intercessions
							H Access
							Peace
Offertory	Offertory	Offertory	Offertory	Offertory	Offertory	Offertory	Offertory
		Intercessions	Intercessions	Intercessions	Intercessions	Intercessions	
		Exhortations	Exhortations	Exhortations	CONFESSION	CONFESSION	
		CONFESSION	CONFESSION	CONFESSION	H Access		
Preface	Preface	Preface	Preface	Preface	Preface	Preface	Preface
Intercessions	Intercessions	H Access	H Access	H Access		H Access	
Consecration	**Consecration**	**Consecration**	**Consecration**	**Consecration**	**Consecration**	**Consecration**	**Consecration**
Our Father	Our Father				Our Father		Our Father
Agnus Dei	Peace				Peace		(Agnus Dei)
Peace	CONFESSION						
	H Access						
	Agnus Dei						
Reception	**Communion**	**Communion**	**Communion**	**Communion**	**Communion**	**Communion**	**Communion**
					Our Father		
PC Prayer	PC Prayer	PC Prayer	PC Prayer	PC Prayer	PC Prayer	PC Prayer	PC Prayer
		Gloria	*Gloria*	*Gloria*	*Gloria*	*Gloria*	
	Blessing	Blessing	Blessing	Blessing	Blessing	Blessing	Blessing
Prayer		Prayers	Prayers	Prayers			

imagine Calvin saying that God's nature is 'always to have mercy', let alone asking God to give us grace to eat the flesh and drink the blood of his Son so that we might dwell in him and he in us. Anglicans consider themselves to be 'reformed catholics' within the unbroken (though zig-zaggy) tradition of the English Church, united in their forms of public worship. Through Prayer Book and Bible, Bishop and King, Anglicanism has sought (in the words of Richard Baxter) 'Unity in things necessary, liberty in things unnecessary, and charity in all'.

Prayer of Humble Access

We do not presume to come to this thy Table, O merciful Lord, trusting in our own righteousness, but in thy manifold and great mercies. We are not worthy so much as to gather up the crumbs under thy Table. But thou art the same Lord, whose property is always to have mercy: Grant us, therefore, gracious Lord, so to eat the flesh of thy dear Son Jesus Christ, and to drink his blood, that our sinful bodies may be made clean by his body, and our souls washed through his most precious blood, and that we may evermore dwell in him, and he in us. Amen.

What has language to do with beauty?
The philosophical foundations of liturgical translations

DANIEL B. GALLAGHER

INTRODUCTION

In a previous essay entitled 'What has beauty to do with reason? The philosophical foundations of liturgical aesthetics',[1] I tried to offer a philosophical basis for affirming the importance – indeed, the necessity – of beauty in the sacred liturgy, and to suggest some criteria for assessing the presence of beauty in the liturgy or the absence thereof. I argued that the Divine Liturgy is an act of worship that fully engages human reason in its broadest sense as urged by Pope Benedict XVI both before and after his election to the papacy. To quote the Pontiff:

> I believe a particularly urgent task of religion today is to unveil the vast potential of human reason ... Belief in the one God, far from stunting our capacity to understand ourselves and the world, broadens it ... Although [God's] infinite glory can never be directly grasped by our finite minds in this life, we nonetheless catch glimpses of it in the beauty that surrounds us. When men and women allow the magnificent order of the world and the splendour of human dignity to illumine their minds, they discover that what is 'reasonable' extends far beyond what mathematics can calculate, logic can deduce and scientific experimentation can demonstrate.[2]

Among those responsible for implanting this broad notion of human reason in the mind of the young Ratzinger were Saints Augustine and Bonaventure, Blessed John Henry Newman, Romano Guardini, Henri de Lubac and Hans Urs von Balthasar. According to them, participation in the liturgy not only brings about a knowledge 'that' (in other words, an apprehension of the

---

1 'What has beauty to do with reason? The philosophical foundations of liturgical aesthetics' in D.V. Twomey and J.E. Rutherford (eds), *Benedict XVI and beauty in sacred art and architecture* (Dublin, 2011), pp 77–93.
2 Meeting with Representatives of the Muslim Community of Cameroon, Yaoundé, 19 March 2009.

content of divine revelation, especially through the proclamation of the Word), nor does it simply entail a knowledge of 'how' (the pronunciation of the words and performance of the gestures indicated by liturgical rubrics and norms); rather, it instils a knowledge 'what', inextricably linked to a knowledge 'who': namely, the God of Abraham who has spoken in his Son Jesus Christ, the Incarnate Word, calling us to share in the divine life and love of the Triune God. Such knowledge and the act of worship that ensues upon it are elegantly suggested by Saint Paul's expression *logiké latreía* (Romans 12:1–2). This relational dimension of Christian faith has pervaded Ratzinger's entire theological output from his *Habilitationschrift* entitled *The theology of history in Saint Bonaventure* to his most recent encyclical *Caritas in veritate*. It is particularly poignant in his liturgical theology. In *Feast of faith*, he asserts that 'the primary characteristic of Christian faith is that ... God is someone who speaks, someone to whom man can speak. The Christian God is characterized by revelation, that is, by the words and deeds in which he addresses man, and the goal of revelation is man's response in word and deed, which thus expands revelation into a dialogue between Creator and creature which guides man toward union with God.'[3]

Among the four implications I presented in my previous essay was the following:

> If beauty pertains primarily to the intellect, such that aesthetic perception is chiefly a form of *understanding*, than beauty is not merely an ornamentation of the liturgy. In other words, beauty engages the intellect such that God's Word and life are apprehended in a way that transcends the mere conveyance of information. This is precisely why a suitable translation of liturgical texts cannot rest merely upon the criterion of 'what will best convey the information contained therein'; it must rather facilitate an encounter with the living God in a way that surpasses sheer discursive communication.[4]

Here I intend to delve further into that implication by converting it from a conclusion to a thesis. As in my previous essay, I do so primarily from a philosophical point of view. This does not, of course, preclude me from speaking about God, since God – at least according to Saint Thomas Aquinas and two millennia of Christian thinking – is a philosophical topic, and philosophy may draw upon the contents of revelation while remaining true to its task.

3 *Feast of faith*, p. 16.   4 'Philosophical foundations of liturgical aesthetics', p. 76.

WHERE IS BEAUTY IN LITURGICAL TRANSLATIONS?

Let me start at the end. It is virtually impossible to capture in any vernacular language the most salient features of the Latin language that render the Roman Rite so beautiful. Whether it is cadence or assonance, syntax or periods ending certain phrases – all of these prosaic and poetical features are so specific to the language that they can hardly be rendered into English without sacrificing quite a lot.

Paragraph 59 of *Liturgiam authenticam* says as much. Though it pertains directly to the oral proclamation of liturgical texts, it nonetheless expresses something unique about the Latin language and what can be expected from vernacular translations:

> [liturgical texts] are characterized by a certain manner of expression that differs from that found in everyday speech ... Examples of this include recurring and recognizable patterns of syntax and style, a solemn or exalted tone, alliteration and assonance ... repetition, parallelism and contrast, a certain rhythm, and at times, the lyric of poetic compositions. If it is sometimes not possible to employ in the translation the same stylistic elements as in the original text (as often happens, for example, in the case of alliteration or assonance), even so, the translator should seek to ascertain the intended effect of such elements in the mind of the hearer as regards thematic content, the expression of contrast between elements, emphasis, and so forth. Then he should employ the full possibilities of the vernacular language skillfully in order to achieve as integrally as possible the same effect as regards not only the conceptual content itself, but the other aspects as well. In poetic texts, greater flexibility will be needed in translation in order to provide for the role played by the literary form itself in expressing the content of the texts. Even so, expressions that have a particular doctrinal or spiritual importance or those that are more widely known are, insofar as possible, to be translated literally.

Presuming that *Liturgiam authenticam* is correct, I would like to suggest that the beauty of liturgical translations consists not so much in the transposition of the literary and poetical features of the original Latin text, but in the clear, precise, elegant expression of the analogical and metaphorical nature of Christian discourse in general.

To make this argument as a Christian philosopher, I will have to go back to the beginning and briefly review the philosophy of language in the twentieth century.

PHILOSOPHY OF LANGUAGE

Only recently has language been considered a philosophical 'problem'. This view arose primarily from developments in analytic philosophy sparked by advances in formal logic, leading to what philosophers call the 'Linguistic Turn', although the philosophy meant by that term ran into serious difficulties in the mid-twentieth century, resulting in major modifications to linguistic theory if not altogether despair of its usefulness.

All the issues concomitant to language as a 'problem' revolve around the relationship between the thing referred to, the concept of the thing, and the word representing the thing. 'Chico' might refer to Pope Benedict XVI's cat (real or imaginary – it doesn't matter), my concept of the cat, and the word 'Chico'. Analytic philosophers tend to consider the word 'Chico' as a 'medium of conceptualization': in other words, as something that enables the existing cat to become a concept in my mind. British empiricism, the epitome of which is represented by John Stuart Mill, holds that the only thing we can receive from external reality are sense impressions; words simply help us to organize or cluster sense impressions into meaningful units. The upshot of this is that language is understood as nothing more than a complex arrangement of signs. When I say 'Chico is perched on Monsignor Gänswein's knee', 'Chico' refers to a 'fuzzy four-legged animal' and 'Monsignor Gänswein's knee' refers to another distinct object. The function of the verb 'is perched' is more difficult to expound, but again, according to analytic philosophy, it boils down to a sign that 'denotes' some object in the world – perhaps in this case the 'object' of the cat's posture.

The shortcomings of a strictly linguistic philosophy are many. The two most obvious are that the theory does not readily account for expressions of wishing, intending, and desiring, and it does little to account for the difference between a really existing cat named Chico and a cat that is merely a figment of Monsignor Gänswein's (and our) imagination. The German mathematician Gottlob Frege tried to overcome the latter difficulty by distinguishing between two semantic aspects: *sense* and *reference*. He called the *sense* of an expression its 'mode of presentation' which is a distinct way of conveying information.

The information conveyed, in turn, has a referent. When it comes to a negative existential expression such as 'Brenda the unicorn', we can flesh out the sense by employing other descriptions, even if the referent of the expression is an empty set.

Frege essentially redrew the map of philosophy in the late-nineteenth century. Senses were not merely psychological entities since, even if their referents do not really exist, they serve a normative function when several people engage in conversation. This opened a new domain for philosophy in a world dominated by the empirical and experimental sciences. It was philosophy's task to perform a logical analysis of the underlying structure of utterances. This paved the way for Bertrand Russell, A.J. Ayer, G.E. Moore, and others to classify different modes of expression based on the various relationships between 'sense' (also referred to as 'intension') and reference (also referred to as 'extension').

Ludwig Wittgenstein carried the idea that language consists of elementary propositions related by the elements of first-order logic to its logical extreme. Namely, he claimed that any sentence that could not become the object of logical analysis had absolutely no sense. The form of every meaningful proposition resembles the form of some fact in the world. An utterance, in a way similar to a picture, yields meaning when its internal elements coordinate with objects outside itself. Though this seems to restrict what language can do, Wittgenstein also believed that language not only 'says' but 'shows'. We cannot 'say' what the conjunction 'and' does in a sentence; we can only 'show' what it does.

The Vienna Circle, founded by Moritz Schlick, proposed the so-called 'verification theory of meaning', which drew upon the distinction between analytic and synthetic sentences. Analytic sentences (those expressing a judgment in which the predicate is covertly contained in the concept of the subject, such as 'all bachelors are unmarried') are true in virtue of the meanings of their terms; while synthetic sentences (those expressing a judgment in which the predicate amplifies or adds something to the concept of the subject, such as 'some bodies are heavy' or 'a green light indicates "go"') must admit some sort of criteria for empirical verification. Any sentence that cannot be verified in one of these two ways must be regarded as meaningless. This, of course, not only excludes theological statements, prayers, and cultic (including liturgical) utterances but a broad swathe of ethics and metaphysics.

As this all too brief summary suggests, the meaning and sense of liturgical language is challenged by not a few philosophical schools, such that the question of its beauty becomes a moot point. As I wished to show in my previous essay, a viable argument can be put on the table for beauty *as* meaning, albeit a meaning different from other kinds of meaning.

The Mind–World–Language Triangle

As a result of the 'linguistic turn', analytic philosophers generally conceive the activity of describing and explaining the world as a triangle, the three points of which are 'language', 'mind', and 'world':

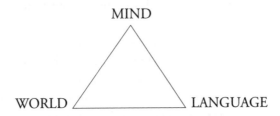

The lines connecting these points represent the relations that are the keys to understanding our place in reality. These relations in one way or another constitute the *meaningfulness* of language. Philosophers then set about studying each of the sides of the triangle as separate entities, even though together they make up a single triangle. Between mind and world, for example, a number of crucial relations are identified including perception, action, the mind's bodily constitution and intentionality (that is, the mind's ability to think *about* what is in the world). In moving from mind to language, philosophers are intent upon studying the mental activity that gives rise to words and syntax. This activity seems to be what the real existence of meaningful language consists in. In short, mind invests *meaning* in language.

The focus of the mind-language connection is the central notion of *understanding*. An account of meaning in a given language is simply an account of what constitutes the ability to understand it. Locke, Frege and the logical positivists were attracted to the view that understanding is a matter of associating the correct ideas or concepts with words. More recently, Donald Davidson and Michael Dummett have equated understanding with knowing the requirements for the accurate or appropriate use of words and sentences. Wittgenstein believed that the key to understanding is one's ability to 'pass' linguistically 'without censure'.

The line connecting the 'language' and 'mind' corners of the triangle implies that if the mind assigns meaning to language, so too language *enables* and *channels* the mind. Acquiring and using a language furnishes the knower with concepts, thoughts, and habits of thought, bearing all sorts of consequences. Indeed, knowing a language is so crucial to our ability to frame the sophisticated thoughts essential to understanding that Donald Davidson began to wonder whether mind is 'prior' to language in any meaningful way. Bertrand Russell expressed a similar concern when we wrote: 'Language serves not only to express thoughts, but to make possible thoughts that could not exist without it'. Although Russell could not assent to the view that there can be no thought without language, 'it cannot be denied that all fairly elaborate thoughts require words'.[5]

What about the line connecting 'language' and 'world'? Philosophers have focused on this line insofar as language, as a vehicle of descriptions and explanations of reality, must prove itself a *true* or *apt* characterization of reality. This gives rise to the notion of *truth-condition* as the preamble for gleaning meaning out of 'meaning'. The meaning of a proposition establishes a condition that must be met if the proposition is to be true. For example, the proposition 'Rome is larger than Cork', given what it means, is true just in case a certain state of affairs obtains (namely, a certain city is larger than a certain other city). According to the truth-conditional picture of meaning, the core of what a statement *means* is its truth-condition – which helps determine the way reality is *said to be* in it – and the core of what a word means is the contribution it makes to obtaining this truth-condition (perhaps, in the case of certain kinds of words, this is simply what the word *refers* to).

Correcting the Triangle

Conceiving the relationship between world, mind, and language in the form of a triangle leads to several pitfalls. It misleadingly establishes three separate entities which seem to be different 'things'.

Aristotle can help us correct this problem.[6] According to the Stagyrite, the central activity of reason is predication or judgment. Aristotle calls this activity *apophansis*, which he describes somewhat cryptically as 'saying something of something'. In short, if nouns and verbs are the fundamental elements of syntax, then predication is its most basic act. Of course, syntax is immensely

---

5 B. Russell, *Human language: its scope and limits* (London, 1948), p. 74.   6 See Robert Sokolowksi, *Phenomenology of the human person* (Cambridge, 2008), pp 48 ff.

rich and varied. If we were to survey all the world's languages – even the Latin language contained in the Roman Missal – we would discover innumerable forms of subordination, conjunction, correlation, reciprocity, reflexives and possessives, tenses and cases, adjectives and adverbs, infinitives and gerunds, but underlying all is the ubiquity of predication by which something is said of something. Everything else hangs on this.

The linguistic turn tends to think of predication as a combination of two different objects or things. This is far too simplistic. The subject and predicate are not to be understood as individual, isolated words but as elements of phrases. Even individual words are latent combinations and hence syntactically structured in principle. Each predication gives rise to further subdivisions and sub-predications in each of its parts. These further subdivisions and sub-predications yield a Russian-doll, hierarchic cascade of phrases that constitutes language and rational articulation.

This rational articulation occurs throughout the World–Mind–Language triangle. That is, syntactic structure occurs in language, in concepts or propositions, and in things. There is a grammatical structure in language, there is a logical structure in concepts and propositions, and there is a formal ontological structure in the things we articulate and present to ourselves and to others. The grammatical ordering of language is correlated with the syntactic structuring of our concepts and propositions, and these in turn are correlated with the formal structures of things. Hence the 'corners' of the triangle are best envisioned as fields: the linguistic, the conceptual or propositional, and the ontological, each of which has its corresponding structure or syntax.

These three domains must be distinguished from one another; but the ways in which they are mutually involved with one another, although philosophically crucial, are difficult to determine. Philosophers often use different scripts or fonts to designate them. *Cat* signifies the word that is the name of the animal; 'cat' signifies the concept; and <u>cat</u> signifies the animal itself. So one and the same word – *cat*, 'cat', and <u>cat</u> – signifies in three different ways:

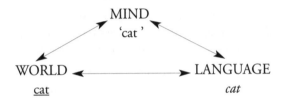

Suppose, for example, that the pope has a cat. Let us further suppose that His Eminence Cardinal Bertone is allergic to cats. In order to protect Cardinal Bertone from having an allergic reaction, Monsignor Gänswein warns him that he should knock before entering the papal apartments so that the cat can be put away. We could then say that Msgr Gänswein used the word *cat* to warn Cardinal Bertone that a <u>cat</u> is in the papal apartments, and his concept of 'cat' led the Cardinal to knock before entering. One word thus means the same thing from three different perspectives: it signifies the thing, its name and its concept.

These differences show up neither to Msgr Gänswein nor to Cardinal Bertone. Each of them focuses on the real cat slinking around the papal apartments. The differences in the use of the term show up only to someone who writes the sentence down or to someone who reads it. They show up to someone who steps back from the situation being described and to what is said within it, but not to someone involved in it. They come into play at a 'second level' of reflection. These shifts in perspective might seem trivial on the surface since they do not introduce new objects into the scenario. But the perspectives and their shifts are not simply 'nothing'. They introduce new dimensions, even though they do not present new things, and it is precisely the introduction of new dimensions that establishes the differences between things, concepts, and words.

The three domains of word, concept and thing come vividly into play when we are not sure whether something we are talking about truly exists. Suppose, for example, we are not sure that there really is a thing such as a cat. In this instance, there may be *cat* (the word) and 'cat' (the concept), but no <u>cat</u> (the thing). But how is it that we can have a word and a concept for something that does not exist, as in the case of unicorns? Recall that this was one of the problems encountered by analytic linguistics. Clearly, without words and syntax we cannot intend such nonentities as unicorns.

To address the triangle problem, we must first note that we move into the domain of categoriality (that is, into the realm of saying something about something) when we do the following: we go back to the identity of the thing, we focus on the identity and on the thing as a whole (we establish a subject, S, 'the cat'), and we focus again on the feature in question – say, the colour – but we now take it explicitly as part of the whole (we establish a predicate, p, 'is white'). We have reached something that has been formalized as S is p. We explicitly embed the feature in the thing, the predicate in the subject, and we now enter the realm of logical inclusion and exclusion, with all its refinements and syntactic complexities. We have moved, in our experience and thoughtful activity, from a perception to an articulated opinion or position. We have reached a proposition or a meaning, something that can be communicated and shared as the very same with other people. If things did not present parts and wholes to us, predication and syntactic articulation would be impossible. Predication takes place between us and things, not within our own consciousness or within a subjective world.

Therefore, in response to the line running from 'mind' to 'language' in our triangle, we can say that logical form or syntactic structure does not have to issue forth from inborn powers in our brains (*à la* Descartes) nor does it have to come from *a priori* structures of the mind (*à la* Kant); it arises through an enhancement of perception, a lifting of perception into thought, and a new way of making things present to us.

In short, the central achievement of articulated speech is that through it, we say something about something. Every syntactic structure is based on this. The structure of predication is the prime example of the hierarchic, Russian-doll, embedding architecture that constitutes syntax. It is not that this embedding begins only after predication has already taken place, or that it happens only when one predicative phrase or clause is embedded in another. There is stacking in predication itself.

We should also note that what is achieved in predication is only achievable at the level of communication. The words we speak and the thoughtful way in which we phrase our utterances occur first and foremost when we are engaged in conversation. Categorical intuition is not perfected within the lonely confines of an isolated mind. It is rather something the speaker does for the listener. The formal structure of subject and predicate (S is p) arises insofar as the speaker focuses the mind of the listener first on the whole object in its identity as something to be articulated and then on a part or a feature of the object in a manner that couples them.

This holds true even when God speaks in divine Revelation. Articulation is a public action mediated by the language available to the persons involved in an encounter. Both speaker and listener are thinking in the medium of words but they are thinking primarily about the thing articulated. They are *not* focused on the concepts or words as such. The 'linguistic triangle' is the furthest thing from their minds. All that is necessary to establish formal structures is the intersubjective context itself. It cannot be done by a single mind imparting a logical structure to sense data. The formation of categorical utterances and their elevation into logic is the achievement not of a single mind but of minds working together, one person working with another, and doing so in public. If the transition from perception to thought happened within the private chamber of the mind, communication would be impossible. We move from the outside to the inside, not from the inside to the outside. We do not move from solitude to interiority to publicness. Even though we tend to think of speech as voiced thought ('thinking out loud'), it would be better to move in the other direction and think of silent thinking as unvoiced speech. The use of language, words, names, and syntactic structures is inherently intersubjective, and predication occurs not when we impose the categories of our understanding on experience, but when speakers bring things into focus and establish references for the audience and for themselves and then determine the salient features of what they have isolated. All of this speaks to the essential 'publicness' of the divine liturgy.

Summary

I hope that the way I have described language above can help us escape the deadly trap of Descartes' mental representations. If we start with them, we never get beyond them. They lock us into subjective isolation. Indeed, it is hard to say exactly what such mental representations are. They never present themselves directly. Mental representations threaten the philosophy of cognition and language because they are taken as the things we know directly. They are posited as intermediaries between us and the things we think about, and we inevitably begin talking about them as if they were the direct targets of our awareness. Once we start talking primarily about mental representations, we run the risk of concluding that what we really and directly know are precisely such representations rather than things themselves. Consequently, we begin to believe that our thoughts are something like images in a dream, except that mental representations are more transparent.

The intersubjective approach circumvents the very notion of mental representations because it understands that the words used in conversation refer to things themselves and formulates them in wholes and parts. Furthermore, with this approach, communication is not something 'added' to words. The communicative dimension is present from the beginning. There would be neither words nor syntax if people were not trying to display or disclose things to one another.

Applying the Triangle to God

Christian discourse is entirely unique with respect to other forms of discourse. Christian discourse is not a species of a generic 'religious discourse'. As Robert Sokolowski explains, religion without biblical revelation takes 'God' or 'the gods' as the best and most powerful beings in the world but part of the world nonetheless.[7] In natural religion, it is not possible to think that the divine could be all there is. Rather, the 'whole' is given, and the divine is the best and the most admirable part of it.

Christianity is unique in that it has received a revelation that gives a distinct sense of the divine. According to Christianity, God *could* have been all there is. God does not have to be conceived as 'part' of the whole. God has in fact created the world, and the world exists as other than God, but in principle it need not have been so. According to the Christian understanding, the world exists 'contingently' as the result of God's free choice. It is not just any kind of 'contingency', but a contingency that depends upon an absolutely free, un-necessitated choice; and not just any kind of choice, but the kind involved in Creation. The logic of parts and wholes discussed above, and the logic of necessity and contingency, are transposed in Christian belief.

ANALYSIS AND METAPHOR

This transposition must be kept in mind lest we equate the functioning of analogy and metaphor in Christian discourse with that of natural discourse. Even in natural discourse, metaphor and analogy seem inevitable. We speak 'about' something, our minds move 'toward' something, arguments 'support' something. These prepositions all have their primary meanings in the realm of space and time. An even more radical inevitability of metaphorical and analogical language emerges in Christian discourse. Our understanding of the divine has an impact on the way we express the contents of Christian faith. Christian discourse must make use of analogy, but a sort of analogy unlike other kinds of analogy. Its use of analogy is 'analogous' to those other uses.

Analogy is employed even at the most basic level of religious discourse: prayer. Prayer is the most important and distinctive form of language present in the liturgy. It is speech addressing an addressee. It is speech directed toward God. It is a form of word-use basic to faith. It is intermixed with the

7 See R. Sokolowski, *The God of faith and reason* (Washington, DC, 1982), pp 12–20.

sacraments and Christian action. This form of speech is even more fundamental than theology just as conversation is more fundamental than linguistic
analysis.

Pope Benedict firmly maintains that prayer is central to Christianity
precisely because the Christian God is such that we cannot believe in him
without praying to him. Since we owe our existence to him, and since he
knows us and has addressed us, we cannot but respond with gratitude and
adoration. Our attitude toward God is quite different from the attitude we
would have, say, toward the god of Aristotle, whom we can admire but would
not address as a person. That the Christian God is such that we cannot believe
in him without praying to him is not just a cultural of psychological fact, nor
is it an expression of piety. It follows, as Benedict insists, from the way God is
understood by Christian faith.

In the *Spirit of the liturgy* he writes:

> This structure of Word and response, which is essential to the liturgy, is
> modelled on the basic structure of the process of divine revelation, in
> which Word and response, the speech of God and the receptive hearing
> of the Bride, the Church, go together.[8]

He then goes on to stress the importance of silence in the liturgy. Listening is
absolutely essential since syntax by its very nature is intersubjective. It springs
from dialogue.

Prayer is speech directed not toward other people nor toward oneself but
toward God. Not all understandings of the divine imply the possibility of
prayer. Aristotle, as noted, conceived god as self-thinking thought, implying
that we neither can nor should pray to God insofar as the divine principle does
not know things in the sublunary world and would not be concerned with
anything that is not permanent and unchanging.

The Christian understanding of God, on the other hand, and of the
relation of the world to God establishes not only the possibility of prayer but
its necessity. Since the world and everything in it, including ourselves, exist
only through divine choice, we cannot but be obliged to render thanks for the
existence of the whole. Not only can we pray, but we ought to pray. The possibility and obligation of prayer are derived theologically from the Christian
understanding of the divine.

---

8 *The spirit of the liturgy* (San Francisco, 2000), p. 208.

The new English translation of the Roman Missal is a source of great encouragement in that this 'oughtness' of prayer is more evident than was previously the case. In the orations, the reason for which God ought to be praised, thanked, and adored is more manifest. The more generous use of subordinate clauses emphasizes that we *do* thank him for who he is and what he has done. The reason for thanking God is clearer precisely because it is formulated as a reason rather that a feeble attempt on our part to remind God of Who He is.

The necessary and ubiquitous use of analogy and metaphor in Christian discourse should not overshadow the fundamental use of narration. The Old and New Testaments are, at their core, narrative. This type of disclosure is indispensible since, according to biblical belief, God has intervened in history: first in his covenants with the Jewish people and providence over them, then in the Incarnation and the life, death and resurrection of Jesus of Nazareth. The structure of narrative is significant because it recounts events without which faith would be impossible. Yet the narrative discourse of scripture subordinates itself to something else. It speaks about something 'outside' itself, something presented as having happened apart from the narration. In this respect, narration differs from a philosophical treatise in that the latter contains within itself the very thought it seeks to express.

Even though we do not live the events of the historical life of Christ, we have access to them through the written word. Reading is thus of fundamental importance to Christianity. Furthermore, the events narrated are not just stories that illustrate general truths, as if the general truths were more basic than the events. Christianity emphasizes the historical event. Worldly events enter into Christian religion, and these events are neither merely illustrations of general truths nor declarations of eternal necessities. Narratives open space for belief. A philosophical treatise simply calls for understanding. It is possible to understand a story without believing it, but such 'mere' understanding is not what the Bible calls for. Moreover, the scriptures are *fundamental* narratives. No piece of writing is more basic to Christian belief, not even a philosophical treatise on the distinction between the God of Christianity and the pagan gods. No verbal composition is prior to them to establish Christian belief since they constitute a verbal response to the events that establish what is believed.

Once we have recognized and pointed out the fundamental place of narrative in Christian discourse, we can more readily flesh out how Christian discourse makes use of analogy and metaphor in a way different from their use in common discourse. It is one thing to recognize analogy in the psalms, prophetic writings and wisdom literature, but another thing to show how these analogies display, make perceptible, and bring out the glory or *doxa* of the divine. Analogy is present at *all* levels of Christian discourse. Words like *God, divine, Creator, Redeemer, goodness, grace, making, response, giving, acting* are ever-present, applied both to God in his own life and to the actions he performs in the world. Christians understand that even the words applying to worldly things take on an analogous meaning once we understand the world as having been created, insofar as the world and everything in it are now seen as contingent in a radical way.

Aristotle spoke of only one kind of analogy, the 'analogy of proper proportionality'. This type of analogy indicates a proportionality of two ratios. A is to B as C is to D. If we take A and C independently, we cannot say that they are the same univocally. However, we can say that the *ratio* of A to B is the same as the ratio of C to D. A point, for example, is to a line as a surface is to a solid. Neither is a point a surface nor a line a solid, but the relationship of point to line is the same as the ratio of surface to solid. They both designate the extremity of the things to which they are related.

Metaphor differs from analogy of proper proportionality. The analogous notion employed in the latter properly consists in both analogates. The former, however, is a type of analogy in which the proper sense of the analogous notion subsists only in the principal or primary analogate. The secondary analogate merely contains the notion in a transferred sense. When I say 'Michael Jordan is a hawk', the nature of a hawk is found only in the bird and not in the man. Accordingly, the notion 'hawk' has its proper notion only in one analogate: namely, the bird in the primary analogate of the implied comparison 'Michael Jordan is to his opponents as a hawk is to its adversaries'. The proper analogous notion is something like 'superbly shrewd hunter'. In a transferred or improper sense the notion 'hawk' is predicated of Michael Jordan by an analogy of metaphorical or improper proportionality. The man Michael Jordan is made the secondary analogate of 'hawk'. There is a difference of proportional likeness between a basketball player and a hawk as hunters.

Metaphor, unlike analogy, is a rhetorical trope. It is situational and personal, even highly subjective. As pleasing and illuminating as it may be, a metaphor does not, strictly speaking, have a place in the natural sciences. Indeed, metaphors can be distracting in the sciences since they lead us to think there are identities where no such identities exist. Analogy, on the other hand, does have a place in science. There are some things that cannot be properly understood unless we know they are analogous to other things. We understand human reasoning better and more fully when we realize that it is analogous to animal cunning. In other words, animals carry out some activities analogous to the exercise of human prudence. Animal cunning and human prudence are not only metaphorically related but analogously related to one another in the real world. Similarly, when we read that Asahel was 'as fleet of foot as a gazelle in the open field' (2 Samuel 2:18), we understand that the beauty of a running gazelle is analogous to the beauty of a running man. The identities that analogies expose are not mere appearances as metaphors are. They are real identities: animal cunning is not the same as human intelligence, but animal cunning is to animals as human prudence is to man. Feathers are not scales, but feathers are to birds as scales are to fish. We can do without metaphor in scientific discourse, but we cannot do without analogy.

An important aspect of analogy is that it prompts us to see things in their wider context. It helps us to resist the modern tendency – clearly present in the analytic philosophy of language – to break things down into discreet particulars and to think we have explained an entity when we have arrived at the ultimate pieces that make it up. In such thinking, all names are ultimately univocal, and things are boiled down to a basic set of core elements as the atomists claimed. Similarly, modern philosophy strives to discover the laws of nature and not natures. If alternatively we take analogies as essential and irreducible, we are more sensitive to the forms of things and see things in their fuller context and environments.

The Christian understanding of the divine creates new space for analogy even though analogy is strained by this new context. The kind of analogy used in the Christian context is analogous to the kind used in normal contexts. However, in the Christian context it is conceivable, though not true, that God could have been all that existed. This requires us to use analogy with caution. We must not allow it to slip into mere metaphor. Christian discourse does not simply point to a mystery or indicate a vague transcendence. It conveys an understanding that is appropriate to this new context and hence only analogous to the understandings we achieve in the natural setting. More specifically, when the analogy of proportionality is applied in Christian discourse, the two ratios (A is to B as C is to D) are no longer the same but similar.

The nature of this similarity has to be spelled out. One of the ratios deals with the divine nature and its features and the other with creatures. We will have to adjust our thinking about both ratios: the divine and the created. The created world and the things within it take on a new meaning in this setting. We might think, for example, that analogy in the Christian context only functions as a way of helping us understand or appreciate something about God. But analogies work in both directions. The world takes on a new intelligibility when seen against the background of the Christian God.

By arguing for the importance of analogy, I do not mean to rule out the place of metaphor in Christian discourse. Indeed, metaphor is perhaps more strongly connected with poetic beauty. I only want to suggest that metaphor must be bound more closely to analogy. Figurative language does not aim to describe things but to connect them: a connection usually forged at the level of feelings and emotions. The connection may be made by way of metaphor, metonymy,[9] simile or personification. Metaphors are not arbitrary since they make connections with the moral life. That is why we feel at home with certain heroic actions in the Old Testament and why we are elevated by them.

The appropriateness of poetical and metaphorical language was a real issue in the Middle Ages when the faithful were surrounded by marvellously ornate, not to mention highly symbolic, works of art. More importantly, theologians were keenly aware of the metaphorical language used in scripture. They were concerned with showing that eternal truths not only *can* be presented in figurative and metaphorical language, but indeed *must* be presented such. Saint Thomas Aquinas distinguishes between the use of metaphors in normal poetry and their use in sacred teaching. Whereas poetry makes use of metaphors for the sake of representation (*propter repraesentationem*) insofar as representation is naturally delightful (*delectabilis*), sacred teaching uses metaphors insofar as they are both necessary and useful (*propter necessitatem et utilitatem*).[10]

Sacramentum caritatis similarly teaches that beauty in the liturgy, including the beauty of metaphor:

> is no mere aestheticism, but the concrete way in which the truth of God's love in Christ encounters us, attracts us and delights us, enabling

---

9 Metonymy is a figure of speech used in rhetoric in which a thing or concept is not called by its own name but by the name of something intimately associated with that thing or concept. For instance, 'Capitol Hill' – is used as a metonym for the United States Congress since it is located there.   10 Cf. *Summa Theologiae* I, 1, 9.

us to emerge from ourselves and drawing us towards our true vocation, which is love.[11]

The beauty of Christ present in the liturgy:

> is not simply a harmony of proportion and form; 'the fairest of the sons of men' (Psalm 45:2) is also, mysteriously, the one 'who had no form or comeliness that we should look at him, and no beauty that we should desire him' (Is 53:2).[12]

It is precisely therein that Christian analogy differs from natural analogy. In the natural world, transposing 'fairest' and 'no beauty' is paradoxical. In the Christian context, it is precisely this seeming contradiction through which we understand that 'the splendour of God's glory surpasses all worldly beauty.'[13]

CONCLUSION

I close with an example from the liturgy, though not from the Roman Missal. It is taken rather from the current English translation of the Lectionary. The Gospel for the Twenty-Fourth Sunday in Ordinary Time of Cycle A is from Matthew, chapter 18. We hear that after the king forgives a servant who owed him 'a huge amount', the same servant meets a fellow servant who 'owed him a much smaller amount'. The *Revised Standard Version* reports the actual amounts, and rightly so, for they appear in the Greek text. The 'huge amount' is actually 'ten thousand talents', and the 'much smaller amount' is 'a hundred denarii'. Granted, the difference between the two is not readily apparent to today's audience. But it is not the translator's job to interpolate the difference between the two sums of money into the text. That's the homilist's job. More to the point, the translator has ignored the essential role of analogous discourse when speaking about divine mysteries. This was acutely brought to my attention by an eight-year-old girl who, after hearing this passage, wanted to know 'how much' the first servant owed. 'A hundred dollars? A million?' She also wanted to know 'how much' the second servant owed. 'Ten cents? A penny?' Those present when Jesus delivered this parable for the first time didn't have to ask him such questions. He told them how much. We, on the other

11 *Sacrosanctum concilium*, 35.   12 Ibid., 35.   13 Ibid., 35.

hand, have managed to de-parabolize the parable of a Master storyteller, sapping it of its potential to spark our imagination and provoke our dismay: 'How could the king forgive such an exorbitant debt? Why couldn't the first servant forgive such a pittance?'

Analogy is essential to Christian discourse. This is particularly true within the divine Liturgy. The privileged *loci* for explaining analogies and metaphors are catechesis and preaching, not worship. Literalness is but one criterion for evaluating the success of the new English translation of the Roman Missal. An elegant rendering of analogy and metaphor into noble, simple, and beautiful English is no less important.

Translating the *Missale Romanum*: towards a sacral vernacular

UWE MICHAEL LANG

The Second Vatican Council granted a significant extension of the use of the vernacular in Catholic worship, with the primary motive to promote 'fully conscious and active participation' of the people in the liturgy.[1] The relevant article of the Constitution on the Sacred Liturgy *Sacrosanctum concilium*, no. 36, strikes a balance that was reached after some debate on the Council floor, asserting in the first paragraph that 'the use of the Latin language is to be preserved in the Latin rite' (§1), and then, secondly, granting that the use of the vernacular may be extended, which 'will apply in the first place to the readings and directives, and to some of the prayers and chants' (§2). Thirdly, 'the competent territorial ecclesiastical authority', which ordinarily would be the Conference of Bishops, is to decide 'whether, and to what extent, the vernacular language is to be used' (§3). Article 54 of *Sacrosanctum concilium* specifies that in 'Masses that are celebrated with the people, a suitable place may be allotted to their mother tongue. This is to apply in the first place to the readings and "the common prayer", but also, as local conditions may warrant, to those parts which pertain to the people'. At the same time, however, 'steps should be taken so that the faithful may also be able to say or to sing together in Latin those parts of the Ordinary of the Mass which pertain to them'.

On 26 September 1964, the *Consilium ad exsequendam constitutionem de sacra liturgia* issued the Instruction *Inter oecumenici*, which came into effect on 7 March 1965 (the First Sunday in Lent) and provided norms for vernacular translations following *Sacrosanctum concilium*, art. 36, §3. *Inter oecumenici* made it clear that: (a) 'the basis of the translations is the Latin liturgical text'; (b) the work of translations should involve institutes of liturgy or persons who are experts in Scripture, liturgy, the biblical languages, Latin, the vernacular, and music; (c) where applicable, 'there should be consultation with bishops of neighbouring regions using the same language'; (d) 'in nations of several languages there should be a translation for each language'; and, finally, 'special attention should be given to the high quality of books used for reading the

1 Second Vatican Council, Constitution on the Sacred Liturgy *Sacrosanctum concilium* (4 December 1963), 14.

liturgical text to the people in the vernacular'.[2] The directives of *Inter oecumenici*, which allowed the use of the vernacular for certain parts of Masses celebrated with a congregation (with reference to *Sacrosanctum concilium* 54) and also included some modifications of the *Ordo Missae*,[3] guided the preparation of bilingual missals in various languages. The first of these 'interim missals', as they have been called with hindsight, was already published and implemented in the US on 29 November 1964 (the First Sunday of Advent).[4]

METHODOLOGY OF LITURGICAL TRANSLATION

In an address to translators of liturgical texts given on 10 November 1965, Paul VI presented the basic principles of liturgical translations. The Pope emphasized that these 'have become part of the rites themselves', unlike previous translations for the use of the faithful, and that for this reason they need to be approved by the local authority and confirmed by the Holy See for liturgical use. The type of language to be used in the liturgy 'should always be worthy of the noble realities it signifies, set apart from the everyday speech of the street and the marketplace'. This requires that translators 'know both Christian Latin and their own modern language', and, given that the liturgy should above all be chanted, the translated prayers need to be constructed in such a way that they can be sung according to the rules of music that obtain in different cultures. The challenge for translators is 'also to make clarity of language and dignity of expression shine forth in the vernacular translations of liturgical texts'.[5]

The question of translation presented itself with greater urgency when in 1969/70 the new, substantially changed *editio typica* of the *Missale Romanum* was released. The key document guiding the translations of the new liturgical

2 Sacred Congregation of Rites, Instruction for the Right Implementation of the Constitution on the Sacred Liturgy *Inter oecumenici* (26 September 1964), in *Acta apostolicae sedis* 56 (1964), 877–900, no. 40; English translation in *Documents on the liturgy, 1963–1979: conciliar, papal, and curial texts* (Collegeville MN, 1982), p. 96.   3 *Inter oecumenici*, 48; English translation: *Documents on the liturgy*, p. 98. The *editio typica* of the revised *Ordo Missae* was published on 27 January 1965; see *Notitiae*, 1 (1965), 101–2.   4 *Roman Missal: Missale Romanum ex decreto Sacrosancti Concilii Tridentini restitutum Summorum Pontificum cura recognitum cum versionibus lingua anglica exaratis et a coetu episcoporum Civitatum Foederatum America Septentrionalis rite approbatis actis ab Apostolica Sede confirmatis* (New York, 1964). Contrary to *Inter oecumenici*, 57, this edition contained only the English, not the Latin text of those parts that could be used in the vernacular. This matter was rectified in the 1966 edition, which had the pertinent parts in Latin and English: *English-Latin Roman Missal for the United States of America: containing the Mass text from the Roman Missal and the prayers of the celebrant together with the Ordinary of the Mass from the English-Latin Sacramentary. English translations approved by the National Conference of Bishops of the United States of America and confirmed by the Apostolic See* (New York, 1966).   5 Paul VI, *Address to translators of liturgical text* (10 November 1965),

books was the Instruction of the *Consilium* of 25 January 1969, *Comme le prévoit*. This instruction shows a few formal irregularities: it was published in six major languages, but not in Latin, the official language of the Holy See; moreover, it bears no official signature and it was not published in the *Acta apostolicae sedis*, the official organ of the Holy See.[6] *Comme le prévoit* is in many ways an elaboration of the above-mentioned address of Paul VI in 1965. However, it introduces significant novelties in the methodology of translation: only 'some euchological and sacramental formularies', above all the Eucharistic Prayers and the Prefaces, 'should be translated integrally and faithfully, without variations, omissions, or insertions'.[7] The other prayers of the Mass, which come from the ancient Roman tradition, 'may need to be rendered somewhat more freely while conserving the original ideas. This can be done by moderately amplifying them or, if necessary, paraphrasing expressions in order to concretize them for the celebration and the needs of today'.[8]

Thus *Comme le prévoit* endorsed a hermeneutics of translation known as 'dynamic equivalence'. This theory was developed by Eugene Nida in order to address the difficulties experienced in the complex work of biblical translation.[9] A word-by-word rendering from the source language into the receptor language often does not make sense and fails to communicate the message of the text. This difficulty is felt particularly when it comes to translating Latin liturgical texts (many of which stem from late antiquity) into contemporary languages. Any translation must naturally aim at translating the spiritual and doctrinal content of these ancient prayers in a way that renders justice to the rules and conventions of the receptor language. However, the theory of 'dynamic equivalence' goes much further, in that it abstracts the content of the text from its linguistic and cultural form and no longer aims at a translation that would reproduce the formal structure of the original as closely as could reasonably be done in a modern language. Rather, the purpose of this approach is to identify the message contained in the original text apart from its linguistic form, which is considered a mere vesture that can be changed according to different cultural contexts. In the process of translation, a new form is to be created that would possess equivalent qualities by means of which the original content can be adequately expressed. By means of this new form,

in *Acta apostolicae sedis*, 57 (1965), 967–70; English translation: *Documents on the liturgy*, pp 273 and 274. **6** *Consilium*, Instruction on the Translation of Liturgical Texts for Celebrations with a Congregation *Comme le prévoit* (25 January 1969), in *Notitiae*, 5 (1969), 3–12.   **7** *Comme le prévoit*, 33; English translation: *Documents on the liturgy*, p. 288.   **8** *Comme le prévoit*, 34; English translation: *Documents on the liturgy*, pp 288–9.   **9** See E.A. Nida, *Toward a science of translating, with special reference to principles and procedures involved in Bible*

the translation intends to create in a reader or audience of the receptor language the same informative and emotive effect that the text in its source language would have had in its original context. Dennis McManus observes that, according to this translation theory: 'the connection between form and meaning is almost completely sacrificed in favour of the immediacy of communicating the meaning derived from a source text.'

McManus also notes that the philosophical roots of this translation theory lie in logical positivism, which:

> maintains that all true statements can be reduced to verifiable propo-sitional forms which relate meaning to the reader. In terms of translation theory, such meanings are then re-clothed in 'equivalent forms' and rendered into a target language.

The primary emphasis is hence on the meaning-response of the reader or hearer of a text. Consequently, 'a translation is considered a failure if the derived meaning of the source text is not communicated immediately, rather than through some linguistic mediation', that is, the 'sacred' register that distinguishes the language of liturgical prayer. In fact, this methodology raises serious questions, above all, how to determine the meaning of a text in abstraction from its form. Thus McManus asks: 'Are there not subjective judgments at play in the translator's estimation, for example, of which 'equivalent forms' will help to create the desired reader-listener response?'[10]

However, these problems do not seem to have been generally recognized in the early years of the post-Conciliar renewal of the liturgy and so the theory of 'dynamic equivalence' guided the translation of the new liturgical books into the vernacular language, especially the English-language edition of the *Missale Romanum* of Paul VI, which was prepared by the International Commission on English in the Liturgy (ICEL) and officially approved in 1973.

LITURGIAM AUTHENTICAM (2001)

In the course of the years the problems of this hermeneutics of translation have become evident both on a pastoral and on a scholarly level.[11] The exigency to

translating (Leiden, 1964). **10** All these citations from D. McManus, 'Translation theory in *Liturgiam authenticam*' in N.J. Roy and J.E. Rutherford (eds), *Benedict XVI and the sacred liturgy* (Dublin, 2010), pp 116–31, at 122. **11** See, for instance, the pertinent critique of E. Duffy, 'Rewriting the liturgy: the

remedy this situation was recognized by the Holy See, and *Comme le prévoit* was replaced in 2001 by the Congregation for Divine Worship and the Discipline of the Sacraments' Instruction, *Liturgiam authenticam*.[12] It is the Fifth Instruction for the correct implementation of the Council's Constitution on the Sacred Liturgy *Sacrosanctum concilium*, and thus stands on a par with the first one in this series, *Inter oecumenici* of 1964. With *Liturgiam authenticam*, previous norms on the translation of liturgical texts are superseded, with the exception of those presented in the Fourth Instruction *Varietates legitimae* of 1994 concerning difficult questions on the Roman Liturgy and inculturation.[13] According to *Liturgiam authenticam*, all translations of liturgical books in use since the Second Vatican Council are to be examined and revised. In order to assure that the translations are authentic and correspond with the original texts, they need the *recognitio* of the Apostolic See, a concept dating from to Pope Sixtus V (1585–90) and his reform of the Roman Curia. The *recognitio* of legal or liturgical texts goes beyond a generic approval and includes a careful and detailed examination whether the universal norms have been correctly applied. Hence the term should not be translated as 'authorization', but rather as 'review'.[14] In the process of reviewing the translations presented by Conferences of Bishops, the Congregation for Divine Worship and the Discipline of the Sacraments can introduce even substantial modifications.[15]

Liturgiam authenticam is a document of considerable length that deals with the translation and publication of liturgical books in the vernacular in a comprehensive way. This is not the place to provide a complete analysis of its rich and nuanced contents; instead, I intend to highlight some principles of the instruction that are meant to guide the revision of vernacular translations of liturgical books.

The Instruction notes that the spiritual and doctrinal patrimony which is contained in the Latin liturgical texts of the Roman Rite is to be preserved and passed on through the centuries. In order to achieve this goal:

theological implications of translation', in S. Caldecott (ed.), *Beyond the prosaic: Renewing the liturgical movement* (Edinburgh, 1998), pp 97–126 (also published in *New Blackfriars*, 78 (1997), 4–27). **12** Congregation for Divine Worship and the Discipline of the Sacraments, Fifth Instruction for the right implementation of the Constitution on the Sacred Liturgy, *Liturgiam authenticam* (28 March 2001), in *Acta apostolicae sedis*, 93 (2001), pp 685–726. **13** Congregation for Divine Worship and the Discipline of the Sacraments, Fourth Instruction for the right implementation of the Constitution on the Sacred Liturgy, *Varietates legitimae* (25 January 1994), in *Acta apostolicae sedis*, 87 (1995), pp 288–314. **14** See Pontifical Council for Legislative Texts, 'Nota Esplicativa X: La natura giuridica e l'estensione della «recognitio» della Santa Sede', *Communicationes*, 38 (2006), 10–17, at 10–11. **15** See *Liturgiam authenticam*, 80; cf. *Code*

it is to be kept in mind from the beginning that the translation of the liturgical texts of the Roman Liturgy is not so much a work of creative innovation as it is of rendering the original texts faithfully and accurately into the vernacular language.

The different methodology that this Instruction requires of translators is made very clear:

> While it is permissible to arrange the wording, the syntax and the style in such a way as to prepare a flowing vernacular text suitable to the rhythm of popular prayer, the original text, insofar as possible, must be translated integrally and in the most exact manner, without omissions or additions in terms of their content, and without paraphrases or glosses. Any adaptation to the characteristics or the nature of the various vernacular languages is to be sober and discreet.[16]

The contents of the liturgical texts should be 'evident and comprehensible even to the faithful who lack any special intellectual formation'; for this reason 'the translations should be characterized by a kind of language which is easily understandable'. At the same time, however, liturgical translations need to preserve the 'dignity, beauty, and doctrinal precision' of the original text. The aim set for liturgical translation is indeed a high one:

> By means of words of praise and adoration that foster reverence and gratitude in the face of God's majesty, his power, his mercy and his transcendent nature, the translations will respond to the hunger and thirst for the living God that is experienced by the people of our own time, while contributing also to the dignity and beauty of the liturgical celebration itself.[17]

The Instruction also addresses the often poorly understood question of inculturation in a reflected and balanced way. Liturgical translation should communicate the Church's perennial treasury of prayer 'by means of language understandable in the cultural context for which it is intended'; however:

> it should also be guided by the conviction that liturgical prayer not only is formed by the genius of a culture, but itself contributes to the

of Canon Law, Can. 838 §1.   **16** *Liturgiam authenticam*, 20.   **17** Ibid., 25.

development of that culture. Consequently it should cause no surprise that such language differs somewhat from ordinary speech. Liturgical translation that takes due account of the authority and integral content of the original texts will facilitate the development of a sacral vernacular, characterized by a vocabulary, syntax and grammar that are proper to divine worship, even though it is not to be excluded that it may exercise an influence even on everyday speech, as has occurred in the languages of peoples evangelized long ago.[18]

This important passage shows an awareness of the complex relationship between faith and culture that takes account of the characteristics of 'sacred language' in the Christian tradition. Elsewhere, I have proposed to follow Christine Mohrmann, whose studies of on 'sacred language' are still essential, despite the valid criticism of the idea of Christian Latin as a 'special language' that would be marked by particularities in morphology, lexis and syntax.[19] Mohrmann sees in sacred language, and in particular in its vocabulary, a specific way of organizing religious experience. She also argues that every form of belief in the supernatural, in the existence of a transcendent being, leads necessarily to adopting a form of sacred language in worship – just as a consistent secularism leads to rejecting any form of it.

In the case of Latin as the language of the Roman Liturgy, a notable distance from the everyday language of the street and of the marketplace existed right from the beginning. As soon as Greek, originally the prevalent language of Christian communities in Rome, was replaced by Latin, a highly stylized medium of worship was created.

The principles of *Liturgiam authenticam* rest on solid philological, historical and theological foundations and are eminently suitable for the critical revision of the post-Conciliar translations, which were produced under great pressure of time and not rarely approved without a due process of examination. According to McManus, the most important aspect of the Instruction from the point of view of translation theory is the claim that:

the Church possesses full authority to self-interpret her own liturgical texts and, furthermore, that in so doing, she best captures her own authorial intent within 'formal equivalency' translation.[20]

---

18 Ibid., 47.   **19** C. Mohrmann, *Liturgical Latin: its origins and character. Three lectures* (London, 1959), and *Études sur le latin des chrétiens*, 4 vols (Rome, 1961–77). Cf. U.M. Lang, *The voice of the church at prayer: reflections on liturgy and language* (San Francisco, 2012).   **20** McManus, 'Translation theory', p. 129.

Developing a sacral vernacular on such principles contributes to the stability of liturgical language and precludes: 'the necessity of frequent revisions when modes of expression may have passed out of popular usage'.[21]

APPLYING *LITURGIAM AUTHENTICAM*: THE ROMAN MISSAL (2011)

The first important result of the process initiated with *Liturgiam authenticam* in the English-speaking world is the thoroughly revised translation of the *Missale Romanum* according to the third *editio typica*.[22] After the liturgical texts had been prepared and approved by various Anglophone Conferences of Bishops all over the world, in a long and at times arduous process, the Holy See gave its *recognitio* in March 2010. The new *Roman Missal* has been implemented in most English-speaking countries in the course of the year 2011.[23]

There are many changes in the liturgical texts that concern not only the celebrant priests themselves, but all the faithful, most notably the people's response to the liturgical greeting 'The Lord be with you' (for *Dominus vobiscum*), which is no longer 'And also with you', but 'And with your spirit' (for *Et cum spiritu tuo*).[24] Moreover, the translation of the *Ordo Missae* has been systematically reworked, following the criteria of *Liturgiam authenticam*. The introduction of the new translation is accompanied by many initiatives and publications to explain its rationale and to provide extensive commentary on the text.[25] Here a brief discussion of a few selected passages will suffice to show the characteristics of the new version in comparison to the older one of 1973.[26]

Liturgical prayer is a form of public speech, and hence it is not surprising that in Christian antiquity, the threefold *officia* of classical rhetoric were applied to it as well. The reasons for this are presented succinctly by Sister Mary Gonzaga Haessly in work on *Rhetoric in the Sunday Collects of the Roman Missal*:

---

21 *Liturgiam authenticam*, p. 27.   22 *Missale Romanum ex decreto Sacrosancti Oecumenici Concilii Vaticani II instauratum auctoritate Pauli PP VI promulgatum Ioannis Pauli PP II cura recognitum*, editio typica tertia (Città del Vaticano, 2002). An emended reprint of this edition was published in 2008.   23 *Roman Missal: renewed by decree of the Most Holy Second Ecumenical Council of the Vatican, promulgated by authority of Pope Paul VI and revised at the direction of Pope John Paul II* (London, 2011).   24 An overdue correction: cf. the compelling article by B. Botte, '*Dominus vobiscum*', *Bible et vie chrétienne*, 62 (1965), 33–8 (a long excerpt in English is now available in *Antiphon*, 14 [2010], 230–5).   25 Here I would just like to single out one book, which serves as the basis for a programme of formation: C. Carstens and D. Martis, *Mystical body, mystical voice: encountering Christ in the words of the mass* (Chicago, 2011).   26 *Roman Missal: revised by decree of the Second Vatican Council and published by authority of Pope Paul VI* (London, 1974).

all these devices of the art of language are necessary for us, for they enable us: (1) to grasp clearly the lessons embodied in the Prayers (*docere*); (2) to make these lessons more acceptable to us through the charm of diction and structure, in a word, through their appeal to our aesthetic sense (*delectare*); (3) to persuade us (movere) to mold our conduct in accordance with the principles of faith set forth in the Prayers. This explains why rhetoric is, and must be, found in the liturgy: it is to dispose us to pray *ut oportet*, as we ought to pray.[27]

My first set of examples is taken from the First Eucharistic Prayer, the Roman Canon. In Latin prose texts, the placing of the various parts of a sentence can be very significant. The post-Sanctus part of the Canon begins with the striking form of address '*Te igitur, clementissime Pater*'. The 1973 version renders this rather blandly as 'We come to you, Father'; thus the emphasis has already shifted from God the Father, to whom the prayer is addressed, to our action ('we come'). By contrast, the new translation is faithful to the unusual beginning of the Latin prayer with 'To you, therefore, most merciful Father', keeping the superlative in the form of address to God.[28]

The choice of the earlier version 'We come to you ... with praise and thanksgiving ... we ask you' is curious, because the Latin Canon only reads '*supplices rogamus ac petimus*' at this point. It has been suggested that this would reflect an opinion current among liturgists in the post-Conciliar period that the Roman Canon was somehow deficient because it gave priority to the elements of petition and intercession over those of praise and thanksgiving. The translators may have tried to remedy this by letting the prayer begin with the words they chose.[29] Be that as it may, the 1973 version does not take into account the formula *rogamus ac petimus*, which is characteristic of Roman euchological style. Here we observe the typical use of consecutive synonyms or near-synonyms. The doubling of the verb increases the force and intensity of

27 M.G. Haessly, *Rhetoric in the Sunday Collects of the Roman Missal: with introduction, text, commentary and translation* (Cleveland, 1938), p. 5. See now also the various contributions in *Appreciating the collect: An irenic methodology*, J.G. Leachman and D.P. McCarthy (Farnborough, 2008). **28** The force of the Latin *igitur* has long been debated among liturgists; it has been argued that this refers back to the Preface, in which God is given thanks and praises for his wonderful work of salvation. Since the *Sanctus* came in at a later stage in the development of the liturgy, it would seem plausible that *igitur* originally connected the petition to make our offering acceptable to the initial act of praise; however, it can now be construed to take up the acclamation of the Benedictus: 'Blessed is he who comes in the name of the Lord. Hosanna in the highest'. **29** Duffy, *Rewriting the liturgy*, p. 102.

the expression. In the 2010 version this is translated as 'we make humble prayer and petition'.

There are other examples of the use of near-synonyms, such as '*accepta habeas et benedicas*' (translated in both versions as 'accept and bless') and '*haec dona, haec munera, haec sancta sacrificia illibata*'. In this latter phrase there is an impressive climax from the simple expression of 'gifts', to a word that implies 'what is due' (and can literally mean 'tributes'), to 'sacrifices'. The 1973 version opts for a more paraphrastic translation ('these gifts we offer you in sacrifice'), not communicating the idea that these sacrifices are indeed *sancta* and *illibata*, whereas the 2010 version does justice to the three different terms and also reproduces the rhetorical movement of the phrase in English: 'these gifts, these offerings, these holy and unblemished sacrifices'.

In the *anamnesis* prayer after the consecration *Unde et memores* there are several outstanding stylistic features, above all in the clause '*offerimus tibi ...*'. The asyndeton '*hostiam puram, hostiam sanctam, hostiam immaculatam*', with three near-synonymous adjectives is once again characteristic of Roman prayer style. Whereas the 1973 translation reduces this to 'this holy and perfect sacrifice', the 2010 version retains the original's rhetorical force: 'this pure victim, this holy victim, this spotless victim'. In the older version, there is a remarkable tendency to leave out certain qualifying adjectives: '*beatae passionis*' is rendered as 'his passion' (new: 'the blessed Passion'), '*in caelos gloriosae ascensionis*' as 'his ascension into glory' (new: 'the glorious Ascension into heaven'), '*plebs tua sancta*' as 'your people' (new: 'your holy people') and '*Panem sanctum vitae aeternae*' as 'the bread of life' (new: 'the holy Bread of eternal life'). In this prayer there is also an instance of the earlier translators' decision to change the respective forms of address for God used in the prayers of the Roman rite (*Deus; Domine; Pater; Domine, Deus noster; Omnipotens aeterne Deus* etc.). There are many such cases in the collects of the Missal. In the *Unde et memores* prayer '*Domine*' was translated as 'Father', no doubt to highlight the fact that this prayer is addressed to the God the Father, while shortly before in the Memorial Acclamation and shortly afterwards *Dominus* is used to refer to the Son. However, it would seem that in the original Canon *Dominus* is used deliberately for both the Father and the Son to underline that both are 'Lord' and thus equal in divinity. Moreover, in the context of the prayer it is clear that the address '*Domine*' refers to the Father, whereas '*Domini nostri*' (left out in the earlier version) means Christ, his Son.

The variable prayers of the Roman Rite are later in origin than the Eucharistic Prayer and may go back as far as the first half of the fifth century.[30] The prayers usually known as 'collects' (a term that is not of Roman but of Gallican origin)[31] have a proper style that is quite distinct from the Canon of the Mass. The characteristics of this style are well established already in the earliest examples that have come down to us in the Verona manuscript, which is from the first quarter of the seventh century, but contains material that is dated variously from 400 to 560.[32] The Verona manuscript (also known as the 'Leonine Sacramentary'), was probably not intended for use in public worship in the form it has come down to us, but should be taken as a private compilation of Roman formularies of different age and authority.

The style of the early Roman collects is terse, well balanced and economical in its expression; each prayer is always a single sentence, even if the syntax can at times be complex. In fact, many of these collects are considered literary masterpieces. In its complete form, the collect has the following structure:

1. an address to God, generally to the Father;
2. a relative or participial clause referring to some attribute of God, or to one of his saving acts;
3. the petition, either in the imperative or in the subjunctive;
4. the reason or desired result, for which the petition is made;
5. the conclusion.[33]

This structure need not always be rigidly observed; some elements may be rearranged, duplicated or omitted.

Parallels have rightly been noted between the characteristic first and second element of the collect, the address to God, followed by a relative clause, and classical Roman prayers.[34] However, Mohrmann would seem correct in arguing this structure simply reflects a general euchological form that is found in many religious traditions.[35] Anton Baumstark has already observed that in

---

30 For a useful overview of recent research in this field, see J.G. Leachman, 'History of Collect Studies' in *Appreciating the collect*, pp 1–25. 31 The history of the term *collecta* is traced by P. Regan, 'The Collect in context', in *Appreciating the collect*, pp 83–103. 32 See C. Vogel, *Medieval liturgy: an introduction to the sources*, tr. W. Storey and N. Rasmussen (Washington DC, 1981), pp 38–45. 33 This structure is adapted from Willis, *A history of early Roman liturgy*, pp 63–4; a similar, more detailed methodology for analysing the prayers is presented by R. De Zan, 'How to interpret a collect' in *Appreciating the collect*, pp 57–82. 34 For instance, Livy, *Ab urbe condita* 29,27,2–4: *Divi divaeque, qui maria terrasque colitis, vos precor quaesoque uti ...* 35 Cf. Mohrmann, *Liturgical Latin*, pp 67–8.

the early Roman collects, the initial form of praise is linked with a prayer of petition, according to the supreme model of the Lord's Prayer: 'Our Father, who art in heaven ...'[36] This structure is indebted to the model of the Jewish *berakah*, where a relative clause follows the invocation 'Blessed are you, Lord our God ...'[37]

Mohrmann describes the style of the collects as closer to the cultural and literary traditions of classical Rome and their vocabulary as further removed from Sacred Scripture than the Canon and the Prefaces.[38] While this observation is generally correct, the biblical provenance of the collects' vocabulary should not be overlooked; this is evident not so much from direct quotations (although there are some), but from general resonances and 'plays' on scriptural words and concepts.[39]

The variable prayers of the Mass in 1973 ICEL translation are particularly problematic, because *Comme le prévoit* dispensed with the need to translate the texts literally and integrally. Hence it is in the collects where the difference between the two versions is most obvious and where the improvements of the new *Roman Missal* are most remarkable. My example is the collect for the Twenty-First Sunday in Ordinary Time (also for the Monday of the Fifth Week of Easter; in the *Missale Romanum* 1570–1962, it is the collect for the Fourth Sunday after Easter):

> <u>Missale Romanum, 1970–2008</u>
> *Deus, qui fidelium mentes unius efficis voluntatis,*
> *da populis tuis id amare quod praecipis,*
> *id desiderare quod promittis,*
> *ut, inter mundanas varietates,*
> *ibi nostra fixa sint corda, ubi vera sunt gaudia.*

> <u>ICEL 1973 (*Roman Missal*, 1974)</u>
> Father,
> help us to seek the values

---

36 See A. Baumstark, *Liturgie comparée. Principes et méthodes pour l'étude historique des liturgies chrétiennes*, troisième édition revue par B. Botte (Chevetogne, 1953), p. 73.   **37** Cf. the collection of Jewish liturgical texts in Hänggi–Pahl, *Prex eucharistica*, vol. I, pp 5–57.   **38** See B. Botte and C. Mohrmann, *L'ordinaire de la messe: Texte critique, traduction et études* (Paris and Louvain, 1953), pp 44–7.   **39** See G. Moore, 'The vocabulary of the collects: retrieving a biblical heritage', in *Appreciating the collect*, pp 175–95 and A.A.R. Bastiaensen, 'Die Bibel in den Gebetsformeln der lateinischen Kirche' in J. den Boeft and M. L. Van Poll-Van De Lisdonk (eds), *The impact of scripture in early Christianity* (Leiden, Boston, Köln, 1999), pp 39–57.

that will bring us lasting joy
in this changing world.
In our desire for what you promise
make us one in mind and heart.

ICEL 2010 (*Roman Missal,* 2011)
O God, who cause the minds of the faithful
to unite in a single purpose,
grant your people to love what you command
and to desire what you promise,
that, amid the uncertainties of this world,
our hearts may be fixed on that place
where true gladness is found.

The 1973 English version re-arranges the structure of the Latin prayer: the *statement of fact* at the beginning, namely that God effects unity of will among the faithful, appears as a *petition* at the end of the prayer. On the other hand, the plea that God may grant the desire for his promises is turned into a phrase that describes the condition of those who make the prayer. Thus the carefully crafted sequence of ideas and their rhetorical expression, which are so characteristic of classical Roman orations, are largely disregarded. There are further problems: the proper form of address is not respected, because 'Father' is not a translation of '*Deus*'; whereas in the Latin the petition is made on behalf of '*populis tuis*', that is, the entire people of God, the older version restricts this to an undetermined 'us', which is presumably identified with the particular worshipping community and so narrows the ecclesiological scope of the prayer. Even though the Latin text later shifts to 'our hearts', when the desired result is expressed, the initial request is of a wider nature. The actual rendering of the petition is highly questionable: 'help us …' introduces a feeble notion of divine causality and smacks of semi-Pelagianism. This point is specifically addressed by *Liturgiam authenticam*:

To be avoided in translations is any psychologizing tendency, especially a tendency to replace words treating of the theological virtues by others expressing merely human emotions. As regards words or expressions conveying a properly divine notion of causality (for example, those expressed in Latin by the words *praesta, ut* …), one should avoid employing words or expressions denoting a merely extrinsic or profane sort of assistance instead.[40]

Equally problematic is 'seek the values ...' for 'love what you command and desire what you promise'. Reducing the concretely biblical concept of love for God's law and a longing for his promises to 'values' can only be described as a step towards self-secularization and possibly even moral relativism (insofar as 'values' is a term that is commonly used to replace discussions of an objective moral order). The mysterious working of divine grace in the human heart, which the Latin prayer expresses in strongly Augustinian terms, is lost in translation. If one asks of what kind these 'values' are, the answer is: those 'that will bring us lasting joy in this changing world'. It should be noted that *inter mundanas varietates* has negative connotations, which are not captured by the insipid phrase 'changing world'. More importantly, however, the original text does precisely *not* ask for lasting joy amid the uncertainties of *this* world, but rather that our hearts should be anchored in that place, where true joy is found: the transcendent reality of heaven. One can easily hear the echo of Luke 12:34: 'For where your treasure is, there will your heart be also'.

It is hard, therefore, to avoid the conclusion that the 1973 ICEL version turns the sense of the Latin prayer upside down. This is evident from the comparison with the 2010 ICEL version, which faithfully renders the original's sequence of ideas and succeeds in presenting them integrally. Of course, even the best translation can only approximate the elegance of the Latin oration[41] with its prose rhythm and its rhetorical elements, such the parallel construction, *id amare quod praecipis* (*cursus tardus*) – *id desiderare quod promittis* (*cursus trispondiacus*), with the use of assonance and alliteration. This graceful composition both relates and distinguishes the precepts and the promises of God.

CONCLUSION

From a theological perspective the use of a sacred language in the liturgy, with its rhetorical forms and its archaic linguistic elements, belongs to the 'solemnity' that is observed in the celebration of the sacraments, especially the

---

40 *Liturgiam authenticam*, p. 54.   41 See the analysis of this particular collect in Haessly, *Rhetoric in the Sunday collects of the Roman Missal*, pp 65–8.

Most Holy Eucharist.[42] The concept of *solemnitas* is in fact is central to Aquinas' understanding of the liturgy as a whole.[43] The German philosopher Josef Pieper proposed a broad definition of 'sacred language', which includes signs and gestures as well as the words used in public worship. In a similar way, the English Dominican Aidan Nichols speaks of 'the idiom of worship'; both concepts cover more or less the same ground as Aquinas' idea of *solemnitas*.[44] Sacred language (both in the wider and in the narrower sense of the term) is part of the sacramental rites ordained by the Church, which are directed 'according to the wisdom of Christ (*secundum sapientiam Christi*)'.[45]

The language used in Christian worship was formed by biblical words and images and has been handed down as well as enriched by the tradition of the Church. Its sacred character, which is so beautifully expressed in the Latin of the Roman Liturgy, also needs to be conveyed in vernacular translations, as the Holy See's instruction *Liturgiam authenticam* of 2001 insisted. Unlike its predecessor, the 2010 ICEL version makes the treasury of the Latin liturgical tradition available to the Church in the English-speaking world. It also contributes greatly to the formation of a 'sacral vernacular', as envisaged by *Liturgiam authenticam*: an idiom of worship that is distinguished from everyday speech and is experienced as the voice of the Church at prayer. For the pastors who are entrusted with the task of introducing the new edition of the *Roman Missal* to their communities, this is also a unique opportunity for teaching the Catholic faith that finds a beautiful and profound expression in these prayers. The revised translation, which represents an important step in the ongoing process of liturgical renewal desired by the Second Vatican Council, can also be considered a major contribution to what the then-Cardinal Joseph Ratzinger called 'reform of the reform'.[46]

---

42 Thomas Aquinas, *Summa Theologiae* IIIa q. 64 a. 2 ad 1, IIIa, q. 83, a. 4, and IIIa, q. 66, a 10, resp. **43** Cf. T.A. Becker, 'The role of Solemnitas in the liturgy according to Saint Thomas Aquinas' in M. Levering and M. Dauphinais (eds), *Rediscovering Aquinas and the sacraments: studies in sacramental theology* (Chicago, 2009), pp 114–35.   **44** J. Pieper, *Religionsphilosophische Schriften*, ed. B. Wald (Hamburg, 2000), pp 477–536; some of Pieper's important contributions are also available in English: *In search of the sacred*, tr. L. Krauth (San Francisco, 1996). A. Nichols, *Looking at the liturgy: a critical view of its contemporary form* (San Francisco, 1996), pp 87–114.   **45** Thomas Aquinas, *Summa theologiae* IIIa, q. 72, a. 12.   **46** See above all his résumé of the important 2001 Fontgombault meeting, 'Bilan et Perspectives' in J. Ratzinger, *Theologie der Liturgie: Die sakramentale Begründung christlicher Existenz* (Freiburg, 2008), pp 657–82, esp. 673–7. English translation in A. Reid (ed.), *Looking again at the question of the liturgy with Cardinal Ratzinger: proceedings of the 2001 Fontgombault liturgical conference* (Farnborough, 2003), pp 145–53.

Why a new translation of the Missal?

GEORGE CARDINAL PELL

INTRODUCTION

The history of translations and translation theory has not been my forte, but it is worth mentioning a few things that happened in the 1960s in this area. Some of you will remember the translation formerly called *Good News for modern man*. Its New Testament came out in 1966 and it was a sincere attempt to get across the saving message of Our Lord to people, in a Protestant perspective; leaving aside, I am sure they would have said, 'churchy' language. It started life with the idea of providing Christians from Asia and Africa through the Bible Societies with a Bible text in English that was easier for them to understand. In the West, it became fashionable as an attempt to get through to young people, to people who were not habitual readers or had little schooling under their belt, to make an impact upon them with the freshness of the message of Jesus.

These ideas, as I have stated them, clearly owe a lot to a Protestant viewpoint, and the idea that you can get rid of the middleman, especially the Church, the priesthood, and put a Christian believer in direct touch with God. A Catholic viewpoint would obviously see the Church as having an important role in transmitting not just the Bible text, but the Word of God understood as embracing also Tradition, and mediating grace in Christ by means of the sacraments. Neither should we ever forget that the New Testament writings were produced under the inspiration of the Holy Spirit, from within the Christian communities. Christ himself left us no writings. Later on, the process took hundreds of years for completion. The Church established the New Testament canon, the list of authorized or inspired books to be distinguished from fine pieces of work like Clement's Epistle and the wilder books of the Apocrypha. I am told that in about five years, the *Good News for modern man* translation had sold some 30 million copies. They later finished the Old Testament and renamed the full Bible the *Good News Bible: the Bible in today's English version*. It is still in print.

Apart from the pastoral and evangelical ideas behind such a translation, there was also a theoretical underpinning, formulated in particular by a man called Eugene Nida, an American Protestant academic and pastor and a major figure at that time in the world of the American Bible Societies. It is from this school of thought that there came phrases like 'dynamic equivalence' (sometimes called 'functional equivalence'), used to describe a certain kind of freer rendering of the original. The opposite approach came to be dubbed 'formal equivalence'.

In our first attempts to produce liturgies in English, we were often short on dynamism and regularly short of equivalence. What was in the Latin texts sometimes, perhaps often, went missing. One extreme example of dynamic equivalence, which does accurately convey the sense, is the Australian translation of *sic transit gloria mundi*: rooster today, feather duster tomorrow!

It just so happened that while the English-speaking Catholic Church (after the Liturgy Constitution, 4 December 1963) was starting to face up to the very new task of translating liturgical texts into English for liturgical use, all this excitement was going on about Bible translations in the Protestant world. In these first times of widespread Catholic ecumenism, Protestant models were important and influential.

The energies of the Holy See were largely occupied in reformulating the Latin books. However, a convention for translators was held in Rome in 1965, and Pope Paul VI, a regular scrutinizer of the signs of the times, addressed it with a speech pointing to the responsibility which liturgical translations represented and saying famously that translations were becoming 'the voice of the Church'.

In 1969 the Roman authorities produced among many liturgical publications a short rather informal set of guidelines in French that was later known from its opening words as *Comme le prévoit* ('As is foreseen by article 36 of the Constitution *Sacrosanctum concilium* …'). It was perhaps a little naive, though it gathered together something of the common experience of liturgical translators to date, and made a plea for a dignified style and for traditional religious language, pointing also to the pitfalls of relying on schoolboy Latin and the importance of letting biblical ideas come through. Fatally, it spoke even if briefly of 'adaptations' to be effected by translations, though on the other hand it was firm in opposing biblical paraphrases.

With hindsight, it was a little of all things to all men, and it provided enough footholds for those who had been attracted and impressed by the very concrete example of *Good News for modern man*. Around the middle 1990s Father Joe Fessio SJ published an article demonstrating that the principle of dynamic equivalence was followed enthusiastically in the English translation of *Comme le prévoit* which emerged with an even looser set of guidelines than the French original. We must also remember that the other example available in the Catholic Church, the translations that people had in their Sunday hand Missals, though done by zealous and well meaning people, were not always very lucid or beautiful.

The idea of explaining the faith in simple terms, coming at it from different angles, using everyday language, is what should happen in the priest's homily, in what you tell your children and grandchildren at home when the occasion arises, or in catechism classes. It is a good thing, a holy thing. It is the business of teaching. However, it is not the whole story when it comes to translating the liturgy.

Our being able to transmit the faith more freely and more intimately relies in the Catholic Church on the fact that we have the Bible, the works of the Fathers of the Church, the documents of the great Church Councils, and especially the texts of the liturgy, which transmit the faith in a more fixed, objective and formal way. Paraphrases which, wrapped in a lot of theory, are what we are really talking about when we speak of 'dynamic equivalence' and the like, will not fit the bill as the foundation we need in the business of handing on the full Catholic faith. We certainly need to explain all these official texts in an effective and lively way, but the real stuff has to be there in the first place for us to explain. If it has been paraphrased away, we are in real trouble.

Let me give you a small but important example. As an auxiliary bishop celebrating more than fifty confirmations a year, I always tried to spend an hour with the grade six, twelve-year-old candidates. I asked questions prompting regular dialogue rather than simply talking. I realized I could reduce many classes to silence by asking what the word *spirit* meant. How is God a spirit, or spiritual? With a smirk one cheeky twelve-year-old-boy volunteered 'unreal' – a slang term then meaning very good. But his amusement suggested he was also affirming the primary meaning. In every class since then I have spoken of God as the spirit of love, to combat a good-willed but *de facto* materialism.

This was one important reason why I welcomed the new response to 'the Lord be with you' – '*And with your spirit*'. All church-goers have to confront the question: What is spiritual?

Some critics of the new translation seem to imply that the Church in her liturgies only has a right to tell people what they already know. The opposite is the case, as the Church is obliged to expand our horizons, lift our hearts and minds to God and, like good children's literature, give us a new word to be learnt every so often.

The Church, and before the Church, the Jewish people, have been engaged in translation for more than two millennia. Before the coming of Jesus Christ, the Hebrew Bible was translated into Greek. We call it the Septuagint. In the early Church many texts were translated into Latin and other languages from the Hebrew Old Testament and the Greek New Testament. We know that St Jerome (*c.*347–420) was given by Pope St Damasus the task of tidying up and correcting, and if necessary re-translating the variety of Latin translations of the Bible that existed in their day. There was little trace of 'dynamic equivalence' in these translations, but rather a recognizable following of biblical style and structure, even if inevitably certain terms underwent shifts and development in the process of translation. The new translations fit well into this ancient and beautiful translation tradition.

It was a surprise to me to hear the claims here in Ireland that the translations are written in American English, or perhaps in Roman English; at any rate they are not written in Irish English.

A few preliminary clarifications might be useful. No Roman was involved in producing the texts, done by ICEL, or in its review by *Vox Clara*. A few English-speakers working in Rome at the Congregation for Divine Worship were important, but only rarely intervened in the *Vox Clara* workings.

Vox Clara members did discuss whether it was possible to have one translation for the whole English-speaking world and it was pointed out that hugely successful films have one text for the whole world. As Catholics we opted for this, unlike the Spanish-speaking nations which use a number of translations.

The majority of English-speaking Catholics, who regularly worship in English, are from the United States, but the translations are remarkable for the extent to which American quirks and particularities have been subordinated to the aspirations for universal English.

A good deal of the finest English has been written, and still is written in North America. Monsignor Moroney's examples of what he called 'great rhetoric' from Lincoln, Kennedy and Reagan are mine also, although I regularly read Lincoln's Gettysburg address before a very important speech or sermon (rather than the Second Inauguration address) and would add Churchill's Second World War speeches in freedom's darkest hour (perhaps a dubious addition here in Ireland) among those I most admire.

The best English transcends its period and country of origin and while the new translation of the Missal cannot regularly equal the language of Heaney, Yeats, Wilde, Hopkins or James Joyce, it aspires to their eloquence and power in ways appropriate to the language of worship of our transcendent God of love.

Very few logicians would claim that a text could simultaneously be both Roman and American. It is certainly not un-Irish, except perhaps that the language used is more precise, eloquent and accurate than much of the day to day conversational language in both Australia and Ireland.

The world has changed dramatically. There are now more English-speakers in the middle class in India than in the British Isles and Ireland. I feel that too many criticisms are made by those ignorant of most of the translation and are based not on linguistic arguments, but ideological or even sub-theological considerations. I suspect that this hostility will disappear among the lay faithful as they come to use and hear the new translations.

WHY A NEW TRANSLATION OF THE MISSAL

This is a wonderful moment in the English-speaking world and in the history of the Church, as we introduce this new English-language translation of the Roman Missal into our dioceses and parishes.

In the light of my introductory comments, you can understand why in 1997 Blessed John Paul II arrived at an evaluation of liturgical translations in general; namely, that they were not up to the mark and further measures were needed to set them on a firmer foundation.[1] He was clearly talking about English, but also about French and Italian and German and a few hundred other languages. This was not the opinion of a single moment, but had matured in the late Pope and in many others over a period of time.

As to the Pope, we may simply note that already in 1988, for the twenty-fifty anniversary of the promulgation of the Council's Liturgy Constitution, *Sacrosanctum concilium*, Blessed John Paul had issued an Apostolic Letter,[2] in which, among other things, he called for the Bishops' Conferences to live up to their responsibilities for the liturgical translations, replacing provisional

---

1 Cf. Cardinal Secretary of State, Letter to the Pro-Prefect of the Congregation for Divine Worship and the Discipline of the Sacraments, 1 February 1997, referred to in a footnote to paragraph 20 of the document: Congregation for Divine Worship and the Discipline of the Sacraments, Instruction *Liturgiam authenticam*, of 28 March 2001.   2 Blessed John Paul II, Apostolic Letter *Vicesimus Quintus Annus*, of 4 December 1988.

translations, completing the range of books, correcting infelicities and errors, ensuring wide co-operation, so that the result might be stable liturgical books of a dignity commensurate with the mysteries of the faith which they serve to celebrate.[3] Quite a programme! We are now a further twenty-three years down the road and we have still not completed it!

However, there *is* a programme and at last something is now moving, and as we shall see, in fact, it is moving well.

It is been moving for at least a decade, since the promulgation on 28 March 2001, at the behest of Blessed John Paul, of the Instruction *Liturgiam authenticam*,[4] which sets out new rules for organizing and carrying out liturgical translations into the vernacular. The Instruction is quite a full document. I would, however, like to quote one essential paragraph that will help us get into the stride of our work in this session of the Conference:

> The Latin liturgical texts of the Roman Rite, while drawing on centuries of ecclesial experience in transmitting the faith of the Church received from the Fathers, are themselves the fruit of the liturgical renewal, just recently brought forth. In order that such a rich patrimony may be preserved and passed on through the centuries, it is to be kept in mind from the beginning that the translation of the liturgical texts of the Roman Liturgy is not so much a work of creative innovation as it is of rendering the original texts faithfully and accurately into the vernacular language. While it is permissible to arrange the wording, the syntax and the style in such a way as to prepare a flowing vernacular text suitable to the rhythm of popular prayer, the original text, insofar as possible, must be translated integrally and in the most exact manner, without omissions or additions in terms of its content, and without paraphrases or glosses. Any adaptation to the characteristics or the nature of the various vernacular languages is to be sober and discreet.

A number of notes are being sounded here and we can paraphrase some of them as follows:

1. Our patrimony of faith, in the expression that is specific to the Roman Rite down the centuries, is to be carefully kept even in translation;

---

3 Ibid., n. 20.   4 Congregation for Divine Worship and the Discipline of the Sacraments, Instruction *Liturgiam authenticam*, of 28 March 2001.

2. Translation is not a superficial business of reinventing the wheel, of making the Church say what some translator wants her to say, but truly of a *carrying across* of a well-honed and well-defined and vital content, guaranteed by the highest authority, into the language we speak today;

3. If we take English as the example, it is clear that the English has to be good English, but not at the cost of mangling the precious original content.

It all seems straightforward enough, and it is. But unfortunately these basic ideas were not faithfully followed and the Church has suffered as a consequence. It is not my allotted task here today, nor frankly is it my temperamental inclination, to rake over the past to see where the strategies went wrong. Rather, let us try to open our eyes to what stands before us as a new fresh, alternative.

Let us get into our stride by looking at one of the early prayers in the present Missal, early in the sense that it comes from the ancient Roman liturgy and predates certainly the year 600. Early, too, in the sense that it comes early in the Missal, since it is assigned to the Second Sunday of Advent. For those of you who have the red book of extracts, it is on page seventy-four.

> *Omnipotens et misericors Deus,*
> *in tui occursum Filii festinantes*
> *nulla opera terreni actus impediant,*
> *sed sapientiae caelestis eruditio*
> *nos faciat eius esse consortes.*
> *Qui tecum vivit.*

Our prayer, though ancient, was not in the Missal arranged after the Council of Trent and so was not in the Missal of Blessed John XXIII. It talks of going out in haste to meet Christ, the Son of God when he comes. This reminds us of the story of the Virgins or Bridesmaids where in the night 'the cry went up: Behold the Bridegroom comes, go out to meet him!' (Matthew 25:6).[5]

Other passages of Scripture, that are read to us at Mass in Advent, often from the very lips of Jesus, tell us that the end will come in the night, when we least expect it. 'Blessed the servant whom the Lord finds doing his duty when he comes' (Luke 12:43–44). You remember how the Apostles ran as fast as

---

5 In this talk I generally cite the RSV version of the Scriptures.

their legs could carry them to the tomb of Jesus, when they heard that he had risen, and that John got there first, impelled by the great love that bound him to the Lord (see John 20:4). You remember, too, how St Paul talks about running the race to make sure of the prize (1 Corinthians 9:24). The prize, of course, is to meet and know Christ and to be saved by his love.

Our prayer, as is the manner of these prayers, plays on a mixture of these reminiscences about going to meet, running, hurrying, being ready, dashing forward to catch the prize, to accompany the Bridegroom into the great feast. It is an Advent prayer and the word *Advent* means a 'coming' or even a 'triumphal entry', like the old Roman Emperors. The four weeks of Advent look forward to Our Lord coming at Christmas, but also cast their gaze beyond, to the final coming of Our Lord in triumph and splendour at the end of time.

There are ideas, here, obviously, but there is also a picture, a word-picture. We pray to God who is almighty, who governs the whole universe, who sustains it in being, who is loving and merciful (and when we say God is merciful, we remember that we are sinners). We ask God to arrange things, to give us warning, to give us the energy to run that race and go out to meet the Son he has sent to us.

So far, these words, these brushstrokes, show us a rough road and people running for their lives in the night to meet someone, and that someone is Jesus Christ. The rest of the prayer fills in the picture, because it is vital that running on that road, we do not trip up. What might trip us up? Deeds and occupations and concerns and thoughts that are too much attached to the things of the earth instead of the heavenly world which, in Jesus, is now descending to meet us. We ask God to set aside these harmful obstacles. We can hear Jesus saying lovingly to good-hearted St Martha, grumbling about her sister while she herself dashed about, doubtless getting a meal ready for him (see Matthew 12:2): 'Martha, Martha, you are anxious and troubled about many things; one thing is needful' (Luke 10:41–2).

Often the prayers are balanced in a wonderful way, imitating in this not rarely the style of the Bible itself. Here, the prayer does not just ask that God clear our path of the obstacle of worldly occupations and concerns, but that he give to us, like he gave, we remember, to the Wise Virgins, heavenly wisdom. St James speaks about Wisdom coming from above (James 3:17–8): 'But the wisdom from above is first pure, then peaceable, gentle, open to reason, full of mercy and good fruits, without uncertainty or insincerity.'

Then the prayer concludes. What will be the result that we can hold up before our eyes in hope, if God grants us the grace? It is that we will be made companions at Christ's great feast, which is at one and the same time his wedding banquet, *and* the meal Jesus gave the weary crowd of five thousand on the hillside when he multiplied loaves and fishes. The feast is also the great meal to which the poor and oppressed stream through history from every corner of the earth, to be sated with the food they could never dream of (Isaiah 2:2; 25:6), and yet in another way to share a simple meal, as they would their family or with a friend (Revelation 3:20), only that now the friend is the Son of God. All these different meals find their high point in the one great meal, the Holy Sacrifice of the Mass, which is the foretaste of heaven.

One last detail. The Latin word *consortes* can mean several things, so when the last line of the prayers asks that we be made 'consortes' of the Son of God, it means made his companions, but also his co-heirs. We remember the promise of Jesus to the Good Thief on the cross: 'This day, you will be with me in paradise' (Luke 23:43) and what Jesus said the Judge will say on the last day to the merciful: 'Come, O blessed of my Father, *inherit* the kingdom prepared for you from the foundation of the world' (Matthew 25:34). St Paul tells the Romans (8:16–17) 'we are children of God, and if children, then *heirs, heirs of God and fellow heirs with Christ,* provided we suffer with him in order that we may also be glorified with him.'

There is a lot in this prayer. The Church went looking for it after the Council in books compiled for Mass by Popes and Church Fathers a millennium and a half ago, because we need deep prayers, prayers that will last. We do not need to be great experts in biblical studies or in the history of the Church to pray this prayer well. However, if we know our Bible a bit better and if we manage to set aside the hustle and bustle of our lives and concentrate for a moment on addressing a short prayer to Almighty God with sincerity, its meaning will be evident enough to us and it will do its work in our heart. The work of a prayer is to bring us into contact, face to face with God.

At this point, we hardly need to remind ourselves that the prayer needs to be properly and sensitively translated. If it was worth handing down 1500 years, it is worth translating with care. It is a treasure, and ordinary Catholic people have a right to this treasure.

The old Missals said this:

> God of power and mercy,
> open our hearts in welcome.
> Remove the things that hinder us from receiving Christ with joy,
> so that we may share his wisdom,
> and become one with him
> when he comes in glory.

Some of the things that we have pointed out are certainly present in this wording. The traditional expression 'Almighty God' has been replaced with a trendy 'God of power', the term 'hearts' has appeared from somewhere (not from the Latin). The idea of hastening to meet our Lord has gone and with it all those allusions that we saw – the Wise Virgins and the rest. There is a mention of wisdom, but it is not called heavenly wisdom and the things that hinder us are not called earthly things. Our being the Lord's companions and co-heirs has become being 'one with him', thus losing as well the reference to all those meals that are the image of the Eucharist.

And the coming of the Lord has been narrowed to when 'he comes in glory', which is partly correct. But it ignores the fact that we are sitting in the benches with our families trying to prepare ourselves for Christmas, too. That is important. There are a lot of people on this planet who live in the hope that things will get better, will one day finally be all right. But sadly not all of them are sustained by the Catholic faith that Jesus has already come once, in his great love, taught us, died for us, has risen, founded his Church, given us the great gift of the sacraments, and remains with us throughout time. That is how *we* have hope of it all ending well, for ourselves and those we love and those we see suffering. You perhaps remember those simple words, which the mediaeval woman mystic, Julian of Norwich, gathered in her mystical experiences from the lips of the Lord: '… sin is the cause of all this pain, but all shall be well, and all shall be well, and all manner of thing shall be well'.[6]

Whoever prepared the old translation was certainly well-meaning, doubtless they looked for a short, well-rounded phrase, and found it. However, the price paid for that neatness was a bit too high.

---

6 Julian of Norwich, *Revelations of divine love*, Chapter 27.

In the new Missal, the prayer sounds like this:

> Almighty and merciful God,
> may no earthly undertaking hinder those
> who set out in haste to meet your Son,
> but may our learning of heavenly wisdom
> gain us admittance to his company.

If you can bear with me, I would like to mention here another prayer, one our grandmothers are unlikely to have known, since it was only discovered in a rare manuscript in a private archive in the North of Italy in the early 1880s. The manuscript is usually called the Rotulus or Scroll of Ravenna, because it was rolled up. It is certainly ancient, but there is no complete agreement about who composed it or where it came from (absolutely nothing to do with the Dead Sea Scrolls, by the way). The forty or so Latin liturgical prayers our Scroll contains are often very beautiful and when Pope Paul VI ordered the Missal to be revised, a large number of these ancient prayers were put to use. My remarks concern one of the prayers now used for the day *after* the first prayer I mentioned above, namely for the Monday of the Second Week of Advent.

We all remember those lines from the Psalms (Psalm 141 [140]) where we pray:

> I have called to you, LORD; hasten to help me!
> Hear my voice when I cry to you.
> *Let my prayer rise like incense before you,*
> *the raising of my hands like an evening oblation.*

These Psalm verses have been very influential in the liturgy in many ways. We can say that the Scroll prayer we are talking about is based on this text, and on the underlying idea of the incense, seen by the Psalmist as a symbol of prayer, rising to where God sits enthroned in the heavens. The prayer as we had it before is partly a quotation of the Psalm but without explicitly mentioning incense.[7]

Then it goes a step further and models the second part of the text on a further application of the same idea. Basically it asks that our prayer may come into the presence of God's majesty (that is, tacitly, that he may hear us, that we

---

7 Cf. also Ps 87, 3: '*intret in conspectu tuo oratio mea inclina aurem tuam ad precem meam*'.

may be in communion with him), but then adapts this and adds the petition that in the same way, our desires, aspirations, prayers or pledges (all possible meanings of the Latin plural noun *vota*), that come from our determination to serve God, may carry across the days between now and the great feast of the Incarnation at Christmas and that we may celebrate that feast worthily, and achieve the same result; that is, the unspoken hope of coming into communion or union with God.

It is quite a sophisticated prayer that, at one level, needs a bit of explaining, but at the same time, it has an evident meaning to anyone who reads it reflectingly.

> *Dirigatur, quaesumus, Domine,*
> *in conspectu tuo nostrae petitionis oratio,*
> *et ad magnum incarnationis Unigeniti tui mysterium*
> *nostra vota servitutis illibata puritate perveniant.*
> *Per Dominum*

The new Missal has this translation:

> May our prayer of petition
> rise before you, we pray, O Lord,
> that, with purity unblemished,
> we, your servants may come, as we desire,
> to celebrate the great mystery
> of the Incarnation of your Only-Begotten Son.
> Who lives and reigns with you.

We see that this translation of our prayer reflects the lines of what we have said. Now let us read the 1970s version:

> Lord, free us from our sins and make us whole.
> Hear our prayer,
> and prepare us to celebrate
> the incarnation of your Son.

While we still have a prayer that says something about celebrating the Incarnation and that mentions something about our prayer, there is no clear link to the biblical text of the Psalm. Moreover the idea of 'purity unblemished', an echo of the usual biblical language about offering acceptable sacrifice, in this case especially of ourselves, is changed to talk about being freed from our sins. This is also legitimate but the thought is not to be found in this Latin prayer. It is hard to forgive the complete jettisoning of a rich expression like 'the great mystery of the Incarnation of your Only-Begotten Son', while extraneous ideas from our contemporary society (forty years ago!) have entered the mix with talk about 'make us whole', a phrase which is totally lacking in the Latin.

As a literary piece, the 1970s prayer is unimpressive, with no elegance to bind ideas and phrases together, to impart stress or emphasis. Prayers should be the vehicle of our inner movement towards God, the Beloved, of the emotion of our meeting with God, our Creator and Father.

Even when not sung, words can have a similar effect to music in elevating our mood, in raising our spirits, in feeding the soul, in prompting our hearts, in bringing us closer to God. What a pity that the 1970s translators achieved this so rarely and turned aside from much biblical imagery. Ironically, at this same period, Pope Paul was reminding us that the Bible is the basic prayer-book of the Church and affirming, 'What is needed is that texts of prayers and chants should draw their inspiration and their wording from the Bible'.[8]

The Pope was only echoing an idea of the Second Vatican Council (*Sacrosanctum concilium* n. 24) taken up in the *General instruction of the Roman Missal*:

> Sacred Scripture is of the greatest importance in the celebration of the liturgy. For it is from Scripture that lessons are read and explained in the homily, and psalms are sung; *the prayers, collects, and liturgical songs are scriptural in their inspiration and their force*, and it is from the Scriptures that actions and signs derive their meaning.[9]

> ... it is out of the Sacred Scripture that the readings are read and are explained in the homily and that Psalms are sung, and it is by the influence of Sacred Scripture and at its prompting that prayers, orations, and liturgical chants are fashioned in such a way that it is from Sacred Scripture that actions and signs derive their meaning.

---

8 Pope Paul VI, Apostolic Exhortation, *Marialis cultus*, of 2 February 1974, n. 30. Pope Paul was as ever faithfully propagating the teaching of the Council: Cf. Second Ecumenical Council of the Vatican, Constitution on the Sacred Liturgy, *Sacrosanctum concilium*, no. 24. See also the Roman Missal.   9 Cited

In our new translation the texts are manifestly steeped in the Scriptures.

I hope that from these words you have been able to taste something of the flavour of these new texts and the necessity for them. I have deliberately not criticized translations that will be used again. My examples from the 1970s texts belong to the past.

Blessed John Paul II, who ordered this whole operation of reworking our liturgical translations, said of it:

> I urge the bishops and the Congregation to make every effort to ensure that liturgical translations are faithful to the original of the respective typical editions in the Latin language. A translation, in fact, is not an exercise in creativity, but a meticulous task of preserving the meaning of the original without changes, omissions or additions. The failure to observe this criterion on occasion makes the work of revising some texts necessary and urgent.[10]

Pope Benedict XVI has followed the development of the translation. On 9 November 2005 he wrote to Cardinal Francis Arinze, then Prefect of the Congregation for Divine Worship: 'I am confident that ... the translation of the *Missale Romanum* into English will succeed in transmitting the treasures of the faith and the liturgical tradition in the specific context of a devout and reverent Eucharistic celebration.'

When the new English translation was presented to him, Pope Benedict acknowledged that some may 'find it hard to adjust to unfamiliar texts after nearly forty years of continuous use of the previous translation'. However, patience, in the words of the Holy Father, will be rewarded by 'a renewal and a deepening of Eucharistic devotion all over the English-speaking world'. The Holy Father has asked that the new translation 'be introduced with due sensitivity, and the opportunity for catechesis that it presents ... be firmly grasped. I pray that in this way any risk of confusion or bewilderment will be averted'.[11] This is our purpose here.

---

more recently also in the important new chapter of the *General instruction of the Roman Missal* (added in 2002), n. 391. The updated text is in the early section of our new Missal.   **10** Blessed John Paul II, Message to the Plenary Meeting of the Congregation for Divine Worship and the Discipline of the Sacraments, from Castel Gandolfo, 21 September 2001.   **11** Pope Benedict XVI, Discourse to the Superiors of the Congregation for Divine Worship and the Discipline of the Sacraments and the Members of the Vox Clara Committee, 28 April 2010.

Our new English-language Missal has been approved by the overwhelming majority votes, often unanimously, of the English-speaking Bishops' Conferences of Europe and North America, of the Caribbean, of Africa, Asia and Oceania. Do not believe newspaper reports and the like that tell you there was no consultation, that it was all imposed from Rome or the like. Total nonsense. If ever in the history of the Church there was a collegial decision affecting a single major language group, this is it. The Bishops' Conferences voted twice on successive versions of the translation.

So we now have a text prepared and then improved by virtually all the Bishops sharing our common English-language, combed through line by line, word by word, in two high-level international committees of Bishops meeting assiduously over the best part of a decade. You can bet, too, that of those Bishops voting on the text, there were few who in their turn did not take further, direct expert advice. Following publicly announced detailed criteria, the work was explicitly encouraged by two Popes, and by three Cardinal Prefects of the Congregation for Divine Worship. And somebody has the effrontery to try to palm off on intelligent Catholic people a story that it was all done in a dark corner by a nameless clique and forced without warning on a shocked public!

Let us leave the fables, and as in the phrase related by the Book of Revelation, 'Hear what the Spirit is saying to the Churches' (Revelation 2:7, 11, 17, 29; 3:6, 13, 22). The enterprise we are concerned with is not petty politics, it is about the vital mysteries of our salvation, in our parishes, in our families, in all we hope for the future of our babes in arms and our young people. It is about the intimate conversation with God in our hearts, the shaping of Christ within our hearts as well as our imagination. It is about the transformation of our world, in love and respect, in steadfast, dogged, self-sacrificing adherence to the one real thing, the truth, the truth about Jesus Christ that St Peter preached to the international crowds in the streets of Jerusalem on the morning of Pentecost (*Acts* 2:22–36), when the Holy Spirit descended to complete the Paschal mystery.

We are privileged to live through a graced moment. So, yes, *carpe diem*, seize the day, seize this great occasion, but with all the love and trust that God has taught us through Our Lord Jesus Christ.

The new Roman Missal: a moment in the Church's liturgical renewal

ARTHUR SERRATELLI

For the past two generations, we have grown very comfortable with the texts we use to celebrate the liturgy. Now the Church in the English-speaking world has undertaken the most significant change in the liturgy since the introduction of the new Order of Mass in 1970. Already the response to the changes has been mixed.

Response to change comes from a number of sources. Sometimes we can become very comfortable with what is familiar and change becomes an annoyance. We have to learn new ways of doing things; and so there is resistance. Sometimes, we do not have sufficient knowledge of the reason or reasons for the changes and we are, therefore, hesitant to embrace them. At other times, there is the honest assessment that not all change is progress. Hopefully, we can address these concerns as we explain the history of the new missal as well as the actual changes in the texts of the missal.

First, change in general. In a word, life is not static. Cardinal John Henry Newman said, 'To live is to change, to be perfect is to have changed often'.[1] To be alive is to change. This applies to people, institutions and even language. Liturgy is people. It is life. Therefore, liturgy changes.[2] But why are our liturgical texts changing now?

In 2000, Pope John Paul II announced the publication of the third edition (*editio typica tertia*) of the *Missale Romanum*. This third edition contains a number of new elements: prayers for the observances of feasts/memorials of recently canonized saints, additional prefaces for the Eucharistic Prayers, additional Masses and Prayers for Various Needs and Intentions, and some minor modifications of rubrics for the celebration of the Mass. Once the third edition of the Roman Missal text was published in Latin, it became the official text to be used in the celebration of the Mass. Hence the need for conferences of Bishops to prepare vernacular translations.

---

1 John Henry Newman, *An essay on the development of christian doctrine*, 1.7. 2 Dennis C. Smolarski, SJ, *Sacred mysteries. Sacramental principles and liturgical practice* (Mahwah, NJ, 1994), pp 7–11.

The fact that a new missal requires a new translation is easy to understand. What poses a problem for some is the fact that the new translation has taken place on the basis of principles different than those used in the texts we are now using. And therefore, the texts sound different.

It is good to remember that we have only been using the vernacular in the liturgy for less than two generations. This means that the translation of liturgical texts into the vernacular has a relatively short history. In these years of using the vernacular, we have learned some things. Since the Second Vatican Council, we have learned more about the sources of these texts, their vocabulary, their structure and even the very art of translation itself.[3] It was inevitable that, based on our understanding, changes would eventually need to be made.

When the Second Vatican Council took up the question of liturgy, the bishops in attendance did something unprecedented in the history of the Church. For the first time ever, an ecumenical council examined the liturgy, an essential part of Church's life, in all its aspects: biblical and theological as well as pastoral. The Council gave great importance to liturgy by making the document on the liturgy, *Sacrosanctum concilium*, the first document it promulgated. This document speaks of the full, active participation of the people.[4] The change from Latin to the vernacular was meant to facilitate this.[5]

On 25 January 1969, *Comme le prévoit*, the Instruction on translating liturgical texts for celebrations with a congregation, was promulgated. From 1969 until 2001, the document *Comme le prévoit* granted translators wide latitude in translations for the liturgy.[6] Rather quickly in the English-speaking world, translators adopted dynamic equivalency as the approach to the texts.[7] Simply stated, dynamic equivalency translates the concepts and ideas of a text, but not necessarily the literal words or expressions. The principle of making the text accessible to the listener at times takes precedence over other considerations.

When the Instruction *Comme le prévoit* provided principles to be followed in the preparation of vernacular translations of the Latin liturgical texts, it also did something else. In its very first paragraph, the Instruction stated that 'after sufficient experiment and passage of time, all translations will need review'. The moment came and a review of the translations was set in motion.

3 Cf. James F. White, *A brief history of christian worship* (Nashville, 1993), pp 86–7.   4 *Sacrosanctum concilium*, 14.   5 A. Reid, *The organic development of the liturgy* (San Francisco, 2005), pp 268–9.
6 *Comme le prévoit, Notitiae* 5 (1969), pp 3–12.   7 See D. McManus, 'Translation theory in *Liturgiam authenticam*', in N.J Roy and J.E. Rutherford (eds), *Benedict XVI and the sacred liturgy* (Dublin, 2010), pp

In 1976, the International Committee on English in the Liturgy began a careful process of reviewing the liturgical books in light of pastoral experience with them. The committee examined both the positive and negative observations made regarding the effectiveness and suitability of the translated texts for public worship. This process of consultation spanned about twenty years.[8] It involved research into the provenance of the texts and the scriptural and patristic allusions contained in them.[9]

In addition to ICEL's evaluation of the texts, the Congregation for Divine Worship and Discipline of the Sacraments had also begun to re-evaluate the principles of translation contained in the instruction on translations. The Congregation had initiated work on a new Latin edition of the Roman Missal. The Congregation wisely decided not to confirm any new translation until a new set of principles could be drawn up and issued and the new Latin edition of the Missal could be completed and published.

As a result of these years of study and consultation, on 28 March 2001 the Congregation issued *Liturgiam authenticam*, the new 'Instruction on the use of the vernacular languages in the publication of the books of the Roman Liturgy'. This document introduced translation principles to refine and, in some ways, replace those principles contained in the 1969 instruction on translations. The new principles emphasize a respect for the scriptural and patristic allusions in the Latin text, the rich vocabulary of the Latin text, its grammar, syntax, rhetorical forms, and word order as far as possible in the vernacular language.

The new instruction did not deny the necessity of making the text accessible to the listener. But it did re-focus the attention of translators on the principle of unearthing the theological and linguistic richness of the original texts. Not just concepts, but words and expression are to be translated faithfully.[10] This approach respects the wealth contained in the original text. Some may find such exactness a bit discomforting. But there is a gain. This new emphasis adds a needed balance that keeps us from suffering an impoverishment of language in terms of our biblical and liturgical tradition.

166–31, especially 121–4. **8** The first fruits of this review and revision process were the revised editions of *Dedication of a church and an altar* (1978), *Pastoral care of the sick* (1982), *Order of Christian funerals* (1985), and *Rite of Christian initiation of adults* (1986). In 1982 ICEL began the process of revising the Missal translation by sending out for the comment of the Conferences of Bishops the first of two consultation books. **9** Paul F. Bradshaw, *The search for the origins of Christian worship*, 2nd ed. (New York, 2002), pp 73–117. **10** '... the translation of the liturgical texts of the Roman Liturgy is not so much a work of creative innovation as it is of rendering the original texts faithfully and accurately into the vernacular

It is important to keep in mind that, in fact, the new instruction has as its stated purpose something wider than translation. It 'envisions and seeks to prepare for a new era of liturgical renewal, which is consonant with the qualities and the traditions of the particular Churches, but which safeguards also the faith and the unity of the whole Church of God'.[11]

Now that we have looked at the reasons for having a new translation of our liturgical texts, we can turn attention to the very art of translation itself. In his popular rhetorical guide, *De duplici copia verborum ac rerum*, the sixteenth century Dutch humanist and theologian Erasmus showed his students that the single Latin sentence *Tuae literae me magnopere delectarunt* ('Your letter has delighted me very much') could be translated in 150 different styles.[12] Thus, he amply demonstrated that no single translation will ever completely satisfy everyone. We need to be honest from the beginning and acknowledge this.

Furthermore, we need to understand the wider implications of translating liturgical texts. Liturgical language is important for the life of the Church. The well-known axiom *Lex orandi, lex credendi*[13] reminds us that what we pray is not only the expression of our sentiment and our reverence directed toward God, but what we pray also speaks to us and articulates for us the faith of the Church. Our words in the liturgy are not simply expressions of one individual in one particular place at one time in history. Rather, they pass on the faith of the Church from one generation to the next.

For this reason, the bishops take seriously their responsibility to provide translations of liturgical texts that are at the same time accurate and inspiring. Hence, they sometimes engage in rather passionate discussions of words, syntax and phrases when approving liturgical texts. With great care, the episcopal conferences of English-speaking countries have provided us with prayers that are theologically accurate, in a language that has dignity and beauty and can be understood.[14] To appreciate these new texts, it is very enlightening to review the careful process that those involved in the work of translation of these texts have used.

---

language. While it is permissible to arrange the wording, the syntax and the style in such a way as to prepare a flowing vernacular text suitable to the rhythm of popular prayer, the original text, insofar as possible, must be translated integrally and in the most exact manner, without omissions or additions in terms of their content, and without paraphrases or glosses. Any adaptation to the characteristics or the nature of the various vernacular languages is to be sober and discreet', *Liturgiam authenticam*, 20. **11** *Liturgiam authenticam*, 7. **12** E.P.J. Corbett, *Classical rhetoric for the modern student* (Oxford, 1990), pp 461–2. **13** Prosper of Aquitaine, *Patrologia Latina* 51:209–10: … *obsecrationum quoque sacerdotalium sacramenta respiciamus, quae ab apostolis tradita, in toto mundo atque in omni catholica Ecclesia uniformiter celebrantur, ut legem credendi lex statuat supplicandi.* **14** 'So that the content of the original texts may be evident and

After the publication of the new Latin Missal, the International Committee on English in the Liturgy worked with scholars to produce a base translation of the texts of the Missal. The International Commission on English in the Liturgy (ICEL) is a mixed commission of Catholic Bishops' Conferences in countries where English is used in the celebration of the sacred liturgy according to the Roman rite. The purpose of the Commission is simple: to prepare English translations of each of the Latin liturgical books and any individual liturgical texts in accord with the directives of the Holy See. Eleven Conferences of Bishops are currently full members of ICEL.[15]

Bishops from English speaking countries attending the Second Vatican Council had set up the commission in Rome in 1963. Most recently, after some reorganization, on 15 September 2003, the Congregation for Divine Worship and the Discipline of the Sacraments formally established ICEL as a mixed commission in accordance with the Holy See's Instruction *Liturgiam authenticam*.

In ICEL's work on the new missal, a base translation of the Latin text was first prepared. Then a review team examined this first translation and commented on its fidelity to the Latin as well as its suitability for public worship. Working from these comments, a new version of the base text was prepared. It was called the proposed text. The Roman Missal editorial committee worked with the proposed text. The members of the committee made adjustments to the text in terms of style, syntax, vocabulary and proclaimability. Their work produced the new version.

Thus, when the commissioners of ICEL met, the members had before them the Latin text, the base text, the proposed text and the Roman Missal editorial committee's text. The bishops of ICEL examined each text according to the same principles of theological accuracy and proclaimablity. Throughout their work, the commissioners of ICEL kept in mind the goal of producing a text that would be accessible to the different language groups within the English-speaking world.

---

comprehensible even to the faithful who lack any special intellectual formation, the translations should be characterized by a kind of language which is easily understandable, yet which at the same time preserves these texts' dignity, beauty, and doctrinal precision. By means of words of praise and adoration that foster reverence and gratitude in the face of God's majesty, his power, his mercy and his transcendent nature, the translations will respond to the hunger and thirst for the living God that is experienced by the people of our own time, while contributing also to the dignity and beauty of the liturgical celebration itself.' *Liturgiam authenticam*, 25.   **15** Australia, Canada, England and Wales, India, Ireland, New Zealand, Pakistan, the Philippines, Scotland, South Africa and the United States of America.

Many people speak English, but not all the same. Our accents differ across the English-speaking world. So do our expressions and vocabulary. Americans take an *elevator*; other English-speakers take a *lift*. In New Jersey and New York, children call their father *pop*; in Kansas, they call soda *pop*. Furthermore, words, like people's dress, change from one generation to the next and from one group to another in the same society. What one individual calls a 'swamp', another more ecologically conscious individual calls 'wetlands'. Today, politically correct as well as linguistically conscious individuals carefully circumvent the word 'man' in order not to offend women.

Translating a Latin text into English for all English-speaking countries therefore requires the expertise of many people. The eleven bishops on the International Committee on English in the Liturgy worked with scholars from different English-speaking countries to produce a final text. Such collaborative work required not only competence in translation, but the art of compromise that comes from humility.

Once ICEL agreed on a text, it was sent to the individual national conferences as a Green Book. So, there was a Green Book for the Order of Mass Part One, for the Proper of Seasons and one for Ritual Masses. Each national conference of bishops used its own process of consultation on both a diocesan and a conference level. Bishops had the opportunity to consult with priests, laypeople and religious. Then, the bishops forwarded their individual consultation and personal work to their respective national conference's Committee on Divine Worship. This committee collated the results, and presented them to all the bishops, who then adopted some of them and forwarded the results to ICEL.

Once again ICEL attentively examined each of these comments and incorporated the insights into the production of the final text that is called the Gray Book. By 13 October 2008 Gray books had been prepared and were in the process of final approval by each national conference. Once a national conference of bishops approved a Gray Book, it was forwarded to the Congregation for Divine Worship and the Sacraments. The Congregation has the responsibility of approving the text in the form in which it is to be used.

The Congregation worked collaboratively both with ICEL and with the national conferences of bishops, and was aided in its work by *Vox Clara*. This commission included bishops from eight English-speaking countries. When texts were presented to the Congregation for approval, *Vox Clara* advised the Congregation with input from English-speaking experts.

I mention this long, careful scholarly, and, I must add, pastoral process in detail for a reason. The production of the final liturgical text is a work of immense importance. It deserves all the attention it is given. It was not left to the competence or preference of a few, because it is the expression of the faith of the whole Church.

The liturgy is the source of the divine life given through the Church as the sacrament of salvation.[16] As Pope Paul VI once said: the liturgy is also 'the first school of the spiritual life, the first gift which we can give to the Christian people who believe and pray with us'.[17] The 'central *actio*' of the Mass is, as Pope Benedict XVI has stated, fundamentally neither that of the priest as such nor of the laity as such, but of Christ the High Priest: This action of God, which takes place through human speech, is the real 'action' for which all creation is in expectation ... This is what is new and distinctive about the Christian liturgy: God himself acts and does what is essential.[18]

Wisely, therefore, the Church does not leave the words used in liturgy to the theology or pastoral sensitivity of any individual celebrant. The words used in the prayers of the liturgy, especially the Eucharistic prayer, cannot be casual or improvised. They are not to be changed by the priest. They are freighted with too much meaning and tradition.

The new translations also have a great respect for the style of the Roman Rite. Certainly, some sentences could be more easily translated to mimic our common speech. But they are not. And with reason. The new translations seek to preserve the general structure of prayers in the Missal. They also keep the particular characteristics of the prayers as well.

In the prayers of the Roman rite, and principally in the collects, there is an easily recognizable structure or pattern. The prayers usually begin with an address to God, followed by a relative clause of description or motivation. Next there is the petition and finally the conclusion.[19] This syntax allows each part clear expression, but carefully subordinates all the elements to a reliance upon God who is addressed in prayer. Each element is meant to flow from the previous one, usually in a single sentence. This allows the prayer to be focused and not overburdened. Thus, when the prayer is recited, the heart, in one continuous thought, pours itself out to God without interruption, directly and simply speaking to God.

---

16 Cf. *Lumen Gentium*, 1.   **17** Pope Paul VI, *Address at the closing of the Second Session of the Council*, 4 December 1963.   **18** Joseph Cardinal Ratzinger, *The spirit of the liturgy*, (tr. J. Saward) (San Francisco, 2000), p. 173.   **19** Cf. *Ratio Translationis*, 32.

The prayers of the Roman Missal are marked by several characteristics worth noting. The new translations preserve these characteristics. In this way, the particular style of the Roman Missal in passing on the faith is not diminished. We will look at some examples where this can be seen.

First of all, I would like to illustrate the biblical richness of the Latin text and the new translation. The collect for the First Sunday of Advent is a good example. The Latin text of this collect is taken from a collection of largely seventh and eighth century Gallican and Roman prayers compiled near Paris around 750, commonly referred to as the Gelasian Sacramentary. The prayer reads:

> *Grant, your faithful, we pray, almighty God,*
> *the resolve to run forth to meet your Christ*
> *with righteous deeds, at his coming,*
> *so that, gathered at his right hand,*
> *they may be worthy to possess the heavenly Kingdom.*
> *Through our Lord Jesus Christ, your Son,*
> *who lives and reigns with you*
> *in the unity of the Holy Spirit,*
> *one God, forever and ever*

The prayer uses the word 'run' in line two. In the Latin prayer, we find the word *occurrentes*, 'running to meet'. Yet, our current text says nothing about running. It was lost in the translation. However, in the newly translated prayer, we now pray for the resolve *to run forth to meet your Christ with righteous deeds*.

Running a race is a Pauline image. In 1 Corinthians 9:24–6, Paul says: 'Do you not know that in a race all the runners compete, but only one receives the prize? So run that you may obtain it.' Again in Galatians 2:2 and 5:7, Paul uses the same image. With the image of the race, Paul reminds us that the Christian life requires discipline and personal effort. Keeping the faith requires the perseverance that prepares us for the Lord when he comes again. We are to 'persevere in running the race that lies before us while keeping our eyes on Jesus, the leader and perfecter of faith'.[20]

We should also note that the prayer says that we are *to run forth with righteous deeds*. If we ask, 'what are these "righteous deeds"?', the prayer itself answers our question biblically. The two phrases found in the prayer – *gathered*

20 Heb 12:1–2.

at his right hand and *to possess (inherit) the heavenly Kingdom* – are taken directly from Matthew's narrative of the final judgment. There, in Chapter 25, we read:

> all the nations will be *gathered* … He will place the sheep on *his right* and the goats on his left. Then the King will say to those on his right, 'Come, you who are blessed by my Father. *Inherit the kingdom* prepared for you from the foundation of the world. *For I was hungry and you gave me food, thirsty and you gave me drink …*'[21]

We run to meet the Lord with our corporal and spiritual works of mercy. Our deeds of love that connect us with each other – that connect us with the most vulnerable and in need – connect us more profoundly to the Lord. Thus, on the very first Sunday in Advent, as we stretch our eyes to the Coming of the Lord and prepare to meet him, the prayer challenges us to connect our prayer, our worship of God, with the way we live out our lives with each other.

The collect for Friday in the Second Week of Advent is another example of a prayer that uses the biblical text as its inspiration. It is taken from the eighth century Old Gelasian Sacramentary. It reads:

> *Grant that your people, we pray, almighty God,*
> *may be ever watchful*
> *for the coming of your Only-Begotten Son,*
> *that, as the author of our salvation himself has taught,*
> *we may hasten, alert, with lighted lamps*
> *to meet him when he comes.*
> *Who lives and reigns with you*
> *in the unity of the Holy Spirit,*
> *One god, for ever and ever.*

The images of hastening, of being watchful and of meeting Christ with lighted lamps are taken right from the parable of the wise and foolish virgins in Matthew 25:1–13.

Perhaps the one text that has been most noticeable as changed in the new missal is the frequently occurring dialogue between priest and people: '*The Lord be with you*' and '*And with your spirit*'.[22] When English was first introduced into

---

21 Mt 25: 32–5.   **22** This greeting and response come in the introductory rites, before the Gospel, at the

the Mass between 1966 and 1970, the priest would say, '*The Lord be with you*' and the people would respond, '*And with your spirit*'. In fact, this is exactly how it is translated in Spanish, French, Italian, Polish, German and Dutch. However, the English translation was changed to the more colloquial form of the greeting and response: '*The Lord be with you*' and '*And also with you*'. We may question why the response is now being changed again. Is it just to be in line with the rest of the world? Not exactly.

There is a very good reason why the other language groups say *with your spirit* and why we are doing the same. The greeting and response are found embedded in the Scriptures. The greeting *Dominus vobiscum* is one of the most ancient of liturgical greetings. It has its scriptural roots in Boaz's greeting of the reapers in Ruth 2:4 and in the angel's greeting of Gideon in Judges 6:12. The response *et cum spiritu tuo* is also biblical.

The Apostle Paul ends four of his letters expressing to the person or community receiving the letter the desire that the grace of the Lord be with their spirit.[23] In Pauline theology, the *pneuma* or 'spirit' is that spiritual part of the human being directly influenced by the Spirit's action. In one of his homilies for Pentecost, St John Chrysostom echoes this Pauline understanding when he explains that, as the Bishop begins the Eucharistic Prayer, he prays that the Lord's grace be given to the people and the people respond 'And with your spirit'. Chrysostom says that this reminds the bishop that the sacrifice to be offered is not accomplished by his own power but by the indwelling power of the Spirit that penetrates his spirit.

Thus, when the greeting and response are given in the Liturgy, '*The Lord be with you ... and with your spirit*', there is being stated the spiritual relationship between priest and people. The Holy Spirit is present as we gather together in the Lord's name. Our greeting each other is not the same as the way we greet each other on other occasions. This occasion is different. A formal, biblical, theological greeting, short and simple, reminds us of this. What is taking place happens because the Holy Spirit is at work. Liturgy is no mere casual gathering of people. It is the assembly called into being by the power of the Holy Spirit. It is a sacred moment.

Some prayers place on our lips the very words of the biblical texts themselves. A few examples will suffice. In Eucharistic Prayer III, we no longer say: '*From east to west, a perfect offering is made to the glory of your name.*'

beginning of the Eucharistic Prayer, at the sign of peace and in Concluding Rites.   **23** Gal 6:18; Phil 4:23; 2 Tim 4:22; and Philem 25.

Instead we pray the words of Malachi 1: 11: '*... from the rising of the sun to its setting*'. Nothing is lost in meaning. A sense of poetry is gained. In the Communion Rite, we now repeat the words of the humble and compassionate centurion, '*Lord, I am not worthy that you should enter under my roof but only say the word ...*'[24]

The examples that we have seen show us that the new texts are richer and fuller because they are more biblical. This is one of the great gifts of the new translation. Formal equivalency as a method of translation works. Unearthing the biblical allusions, images and words helps us to make the words of Scripture our own. The Word that God speaks to us in Revelation, we speak to him in prayer.

Second, the new texts not only are careful to keep biblical allusions but those also from patristic writings. Two examples will suffice. *Ex pede Hercule!*

In the post communion prayer for 28 August, the memorial of St Augustine, we pray:

> *May partaking of the table of Christ*
> *sanctify us, we pray, O Lord,*
> *that, being made members of his body,*
> *we may be what we have received.*
> *Through Christ our Lord.*

Our words asking God that we may be what we receive play on St Augustine's dictum: 'If you have received worthily, you are what you have received.'[25]

In the prayer over the offering for Saint Ignatius of Antioch (October 17), we pray:

> *May this oblation and our homage be pleasing to you, O Lord,*
> *Just as you accepted Saint Ignatius, the wheat of Christ,*
> *made pure bread through his martyrdom and passion.*
> *Through Christ our Lord.*

This prayer places on our lips the words of the courageous bishop of Antioch who, more than any other Church father, expressed his desire for union with Christ. St Ignatius wrote: 'Suffer me to become food for the wild beasts, through whose instrumentality it will be granted me to attain to God.

24 Mt 8:8. **25** *Sermons*, 227.

I am the wheat of God, and let me be ground by the teeth of the wild beasts, that I may be found the pure bread of Christ.'[26]

A third characteristic of new texts is a greater adherence to the structure of the Latin. The new translation of the *Gloria* follows the exact order of the phrases found in the Latin. It does not omit, as the present text does, any of the phrases that express our response to the goodness of God. We now say: 'We praise you. We bless you. We adore you. We glorify you. We give you thanks for your great glory …'

By piling up five parallel phrases one on top of the other, as opposed to the three in the present translation, the new text builds up a crescendo of praising God. One word of praise after another in rapid succession creates the feeling not only of exuberant joy, but also conveys the feeling of our inability to say enough in praise of God. The prayer is more than words. It is sentiment. It is feeling. It is the expression of our extravagant praise that is due to God.

The prayers at the offertory give us another example of a greater adherence to the Latin in the new texts. Where we said: *We have this bread to offer*, we now say: *We have received the bread we offer you*. In the English as it was before, we literally said that we have bread to offer, but we did not literally say that we are offering the bread.

The Latin uses for both bread and wine a relative clause, the bread or the wine *which we offer*. The Latin emphasizes that the very act of our offering the elements is occurring. The relative clause in the Latin – *which we offer* – was added to the text by Pope Paul VI. He wanted to indicate that all present – people and priest – are making the offering to God at this moment. The new translation brings out more everyone's share in the one priesthood of Christ.

Furthermore, where the English said the bread which earth has given, the new translation uses the expression *fruit of the earth*. This is a somewhat strange expression to find here. It is used metaphorically now to express that the bread we are offering is the fruit, that is, the result of much labour. With the new texts, both prayers for the offering of the bread and wine will use the same expression, *fruit of the earth*, and thus have a clear parallelism.

A fourth characteristic of the Roman Missal is the particular way that many of the Post-communion prayers are concluded. These prayers tend to conclude strongly with a teleological or eschatological point. For example, the Post-Communion prayer for Tuesday of the first week of Lent read:

---

26 *Epistle to the Romans*, 4.

> *Grant us through these mysteries, Lord,*
> *that by moderating earthly desires*
> *we may learn to love the things of heaven.*
> *Through Christ our Lord.*

In everyday speech, we would say: *that we may learn to love the things of heaven by moderating earthly desires.* Yet, *by moderating earthly desires* comes first. The order is reversed. As a result, there is now a strong teleological emphasis on *the things of heaven.*

The prayer after communion for the eighth Sunday in Ordinary time reads:

> *Nourished by your saving gifts,*
> *we beseech you mercy, Lord,*
> *that by this same Sacrament*
> *with which you feed us in the present age,*
> *You may make us partakers of life eternal.*
> *Through Christ our Lord.*

The phrase *by this same Sacrament with which you feed us in the present age* does not follow the normal pattern of ordinary conversation. But its present position allows the prayer to end with the emphasis on *life eternal.*

This use of inversion is a characteristic of the Latin Missal. In the Proper of Time, about 14 per cent of the Prayers after Communion use inversions. By placing the adverbial prepositional phrase at the beginning of the clause, the result is powerful. When recited, the prayer does not simply dribble off into insignificance. Rather, the new text keeps the distinctive theological emphasis of the Latin text and concludes with focused attention on the point of the prayer.

A fifth characteristic of the new translation is its respect for the rich vocabulary of the Roman rite. The Post-Communion prayers employ a variety of words such as *nourished, fed, recreated* and *made new.* The collects use words such as: *we pray, we beseech* and *we ask.* The many different words of the Latin text are not monotonously translated with the same English words. Thus, by being faithful to the Latin text, the new translation enriches the use of our liturgical language in English.

A sixth characteristic of the new texts is the presence of concrete images. In biblical language, anthropomorphisms are not uncommon. The new texts keep these vivid ways of speaking about God as well as maintaining other concrete images in speaking about the Christian life.[27]

It is perfectly good English to say: *in your pity hear our prayers.* But the new text for the blessing of ashes respects the poetry of the text and says: *in your pity give ear to our prayers.*

The collect for Ash Wednesday reads:

> *Grant, O Lord, that we may begin with holy fasting*
> *this campaign of Christian service,*
> *so that, as we take up battle against spiritual evils,*
> *we may be armed with weapons of self-restraint.*
> *Through our Lord Jesus Christ, your Son,*
> *who lives and reigns with you,*
> *In the unity of the Holy Spirit,*
> *one God for ever and ever.*

The images of a military *campaign, a battle* and *weapons* are certainly appropriate for the struggle of Lenten discipline against evil. These are not suppressed in the new translation

A seventh characteristic of the new translation is the concern for an exactness of vocabulary. In the Introductory Rites, we say, *let us acknowledge our sins, and so prepare ourselves to celebrate the sacred mysteries.* Acknowledge was chosen because this word (*agnoscamus*) implies not simply remembering – calling to mind – our sins interiorly but also confessing them openly.

A fuller example of this attention to exactness is found in the preface of Eucharistic Prayer II. In our old translation, we said;

> *For our sake he opened his arms on the cross,*
> *He put an end to death*
> *and revealed the resurrection.*
> *in this he fulfilled your will*
> *and won for you a holy people.*

27 'Modes of speech by which heavenly realities and actions are depicted in human form, or designated by means of limited, concrete terminology – as happens quite frequently in biblical language (i.e., anthropomorphisms) – often maintain their full force only if translated somewhat literally ... such as *ambulare, brachium, digitus, manus,* or *vultus [Dei]*, as well as *caro, cornu, os, semen,* and *visitare.* Thus it is best that such terms not be explained or interpreted by more abstract or general vernacular expressions ... It should be borne in mind that a literal translation of terms which may initially sound odd in a vernacular

The new text reads:

> *Fulfilling your will and gaining for you a holy people,*
> *he stretched out his hands as he endured his Passion,*
> *so as to break the bonds of death and manifest the resurrection.*

By saying *Fulfilling your will and gaining for you a holy people*, the text places an emphasis on the process of gathering a holy people as something that is still continuing. Thus, this preface comes closer to the opening paragraph of Eucharistic Prayer III. Both of which are based of 1 Peter 2:9.

Furthermore, by saying *he stretched out his hands as he endured his Passion*, the text draws greater attention to the suffering of Christ. The present text simply says: *he opened his arms on the cross*. Lastly, the new text retains the image of *breaking the bonds of death*. This is totally lacking in the current version.

An eight characteristic of the new translation is its safeguarding the cate-chetical aspect of public prayer. One simple example may suffice to illustrate this point. In the old text of the *Sanctus*, we said: *Lord God of power and might*. The new text says more exactly *Lord God of hosts*. The present wording, 'power and might', ignores the underlying scriptural reference. The Latin *Dominus Deus Sabbaoth* comes from Isaiah 6:1–3. *Dominus Deus Sabbaoth* is a name for God found a total of 279 times in the Old Testament. *Sabbaoth* can refer to the hosts which are the armies of this world or the hosts which are the heavenly bodies. God is the one who commands the armies of Israel and even of her enemies. God is the Creator who made the heavens and all their hosts. The hosts of heaven, like the armies on earth, are subject to his power.

Theologically, the name *Dominus Deus Sabbaoth* means that God is Lord, Sovereign and Ruler over every kind of force imaginable, over military, political or other-worldly. *Dominus Deus Sabbaoth* is a very exalted title, that does say *power and might*, but in an exponential way. When we now say, *God of hosts* instead of *God of power and might*, we regain more of the biblical tradition. We are reminded, even as Jesus taught, that God who is all powerful is all-embracing in his care for us.[28]

A ninth and last characteristic of the Roman Missal is the noble tone of its prayers. The new texts are careful to keep this style. In our present prayers,

language may for this very reason provoke inquisitiveness in the hearer and provide an occasion for catechesis.' *Liturgian authenticam*, 43.   **28** Lk 12:4–7.

Lord is often said at the very beginning of a sentence. Yet, the Latin does not put *Domine* as the first word. The new translations will follow Latin word-order more carefully. By not beginning with the appellative *Lord,* our way of addressing God becomes less peremptory.

When we frame our prayers in liturgy, the language of the street is not appropriate. The vocabulary of the person in the supermarket, in the gym or around the kitchen table should not be the standard for liturgical language. There is a difference between the language of public discourse used in a presidential address and the language we use in everyday conversation. It is the difference between our active vocabulary and our passive vocabulary. There are many words that we may not use every day, words such as *penitence* and *oblation.* Yet these words are in our passive vocabulary. We can understand them. Rightly do the translations respect the difference and consistently maintain a noble style of speech befitting the Divine Liturgy.

Lastly, as we welcome the new texts, it is helpful to keep in mind certain facts. First, the new texts will be used in many different English-speaking countries. Therefore, the language will not bear the cultural stamp or preference of one particular country. This calls for certain openness on the part of all of us to use words that may be understood, but are not commonly used in our own particular country.

Second, the language of the liturgy to address God, it should be intelligible. This does not, however, mean every word has to be part of the active vocabulary of everyone.

Third, in Liturgy, we should use a noble language that lifts us up as well as honours God. From the earliest Latin texts from the fourth century, the style of the language used in prayer differed from street language. In the new translation, the noble, heightened style of prayer at Liturgy is certainly a gain for all.

Fourth, the new translation of the Roman Missal for the English-speaking world gives us texts that are exact translations, though not slavishly literal translations. The prayers are theologically accurate in expression and free from ideological influences so that 'the sacred mysteries of salvation and the indefectible faith of the Church are efficaciously transmitted by means of human language …'[29]

Fifth, the common English text for all English-speaking countries reaffirms in a tangible manner the breadth of our Catholic identity.

---

29 *Liturgiam authenticam,* 3.

In conclusion, we should note that the new Missal comes as the result of years of growth and understanding. It will improve our liturgical prayer, but it will not be perfect. Perfection will come when the Liturgy on earth gives way to that of heaven where all the saints praise God with one voice.

The introduction of a new edition of the Roman Missal and a new translation is a moment of organic growth within the liturgical renewal of the Church. While individuals inevitably differ in their judgment on the quality of particular words or phrases, there is no dissent on the vital importance that proper texts have in the Church's life. The very preparation of an English version of the third edition of the Missal has not been simply a matter of translation. Scholars and pastors debated the value of particular words and styles because a new translation of the Roman Missal is an important moment to enter into a fresh appreciation of the Roman rite. It is the occasion to understand more deeply its particular style and language of prayer. As Pope John Paul II said on the occasion of the 25th anniversary of the Second Vatican Council's *Constitution on the Sacred Liturgy*:

> The time has come to renew that spirit which inspired the Church at the moment when the Constitution *Sacrosanctum Concilium* was ... promulgated ... The seed was sown; it has known the rigors of winter, but the seed has sprouted ...[30]

This is the graced moment to sink our roots deeper into the rich soil of tradition handed on in the Roman Missal.[31]

---

30 *Vicesimus Quintus Annus*, 23.　**31** See Ibid.

The *Ordo Missae* of 1965: the Latin-German altar missal and liturgical renewal

HELMUT HOPING

For a long time, the *Ordo Missae* of 1965, and the published bilingual missals based on it, did not meet with great interest in the field of liturgical studies. This changed with the call by Joseph Ratzinger for a 'new liturgical movement', as well as for a 'reform of the reform'. At the moment, a number of dissertations are being written about the so-called 'interim missals'.[1] My interest in the Latin-German altar missal of 1965[2] goes back to my analysis of the *usus antiquior* of the Roman Mass, which Pope Benedict XVI reintroduced with permission for its use by all priests of the Roman Catholic Church, with his *motu proprio Summorum pontificum* (2007).[3] I would like to begin this essay by recalling the process that led to the *Novus Ordo Missae* of 1969. I will then call attention to significant differences between the versions of the *Ordo Missae* of 1962, 1965 and 1969, and conclude by highlighting the different hermeneutics of translation that formed the basis of the 1965 Latin-German altar missal and the missal for the German language areas of 1975.

FROM THE *ORDO MISSAE* (1962) TO THE *NOVUS ORDO MISSAE* (1969)

At the constitutent meeting on 15 January 1964 of the *Consilium ad exsequendam constitutionem de sacra liturgia*, which directed the implementation of the liturgical reform, an agreement was reached to begin reforming liturgical books, particularly the Breviary and the Missal. In reaction to numerous pleas for him to do so, Pope Paul VI (1963–78) replaced the traditional formula of administration at the communion of the faithful with the simple formula *Corpus Christi*.[4] The *Coetus X, De ordine missae*, of the

---

1 Under the patronage of Bishop Thomas Olmsted (Phoenix) and Bishop Salvatore Cordileone (Oakland) a conference took place in Phoenix, Arizona 3–4 October 2012, where preliminary results of the ongoing research on the interim missals were presented. 2 See *Lateinisch-deutsches Altarmessbuch. Ausgabe für den liturgischen Gebrauch. Im Auftrag der Fuldaer und der Schweizer Bischofskonferenz. Besorgt von den liturgischen Kommissionen Deutschlands und der Schweiz* (Einsiedeln, Köln, Freiburg, Basel, 1965). 3 On 13 May 2011 an instruction was published that specified how the *motu proprio Summorum pontificum* was to be put into practice. 4 See *AAS* 56 (1964) 337f (= DEL I, 100).

Consilium held its first meeting between 7 and 10 May 1964 in Trier. In the same year further meetings took place in Rome (from 4 to 7 June), in Freiburg, Switzerland (from 23 to 28 August) and again in Rome (from 21 to 23 September). At the fourth meeting, the draft of a renewed Order of Mass was presented.

A few days later, the first instruction for the implementation of the liturgical reform, *Inter oecumenici*, was released (26 September 1964).[5] The instruction brought initial changes of the *Ordo Missae*[6] and established norms on the extent to which local languages were to be used in the Mass.[7] The instruction also contained directives for the translation of liturgical texts based on article 36 §3 of the liturgical constitution. The instruction does not comment on the relationship between the source and the target language.[8] Following the Constitution on the Sacred Liturgy *Sacrosanctum concilium*, Latin as the language of worship was maintained for the Eucharistic Prayer.[9] Many Bishops' Conferences, however, were very vocal in demanding that the local language should be allowed here, too.[10] As early as 27 April 1964 permission was given for the vernacular Preface.

On 27 January 1965, the new *editio typica* of the *Ordo Missae*[11] was published with the Roman Canon unchanged. The prayers at the foot of the altar also remained unchanged apart from the psalm *Iudica*, which was dropped. The first two bilingual altar missals were published in the same year, according to the norms of *Inter oecumenici* pertaining to the use of local languages in the liturgy of the Mass. The bilingual altar missal had, as a prefix, an edited version of Johannes Burkhard's († 1506) essay *Ritus servandus in celebratione missae*, supplemented with the essay *De defectibus missae celebratione occurentibus*. The Latin-German altar missal was approved on 25 September 1965.

The first volume of the Latin-German altar missal contained the texts for Mass from the First Sunday in Advent to the Saturday after the First Passion Sunday. At the beginning of 1966 the archabbey of Beuron published a new edition of its very popular bilingual missal for use by the faithful, known

---

5 See *AAS* 56 (1964) 877–900 (= DEL I, 102–138). The document came into effect on 7 March 1965. 6 See *Inter oecumenici* No. 48 (= DEL I, 118f). 7 Parts which were not permitted for use in the local language were the Collect *Oratio super oblata*, the *Postcommunio* and the Eucharistic Prayer. Cf. *Congregation of Rites, Inter oecumenici* No. 57 (= DEL I, 122–4). This is an interpretation of SC 54. 8 See *Inter oecumenici* No. 40 (DEL I, 114–6). 9 See SC 36. Care is to be taken 'that those believing in Christ are able to sing or pray the parts belonging to them in the Ordinary of the Mass with each other in Latin, too' (SC 54). 10 They based this on SC 40, 54. 11 See *Ordo Missae. Ritus servandus in celebratione Missae. De defectibus in celebratione Missae occurentibus. Editio typica*, Typis Polyglottis Vaticanis 1965; See *Notitiae*,

simply as the 'Schott', on the basis of the Latin-German altar missal, with a new liturgical introduction.[12] Included is a letter from the Cardinal Secretary of State Amleto Giovanni Cicogniani († 1973) to the Archabbot of Beuron. In it, Cardinal Cicogniani explains that the Latin-German altar missal and the new missal for the people were conducive to the *actuosa participatio* of the faithful, and were in accordance with the spirit of the Constitution on the Sacred Liturgy.[13] According to the Cardinal, the altar missal and the missal for the people make it clear that 'the liturgy is the summit towards which the actions of the Church are directed, and, at the same time, the source out of which all its power flows'.[14] It is not possible to tell from the Cardinal Secretary of State's letter whether the *Ordo Missae* of 1965 was meant to be a trial or an intermediate stage of the liturgical reform. The reform of the Missal was not finished with the reform of the *Ordo Missae* of 1965, even if the Sacred Congregation for Rites regarded it as its conclusion. One year after the publication of the *Ordo Missae* of 1965 the Congregation declared:

> Sometimes it is circulated that a reform of the Ordo Missae is imminent, or the whole Missal should be renewed; that is completely unfounded. The liturgical renewal needs additional efforts and further years of research.[15]

Yet further meetings of *Coetus X* for the reform of the *Ordo Missae* had already taken place in 1965.[16] Josef Andreas Jungmann SJ († 1975) advocated a reform of the Roman Canon; Cipriano Vagaggini OSB († 1999) advocated abolishing it, and replacing it with a new one. Aimé-Georges Martimort († 2000) took a position against this at a plenary session of the *Consilium* between 18 and 22 October 1965 in Rome. Louis Bouyer († 2004), a friend of Pope Paul VI's, who was appointed to join the working group on the *Ordo Missae* in 1966, also voiced doubts about the work of *Coetus X*. At the meetings in Le Saulchoir and Nemi, a new scheme, *De ordine missae*, was discussed. The scheme was to be presented to the Synod of Bishops, which had been newly created by Pope Paul VI with the *motu proprio Apostolica sollicitudo* (15 September 1965).

1 (1965), 101–2.   12 See A. Schott, *Das Messbuch der heiligen Kirche. Mit neuen liturgischen Einführungen. In Übereinstimmung mit dem Altarmeßbuch. Neubearbeitet von den Benediktinern der Erzabtei Beuron* (Freiburg, Basel, Vienna, 1966), with a letter from Amleto Giovanni Cardinal Ciogniani of 28 May 1966 to the archbot of Beuron.   13 See SC 14, 21.   14 SC 10.   15 *Notitiae*, 2 (1966), 32, n. 97: 'Notitia aliquando passim diffunditur circa imminentem reformationem Ordinis Missae, vel definitivam instaurationem totius Missalis; quae serio fundamento caret. Instauratio liturgica pluribus indiget studiis et studiorum annis.'   16 Le Saulchoir (8–23 June 1965) and Nemi (16–19 September 1965).

Since 1965, non-approved translations of the Roman Canon and new Eucharistic Prayers for use in the liturgy had been circulating in the Netherlands. On 20 January 1966 Paul VI decided that the Roman Canon was to remain unchanged, but that two or three new Eucharistic Prayers were to be added to the *Ordo Missae*.[17] Following this signal of the Pope, *Coetus X* immediately took up its work again, which had been interrupted in autumn 1965.[18] On 4 May 1967 the second instruction of the Sacred Congregation for Rites on the implementation of the liturgical reform, *Tres abhinc annos*,[19] was published. The name *Novus Ordo Missae* was now used. The new instruction mainly dealt with changes concerning rubrics. The permission to read the Canon of the Mass at the *missa cum populo* (also in the case of concelebration) at an audible volume is significant.[20] Deviating from the *Ordo Missae* of 1965, the instruction specifies that the priest says the *Domine, non sum dignus* three times, together with the faithful.[21] It is recommended that the priest reads the prayer *Placeat, tibi* during the exit.[22] The competent territorial authority can decide on the use of the local language for the Canon of the Mass, too.[23]

With this, permission was given for using the local language for the Canon of the Mass. Two weeks later, the first translations of the Roman Canon had been submitted to the Holy See for approval. The Congregation for the Doctrine of the Faith rejected these translations as too loose and insisted on an accurate and complete translation. *Ad interim*, the approved translations of the missals for the faithful were permitted, which had not originally been intended for liturgical use.[24] The approval of the first German translation of the Roman Canon for liturgical use was given on 5 December 1967, after the text had been confirmed by the Holy See (14 November 1967).[25] The translation was prepared by a commission led by the Munich professor for liturgy Joseph Pascher († 1979), but was changed in some places by the German-speaking bishops.[26]

17 According to Johannes Wagner, *Mein Weg zur Liturgiereform* (1936–1986) (Freiburg, Basel, Vienna, 1993), p. 95 after a note of Paul VI's to Bugnini, sent to Wagner on 2 July 1966. **18** See A. Bugnini, *Die Liturgiereform, 1948–75* (Freiburg i.Br., 1988), p. 371. **19** See *Ritenkongregation, Instructio altera* Tres abhinc annos *ad exsecutionem Constitutionis de Sacra Liturgia recte ordinandam*, in: *Notitiae*, 3 (1967) 167–94 (= DEL I, 429–37). **20** See *Tres abhinc annos* No. 10 (= DEL I, 432). The permission is corroborated by the instruction *Eucharisticum mysterium* (Nr. 21) of the Commission of Rites on 25 May 1967 (= DEL I, 474). **21** See *Tres abhinc annos*, No. 13 (= DEL I, 433). **22** See *Tres abhinc annos*, No. 16 (= DEL I, 433f). **23** See *Tres abhinc annos*, No. 28 (= DEL I, 436f). **24** See *Notitiae*, 3 (1967), 326. See also the decree of the Congregation of Rites, *De editione librorum liturgicorum* of 27 January 1966, No. 5 (= DEL I, 314). **25** See *Gottesdienst*, 1 (1967), 28–30. The translation was checked by the *Consilium*, the Congregation for the Doctrine of Faith and the Congregation of Rites. **26** See T. Schnitzler, *Der römische Meßkanon. In Betrachtung, Verkündigung und Gebet* (Freiburg, Basel, Vienna, 1968), p. 40. Schnitzler († 1982) was a

On 18 May 1967, the Sacred Congregation for Rites gave an overview of the new modifications to *Ordo Missae*. On two pages, the relevant texts of the *Novus Ordo Missae* were contrasted with those of the *Vetus Ordo Missae*, so that the changes are immediately obvious.[27] The first Bishops' Synod, at which the scheme *Novus Ordo Missae* was discussed, took place in October 1967. The scheme met with considerable resistance by the synod fathers.[28] In January 1968 experimental celebrations of the so-called *missa normativa* were carried out in the Sistine Chapel for the synod fathers and for the Pope, who could not take part in the synodal deliberations due to illness. The new form of the offertory met with particular criticism by the Pope. He desired as few changes as possible to the order of the Mass.[29] On 23 May 1968 the Congregation for Rites published three new Eucharistic Prayers as well as eight new Prefaces.[30] The corrections to the Roman Canon were approved by Pope Paul VI (6 November 1968).[31] On 6 April 1969 the Congregation for Rites published the *Novus Ordo Missae* together with the *Institutio generalis*,[32] three days after Pope Paul VI's Apostolic Constitution *Missale romanum*, on the publication of the new Roman Missal, had been released. On the basis of the *editio typica* of the *Missale Romanum* (26 March 1970), the new altar missals in local languages evolved. The first volume of the Missal for the Dioceses of the German language area of 1975 still contained, in the second part, the Mass in Latin for Sundays and holidays.[33] In contrast, the second edition of the missal of 1988 merely gives the German text.

THE IMPORTANT CHANGES TO THE *ORDO MISSAE* IN THE NINETEEN-SIXTIES

The first thing that strikes the eye when comparing the *Ordo Missae* in its editions of 1962, 1965 and 1969 are the changes to the introductory part of

---

consultor to the Consilium and of the Congregation for Worship.   **27** See *Variationes in Ordinem Missae inducendae ad normam Instructionis S.R.C. diei 4 maii 1967* (Città del Vaticano, 1967). The entire text is also printed in *Notitiae*, 3 (1967), 195–211.   **28** See Bugnini, *Die Liturgiereform*, pp 371–85.   **29** See Bugnini, *Die Liturgiereform*, p. 390.   **30** See *Preces eucharistica et praefationis*, in *Notitia*, 4 (1968), 156–60 (= DEL I, 529–34). See also the letter and the notes of the chairman of the *Consilium, Benno Cardinal Gut*, to the chairs of the Bishops' Conferences: *Notitiae*, 4 (1968), 146–55 (= DEL I, 535–46).   **31** See Bugnini, *Die Liturgiereform*, p. 409.   **32** See *Missale romanum ex decreto sacrosancti oecumenici concilii Vaticani II instauratum auctoritate Pauli Pp VI promulgatum, Ordo Missae* (Città del Vaticano, 1970).   **33** See *Die Feier der Heiligen Messe. Messbuch für die Bistümer des deutschen Sprachgebiets. Teil I: Die Sonn- und Feiertag deutsch und lateinisch. Die Karwoche deutsch* (Einsiedeln, Freiburg u.a., 1975), pp 355–657.

Mass. While there were only moderate changes in the *Ordo Missae* of 1965, the *Ordo Missae* of 1969 had a fundamentally different shape. This becomes apparent in the prayers at the foot of the altar, which had remained in the *Ordo Missae* of 1965, and also after the changes of 1967, in its essence, with the parts *Introibo ad altare Dei, Confiteor* of the priest and the response *Misereatur tui* as well as the silent prayers of the priest *Aufer a nobis* and *Oramus te*. The psalm *Iudica me* and the repetition of the antiphon *Introibo ad altare*, however, were dropped. The prayer at the foot of the altar could be prayed by the priest with the *ministri* or the *circumstantes* in the sense of a *missa dialogata* in Latin or in German.

The opening with the sign of the cross and the prayer at the foot of the altar are said by the priest *versus orientem* or *absidem*. It is only after the *Kyrie* (nine instances) and the *Gloria* that the priest turns to the faithful (*versus populum*). The prayers *Munda cor meum* and *Dominus sit in corde* also remained in the *Ordo Missae* of 1965, which, like the other prayers, are to be said silently by the priest, in Latin. The *oratio fidelium* is new, at which the priest, with the exception of the liturgical greeting, is standing at the altar *versus absidem*. Everything stays the same for the *Offertorium*. The Latin-German altar missal does specify that the request for prayer *Orate fratres* and the *Suscipiat* will be said in local languages during spoken Masses.

For the Eucharistic Prayer, the Latin-German altar missal gives the opportunity to sing the Preface, including the liturgical greeting that precedes it, in Latin or in the local language. This is also true for the *Sanctus* and *Benedictus*. From the *Te igitur* onwards, part of the Eucharistic Prayer is sung in Latin. The silent Canon is no longer to be observed at the *missa cum populo*. The *Mysterium fidei* is still a part of the dominical words referring to the chalice in the Latin-German altar missal of 1967. Equally, the addition of the *quod pro vobis tradetur*, as witnessed by Luke for Jesus' words referring to the bread (Luke 22:19), is still missing. The prayers of the Communion rite can be prayed in Latin or in the local language. The *Pater noster* is, as already laid down in the first instruction on the implementation of the liturgical reform, prayed together by the priest and the faithful, following the example of the eastern rites. The prayer for peace *Domine Jesu Christe*, which had followed the *Pax tecum* as a silent prayer by the priest since the eleventh century, was placed in front of the *Pax tecum* in the *Ordo Missae* of 1965, without the faithful giving a sign of peace to each other. Like the *Pater noster*, the *Agnus Dei* could also be prayed in the local language, as well as the *Ecce Agnus Dei* and the

Domine, non sum dignus. The formula of administration for the Communion of the faithful had already been changed in 1964: *Corpus Christi* or 'The Body of Christ'. The person receiving Communion answers with 'Amen'. For the *Postcommunio*, the dismissal formula (*Ite missa est*) and the *Benedictio* of the old order still applies. For all three elements, the local language can be used as well as the Latin language of worship. The final Gospel is omitted in the *Ordo Missae* of 1965.

If you compare the *Ordo Missae* of 1965 with the one of 1969 it is easy to see that it gained an entirely new form between 1965 and 1969, so that Pope Paul VI was entirely correct in calling it a *Novus Ordo*. The biggest changes, with the exception of the Eucharistic Prayer, were made to the *ritus initiales* and the *Offertorium*. Some of the changes raise questions; for example, the elimination of the prayer at the foot of the altar in the *Novus Ordo Missae*, without providing a replacement, is a significant loss with regard to the theology of prayer. This is because, in place of the prayer spoken in turns, there is now a short facultative introduction to the celebration of Mass. The *Antiphon* to the *Introitus* was retained, but was dropped in most cases in liturgical practice. Pope Paul VI and Franjo Cardinal Šeper, the prefect of the Congregation for the Doctrine of the Faith who was newly appointed in 1968, voiced concerns with the third form of the penitential rite with an integrated *Kyrie eleison*. Bugnini defended this form and finally prevailed.[34]

The new shape of the *Offertorium* leads to the fact that all but one (*In spiritu humilitatis*) of the offertory prayers were abandoned. It is understandable that the accompanying prayers for the offering of the oblations of bread (*Suscipe, sancte Pater*) and wine (*Offerimus, tibi*) were not kept, as they speak, in a theologically difficult manner, of the anticipation of the perfect sacrifice (*immaculata hostia*) and the chalice of salvation (*calix salutaris*). Even before the Council of Trent there was criticism about the fact that, during the *Offertorium*, the bread was already called a *hostia immaculata* (during the prayer *Suscipe, sancte Pater*) and the wine was called *calix salutaris* (during the prayer *Offerimus tibi*).[35] The post-Tridentine reform of the missals retained these prayers, however. It was only after the Second Vatican Council that they were replaced in the *Novus Ordo Missae* with new prayers that were modelled on the Jewish *berakhot*. These prayers are undoubtedly very beautiful, but are, normally, said silently by the priest. If they are spoken at an audible volume,

---

34 See Bugnini, *Die Liturgiereform*, p. 405f.   35 See *Concilium Tridentinum* VIII, 917.

the offering of bread and wine during the *Offertorium* is expressed more clearly. Rubrically, however, the praying of the accompanying prayers for the offering is specified as *submissa voce*, not as *secreto*.

The prayer for blessing *Veni, sanctificator*, spoken over the offerings, was eliminated without replacement in comparison to the *Ordo Missae* of 1965, as it was seen as an anticipation of the transformation epiclesis of the Eucharistic Prayer. It is possible to say that the praises over the bread and wine take on the function of a blessing. This, too, calls for saying the accompanying prayers in an audible voice. As the *Offertorium* is more than a 'ceremonial laying of the table' (Alex Stock), a blessing of the offerings that have been singled out and prepared for the sacrifice of the Eucharist does make good sense. The prayer *Suscipe, sancta Trinitas*,[36] documented for the first time in the ninth century, which was also eliminated in the *Novus Ordo Missae* without any replacement, had still been present in the *Ordo Missae* of 1965. The prayer makes it clear that the offering of the Eucharist takes place within the living space of the triune God, in unity with the saints.

Permission to say the Roman Canon in the local language was not without its adversaries like Louis Bouyer[37] or Hubert Jedin.[38] Annibale Bugnini accused the critics of using the local language of 'folly' and of complete incomprehension of the 'pastoral aim of the reform'.[39] Whichever way one chooses to answer the question as to whether saying the whole liturgy of the Mass in the local language is in the spirit of *Sacrosanctum concilium*,[40] the rejection of the bilingual missal in favour of the purely vernacular missal did lead to the disappearance from local churches of Latin as a language of worship, for the most part, and as time passed, Latin became increasingly identified with the Roman Mass of the *usus antiquior*.

36 See Josef Andreas Jungmann, *Missarum sollemnia. Eine genetische Erklärung der Messe*, Bd. II: *Opfermesse* (Vienna, 1949), pp 54f. 37 See Louis Bouyer, *Der Verfall des Katholizismus* (Munich, 1970); French translation, *La décomposition du catholicisme* (Ligugé, 1968), pp 40f : 'This is the most paradox thing about the present situation: in the instance that all sense of authority has been lost, a neo-clericalism develops, with the lay person as well with the priest, which is more limited, more intolerant and more aggressive than anything that was shown up until now. Liturgical Latin is a typical example of this. The Council decided very clearly and unambiguously to keep this language that has been normal in western countries from ancient times, but did, generously, give the permission to deviate from this principle in cases in which the requirement of the pastoral service suggest the more or less wide-reaching usage of the local language. Afterwards, up to now, it was not even imaginable that the local language would have a place in the liturgy, even in the proclamation of the word of God, the greater number of priests now go from one extreme to the other and don't want to tolerate a single word of Latin in church any more.' 38 See H. Jedin, 'Storia della chiesa e crisi della chiesa', *Osservatore Romano*, 15 January 1969, No. 11, 5. 39 Bugnini, *Die Liturgiereform*, p. 305. 40 According to *Winfried Haunerland* the complete liturgy of the Mass in the local language is in accordance with the principle of *actuosa participatio* and is thus in the spirit of the liturgical

At the Communion rite of the *Ordo Missae* of 1969, it was intended that the prayer for peace *Domine Iesu Christi* should be spoken audibly by the priest. The deacon, with the call *Offerte vobis pacem*, subsequently invites the faithful to give each other a sign of peace, which is to be determined by the Bishops' Conference. For the singing of *Agnus Dei* in the *Novus Ordo Missae*, the connection to the *fractio panis* is re-established, and with that, the original meaning of the *Agnus Dei* is regained.[41] The prayer *Domine, non sum dignus*, which was still intended to be said three times by the faithful according to the *Ordo Missae* of 1965, and was permitted in Latin or in the local language,[42] is only prescribed once by the *Novus Ordo Missae*.[43] The traditional formula for the priest's communion, *Corpus Domini nostri Iesu Christi custodiat animam meam in vitam aeternam* was eliminated in the *Novus Ordo Missae*.

It is likely that post-Conciliar theology's criticism of the concept of the soul played a role in this. The changed formula is: *Corpus Domini Iesu Christi custodiat me in vitam aeternam*. The new order of blessing and the *Ite missa est* were only introduced with the *Ordo missae* of 1969. The dismissal at the end does seem to make more sense looking at the structure of the Mass. There are, however, also good reasons for the traditional order, as the sober *Ite missa est*, unless sung in a ceremonial fashion, forms a noticeable anticlimax to the blessing. It is important to note the new dismissal formulas added to the *Ite missa est* by Benedict XVI, which have hardly been tried and tested as yet.

FORMAL VERSUS DYNAMIC EQUIVALENCE?

During the Second Vatican Council, a congress for translators of liturgical texts took place in Rome. In his address to participants in this congress on 10 November 1965, Pope Paul VI pointed out the difficulties of translation, quoting Saint Jerome:

> If I translate word for word, it goes against the meaning of the text; if I changed anything, urged by necessity, in the syntax and in the text, it looks as if I did not do the translator's task justice.[44]

consititution *Sacrosanctum concilium*. See '*Participatio actuosa*. Programmwort liturgischer Erneuerung', *Communio*, 38 (2009), 585–95.   **41** See *Missale Romanum*, No. 130.   **42** See *Lateinisch-deutsches Altarmessbuch*, no. 133.   **43** See *Missale Romanum*, no. 132.   **44** Pope Paul VI, *Allocutio ad interpretes* of 10 November 1965, in *Notitiae* 1 (1965), 378–81, 378 (= DEL I, 262). See Jerome, *Praefatio ad Chronicam Eusebii Pamphilii* (PL 26, 35).

This quote by Jerome makes it clear that, for translations of liturgical texts, as well as for translation of biblical texts, the problem of translation theory is to maintain a balance between formal and dynamic equivalence. The new translations are to become (as the missals for the faithful do not) part of the Roman rite of Mass, and thus the voice of the Church.[45] This poses a particular challenge to the translators. The translation of liturgical texts should not use colloquial language, and needs to vocalize appropriately the depths of the divine mystery. For this, it is necessary to find a careful balance between Christian Latinate language and the local language, and to take into account that the texts have to lend themselves to being sung.[46] When translating liturgical texts, it is also important to ensure that they are translated completely, so that no parts are left out which can be translated without difficulty.[47]

On 21 June 1967 Giacomo Cardinal Lercaro († 1976), in a letter from the *Consilium* to the presidents of the Bishops' Conferences, confirmed that translations of the Canon had to be *litterale et integrale*, and that the texts had to be approached 'as they are, without any shortening or simplification. The adjustment to modern language has to be simple and restrained'.[48] In a note of 10 August 1967, the secretary of the *Consilium* pointed out that the Holy See desired 'that the different translations of the Roman Canon be consistent with each other, to preserve in this way a certain uniformity, at least for this most holy text of the eucharistic celebration.[49] Bugnini also reminds his recipients of the Pope's wish 'that the missals ... should always contain the Latin text together with the text in the native language, in complete as well as in the partial editions'.[50]

On 10 August 1967, the *Consilium* asked for a consistent translation of the Roman Canon into all languages, as this was the core of the eucharistic liturgy. When translating the texts, the extremes of a language that is too antiquated or too modern were to be avoided.[51] For the *pro multis* of Jesus' words referring to the chalice, the Congregation for the Doctrine of the Faith and the Secretariat of State insisted on a literally translation in all bilingual altar missals. There were also voices that expressed the view that the *Verba*

---

45 See Pope Paul VI, *Allocutio ad interpretes* of 10 November 1965, *Notitiae*, 1 (1965), 379–81, 380 (= DEL I, 263).   46 See Pope Paul VI, *Allocutio ad interpretes* of 10 November 1965, in *Notitiae*, 1 (1965), 379 (= DEL I, 263).   47 Pope Paul VI, *Allocutio ad interpretes* of 10 November 1965, in *Notitiae*, 1 (1965), 381 (= DEL I, 265).   48 Giacomo Cardinal Lercaro, *Epistula 'Consilii'*, in *Notitiae*, 3 (1967), 289–96, 296 (= DEL I, 503–510: 510).   49 A. Bugnini, *De interpretatione canonis romani*, in *Notitiae*, 3 (1967), 326–7, 326 (= DEL I, 512–513: 512).   50 Bugnini, *De interpretatione canonis romani*, 327 (= DEL I, 513).   51 See the *Consilium*'s *De interpretatione canonis romani* of 10 August 1967, *Prooemium* and No. 2 (DEL I, 512f).

Testamenti should not be translated.[52] The 25 January 1969 instruction of the *Consilium*, *De interpretatione textuum liturgicorum* (*Comme le prévoit*), made a significant change.[53] The instruction only asks for a translation of the Eucharistic Prayers that is *integre et fideliter*.[54] The orations can, in contrast, be translated freely, using colloquial language. It stated that it was not necessary to have a complete translation either, just like the other parts of Mass.[55] The instruction gives predominance to dynamic equivalence in this instance.[56] On the basis of the translation hermeneutics of the instruction, the work on the translation of the *Missale Romanum* into local languages was carried out in the seventies. A necessary correction to the 1969 instruction of the *Consilium* resulted on 28 March 2001 in the fifth instruction for the correct interpretation of the Constitution of the Second Vatican Council on the Sacred Liturgy: *Liturgiam authenticam*. This initiated a comprehensive revision of the translations of the *Missale Romanum* into local languages.[57]

According to *Liturgiam authenticam*, revision of the translations could be evaluated using a variety of criteria.[58] The central guidelines are 'adherence to the text' and 'comprehensibility'. It is thought necessary for all liturgical texts to be translated into local languages *fideliter et accurate* (accurately and exactly).[59] As far as this is possible, the original text has to be translated *integerimme et peraccurate* (fully complete and fully exact); this means 'without omissions and additions regarding the content, and without paraphrasing or explaining'.[60] Attention needs to be paid to the fact that the sacral character of the Latin language of worship stays intact in the target language. At the same time it is often overlooked that *Liturgiam authenticam* does stipulate 'a fluent text in the local language that is adjusted to the rhythm of the congregation's prayer'.[61] To achieve this, it might be necessary to make changes to the syntax, and to the position of words in the sentence.[62] *Liturgiam authenticam* is not, accordingly, about formal equivalence at any price. The aim of the revision of

---

52 See Bugnini, *Die Liturgiereform*, pp 130f.   **53** See the *Consilium's*, *De interpretione textuum liturgicorum* of 25 January 1969, in *Notitiae*, 5 (1969), 3–12 (= DEL I, 592–605).   **54** See *De interpretione textuum liturgicorum*, no. 33.   **55** See *De intepretatione textuum liturgicorum*, nos. 15; 34.   **56** For translation theory in the twentieth century and its influence on the translation of the Roman Missal see D. McManus, 'Translation theory in *Liturgiam authenticam*' in N.J. Roy and J.E. Rutherford (eds), *Benedict XVI and the sacred liturgy* (Dublin, 2010), pp 116–31, especially pp 119–27.   **57** See McManus, 'Translation theory in *Liturgiam authenticam*', pp 127–31.   **58** See D. Böhler, 'Anmerkungen eines Exegeten zur Instructio Quinta „Liturgiam Authenticam",' *Liturgisches Jahrbuch*, 54 (2004), 205–22; W. Haunerland, 'Die Leitlinien der Revision: Texttreue und Verständlichkeit. Referat zur Auftaktveran-staltung der Kommission „Ecclesia Celebrans" in Bensberg (30–31 March 2005)': http://www.alt.dbk. de/imperia/md/content/aktionen/ecclesia_celebrans/ec_haunerland.pdf.   **59** *Liturgiam authenticam*, no. 20.   **60** See *Liturgiam authenticam*, no. 20.   **61** *Liturgiam authenticam*, no. 20.   **62** See *Liturgiam authenticam*, no. 20.

translations can only be a shrewd balance between formal and dynamic equivalence. That a revision of the translation is necessary is, however, irrefutable. This is because, while the translation in the Latin-German altar missal of 1965 tried to achieve a balance between formal and dynamic equivalence, the missal for the German language area of 1975 is dominated by the principle of dynamic equivalence to the point of paraphrases, omissions and additions to the content. To conclude, this can be demonstrated by the Roman Canon, the *Offertorium* and the three orations.

Canon romanus

For the translation of the Roman Canon attention needs to be drawn, first, to the *Memento, Domine*. Here the missal for the German language area (1975) suppresses the formula *redemptio animarum salutis*, which was still present in the translation of 1967.[63] Avoiding the concept of the soul in liturgical texts as much as possible chimed perfectly with popular attitudes at the time, as even well-regarded theologians thought that the differentiation between soul (*anima*) and body (*corpus*) was unbiblical and dualistic. This is one of the blind spots of the translation of liturgical books after 1970. In the German order of funeral rites of 1973 the concept of the soul does not make an appearance any more, apart from a mention in a psalm, in contrast to the Roman *Ordo exsequiarum*. This was rightly corrected in the revised edition.[64] This is because the anthropology of the intransient soul and the transient body cannot be described as dualism by any definition; it does rather stress the unity of the human being as constituted by soul and body.

In the *Hanc igitur* and the *Quam oblationem*, the oblation (*oblatio*) becomes a gift, or gifts, just as it does during the *Offertorium*; similarly, in *Supra quae* the *immaculata hostia* of the priest Melchisedech is represented as 'the holy gift'. The *pro multis* is translated first, in the 'Schott', as 'for many' ('für viele'), then in the Latin-German missal of 1965 as 'for the multitude' ('für die vielen') and finally as 'for all' ('für alle'), which was based on Joachim Jeremias' study of the accounts of the Last Supper, which is, nowadays, outdated in many

---

63 In the *Memento, Domine* the following is said: *Pro redemptione animarum suarum, pro spe salutis et incolumitatis suae.* The translation of 1967 says: 'They hope for the salvation of soul and body' (German: 'Sie hoffen auf Heil und Erlösung für Seele und Leib'). In contrast, the translation of 1975 reads: 'for their salvation and for their hope of the salvation that cannot be lost' (German: 'für ihre Erlösung und für ihre Hoffnung auf das unverlierbare Heil'). 64 See H. Hoping, 'Begraben auf Hoffnung hin. Die Identität des Verstorbenen im Spiegel der kirchlichen Begräbnisliturgie' in H. Hoping and St Wahle (eds), *Der Herr aber wird dich auferwecken. Begleitbuch zum neuen Begräbnisrituale* (Freiburg, Basel, Vienna, 2009), pp 71–88.

respects.[65] In the *Memento* for the deceased the *locum refrigerii* (place of refreshment) is rendered as 'land of promise', thus evoking associations with the land flowing with milk and honey. Finally, the eternity formula (*per omnia saecula saeculorum*) in the final doxology is represented, without necessity, in a mutilated form (now and forever). The more precise translation of 'from eternity to eternity' is offered in the missal for the faithful as published by Schott.

Offertorium

The version of the prayers that accompany the offering of bread and wine that was presented for approval to Paul VI no longer contained any reference to offering. The addition *quem (quod) tibi offerimus* (the bread which we sacrifice to you and the chalice that we offer to you) was only added because the Pope insisted on it.[66] The Pope falls back on the 1962 form of the prayer for the offering of the chalice, *offerimus tibi*. The majority of the *Consilium* voted against the insertion of the *offerimus* to the very end. Bugnini was against any statement of offering, along with the majority of the members of the *Consilium*. The secretary of the *Consilium* was, accordingly, content with the fact that, in most of the translations into local languages, the *offerimus* was not translated.[67]

Like the Italian and other translations, the German translation also rendered unrecognizable the statement of offering that was desired by Paul VI. This is because it says: 'we bring this bread and this chalice into your presence' ('wir bringen dieses Brot bzw. diesen Kelch vor dein Angesicht'). The German translation avoids the term 'sacrifice', but does choose an image from the language of worship of the Old Testament. The background for the translation are Exodus 25:30 (the showbreads that lay in God's presence) and the formula *in conspectu divinae maiestatis tuae* in the second part of the traditional accompanying prayer for the offering of the chalice. As the Pope himself wanted the language of sacrifice to be kept in the prayers accompanying the offering of bread and wine, the following translation would have fulfilled this justified desire more appropriately: 'we offer you'[68]. There was, however, a trend at the time to curtail the language of sacrifice as much as possible in the *Offertorium*.

---

65 See J. Jeremias, *Die Abendmahlsworte Jesu* (Göttingen, 1967).   66 See Bugnini, *Die Liturgiereform*, p. 398.   67 Ibid., p. 406.   68 See A. Stock, *Liturgie und Poesie. Zur Sprache des Gottesdienstes* (Kevelear, 2010), p. 166.

The reservations regarding the liturgical language of sacrifice also becomes clear when looking at the fact that *offertorium* was translated in German as 'preparation of the gifts' instead of 'offering of the oblation', which was proposed by the post-Conciliar edition of Schott's missal for the faithful (1966),[69] and *oratio super oblata* as 'prayer of the gifts' instead of 'prayer of the offerings'.[70] In the Latin-German altar missal, which prints the *oratio super oblata* in Latin and in German, the name of the oration to the *offertorium* remains untranslated. The Church does of course first have to receive that which she sacrifices, bread and wine, and allow it to be given to her anew again and again.[71] At the Offertory, however, a differentiation needs to be made between *praeparatio donorum* and the offering of the gifts. The gifts of bread and wine are not only placed on the altar, but offered to God (*offere*), so that they may become the body and blood of Christ. This is, however, the 'elementary act of the sacrifice'.[72] The translations 'preparation of the gifts' and 'prayer of the gifts', as offered by the German-language missal of 1975, should be corrected because of that. Correctly, it should say 'offering of oblations' and 'prayer over the offerings'. Josef Andreas Jungmann rightly notes that the German translation of the *Offertorium* disregards the symbolic value of the act.[73]

Roman Orations

It is not only the ending *per Christum* that is characteristic of the Roman orations, but also their character as a bidding prayer, at least in the second part of the oration. As the first example of the occasionally very free translations of the orations in the German missal of 1975, I will mention the *Postcommunio* of the daytime Christmas Mass, which remained the same from 1962 to 1970, with the exception of one change in the *Missale Romanum*. The oration can be traced back to the Verona manuscript also known as the Leonine Sacramentary (end of the sixth–beginning of the seventh century)[74]. The Latin text of the oration is as follows:

---

69 See Schott, *Das Messbuch der heiligen Kirche*, pp 626f. For an excellent new translation of the Collects of the Liturgical Year into German see A. Stock, *Orationen, Die Tagesgebete im Jahreskreis. Neu übersetzt und erklärt* (Regensburg, 2011).   **70** 'Prayer over the Offerings' is the new English translation too.   **71** See H. Hoping, *Kreuz und Altar. Die Gegenwart des Kreuzesopfers in der Eucharistie* (Augsburg, 2012), p. 21.   **72** Stock, *Liturgie und Poesie*, p. 166.   **73** See J.A. Jungmann, *Messe im Gottesvolk. Ein nachkonziliarer Durchblick durch Missarum Sollemnia* (Freiburg, Basel, Vienna, 1970), p. 60.   **74** See *Sacramentarium Veronense* (*Leonianum*) [N:1271].

> *Praesta, quaesumus, omnipotens Deus: ut natus hodie Salvator mundi, sicut*
> *divinae nobis generationis est auctor; ita et immortalitatis sit ipse largitor.*[75]

The Latin-German altar missal of 1965 translates, both elegantly and at the
same time true to the word:

> Today was born to us the saviour of the world, through whom we are
> born to eternal life; grant, omnipotent God, that he may give us the gift
> of immortality.[76]

In the revised Latin text, *Deus omnipotens* was replaced by *Misericors Deus*.
No other changes were made. The translation in the 1975 missal does,
however, look completely different to the one in the Latin-German missal of
1965. The gift of 'immortality' (*immortalitas*) was dropped, as was the *Salvator*
mundi. For the explanation of the liturgical *hodie*, an extra subordinate clause
was added. Accordingly, the translation today goes as follows:

> Merciful God, in this holy celebration you have given us your Son, who
> was born today as the saviour of the world. Through him, we are reborn
> to divine life.[77]

There will be little temptation to call this translation *integerrime et peraccurate*
(*Liturgiam authenticam*) or *litterale et integrale*, which is what Cardinal Lercaro
asked for in a translation of liturgical prayers.

The same is true for two other examples, which I take from the Alex Stock's
book (the reading of which I highly recommend), *Liturgie und Poesie. Zur*
Sprache des Gottesdienstes (Liturgy and poetry. On the language of worship).[78]

In the *Missale Romanum* of 1970 the Prayer of the Day for the Fourth
Sunday of Ordinary Time is:

> *Concede nobis, Domine Deus noster, ut te tota mente veneremur, et omnes*
> *homines rationabili diligamus affectu.*

---

75 *Missale Romanum* (1962), no. 22.   **76** *Lateinisch-deutsches Altarmessbuch*, no. 30: 'Heute ist uns geboren
der Heiland der Welt, durch den wir geboren sind zum ewigen Leben; verleihe, allmächtiger Gott, dass er
uns einst die Gabe der Unsterblichkeit schenke.'   **77** *Messbuch* (1975), no. 41: 'Barmherziger Gott, in
dieser heiligen Feier hast du uns deinen Sohn geschenkt, der heute als Heiland der Welt geboren wurde.
Durch ihn sind wir wiedergeboren zum göttlichen Leben.'   **78** See Stock, *Liturgie und Poesie*, pp 122–50.

This is a very old oration, which can also already be found in the Veronese, and which was taken up afresh for the Missal of 1970.[79] The missal for the German language area translates:

> Lord, our God, you created us so that we may praise you. Grant that we adore you with undivided hearts and that we love all people as you love them.[80]

The thought that God created us is added; the Latin text does not contain such a statement about the creation. It is possible that the intention was to make an anamnetic-epicleptic prayer of the epicleptic oration. The worship of God (*venerare*) becomes his adoration (*adorare*). With *rationabili affectu* the 'rational service' as mentioned in Romans 12:1 is hinted at (*logikē latreia* / Vulgate: *rationabile obsequeium*). In the German text, the *rationabili affectu* is dropped. In addition, *tota mente* is not translated as 'with the whole power of reason', but with 'undivided hearts'. The motif is supplemented with the love of God for us and the love of our neighbour. This is not a translation *fideliter et accurate*. Alex Stock suggest as a translation:

> Grant us, Lord, our God, that we honour you with all the power of our reason and that we love all people with heart and mind.[81]

The Prayer of the Day of the Seventh Sunday in Ordinary Time is, in the Latin text:

> *Praesta, quaesumus, omnipotens Deus, ut semper rationabilia meditantes, quae tibi sunt placita, et dictis exsequamur et factis.*

The oration can be traced back to the Gelasian Sacramentary (eighth century). In the Missal of 1962, it is given as the oration for the Sixth Sunday after Epiphany.[82] The German missal translates:

---

79 In the Sacramentarium Veronense the oratation appears as one of the *orationes diurnae* for the month of July. See A. Bauer and H. Feifel, *Mit der Kirche beten 1: Betrachtungen zu den Tagesgebeten der Sonntage im Jahreskreis* (Stuttgart, 1978), p. 16. 80 'Herr, unser Gott, du hast uns erschaffen, damit wir dich preisen. Gib, dass wir dich mit ungeteiltem Herzen anbeten und die Menschen lieben, wie du sie liebst.' 81 Stock, *Liturgie und Poesie*, p. 148: 'Gewähre uns, Herr, unser Gott, dass wir mit aller Kraft unseres Geistes dir die Ehre geben und alle Menschen lieben mit Herz und mit Verstand.' 82 See Bauer, Feifel, *Mit der Kirche beten*, p. 28.

Merciful God, you have spoken to us through your Son. Let us think about your word again and again, so that we speak and do that which pleases you.[83]

The 'omnipotent God' becomes the 'merciful God'. That is not the only instance in the German missal. The statement that God's Son spoke to us is added. The *semper rationabilia mediantes* is left out, just like the *rationabili affectu* in the last example. The reason-based thought becomes, according to Stock, a meditation on the Scripture that considers the words of God.[84] With a slight change to Stock's translation[85] the prayer of the day could be as follows:

Omnipotent God, we ask you to grant us enough reason to speak and act as it pleases you.

CONCLUSION

Between 1965 and 1969, significant changes were made to the *Missale Romanum*. While the *Ordo Missae* of 1965 led to only moderate adjustment, after that a *Novus Ordo Missae* developed, which was felt to be such by critics as well as by those who endorsed it. When translating the liturgical prayers, the hermeneutics of translation changed in the 1960s. With the *Consilium's* instruction *De interpretatione textuum liturgicorum* of 25 January 1969, the principle of dynamic equivalence asserted itself, which we have illustrated by a number of examples. The translation hermeneutics of *Liturgiam authenticam* were a necessary correction. This is only part of a reform of the liturgical reform that will involve more than just revising local language missals in a way that is mindful of a balance between formal and dynamical equivalence. It is necessary not only to correct the omissions of the translations (such as the concept of the soul, the language of sacrifice, and so on). Of equal importance will be a critical review of the individual parts of the reform of the Missal.

There are weaknesses with the new form of the opening rites and the *Offertorium*. In contrast to that, the new order of the pericopes for the

---

83 See *Messbuch*, no. 217: 'Barmherziger Gott, du hast durch deinen Sohn zu uns gesprochen. Lass uns immer wieder über dein Wort nachsinnen, damit wir reden und tun, was dir gefällt.'   84 See Stock, *Liturgie und Poesie*, p. 147.   85 See Stock, *Liturgie und Poesie*, p. 148: 'Gib uns doch immer, allmächtiger Gott, genügend Verstand, zu reden und auch zu handeln, wie es dir gefällt.' ('Grant us always, omnipotent God, enough reason to talk and also to act in a way that pleases you.')

celebration of Mass on Sundays and days of the week, as well as the three new Eucharistic Prayers are an enrichment. The position of the sign of peace, which was only integrated later on, has become contested within the Communion rite, since in most cases it disturbs preparation for communion. There are a number of reasons for taking it out of the Communion rite and putting it at the end of the Liturgy of the Word. It is decisive for the future of the renewed liturgy of the Mass that its sacral character is retained, or regained in the *ars celebrandi*, regarding the language of prayer as well as the execution of the ritual. It is also necessary to rediscover the character of the eucharistic liturgy as *oblatio*, offering.

Homily for Pontifical High Mass on the fourth Sunday after Pentecost 2011

(Romans 8:18–23; Luke 5:1–11)

RAYMOND LEO CARDINAL BURKE

One can imagine the great fatigue and profound discouragement of Simon Peter and the other fishermen after labouring throughout the night and catching nothing. Having given up hope of any catch on that day, they were washing their nets to put them away. In the context of their discouragement and loss of hope, Our Lord Jesus Christ approached and asked for the use of Simon Peter's boat, so that he could teach the large crowd that was pressing upon him.

Many desired to hear him teach the Word of God, for he 'taught them as one who had authority, and not as the scribes'.[1] His teaching gave them hope in the seemingly hopeless situations of daily living. Although the Gospel does not provide us a record of the content of his teaching on that occasion, we can be certain that his words opened the minds and hearts of the people to know the immeasurable and unceasing love of God for them, so that they might offer to God, in return, their faithful and enduring love. We can be certain that his teaching gave them the hope for which they were seeking in the depths of their being. The profound thirst and hunger for hope was the reason for which they pressed upon him.

Having concluded his teaching, Our Lord invited Simon Peter to put out his nets for a catch, a seemingly absurd request, given the failure of the fisherman to catch any fish during an entire night of intense labour. Simon Peter, in fact, commented on the unusual nature of Our Lord's request, while at the same time he did not hesitate to do immediately what his Master had requested. Surely, the promptness of Peter's response was inspired by Our Lord's teaching of the Word of God, which always calls forth in us, at one and the same time, both humility before God and complete trust in his providence. Notwithstanding the seeming hopelessness of the situation, Our Lord gave

---

[1] Mk 1:22.

Saint Peter hope. Simon Peter stopped putting away his nets and instead put them out for a catch. The Gospel, in fact, tells us that, when Simon Peter lowered his nets at the direction of Our Lord, he took in a catch so large that he had to call upon the help of the other fishermen, with their boats, in order to bring the catch to shore.

Simon Peter, witnessing the power of Divine Love in the miraculous catch of fish, was filled with even greater humility, asking Our Lord to leave him, not because he did not want to remain in the company of Christ but because he felt so completely unworthy of Christ, for he was a sinner in the presence of Divine Love. Our Lord, for his part, responded by inviting Peter to trust in the unfailing gift of God's love, miraculously manifested in the catch of fish, and to follow him as his apostle. He declared to Simon Peter, and to James and John: 'Do not be afraid; henceforth you will be fishers of men'.[2] In truth, Simon Peter, the 'sinful man', became the head of the Apostles, winning innumerable souls for Christ by his apostolic ministry and ultimately by martyrdom. What is more, he continues to win souls for Christ by his intercession for the needs of the universal Church and, above all, of her Supreme Pastor, his Successor, the Roman Pontiff.

By the miracle of the miraculous catch of fish, Our Lord showed us that he is with us always in the struggles of daily living, in the situations of our daily life, which tempt us to lose hope. What is more, the miracle uncovers for us the truth that not only our individual lives but the whole of creation is governed by the mystery of his immeasurable and unceasing love. At Christ's direction, nature provides for man, in accord with God's law, what man, on his own, could not obtain. Saint Paul, in his Letter to the Romans, reminds us that 'the sufferings of this time are not worthy to be compared with the glory to come, that shall be revealed in us'.[3] Christ, Lord of creation and Lord of history, has poured out his life for our salvation, for the salvation of the world. He has poured out upon us and upon the world the seven-fold gift of the Holy Spirit, by which he lovingly guides us along the pilgrim way to our eternal glory, to 'the new heavens and the new earth',[4] which he will inaugurate at his second coming.

The struggles of our daily living in Christ and the struggles of creation itself are not for us a source of discouragement and despair. Rather, in the company of Our Lord and at his command, we put out our nets each day for a catch, even when we have been labouring long and hard without accomplishing

2 Lk 5:10.   3 Rom 8:18.   4 2 Pet 3:13; cf. Rev 21:1.

anything, confident that Our Lord will render our humble act abundantly fruitful. We, with the Psalmist, pray every day, and especially before the challenges of each day, as we have prayed in the Introit of today's Holy Mass: 'The Lord is my light and my salvation: whom shall I fear? The Lord is the protector of my life: of whom shall I be afraid?'[5]

The challenges and struggles are real, and, without faith, they would cause discouragement and despair. But Saint Paul reminds us that, through the very struggles that we experience in our personal lives and that we witness in creation, Our Lord is accomplishing the victory of life and love, which he will bring to fullness at the end of time, at his second coming:

> For we know that every creature groans, and travails in pain, even till now; and not only it, but ourselves also, who have the first fruits of the Spirit, even we ourselves groan within ourselves, waiting for the adoption of the sons of God, the redemption of our body, in Christ Jesus Our Lord.[6]

The struggles that we endure, just as the struggles of creation, are for us a cause of hope, for we are confident that Our Lord is with us to accomplish the Father's will, a will filled with love of us and of all his creation 'to the end'.[7]

Commenting on the texts of the Holy Mass for the Fourth Sunday of Pentecost, Dom Prosper Guéranger wrote:

> The present condition of this world, therefore, furnishes a special and most telling motive, inviting us to the holy virtue of *hope*. They alone can find anything strange in such teaching who have no idea of how man's being raised up to the supernatural order was, from the beginning, a real ennobling of the world that was made for man's service. Men of this stamp have their own ways of explaining God's creation; but the truth that explains everything both on earth and in heaven – the divine axiom that is the principle and reason of everything that has been made – is this: that God, who of necessity does everything for his own glory, has, of his own free choice, appointed that the perfection of this his glory shall consist in the triumph of his love, by the ineffable mystery of divine union realized in his creature. To bring this divine union about is, consequently, by God's gracious will, not only the one sole end, but, moreover, the one only law, the vital and constitutive law, of creation.[8]

---

5 Ps 26 [27]:1.   **6** Rom 8:22–3.   **7** Jn 13:1.   **8** P. Guéranger, *The liturgical year: time after Pentecost*, Book II, tr. L. Shepherd (Fitzwilliam, NH: Loreto 2000), pp 122–3.

Our hope is not, therefore, a product of our fantasy, of our invention, but rather the fruit of the salvation won for us in our human nature by Our Lord Jesus Christ, God the Son made man, through his suffering and dying on the Cross.

Our Lord now makes present for us the Mystery of Faith, the gift of his divine life and love poured out for us on the Cross, from his Heart, pierced by the Roman soldier's spear, after he had died for our eternal salvation. In the Holy Sacrifice of the Mass, handed down to us in an unbroken line from Our Lord through the priestly ministry of his Apostles and their successors – our Holy Father, the bishops in communion with him, and the priests, their co-workers – we witness the truth that God, by 'his own free choice', has made our communion with him 'the one sole end', 'the one only law, the vital and constitutive law, of creation'.[9] At the Lord's Supper, he made sacramentally present the outpouring of his life for us, which he would accomplish on the following day, and consecrated the Apostles and their successors to do the same, so that his sacrifice on Calvary would reach men of every time and place, so that men of every time and place could unite themselves to him in the sacrifice through which our hearts rest, are healed of sin and are filled with Divine Love, in his glorious pierced Heart. In the Eucharistic Sacrifice, Our Lord accomplishes his one only desire, fulfills his sole law, namely, our communion with him in faithful and enduring love.

These reflections help us to understand why our Holy Father, the Successor of Saint Peter as Supreme Pastor of the Universal Church, has placed at the centre of his pastoral care of the Church – and indeed of the world – the reform of the Sacred Liturgy, so that the Mystery of Faith may be celebrated in the most worthy manner possible, as it was instituted by Our Lord at his Last Supper and as the Church, in an unbroken line, in a continuity of reform and growth, has done throughout the Christian centuries, not according to her invention, but in accord with the gift of Our Lord and his command to the Apostles: 'Do this in remembrance of me ... Do this, as often as you drink it, in remembrance of me'.[10]

Through his Apostolic Letter, given *motu proprio, Summorum pontificum,* of 7 July 2007, and the Instruction on the Application of the Apostolic Letter, *Universae ecclesiae,* approved by him and published by the Pontifical Commission *Ecclesia Dei* on 30 April of this year, our Holy Father, in continuity with his predecessors in the office of Saint Peter, has shown a

9 Ibid.   **10** I Cor 11:24–5.

particular care for the Sacred Liturgy as the highest and most perfect expression of the Mystery of Faith, the law of Divine Love that governs all creation and is fulfilled in Our Lord's redemptive Incarnation. Our Holy Father, at the very beginning of *Summorum pontificum*, makes clear the motive of pastoral charity for the universal Church which has inspired his care to provide for the celebration of the Roman Rite in two forms:

> Since time immemorial it has been necessary – as it is also for the future – to maintain the principle according to which 'each particular Church must concur with the universal Church, not only as regards the doctrine of the faith and the sacramental signs, but also as regard the usages universally accepted by uninterrupted apostolic tradition, which must be observed not only to avoid errors but also to transmit the integrity of the faith, because the Church's law of prayer corresponds to her law of faith.'[11]

Following the mind of the Pastor of the Universal Church, we are led to a new knowledge and love of the Mystery of Faith. We grow in the virtue of hope, for we experience sacramentally the presence of Our Lord with us, especially in the struggles of the present time and of his creation, to fulfill his law of pure and selfless love of man 'to the end'.[12]

The great richness of the Roman Rite, as it has been faithfully handed on to us, down the centuries, under the care and direction of Saint Peter and his successors, makes possible our participation in the Mystery of Faith, by which we are given the grace to express in our personal lives the one law of God, his will for the salvation of man and of the world. Let us pray in a special way today for an ever greater understanding of the teaching of our Holy Father for the sake of a more worthy celebration of the Sacred Liturgy, of the Mystery of Faith, of our communion of love with Our Lord.

Let us now lift up our hearts, together with the Immaculate Heart of the Blessed Virgin Mary, to the glorious pierced Heart of Jesus, opened by the soldier's spear on Calvary and remaining forever open in glory at the right

---

[11] *Ab immemorabili tempore sicut etiam in futurum, principium servandum est "iuxta quod unaquaeque Ecclesia particularis concordare debet cum universali Ecclesia non solum quoad fidei doctrinam et signa sacramentalia, sed etiam quoad usus universaliter acceptos ab apostolica et continua traditione, qui servandi sunt non solum ut errores vitentur, verum etiam ad fidei integritatem tradendam, quia Ecclesiae lex orandi eius legi credendi respondet."* Benedictus PP XVI, Litterae Apostolicae *motu proprio* datae, *Summorum pontificum*, 7 iulii 2007, *Acta Apostolicae Sedis* 99 (2007), p. 777. English translation: Libreria Editrice Vaticana. [12] Jn 13:1.

hand of the Father, in order to receive all men with immeasurable and ceaseless love, purifying them of all sin and strengthening them to love as he loves. In the eucharistic Heart of Jesus, our hearts will discover anew the sure anchor of our hope, the Mystery of Faith, and will be filled with courage to have hope, to put out our nets once again for the catch that is our salvation and the salvation of the world.

> *Heart of Jesus, fountain of life and holiness, have mercy on us.*
> *Our Lady of Knock, pray for us.*
> *Saints Peter and Paul, pray for us.*
> *Saint Patrick, Apostle of Ireland, pray for us.*

Contributors

DIETER BÖHLER is Professor of Old Testament Exegesis at the Philosophisch-Theologische Hochschule Sankt Georgen, Frankfurt (Germany).

RAYMOND LEO CARDINAL BURKE is Prefect of the Supreme Tribunal of the Apostolic Signatura.

SVEN CONRAD is a member of the Priestly Fraternity of St Peter.

CASSIAN FOLSOM is Prior of the Monastero di San Benedetto in Norcia (Italy) and a liturgical scholar.

DANIEL GALLAGHER is currently assigned to the Latin section of the Vatican Secretariat of State.

PAUL GUNTER is a monk of Duai Abbey (England), Professor at the Pontifical Liturgical Institute of San'Anselmo, Rome, and Consultor of the Office of Liturgical Celebrations of the Supreme Pontiff.

MANFRED HAUKE is Professor of Dogmatic Theology at the Theological Faculty in Lugano (Switzerland).

HELMUT HOPING is Professor in ordinary of Dogmatic Theology and Liturgy of the Theology Faculty of the University of Freiburg (Germany).

UWE MICHAEL LANG is a member of the London Oratory and a liturgical scholar.

WILLIAM MAHRT is Associate Professor of Music at Stanford University, President of the Church Music Association of America and editor of its journal *Sacred Music*.

GEORGE CARDINAL PELL is Archbishop of Sydney (Australia).

LAUREN PRISTAS is Professor and Chairman of the Department of Theology and Philosophy at Caldwell College in Caldwell, New Jersey (USA).

JANET RUTHERFORD is Secretary of the Patristic Symposium, Maynooth, and Irish Correspondent to the International Association of Patristic Studies.

ARTHUR SERRATELLI is the Bishop of Paterson, New Jersey (USA) and Chairman of the International Commission on English in the Liturgy (ICEL).

VINCENT TWOMEY is Professor Emeritus of Moral Theology, St Patrick's College Maynooth, and founder of its Patristic Symposium, a forum for advanced scholarship in patrology.

Index